Critical Play

Critical Play

Radical Game Design

Mary Flanagan

The MIT Press Cambridge, Massachusetts London, England

First MIT Press paperback edition, 2013
© 2009 Massachusetts Institute of Technology

This book was set in Janson and Rotis Sans by Graphic Composition, Inc., Bogart, Georgia.

Library of Congress Cataloging-in-Publication Data

Flanagan, Mary, 1969–
Critical play : radical game design / Mary Flanagan.
    p. cm.
Includes bibliographical references and index.
ISBN 978-0-262-06268-8 (hardcover : alk. paper)—978-0-262-51865-9 (paperback)
1. Games—Design and construction. 2. Games—Sociological aspects.
3. Art and popular culture. I. Title.

GV1230.F53 2009
794.8'1536—dc22

2008041726

Contents

Preface and Acknowledgments

As both an artist and a writer, in order to give due focus on some of the ideas for *Critical Play*, I have for the most part avoided discussion of my own work. It is the case, however, that much of my own creative work parallels the various concerns in this book, as the book was developed in concert to my own creative practice. Further, it is to my own creative practice that I owe the concept of "critical play," and this book is an attempt to propose this approach and give ample background material for its set of methods.

I am deeply indebted to friends and colleagues who helped make this book possible through the years of research. *Critical Play* emerged from my doctoral work in theory and practice at Central Saint Martins College of Art and Design, London, and I am deeply indebted to my supervisors: Dr. Lizbeth Goodman, Patricia Austin, and James Swinson, as well as the community of scholars working in and around the SMARTlab center in London. Many thanks to my supportive colleagues at the University of Oregon and Hunter College for their encouragement during my research. Thanks are especially due to those working with the Tiltfactor Laboratory at Hunter College in New York from 2004 to 2008.

Gratitude floats out to the artists who have shared their work with me, and provided images of their work to offer a rich text. Their contributions need be celebrated as they forge playful interventions and games.

I greatly appreciate all the people who have shown an interest in the work, and pay tribute in particular to those who have given their time and energy to discussion. In this, I would like to especially thank Helen Nissenbaum and our Values at Play work that has helped critical play cross into new disciplines through a values approach.

I should not forget to thank my mentors, the practitioners and scholars who have influenced my work tremendously over the years. Alison Knowles was generous in sharing her important work and insight for this, and future, work.

Angela Ferraiolo read the manuscript with a discerning eye, and her insight is appreciated. Alice Bonvicini and Suyin Looui have helped keep the laboratory growing and useful along the way; Jarah Moesch and Steven Kowalik assisted with some key images for the text. James Bachhuber pitched in with enthusiasm to support critical thinking and play. Gratitude is also due to the CUNY Faculty Fellowship Publication Program, which provided me with valuable time to write this book, and the National Science Foundation, because the project continued to be inspired by my funded research into games and human values.

Special thanks go to my parents, family, and friends, who brought to me all sorts of influential games! Much gratitude goes to colleagues who are artists and game designers themselves. Tracy Fullerton and Celia Pearce were particularly supportive, and I send them my infinite gratitude.

Preface and Acknowledgments

INTRODUCTION TO CRITICAL PLAY

By the madness which interrupts it, a work of art opens a void, a moment of silence, a question without answer, provokes a breach without reconciliation where the world is forced to question itself.

—Michel Foucault, *Politics, Philosophy and Culture: Interviews and Other Writings, 1977–1984*

For many game players, games exist for entertainment, for passing the time, for fun. They are a diversionary activity, meant for relaxation or distraction—a "not-work" space where players are free to engage in fantasy narratives, amazing feats, and rewarding tasks. But what if certain games have become something *more*? What if some games, and the more general concept of "play," not only provide outlets for entertainment but also function as means for creative expression, as instruments for conceptual thinking, or as tools to help examine or work through social issues?

Each day, computer users check email, search for movie trailers or the news, and perhaps blog, balance a budget, or download digital camera images. They also play computer games—simultaneously during these other tasks, as in casual games, or in more comprehensive games both on- and offline, such as the multiplayer PC game *World of Warcraft* or a console game such as *Katamari Damashii*. Computer and console games have become a significant cultural medium across a wide range of social, economic, age, and gender categories.[1] As the game industry involves an increasing number of educators, designers, and scientists, there is considerable need for games that take on, and challenge, the accepted norms embedded in the gaming industry. There is a need for a critical approach not only in examining such games but also in creating them.

Critical Play is the first book to examine alternative games and use such games as models to propose a theory of avant-garde game design—that is, like alternative theories of narrative texts, poetry, and film, a theory that focuses on the reworking of contemporary, popular game practices to propose an alternative, or "radical," game design. Specifically, this book investigates games designed for artistic, political, and social critique or intervention, in order to propose ways of understanding larger cultural issues as well as the games themselves.

The research for *Critical Play* grew out of an avid interest in popular computer games technology, history, and cultural studies, as well as my own creative work: I use play and game fundamentals in projects as diverse as activist software design, classroom teaching, and drawings, installation, and sculpture that appear in more traditional art venues. The games and other works I discovered while investigating my interests in social issues are collected in this book. In the course of so much play, I became fascinated with observing how ideas about politics, play, and games were most interesting in those projects operating outside the software, board-game, or theme park industries—not only among those who are independent game developers but also those who thought of making play scenarios or games within the context of being artists. Art has long been intertwined with politics; the twentieth century has witnessed provocative materials produced during the Mexican Revolution of 1910, the Constructivist political design used in the Russian Revolution of 1917, the theatrical protests in World Wars I and II, the 1968 student postering campaigns, and the U.S. civil rights campaigns that used mixed media. *Critical Play* outlines how play has influenced the history of creative exploration of the social and the political. The book's arrival is well timed, for this is a significant era in which to learn how to play in ways that break the mold and open up what play can be, and at the same time possibly benefit someone or something.

Prior to this project, few researchers had advanced gaming scholarship from the point of view of art history. Numerous scholarly studies have focused on the early forms of computer gaming as a field, in topics such as early console games or the history of gaming at Atari. In this book, I have studiously avoided these too-common examples, for several reasons. First, typical histories of computer games have not examined the practice of play outside the realm of computers. Second, these historical studies do not generally involve artists and their social and cultural roles, either in the making or the playing capacity. Third, few of these studies have made any serious attempt to ground contemporary gaming in creative and aesthetic origins rather than a primarily technological context; and fourth, few have made the connection between games and art.

On first glance, it may seem a stretch to perceive how artists working in a very different place and during very different eras would be able to significantly contribute to the manners, modes, and processes for making games today. Computer games are often seen as a new medium, and not necessarily aligned with other forms of play. Few would imagine that such play could also be related to ancient divination, psychoanalysis, utopian tax laws, social protest, or environmentalism. While recognizing certain distinctions, *Critical Play* looks to the commonalities among play activities, game genres, and important historical contexts to discover thematic ways in which play can continue to manifest critical thinking.

As Marcel Duchamp said in 1946,

The great trouble with art in this country [the United States] at present, and apparently in France also, is that there is no spirit of revolt—no new ideas appearing among the younger artists. They are following along the paths beaten out by their predecessors, trying to do better what their predecessors have already done. In art there is no such thing as perfection. And a creative lull occurs always when artists of a period are satisfied to pick up a predecessor's work where he dropped it and attempt to continue what he was doing. When on the other hand you pick up something from an earlier period and adapt it to your own work an approach can be creative. The result is not new; but it is new insomuch as it is a different approach.[2]

Whether one believes Duchamp's criticism could apply today, his call for innovation is one that can speak to many. In this book, I will explore historic instances of artists using play in their work. I consider given projects amid the shifting historical context for play, the political use of play, and look also to contemporary artists using physical, locative, and computer games in their work. In the spirit of activist art, *Critical Play* primarily focuses on individual artists or collectives of artists making work because they have something to say.[3] The creative experiments with games described in this book help provide a provocative look at how artists can challenge ideas, beliefs, and social expectations and subsequently transform them in their work. These experiments are particularly worthy of note in an era of increasing financial stakes in the games industry, the decline in "street protest" and civil actions, and citizens' overall lack of time and sense of agency. Taking wild chances to provoke, disrupt, and change even in play appears to be risky business.

Using the term *artist* to describe anyone making creative work can be off-putting to some readers, particularly readers in the various professional fields who might find the term exclusionary. The term *artist* is used here with a particular meaning in mind, to refer to those who are creating outside commercial establishments, and often, those who are "making" for "making's sake." Therefore, while a short section on social impact games is included in the book, these may tend to be more focused in scope and scale and work with more traditional "industry-style" methods instead of the more avant-garde practices that have become many artists' focus. The voices of the alternative social impact game makers, however, represent a voice of critical play that needs to be explored.

Critical Play is built on the premise that, as with other media, games carry beliefs within their representation systems and mechanics. Artists using games as a *medium of expression*, then, manipulate elements common to games—representation systems and styles, rules of progress, codes of conduct, context of reception, winning and losing paradigms, ways of interacting in a game—for they are the material properties of games, much like marble and chisel or pen and ink bring with them their own intended possibilities, limitations, and conventions. Artists have indeed "revolted" effectively before, transforming popular culture around the globe for the last century and a half. *Critical Play* documents this promise of large-scale transformation.

Defining Some Key Terms

What is, for the purposes of this study, the first key term, *play*? And what does it mean to play *critically*? Play is a notoriously difficult concept to define; it is a culturally and socially specific idea. Anthropologist Brian Sutton-Smith, a leader in twentieth-century research in play, and one of the core play theorists used in this book, has defined play consistently through the years as an activity that is fun, voluntary, intrinsically motivated, incorporates free choices/free will, offers escape, and is fundamentally exciting.[4] He has argued that play activities can be grouped in four categories: play as learning, play as power, play as fantasy, and play as self.[5] While quick to recognize the dark side of play, including bullying, abusive situations, and frightening circumstances, Sutton-Smith also notes that play can be defined as a variety of activities: as exchanges of power, or "power plays" that prioritize competition and traditionally aggressive play styles; as the act of bonding and belonging; as a practice of real-life functions; and as "fun," being with friends, and choosing freely.[6] Play is recognized as one of the most fundamental aspects of the human condition.[7] While play spaces are generally fantasy spaces, players often experience real stakes when inside them. One might easily find examples of the "serious" aspects of play in sport and gambling.

Play is an integral and vital part of mental development and learning, and playful activities are essential aspects of learning and creative acts. Historically, there have been two "camps" in the study of play: those who see play as voluntary, intrinsic, and important to class structure (leisure) and socialization (members of this camp Sutton-Smith calls "the idealizers"), such as Huizinga and Caillois; and those who look more to ritual, to communication, and who study play in natural settings, such as Bateson, Turner, and Sutton-Smith himself. In this look at critical play, I use the strengths of both camps. In *The Ambiguity of Play*, Sutton-Smith suggests that play provides a working model of species variability by incorporating mental feedback that keeps a species flexible in evolution. He particularly focuses on play's potential to help define social norms and identity, noting that the "use of play forms as forms of bonding, including the exhibition and validation or parody of membership and traditions in a community" is essential to cultural formation.[8] By playing together, people form close communities and develop a group identity and a sense of belonging. Play can also function as a tool to understand the self. Many anthropologists like Sutton-Smith have argued that play is the way children work out social and cultural norms. "Play can cure children of the hypocrisies of adult life," notes Sutton-Smith, arguing that children's play spanning from early childhood to teenage years offers narratives that negotiate the risks of the real world: "These stories exhibit anger, fear, shock, sadness, and disgust."[9]

Johan Huizinga, in his 1938 book *Homo Ludens: A Study of the Play Element in Culture*, defines play in an extraordinarily loose way: play is a "function of the living, but is not susceptible of exact definition either logically, biologically, or aesthetically."[10] Huizinga rather defines the formal characteristics of play as "a free activity standing quite consciously outside "ordinary" life."[11] Other aspects include play as a voluntary activity, executed within certain fixed limits of time and place, having rules freely accepted but absolutely binding.[12] In play, the aim is play itself, not success or interaction in ordinary life. Unlike Sutton-Smith, Huizinga focuses on adult play, and he argues that play activities tend not to be serious in and of themselves but shape culture nonetheless through ritual and social custom. At the same time, they absorb the player utterly in a special time and place set aside for play: "a closed space is marked out for it, either materially or ideally, hedged off from the everyday surroundings" that he later famously refers to as "the magic circle."[13]

Distinct themes emerge in scholarship attempting to define play. Most anthropologists and historians agree that play is central to human and animal life; is generally a voluntary act; offers pleasure in its own right (and by its own rules); is mentally or physically challenging; and is separated from reality, either through a sanctioned play space or through an agreed upon fantasy or rule set.[14] Because play and the ordinary world are intermingled amid the increasing popularity of games (specifically, at present, computer games and sports), games are becoming the "sacred spots" Huizinga identifies in his anthropological writing.[15]

Critical Play

Games ultimately create cognitive and epistemological environments that position the player or participant with the experiences previously described in meaningful ways. So what does it mean to "play critically"? Critical play means to create or occupy play environments and activities that represent one or more questions about aspects of human life. These questions can be abstract, such as rethinking cooperation, or winning, or losing; or concrete, involved with content issues such as looking at the U.S. military actions in Cambodia in the early 1970s. Criticality in play can be fostered in order to question an aspect of a game's "content," or an aspect of a play scenario's function that might otherwise be considered a given or necessary. Criticality can provide an essential viewpoint or an analytical framework. Those using critical play as an approach might create a platform of rules by which to examine a specific issue—rules that would be somehow relevant to the issue itself. Critical play is characterized by a careful examination of social, cultural, political, or even personal themes that function as alternates to popular play spaces.

The challenge, then, is to find ways to make compelling, complex play environments using the intricacies of critical thinking to offer novel possibilities in games, and for a wide range of players. Thus the goal in theorizing a critical game-design paradigm is as much about the creative person's interest in critiquing the status quo as it is about using play for such a phase change.

Games

Another key term used throughout this text is *games*, to refer to those instances of more-or-less constructed play scenarios. Katie Salen and Eric Zimmerman (2004), among other games scholars, note the wide variety of definitions of the term "game." Historically speaking, the challenge of defining games has occurred throughout 150 years of game scholarship and research, with the most recent turn in computer games studies yielding related questions. In his 1984 book *The Art of Computer Game Design*, one of the first books detailing the intricacies of thinking about computers as gaming platforms, Chris Crawford contrasts what he calls "games" with "puzzles." Puzzles are static; they present the player with a logical puzzle to be solved with the assistance of clues. Games, however, can evolve, and rules may shift at certain points in a game and can change with the player's actions.

Greg Costikyan (1994) also has a concrete definition of what constitutes a game, which he describes as "a form of art in which participants, termed players, make decisions in order to manage resources through game tokens in the pursuit of a goal."[16] In much of game scholarship, it has been argued that games are by their definition competitive in that they always have an end point—a winning or losing state. But Costikyan avoids the "win/lose" dichotomy as the only possible goal for players. He additionally details how the structure of games compares to other kinds of experiences, such as stories:

Stories are inherently linear. However much characters may agonize over the decisions they make, they make them the same way every time we reread the story, and the outcome is always the same. . . . Games are inherently non-linear. They depend on decision-making. Decisions have to pose real, plausible alternatives, or they aren't real decisions. It must be entirely reasonable for a player to make a decision one way in one game, and a different way in the next. To the degree that you make a game more like a story—more linear, fewer real options—you make it less like a game.[17]

While Costikyan believes that stories are linear but games are not, the key to the preceding text is his attention to "real options" for players to pursue. Generally, this is referred to as player agency, or the player's ability to make choices that mean something to him or her.[18] Salen and Zimmerman (2003) also discuss the designer's ability to create situations for "meaningful play." They have provided students of game design perhaps the most codified definition of a game: "a system in which players engage in an artificial conflict, defined by rules, that results in a quantifiable outcome."[19] Salen and Zimmerman offer six key game concepts in their influential game creation book, *Rules of Play*:

1. a game is a system
2. it is artificial
3. it has players
4. it has conflict
5. it has rules
6. it contains a quantifiable outcome/goal, an ending state in which players can either be considered the "winners" or the "losers."[20]

Each of these canonical authors in the field of digital game design—Crawford, Costikyan, and Salen and Zimmerman—notes the importance of rules in constructing games, with varying degrees of storytelling, conflict, and competition added into the (often, technology driven) system. In this book, I choose not to follow such strict definitions. Games can be thought of more productively as situations with guidelines and procedures. Perhaps games are *themselves* a technology.

———

Technology

In organized play and games, rules have a mechanical rigor and are followed as procedures. These take on a kind of algorithmic specificity as players enact meaning through following rule sets. In this way, technological change has been interlinked with changes in play and gaming practices. "All art derives from play," noted Johan Huizinga in *Homo Ludens*, his famous book exploring the human interest in play. This sentiment inspires one to examine both the notion of "art" and the notion of "play" within twentieth-century creative practices.

Shifts in play have historically mirrored shifts in technologies. This is evident in the invention of organized doll play and "playing house" during the U.S. industrial revolution, when gender roles needed to be reasserted due to changing labor conditions.[21] The link among the reorganization of banking, financial systems, and property ownership in twentieth-century U.S. culture mirrored the rise of financially focused board games such as *Monopoly*.[22] Later chapters will examine inventions such as Edison's mechanical doll and other, literal "play" technologies. But play shifts have done more than utilize such new inventions. Even play that does not involve gadgets or devices might be considered a technology. Games and play activities themselves, with their emphasis on order and conventions, act as technologies that produce sets of relationships, governed by time and rules, played out in behavioral patterns. Even a simple game of hopscotch (figure 1.1), in the hands of an artist, could become a kind of technology.

In the age-old playground game of hopscotch, a play space is drawn on the ground and shared among players. Each takes a turn tossing the potsy, hopping the length of the "map," and returning to the beginning. Hopscotch is one of those universal games that many people seem to recognize. As respected twentieth-century media theorist Marshall McLuhan noted, such "games as popular art forms offer to all an immediate means of participation in the full life of a society, such as no single role or job can offer to any man."[23]

If the hopscotch map contained numbers, the sequence would likely take on meaning for players (marking spaces toward the end of the map, or representing points to add or subtract) but this very simple game could also affect or create social relations. What if the numbers were a collection of points, and the person who had the highest (or fewest) won, regardless of order? If the map size is scaled much larger than is typical, some players would have unfair advantage to win over others (by having longer legs, for example). If two hopscotch maps are laid side-by-side, players might play for speed, one racing against another. Players waiting in line might try to distract the hopping player, waving arms or mocking to make the hopper miss the target square;

| Figure 1.1 |
[mapscotch], 2007, artist's reworking of hopscotch, by the author.

this type of activity would not be explicitly forbidden by the rules and would thus fall into the realm of peer sanctioned or accepted play. In other words, how the game is designed and presented carries implications for the social group. Some players might opt not to play (and become perhaps an onlooker, witness, or referee); some players might choose to compete. Other players might choose to break the explicit game rules by skipping ahead in line or by jumping on the wrong spaces in order to get ahead. Games, functioning as an ordering logic—a machine, or a technology—for creating social relations, work to distill or abstract the everyday actions of the players into easy-to-understand instruments where context is defamiliarized just enough to allow Huizinga's magic circle of play to manifest. From this one example, it is possible to see how games in and of themselves function as *social technologies*.

If games themselves act as types of technologies, then technological games are twofold in their capacity for meaning making. Most students of the evolution of digital gaming begin their studies among the technological milestones of computing: Vannevar Bush's technological fantasies, the ENIAC computer, the 1961 *SpaceWars!* game at MIT, the release of *Pong* by Atari in 1972, or the success of *Pac-Man* when the Buckner and Garcia song "Pac-Man Fever" hit the charts in 1982. Those studying contemporary game design, especially in programs highlighting the role of technology, rarely tap links to the seemingly distant domain of the arts. Likewise, those studying popular culture rarely cross into the realm of institutions such as galleries, museums, and private collections. One of the most important reasons to make such a crossing is that shifts in art movements, like technologies, also indicate (and mirror) world events; these specifically include international events such as the world wars, as well as the cultural and social movements affecting everyday citizens and arts practitioners. For example, at the same time in the early twentieth century that Marcel Duchamp was engaging "high art" audiences to make their own decisions about the nature of art—his famous quote "The spectator makes the picture," is an example of this philosophy—through his multitemporal paintings and "readymade" found art objects, American cinema fans were participating similarly in early "low art" media culture through newly created fan discourse. Meanwhile, still other avant-garde artists were adopting and reconfiguring themes from culture altogether in their work—take, for example, the board games critical of war by Alberto Giacometti and compare them to the origins of *Monopoly*, the famous Parker Brothers game originally created by a social activist to protest landlords and tax policies. These are examples of the interesting juxtapositions and discoveries the reader will make in this book.

Subversion

Notions of subversion, disruption, and intervention are bandied about along with notions of the critical by artists and activists, and need further articulation. Artists have long reused, worked against, or invented new media forms and conventions: early twentieth-century innovator Marcel Duchamp turned urinals into scandalous "readymade" sculpture.[24] Photographer Claude Cahun, cross-dressing and infantilizing herself, performed over-the-top gender stereotypes in her self-portrait photographs dating from the 1930s to the 1940s.[25] Surrealists fashioned experimental films, inverting trends in cinematic narrative and visual conventions, even "cutting the eye" (such as in the famed Surrealist film *Un chien andalou* of 1929) for both shock value and as a statement against overly controlling aesthetics.[26] These are only a few examples from myriad artistic practices that survive in significance because they broke the rules.

According to the *Oxford English Dictionary*, subversion is "the turning (of a thing) upside down or uprooting it from its position; overturning, upsetting; overthrow of a law, rule, system, condition."[27] A subversion is an action, plan, or activity intended to undermine an institution, event, or object. When discussing subversion, it is necessary to know what system or phenomenon in particular one is working against, be it political, social, legal, or cultural. In this book I extend the term *subversion* from the definitions provided by Raymond Williams and Antonio Gramsci,[28] Michel Foucault,[29] Judith Butler,[30] and others.[31] The core ideas regarding this term evolved from Antonio Negri's work on subversion (2001) as well as themes of disruption and intervention from decades of art practices. Subversion has been identified by several theorists and practitioners as a powerful means for marginalized groups to have a voice.[32] Likely this focus is due to the activist call to examine how power relationships play out and how social change is actually orchestrated. Much of Negri's writing emerged during his long house arrest in Italy for his political acts, and his ideas are a culmination of much contemplation on how contemporary culture operates. Negri's is a dual view; he writes of both the difficulty of "breaking out" against power, and the inherent encapsulation and control by those in power of subversive acts. When working against pervasive systems of power, he notes that subversive practices *still* have the power to trigger social change when used on the right scale and with the right tools. Perhaps games are such a tool: Negri notes that subversion is *necessary* within a multitude of organizations in myriad types of forms, and not merely for the functioning of such organizations but for individual and collective well-being.[33] Negri and others use the term *subversion* to mean a creative act rather than a destructive act.

Because they primarily exist as rule systems, games are particularly ripe for subversive practices. A hallmark of games is that they are structured by their rule sets, and every game has its "cheats"—even play itself, pushing at the boundaries of a game system, could be said to involve a kind of subversion. This idea is supported by games scholarship; to scholars of play such as Brian Sutton-Smith, play is associated, at least in part, with transgressive and subversive actions.

"Interventions" are specific types of subversions that rely upon direct action and engage with political or social issues—a "'stepping in', or interfering in any affair, so as to affect its course or issue."[34] Rather than reducing these actions to limiting categories, it is more fitting to situate the actions of artists among a loose set of principles that guide interventions. The introduction of art objects and performance into public spaces, for example, is a way that artists appropriate the cognitive space of public space, of everyday space, and functions in an interventionist fashion. Artists practicing intervention often have social or political goals, and may seek to open up dialogue by transgressing the boundaries between art and everyday life. With the exception of purely aesthetic movements (abstract expressionism comes to mind), most twentieth-century art movements fostered interventionist activities and strategies, particularly those identified as the avant-garde. Numerous twentieth-century avant-garde artists had the shared goal of bringing about private and public transformation through crea-tive acts.[35] Thus some artistic intervention takes the form of performance, parody, simulation, game, activist, and "hacktivist" strategies. Intervention has been a popular strategy with street performance and activism: feminist theater groups reworked per-formance practices, for example, and turned to street theater for intervention.[36] Guer-rilla street theater of the 1960s and 1970s by El Teatro Campesino, the Farmworkers' theater, The Black Revolutionary Theatre (BRT) led by Amiri Baraka, or the media interventions of Nikki Craft, Martha Rosler, or Joan Braderman were able to disrupt everyday activities when the "street," not the computer, was the gateway to cultural intervention.[37]

A number of artists have invested in interventionist strategies, and they are docu-mented in this book. These artists, and many more, intervened in contemporary art venues, took over traditional art styles to change them, or depicted narratives that operated against social norms. Since the 1960s, numerous artists have furthered these interests without a particular art movement identity, such as Jenny Holzer and Rachel Whiteread, but who reflect an international current in art that subverts everyday lived experience by exposing negative or unexpected visions of the everyday.[38]

Finally, contemporary electronic artists negotiate between traditional, institution-alized aesthetic discourses and emergent, organic forms of social communication. If electronic art has become an experimental laboratory, not so much for new technology as for new social relations of communication, then perhaps electronic games might operate in an interventionist way within electronic spaces and discourses.[39]

The definition of the term *disruption* lies somewhere in between the concepts of intervention and subversion. A useful term derived from "Disruption-Innovation" theory in the IT business innovation field, a disruption is a creative act that shifts the way a particular logic or paradigm is operating.[40] In the high-tech arena, disruptive innovators are those who introduce relatively simple yet "paradigm-shifting" solu-tions to a particular market. Examples in business include Dell computer's direct-to-customer sales model or its "song per song" online music sales, which are examples of low-end disruption.[41] Other disruptive innovations create entirely new markets. By creating need and new venues for products, the disruption effectively competes against very little. Businesses spawned from such an approach include Starbucks and eBay (which Harvard innovation theorist Clayton Christensen and his collaborators, Erik Roth and Scott Anthony, argue "democratized" the auction process). Disruption-Innovation theory influences game design, for if it is intervention and subversion that artists seek, they create this within the confines of a new kind of game design.

As detailed later, a great deal of pleasure for players can be derived from subverting set interaction norms in both simple play environments and highly complex games. Players will consistently explore what is permissible and what pushes at that boundary between rules and expectations, and a player's own agency, within any given play environment—no matter how structured that play is. From hockey, to chess, to playing dolls or "house," player subversion—as cheating, as open play, as social critique—is an intrinsic part of play. [42] If digital artifacts have truly become a magic circle in which players enter a sanctioned play space, then this culture of play, or playculture, as it is commonly termed, is one in which participants find a space for permission, experimentation, and subversion. In the following chapters, I will postulate the possible historic reasons for the necessity of this stance.

What Are Activist Games?

In this book I use the terms *activist game* and *activist game design*. Activist games can be characterized by their emphasis on social issues, education, and, occasionally, intervention. In other words, they are not purely conceptual exercises, but rather, games that engage in a social issue through, most commonly, themes, narratives, roles, settings, goals, and characters; and less commonly, through game mechanics, play paradigms, interactions, or win states to benefit an intended outcome beyond a game's entertainment or experiential value alone. This is not to say that activist games cannot, or should not, be "fun," though this has been a critique of many activist games to date. The term "activist game," however, is meant to specify the game theme and sometimes-desired outcomes for playing the game, and only one of the desired outcomes would be entertainment.

Activist approaches to media are important to the study of digital culture precisely because of media's inherent imbalances. Indeed, issues of gender, racial, ethnic, language, and class inequities and imbalances are also manifest in the historic imbalances with technology production and use. Take, for example, the fact that women constitute only 10 percent of the computer-game industry workforce, or that less than 10 percent of all programmers in the United States are women. These imbalances extend in a sometimes subtle fashion to who uses these tools and spaces on a daily basis. Even renowned media scholar Henry Jenkins, among others, noted over a decade ago that video game spaces are gendered spaces. [43] Gender imbalance in technical and visual culture triggered one of the most significant critiques of film and visual representation: Laura Mulvey, in her 1970s analysis of the visual representation of woman in cinema, inspired myriad progressive experiments calling attention to the representation of women in commercial imagery and film.[44] In the area of video games, significant essays critiquing the continued problematic representation of gender in video games (Flanagan, Anne-Marie Schleiner) and race (Jennifer González, Lisa Nakamura) continue to call these issues into question.

Design Actions and Design Methods

One of the most important things *Critical Play* provides is a range of examples demonstrating what artists have done in their creation of games and play. These can inspire other artists, designers, and innovators. Some artists make instructions for actions, and even paintings; some playful disruptors use obnoxious language and make humans into puppets; while others write computer programs that write poems. Some even project their games onto bridges or have players dress up as chickens. Artists make words touchable, create palindromes, do street intervention, and even skywrite from airplanes to disrupt the everyday actions in the city. These activities are spurred on by the methods developed over the last century, including Simultanism, which means a telescoping of time; free verse/free visual verse; automatism and automatic writing; exquisite corpse; and the drift of psychogeography fame (all explained more fully in later chapters).

The Chapters

The games explored in the following chapters range from playing doll and playing house to board games, performative games, locative media games, and computer games. Each chapter explores historic instances of a particular game genre, as well as how art and social movements have engaged with it.

In chapter 2, I review the history of domestic play as particularly relevant to game design, especially given that the majority of contemporary computer-based games are experienced in domestic environments. I look at the resurgence of popular domestic play in games such as *The Sims* and artists' projects that function as critical play in domestic space, and I present a variety of forms of doll play, proposing the subversive methods of reskinning, rewriting, and unplaying.

In chapter 3, I examine the various ways in which board games have worked as critical documents and experiences, and discuss several artists' board games. I look at the spiritual practices of play and chance and how board games developed. I will also look at how board games reflect changes in society, for they also provide a window on the values, hopes, and beliefs of a given culture. The *Landlord* and *Anti-Monopoly* games, for example, showed how designers could invite player modifications to the games for mass-distributed, alternative game hacks.

I turn to language games in chapter 4. Puns and jokes, sound games, the historic methods of Simultanism and automatism, and the use of textual instructions and rules (including public disruptions) and embodiment are explored.

In chapter 5, I look at performative objects and games, including sculpture and photography, and study how critical game makers are approaching their games as physical interventions. Examining play that uses the body or the object in compelling ways, this chapter emphasizes collage, surrealist game methods, artists taking to the street with performative games, and the New Games Movement.

I explore locative games in chapter 6 as artistic practices expand to take play into environments in which player-participants can make meaning in public spaces. This chapter refers to play that is generally outside or in unusual locations, and examines the work of the Situationists and their method of the drift.

Chapter 7 focuses on artists' alternative computer-based games, including online and offline games. I provide an analysis of projects from Persuasive Games and those of Gonzalo Frasca, as well as other games created through the use of interventionist strategies in the design process.

To conclude, in chapter 8, I explore games for change, considering the ways in which activist concerns can be incorporated into game design. If a hypothesis for activist gaming is that a well-crafted approach to embedding certain ideologies (interventionist strategies) in design will have the capacity to alter the practices on both the part of conscientious designers and artists as well as the players, the goal of this chapter is to support makers who make real the systems that support an array of such choices. I conclude by discussing several methodologies for designing critical play as revealed in prior examples and analysis.

Rather than provide a comprehensive analysis of all games, this book aims to uncover some of the more interesting instances of artists' works where play and criticality manifest. Along the way, historical innovations in game play as they reflect social mores will be highlighted. The goal of *Critical Play* is to examine the ways in which individuals and groups involved in creating and playing games have worked, and are working within, social, political, and cultural systems. Their critical, radical play can be considered the avant-garde of the game as a medium.

PLAYING HOUSE

Play customs are wide-reaching forces that can be mapped through a society's art, media, and institutionalized forms of leisure. From the Olympic games of Hellenic Greece to the public spectacles of the Roman Empire to the chivalries of medieval tournaments and jousts, sports and sporting events have traditionally fostered public involvement. In addition, cockfights, fistfights, boxing, horse racing, and similar types of spectator sports encouraged interaction with risk via wagering, especially during the cultural shifts accompanying the British industrial revolution.[1] However, while sports, athletics, and other contests of skill offer familiar opportunities for social analysis, it is less well documented that these presentations are also examples of *critical* play. Instead, in an early and continuous line of intervention, the site of recreation where activities reach the value of critical play is the home. In eighteenth-century Europe, French artists developed an elaborate and incisive art style known as Rococo, infusing a pointedly domestic materiality into what was traditionally accepted as "high" art.[2] In nineteenth-century England, children "hacked" the household norms of the Victorian period through their own critical forms of doll play. Early in the twentieth century, the artists of the Dada movement created toys and puppet shows that mocked, among other things, familial conventions. The impulse to examine through play remains alive in our own era as participants in virtual worlds and computer games simultaneously feed, heal, and maintain their virtual characters while also posing amusing challenges or problems for them. In this way, gamers still "play house," reworking paradigms of the status quo by experimenting with artificial identities, self-expressive environments, and humorous scenarios. Today, artists frequently position themselves at the margins of computer culture using play as critical intervention. By examining historical instances of arts culture and how popular culture practices can become a vehicle for larger concerns, new parameters for understanding mischievous, even rebellious play begin to emerge.

Looking at Games

In the Middle Ages and Early Renaissance, engravers and painters relied on scenes of play to charm and illuminate. Examples include the Ghent-Bruges calendar *Horae* (1520–1525 AD) as well as the miniatures found in the Dutch manuscripts of Antwerp and the Venetian Grimani Breviaries (1490–1510 AD). In these contexts, games were reminiscent of the seasons, depicting summer games of celebration or games of abundance for harvest, and play reinforced the significance of the cycle of the year. Pieter Bruegel's painting *Khinderspil*, or *Children's Games* (1560, Vienna Kunsthistorisches Museum) includes depictions of over ninety games common to his time. Art historian Sandra Hindman has read the symbolic associations in this work as a means of conveying a range of human experience: ill fortune in marriage, luck's sometime triumph over skill, and the ways in which traditional holidays marked by the Catholic Church may, in fact, have been days of folly rather than introspection.[3] Bruegel's incorporation of a mask, of blue cloaks for blind man's bluff, and of fools sporting whirligigs are said to connote human fallibility and self-deception as well as standard phases of adult life such as marriage and childbirth. Through his depiction of a courtship, a baptismal procession, a true-to-the-time bridal party, and the doll play that acted as a model for motherhood, Bruegel uses play to critique norms of sixteenth-century Dutch life, capturing in a single moment not only the notions of youth but also a foreshadowing of the most profound events the children portrayed would come to experience as their lives unfolded.[4] Bruegel also documents the unpleasant through the nasty play he saw among those same children, giving us an even more damning critique. The performance of myriad children's games like knucklebones and its more violent counterparts, tug-of-war or plain fighting and pulling hair, signal that children's activities may be more than folly and, in fact, represent the darker aspects of the human experience.

Shifts in Perspective

No matter how revealing, after the Renaissance, games and artworks concerning play continued to be marginalized as irrational, whimsical parts of culture, unworthy of the advanced scholarship of the day.[5] Ever reasonable, scholars and philosophers of the European Enlightenment (1650–1800) emphasized scientific and technological solutions to problems and, in general, banished ritual, superstition, and folk knowledge in favor of developments in logic. Nevertheless, games of the period began to proliferate beyond their "serious" use in warfare and military training across Europe as the Enlightenment's cold rationality was countered by the playfulness of artists, performers, and others who continued to find themselves preoccupied with domestic space.

Baroque-era Dutch painter Samuel Dirksz van Hoogstraten (1627–1678) is an excellent example of these countercultural artists. A student of Rembrandt, van Hoogstraten was a phenomenal painter adept in many styles, and he used his gift to create a portfolio of illusionist visual experiments. These feature everyday objects—desks, quills, and furniture—showcasing his mastery of perspective and light. Van Hoogstraten painted perspective boxes and amusing trompe-l'oeil, experimenting with craft and playing with the conventions reflected by Europe's dominant worldview.[6] For example, humorous touches such as a pet dog painted into a corner of a scene speak to the everyday focus of his gaze. The jocular inventiveness of his style traversed the rift between popular culture and the high-art world in compelling and meaningful ways while critiquing lofty Enlightenment values.

What is extraordinary about van Hoogstraten's works is the sense of quickness, cleverness, and creative perspective with which he pictured domestic space and activities. In *View of an Interior* or *The Slippers* (1654–1662), the artist painted a colorful scene that evidences a recent change in an everyday environment. There is a marked absence of people in these rooms; the painting seems to mimic a playhouse. The artist devoted himself to an accurate depiction of spatiality with nesting wall pictures, shadows of upper- or middle-class furnishings, and doorframes in an attempt to emphasize depth from the point of view of the painting's observer until van Hoogstraten approaches the point where the absence of figure itself implies movement. As in the artist's other trompe l'oeil paintings, his careful illusion marks everyday space with the potential for a subject, a space waiting to be "played out." One analysis of the painting could be that the evidence in the house—for example, the slippers and the broom left behind in the room—show that the mistress of the house may be neglecting her household duties and has left the scene to carry out an affair. Is she at home, in another room? With whom? The slippers as a symbol were often used to connote romantic liaisons. In these configurations, van Hoogstraten plays a guessing game with viewers to tease out questions concerning domestic norms and their rituals.

In another, even more striking series, van Hoogstraten went so far as to make paintings into viewing-boxes. These were called "peepshow boxes" by fans and collectors,[7] building on the work of Filippo Brunelleschi (1377–1446) and Carel Fabritius (1622–1654) and their experiments with perspective. Van Hoogstraten's examples are desktop-sized wooden containers inset with paintings cleverly positioned to create the illusion of real, three-dimensional space.[8] In Brunelleschi's work, Italian piazzas conjure distance, but in van Hoogstraten's *Perspective Box of a Dutch Interior* (ca. 1660), a domestic scene unfolds (figure 2.1). There are no separate physical objects placed within the house; rather, all elements of the house are painted into the scene with just

| Figure 2.1 |

Perspective Box of a Dutch Interior, ca. 1660, by Samuel Dirksz van Hoogstraten (1627–1678). The National Gallery, London.

the proper alignment, rendering them believable to viewers. Any human figure or item that might detract from believability is avoided, and any object that could normally be found in a house—wall pictures, furniture, décor, even the pet dog—are painted directly into the box. Created from a central perspective, each room looks perfectly correct from one angle, yet is a distortion of scale, light, and line from another.

The example of van Hoogstraten's peepshow paintings reflects a playful attitude about space and painting but also serves to reference playhouses as sites for adult play. The compulsion toward creating miniature houses and replicas of household goods is hundreds of years old, but so is the idea that domestic games can be mechanisms for identifying particular themes in culture.[9] Indeed, Roger Caillois has argued for a strong link between the culture in which a game is played and the game itself.[10] Van Hoogstraten's fantasy and whimsy also demonstrate ideas expressed by Sutton-Smith, who discusses the rhetoric of frivolity associated with play. Witty boxes interpreted to be play also manifest ideas of progress, identity, power, and perception, and the treatment of everyday subjects can critique dominant Enlightenment ideologies of state, science, rationality, and order. Viewed this way, van Hoogstraten was practicing a critical type of play in his very deliberate creation of peepshows that are rendered believable, but are by all intents and purposes much like the playhouses created by his craft-inspired contemporaries—that is, a window onto domestic space as a place for the reflection on the norms and behaviors in that space. There are many examples of artistic styles that reflect the influence of their social and political times. The artistic directives of Egyptian Pharaoh Akhenaten (1369–1332 BC), for example, altered Egyptian representational practices based on a dramatic shift in religious belief. The radical graphic style represented by Russian Constructivism embodied a fluid, changing model of visual culture. Historians who see representational practices as mirrors of culture can also look to play for cultural clues, paying special attention to the intersection of play and art.

A New Focus on Play

While artists had long referenced games in their scenes, the whimsical artists of the Rococo (1725–1775) were the first to use play as a central subject; the artists Chardin, Boucher, and Fragonard are of note for their exploration of play in lavish everyday settings. In exploring the eighteenth-century paintings of Jean-Honoré Fragonard (1732–1806), Jennifer Milam notes a playful, almost gaudy, style.[11] Enlightenment developments spurred social and political developments and industrialization, but fostered a creative outcry for the irrational, the merry, and the epigrammatic, themes most of the esteemed thinkers of the time resisted.

François Boucher (1703–1770) recorded eighteenth-century life by painting the pastoral and the common scene. In his work Le Déjeuner (1739), a domestic moment unfolds in the soft lines of household women tending to children (figure 2.2). The girl seated on the floor holds her doll and the doll's horse. In other examples from the period—namely, several by Fragonard—female subjects are depicted seated on outdoor garden swings; Milam notes that swinging was a game sanctioned by doctors of the ruling class, who diagnosed exercises such as swinging or strolling as those worthy of a certain sense of propriety and sensitivity to station.

Sutton-Smith has argued that a group's preference for specific activities is one important way values emerge in a culture.[12] The leisure habits of the rich are framed as activities to see and to be seen at. They provide exercise, but not exertion; they are a courtly site of sociality and pleasure. In Fragonard's day, swinging was a play activity that liberated men and women to touch each other, view each other, and rendezvous. Milam notes that in Rococo painting "swinging alludes to the fickleness of women in the emblematic tradition, but also, with its rhythmic motion, to the act of lovemaking."[13] Milam goes on to describe the details found in Fragonard's "swing" paintings (such as figure 2.3, The Swing, from 1767) more specifically: a tossed shoe

| Figure 2.2 |

Le Déjeuner, 1739, by François Boucher (1703–1770) features elements of the Rococo style. Musée du Louvre, Paris. Image courtesy of the Art Renewal Center.

| Figure 2.3 |
Jean-Honoré Fragonard (1732–1806), *The Swing*, 1767, oil on canvas. Wallace Collection, London. Image courtesy of the Art Renewal Center.

signals female abandon to passion, an unshod foot denotes lost virginity, an eager lap dog can stand for impatient desire, a statue of Cupid, who silences with one hand and pulls arrows from his quiver with another, may mean love at work, and a hat that caps a budding bush, sexual engagement.[14] These references, Milam argues, help viewers piece together a coded, erotic scene in which participants play with each other, their environment, and larger social rules, while the artist who captures them plays with visual conventions, symbolism, perspective, and the limits of the times. Milam goes so far as to label Fragonard's works "interactive paintings," that is to say, art that encourages viewers to engage in their own visual games, crossing categories of form, subject, and belief. As is the case of van Hoogstraten, the artists of the Rococo establish a clear link between play and investigation both in the art world and in vernacular space.

Play patterns themselves reflect cultural change. While Fragonard's Enlightenment high society seems to flirt and swing far from the concerns of the Enlightenment and the establishment of scientific thinking, its very ability to play hinted at the promises offered by industrialization and the coming leisure class. In the West, play became organized and structured around objects at the onset of industrialization. Henri Lefebvre (1901–1991), noted twentieth-century Marxist critic and philosopher, whose influential writings connect social systems to space, noted that the construction of the concept of "leisure" was key to contemporary notions of the everyday and that it took the development of a bourgeois culture to create the idea of leisure for all. While the ruling class enjoyed free time, changing class relations and a growing desire for leisure combined among the masses, creating a "culture of the consumer." In turn, the commodities and goods developed to satisfy the masses' desires for leisure time came to reflect the power structure of a developing elite. Play cannot erase these distinctions, but play may often reinforce established power or challenge it.[15] In many cases, the activities of play carry nostalgic and class-informed notions of free time, leisure, and access—a tendency still inadequately addressed by most theorists of play; studies of play have been relegated to the nursery, with a significant body of scholarship in the field of play research emerging from developmental theories emphasizing childhood play.[16] From this perspective, play becomes "a primary vehicle for and indicator of [children's] mental growth. Play enables children to progress along the developmental sequence from the sensorimotor intelligence of infancy to preoperational thought in the preschool years to the concrete operational thinking exhibited by primary children . . . play also serves important functions in children's physical, emotional, and social development."[17]

Moreover, even this limited view of play's significance and function finds itself dependent on cultural shifts. First was the conceptualization of childhood as a specific time with specific needs and goals: the idea of "childhood" itself is a cultural invention, existing in Europe and North America for about four hundred years. The concept gained influence during the industrial revolution, as debates raged over child labor in factories.[18] The new awareness of childhood as a category of experience was emphasized in the nineteenth century by the burgeoning areas of educational theory and the corresponding establishment of the Montessori, Catholic, and Steiner schools. One theorist who has considered the effects of a cultural split between childhood and adulthood is the developmental psychologist Bruno Bettelheim: "Until the 18th century (and even more recently in some parts of the world), the play and games of children were also the play and games of adults."[19] Arguing that adult activities have become too far removed from the places where a child's world unfolds, Bettelheim goes on to note that the adult world is now separated from the world of children in deep ways.

Second, play would not be as popular without the "invention" of leisure time due, in part, to the industrial revolution's separation of the social from the occupational. In this new culture, games, whether public spectacles or parlor amusements, emerged as necessary interaction mediators.

At this point, *leisure* must be defined as an operationalized term. Sports, fairs, rodeos, crafts, music—all of these could be considered contemporary adult forms of leisure. They are activities that are intentional, voluntary, and active. In other words, participants in leisure activities must *choose* to pursue them. As Aristotle theorized, leisure is a decidedly adult activity, an extension of child's play. This play is often collectivized in terms of competitions, exhibitions, or teams, becoming an activity for groups as well as individuals. The social role of leisure has been well articulated through Veblen's notion of conspicuous consumption (1899), which interprets free time as spectacle.[20] It can be argued that leisure is an "object," or goal, as well as a process—one that is born out of the interaction between individual and collective actions within the larger context of a consumption-oriented economy. A great deal of institutionalized play emerges from this "goal-oriented" notion. In a sharp observation of play research, Sutton-Smith critiques much of the play literature of the twentieth century, noting that play has consistently been framed within a Western notion of progress where play, especially children's play, is justified as educational and moral, helping to build intelligence and good behavior, and preparing children to take part as good citizens of the adult world.[21]

Playing House and Doll Play

While the artist van Hoogstraten was painting domestic scenes and creating his peepshow boxes, fine dollhouses were a leisure fashion in Europe.[22] Designed to play with

| Figure 2.4 |
Poppenhuis van Petronella Oortman. Rijksmuseum, the Netherlands.

and reimagine domestic spaces along with children's future roles within them, these toys drew on an ancient practice, particularly represented through games and doll play. Dolls have been found in children's graves from the Roman Empire, Ancient Egypt, and Ancient Greece, and wooden peg dolls were popular in sixteenth- and seventeenth-century Europe. Three hundred years ago, dollhouses in the Netherlands were large—up to two meters tall. These wooden structures fashioned as cupboards opening onto all rooms of a house. The *Poppenhuis van Petronella Oortman* (Doll's House of Petronella Oortman), in Amsterdam, created sometime between 1686 and 1705, is among the earliest and most ornate of dollhouses (figure 2.4). The finest examples of Dutch dollhouses were created for adult women, particularly for women about to be married. A complete example of an early Dutch dollhouse is *Het Poppenhuis van Petronella de la Court*, 1670–1690 (also known as the Utrecht Dollhouse), which featured over ten rooms and was filled with miniature furniture and household objects.

This example references paintings like those produced by van Hoogstraten in its carefully painted interiors—some walls have oil murals and meticulously painted ceilings done in perspective. Like most of this grand dollhouse genre, the Poppenhuis also mimicked the upper-class fashions of the times. The materials used to create the miniature objects were authentic: animal fur and leather seat coverings, marble mantelpieces, and linen in the washroom.

Over the years, elaborate European dolls and dollhouses proliferated, and similar types of play artifacts were created in the growing American colonies where dolls and dollhouses became a prominent industry in just a few centuries. During America's Civil War era, dolls, dollhouses, and toy stores reflected changes in work patterns due to immigration and industrialization as well as shifts in the categories of social classification, the solidification of familial roles, and an overall increase in leisure time.[23] Playing house in miniature became a popular nineteenth-century children's pastime. Dolls and other commercial play items were consistently featured in the emerging genre of magazines dedicated to home life in the United States and United Kingdom throughout the late nineteenth and early twentieth centuries. During the Victorian era (1837–1901), social mores and play styles also moved from public spectacle into the home, as middle-class and upper-class women and children were freed from the time and labor demands made on the working populace.[24] Play and domesticity, therefore, became linked to the very notion of "free time." This shift in play to domestic space would set the stage for later trends in computer culture where hacking, BBS communication, fan culture, and open software, and online games would become highly "domestic" forms of play.

Meanwhile, the actual production of toys shifted from the home to the factory. In the 1800s, play became a formalized part of popular culture through board games, card games, parlor games, and, after the U.S. Civil War, an increasing number of commercially available toys. According to toy scholar Cross, as handmade toys gave way to mass-produced, commercial toy "products," dolls and teddy bears helped romanticize childhood.[25] One result was the separation of childhood play from adult experience in a way that "made it innocent and pure."

Though a central part of childhood for countless years, the doll is a subject of study for only a handful of theorists. Francis Armstrong, Miriam Formanek-Brunell, and Lois Kuznets are three of the leading researchers. Others note the significance of playing house in the normalization, and moreover, the institutionalization of Victorian social and cultural norms.[26] Before examining these issues as they manifest in play environments, however, it is useful to recall and perhaps reconcile the two different interpretations of "normative" behavior: Sigmund Freud's psychoanalytic model of normalization and desire, and Michel Foucault's ideas concerning desire and its social control.

Contrary to Freud, who suggested that the unconscious was the seat of one's "dark matters" including sexuality, death, and the repression of desire, Foucault, in his *History of Sexuality* and in his work on nineteenth-century discourses of social regulation, challenged the linkages between personal "regulation" and external power structures, namely, the hegemony of the state.[27] The state, Foucault argued, has a direct, vested interest in controlling a population's repressed desires and sexual urges. He went on to detail the power relations employed by states in the ongoing pursuit of higher levels of control. During the Victorian era, important mechanisms of control included social and cultural institutions such as marriage, the church, and the traditional activities and social roles associated with the home. Here, some of most provocative and compelling examples of nineteenth-century play represent the ways individuals might work out, or rebel against, normative, prescriptive behaviors.[28] A great deal of the "regulation" could be achieved through the assertion of traditional activities within the home. From the Victorian era until the present, playing house has constituted a symbolic act whose meaning is culturally negotiated. For example, the house has long been the central icon of the American dream, representing class fluidity as well as the egalitarian promises of capitalism. While Marxist critic Henri Lefebvre critiqued the consumption of space as a capitalist endeavor, even he, like many other theorists and writers, falls into romanticizing the house: "The House is as much cosmic as it is human. From cellar to attic, from foundations to roof, it has a density at once dreamy and rational, earthly and celestial."[29]

These themes may appear obvious in the play artifacts of the affluent classes, but they were just as readily translated to poorer children and children in rural areas with less access to the Victorian commercial toy boom, through scrapbook houses and paper doll play. For U.S. families living in remote locations, a booming catalog-sales industry represented a link to the larger world of fashion in furniture, clothing, and home goods. Leftover catalogs, such as those issued by Sears Roebuck, became precious commodities for playing "scrapbook house." To play, children used old ledgers or albums as the basis to create paste-up, collaged domestic spaces. Often an entire ledger book would be filled with various upper-middle-class styled rooms. Most scrapbook houses were consistent in that one room would occupy an open ledger page, but some examples, such as the Grace Curtis Stevens house (as the 1880s scrapbook house is known), further miniaturized the domestic environment so that a cross-section of the house could be seen in its entirety.

The furnishings, layout, and paper characters that "lived" in the domestic spaces of the scrapbook house created by small hands provide a snapshot of how ideal houses

| Figure 2.5 |

Emilie P. Hickey's Paper Dolls, United States, ca. 1870, glue/cut/painted/paper/ cardboard. On the dark red cover inscribed in gold is "Paper Dolls House, Emilie P. Hickey." This scrapbook contains six double-page spreads of room interiors including two parlors, one bedroom or dressing room, a man's room, a trunk room, and the children's playroom or nursery. Margaret Woodbury Strong Museum, Rochester, NY.

were imagined by a particular class at a particular time and geography. The players were typically girls and were expected to imitate their parents' tastes by "shopping" for desirable goods in the catalogs. Often, girls playing scrapbook house would add paper human characters to the houses, clipping out servants such as butlers and maids in addition to family members. In some cases, all furniture and human figures were glued completely in place. In others, characters remained loose, and players were able to move them about the rooms. Scenes included home furnishings, wallpaper, and exterior images found in magazines. In design, the houses incorporated all of the functional items needed for the family and staff to perform domestic labor. The presence of maids and butlers suggests the theme of household management as well: the goal was for players to learn how to manage effectively all aspects of this early version of a virtual household. The sample of artwork exemplifies this theme: Emilie P. Hickey's paper dollhouse from ca. 1870 (figure 2.5), focused on home-based play, featuring scenarious of tea parties, dressup, hide-and-seek, and the like while incorporating family members and domestic staff.

Doll play scholar Frances Armstrong notes that historic documents demonstrate that the events occurring within the dolls' homes were a faithful mirror of what happened in real homes. Such repetition was similar to record keeping or cultural documentation disguised as play. Armstrong relays an anonymous account written in 1888 that gives a detailed example of the rules enacted in this style of doll play as occurred over an entire day: the girl of the household would get her dolls out of bed in the morning, dress them, and give them breakfast before their "school lessons." These followed immediately, using small textbooks the child had designed. The dolls studied at the same time the girl did, and, like her, had dinner, did more homework, bathed, and went to bed. The doll parents played cards, and eventually, all of the dolls and their owner retired for the night. Afterwards, the girl might expect her mother to commend her "for doing the duty of this toy house."[30]

With this example, the complex relationship between play and daily life that the idea of playculture encapsulates develops, as players intertwine play and domestic life well over a century ago.[31] Through the exploration of the rules of domestic life, those playing house through scrapbooking maintained traditions of cultural, material, and symbolic importance that reinstated traditional roles within the home, which in turn becomes the site of instantiation of traditional gender roles surrounding work, play, and consumption. Flat, paper model houses "were an ideal medium to introduce girls to their future roles as wives, mothers, and homemakers" since a house, as play scholar Roth has noted, "in a scrapbook, just as much as an actual one, had to be run and maintained properly."[32] Paper dollhouse makers even seemed to try to capture some of the spatial complexity of real houses through their inset layers, cutouts, and outlines (such as figure 2.6). Play housekeeping thus acted as a continuous symbolic reinforcement of Western household tradition, and the practical and ritualistic function of housekeeping became a desired focus of play. Inexpensive to make and prudently imaginative in their recycling of materials, the scrapbook houses could be made by anyone who could afford time, paste, and scissors, making the trend a democratic form not only of play but also of normative reinforcement.[33]

At the same time, nineteenth- and twentieth-century children's magazines, books, and songs reveal that children were encouraged to develop strong bonds with their dolls. Magazines generally focused on the more expensive dolls—often European, French-styled ceramic dolls possessing detailed features.[34] The doll boom in the late nineteenth century included innovations like the European L'Intrépide Bébé, a walking doll (1880s), the Edison talking doll (1886), the Campbell Kids dolls (1910) (figure 2.7), and, in a popular sensation, the Dolly Dingle Paper Dolls (1913) and, later, the Madame Alexander dolls (1930s).[35]

| Figure 2.6 |

Scrapbook dollhouse, ca. 1890. Ledger book with tan leather spine and corners and covers of yellow marbleized paper on heavy cardboard. Book creates entire house. Outlines of room interiors in ink embellished with scrap, newspaper and magazine cutouts, watercolor. Many pages have door or window openings cut out to reveal part of the next room. Begins with front door, opening to many specialized rooms: dining, library, nursery, bath, kitchen, ballroom, billiard room, attic, servants' hall, and conservatory. Most rooms include cutout figures displaying careful attention to proportion. See jacket file for identification of one figure used in the book. Acquired by D. Smith. Purchased from Bromer Booksellers, Boston, MA. Margaret Woodbury Strong Museum, Rochester, NY.

Despite the best efforts of marketing and commercial culture, the unexpected yet striking fact is that there is evidence that girls in particular were resistant to, even critical of, the social roles being ascribed through doll play. As Sutton-Smith has noted, because games, sports, and festivals are in part an exercise in the identity formation and display of power of kings, the aristocracy, heterosexuals, and men, "the games of the less powerful groups are excluded and even ridiculed."[36] Typically then, we would expect that the games of women and girls have not been validated or recorded since they have not been a part of popular or public contests. Nevertheless, even in everyday play, nineteenth-century girls met the emphasis on "normative" domestic behavior for women with subversive resistance. Here, the work of Miriam Formanek-Brunell, a central figure in research in historic play patterns, is an essential resource. In her book *Made to Play House*, Formanek-Brunell notes that while adults saw playing with dolls as useful for social "feminization," some children would use the dolls for purposes distinctly different than their intended use.[37] When domestic roles needed to be

| Figure 2.7 |

Victorian-era children playing with Campbell Kids dolls. New York, March 1912. Photographed by Lewis Wickes Hine (1874–1940).

reasserted due to changing labor conditions, reorganization of banking and financial systems, or changes in property ownership, doll play changed with them.[38] Rather than focus on mothering and household management skills, players often opted to play out scenes of strife, family fights, incidents that broke strict social etiquette, and illness. In scenes rather resembling television crime dramas, these play sessions might result in the punishment, dismemberment, or death of a doll. Players staged doll funerals, perhaps in an effort to work out deeper issues imbedded in Victorian social customs and rituals. States Formanek-Brunell, "For some, a doll's worth was determined by its ability to subvert convention, mock materialism, and undermine restrictions."[39]

Types of Critical Play

At this point then, I would propose terms for the types of critical play enacted by Victorian girls, acknowledging that the space in play for reworking cultural conventions reflects Turner's notion that play creates "liminal" periods for the community of play participants.[40] Furthermore, the enactment of critical play exhibits at least three kinds of action: unplaying, re-dressing or reskinning, and rewriting.

Unplaying

In this play action, players specifically enact "forbidden" or secret scenes, unfortunate scenarios, or other unanticipated conclusions often in opposition to an acceptable or expected adult-play script. In doll play, *unplaying* manifests in children abusing their dolls, "killing" them, or some other revision of the "care giving" framework of expected play. This critical kind of play reverses traditional expectations regarding care-giving behaviors and allows players to rethink the conventions involved in these social roles. While at first the gruesome act of killing dolls was seen as subversive, parents eventually encouraged doll death ceremonies in order to instruct girls on family funeral etiquette.[41]

Re-dressing or Reskinning

Players make alternative arrangements and disguise their dolls for subversive roles, altering the appearance or the presentation of dolls in a way that allows dolls to enter the forbidden scene. Dolls could merely change costumes, or they could be reskinned with makeup or masks to literally efface the surface of the body. For instance, girls who enacted doll funerals might construct clothing ensembles appropriate for death scenes. Parents eventually addressed these preferences by providing girls with doll caskets and doll manufacturers began packaging their fashion dolls to appeal to such subversion by creating new doll products that catered to critical types of play. Some dolls, for example, were sold together with elaborate black mourning outfits.[42]

Rewriting

While many scenarios document "normal" kinds of play, in American fiction publications for children in the later half of the nineteenth century, short stories about death, dying dolls, and mourning proliferated in books and magazines. In fact, many books and essays were marketed to the dolls themselves, with titles such as *The Dolls' Own Book* or *Playday Stories* (figure 2.8); both had narratives purportedly written by doll authors.[43] In this way, those involved in the manufacture of dolls and doll culture (including children, as they wrote letters to such publications) could constantly revise or rewrite the narratives surrounding dolls. This fiction surrounding a burgeoning doll culture was powerful for a number of reasons. First, it celebrated the critical aspects that girls themselves had brought to "straight" play. Second, it reinforced and validated the existence of the dolls and the importance of imaginative playtime. Finally, doll fiction was a way for girls to explore deeper social and personal meanings in play. As Formanek-Brunell notes, "It was the fictional literature of 'doll culture' that broached the more powerful feelings of love and violence."[44] These "rewritten"

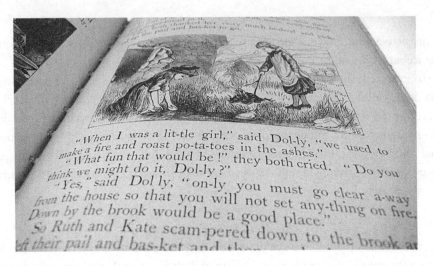

"When I was a lit-tle girl," said Dol-ly, "we used to make a fire and roast po-ta-toes in the ashes."
"What fun that would be !" they both cried. "Do you think we might do it, Dol-ly ?"
"Yes," said Dol-ly, "on-ly you must go clear a-way from the house so that you will not set any-thing on fire. Down by the brook would be a good place."
So Ruth and Kate scam-pered down to the brook an of their pail and bas-ket and th——

| Figure 2.8 |
The children's book *Playday Stories* was purportedly written from the point of view of "Dol-ly."

texts helped expand parental approval over the various ways children were allowed to play. Participant narratives were important, then, on a number of levels, from merchandising to defining playculture itself.

In other cases of rewriting, a fascination with dolls and the macabre goes beyond the playrooms of Victorian childhood. The 1940s dollhouse of Chicago heiress and volunteer police officer Frances Glessner Lee is one of many examples of adults engaged with doll culture. As a doll maker, Glessner Lee produced ghoulish scenes, called the *Nutshell Studies of Unexplained Death*. These toys were used as models to train police officers in forensics and crime scene investigation. Giving each diorama an unsettling name like "Burned Cabin" or "Dark Bathroom," Glessner Lee created custom clothing, crime weapons, and gore, and was assisted by a professional carpenter who followed the details Glessner Lee derived from true crime stories to create the opulent structures that stood for the doll rooms (see figure 2.9). Jennifer Doublet, an architect researching Glessner Lee's work, was quoted in Eve Kahn's *San Francisco Chronicle* article as saying: "For me there is perhaps nothing more satisfying in the Nutshells than the subversive pleasure of seeing the world of male detecting [*sic*] blown wide apart by the macabre depiction of domestic violence in the precious, controlled, feminine space of a doll's house."[45]

Glessner Lee, then, enacted all three styles of critical play described earlier. She "reskinned" the dollhouse itself to be the scene of macabre crimes by using real life

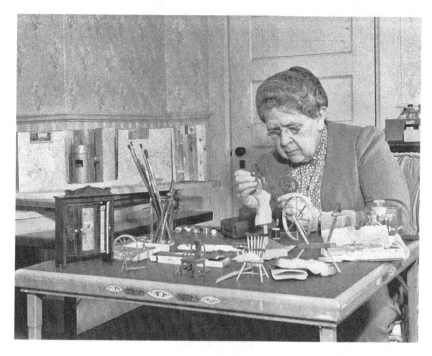

| **Figure 2.9** |
Fanny Glessner Lee shown working on miniatures for her *Nutshell Studies of Unexplained Death*. Photograph courtesy of the Glessner House Museum, Chicago, IL.

descriptions. She "unplayed" the conventions of police work and confronted notions of the appropriate through doll play activities. Glessner Lee also "rewrote" her own role and the importance of doll playing within her surrounding society. Just as Henrik Ibsen's play *A Doll's House* (1879) features a troubled heroine who longs to leave the trap of domesticity, Glessner Lee's inversions demonstrate some of the ways dollhouses signify a controlling repression at work in cultural discourse, a repression enforced by the rule set generated by domestic norms. By pushing the boundaries of the permissible, these acts of critical play are linked to historical models of play in domestic space. Agency is thus a central factor in the construction of doll play, whether virtual or physical.

Inventor's Dolls

Cultural roles also play a part in the production of a toy. In *Made to Play House*, Formanek-Brunell explores the production of dolls and the creation of the doll

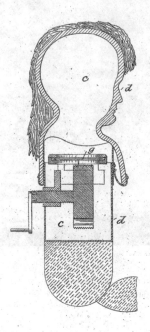

(No Model.)   2 Sheets—Sheet 1.

W. W. JACQUES.
PHONOGRAPH DOLL.

No. 400,851.   Patented Apr. 2, 1889.

Fig. 1.

Witnesses.   *Inventor.*

| Figure 2.10 |

W. W. Jacques's file for Phonograph Doll, from his April 2, 1889, patent, the Edison Phonography Toy Manufacturing Company of Maine.

industry, to argue that while dolls may be seen in some circles as trivial artifacts, the doll business became an incredibly lucrative and competitive industry, which reflected specific social and political agendas. In the United States, early doll makers were women, often sisters, working out of their homes. These artisans typically made dolls at home until they had the funds to create factories.[46] Generally, however, once doll making entered the phase of mass production, it became a male-dominated business. Several inventors became interested in doll making in the nineteenth century, and dolls soon emerged as products of clockmakers and machinists.[47] Instead of the plush comfort of the rag doll and an array of clothing that female doll makers might wish to offer girls, inventors-turned-doll makers were interested in doll functionality. Twentieth-century doll making in North America was not based on an apprentice system or family business as it had been in the past, but rather, on a profit-seeking toy industry that attracted male entrepreneurs.[48]

Inspired by late-nineteenth-century innovations in animation and the creation of lifelike products such as cinema and photography, doll makers specialized in creating animated features or limbs. Locomotion was a special source of fascination.[49] Edison is credited with inventing the first talking doll, the Phonograph Doll (figure 2.10). It is a mechanical doll created almost entirely of metal that contained a miniature cylinder phonograph, and it was patented in 1889.[50]

Other dolls had adjustable mouths, eyes, or mechanized limbs. Materials also changed. Dolls with wooden, ceramic, or metal bodies gradually replaced rag dolls. Patents filed by various inventors from 1871 to 1901 show numerous mechanical dolls, such as George Pemberton Clarke's Natural Creeping Baby Doll, patented in 1871 (figures 2.11 and 2.12).[51] In parallel to an industrial revolution that brought mechanical gadgets to the center of everyday life and promoted the idea that pleasure could be derived from mechanical devices, the culture of technology collided with more traditional forms of doll making.[52] The mechanically controlled dolls, however, were unpopular with girls, and early mechanical dolls often failed to function.[53] Without the pleasure of a mechanical doll appearing "alive," the broken dolls were mere heavy objects, which did not foster engagement.

Artists' Dolls

Artists have explored domestic themes more fully and in more media throughout the last century, but despite these efforts there is a somewhat peculiar emergence of dolls in twentieth-century art. Among the artists who worked with dolls early on and in an explicit arts context were those who inspired or were associated with twentieth-century Dada movement. Banding together in the heart of Europe during World

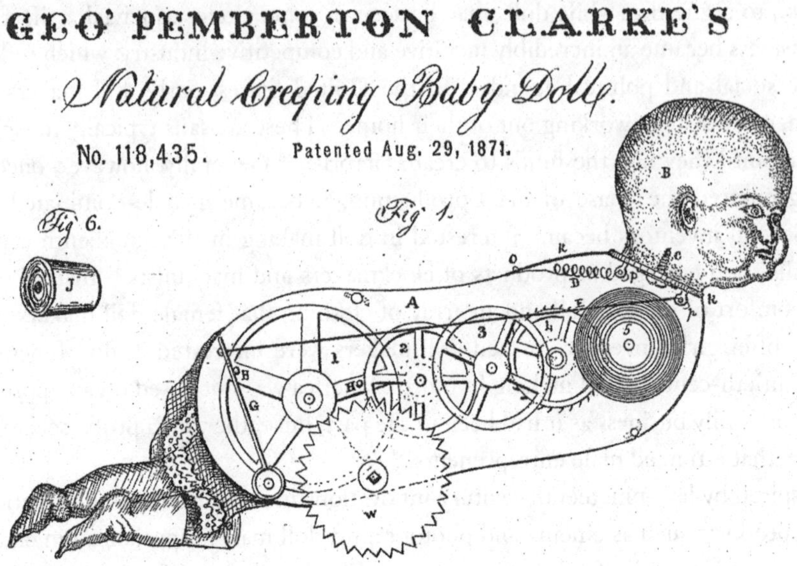

| Figure 2.11 |
George Pemberton Clarke's Natural Creeping Baby Doll, from his August 29, 1871, patent.

War I, the Dadaists' aim was to give voice to "a raucous skepticism about accepted values."[54] While Dada emerged in Zurich, Paris, Berlin, Hanover, Cologne, and New York in differing ways, consistent Dada innovations include the creation of a global network of artists who used new forms to communicate and to create art itself. These forms included letters, postcards, and publications, some of which resemble more contemporary zines. The context of the Dada artist was the large-scale mutilation and killing of World War I, the paradigm-shifting developments in psychology and medicine, advances in technology, and fascism. Cultural and political upheaval set the stage for a cultural production that could express the severe and very real repercussions of moral and intellectual crisis. Dada artists responded to the shock of the twentieth century with a diverse range of writing, painting, performance, photo-collage, object making, and sound recording, all of which reflected the collapse of the rationality so beloved to Enlightenment thinkers. Promising to "put an end to 'culture' as something distinct from everyday life," Dada embodied the irony of an antilaw antiwar antiart that was created by those who were to become central figures in the move toward modernism.[55]

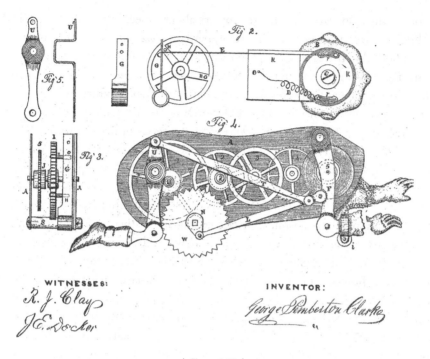

| Figure 2.12 |
Natural Creeping Baby Doll patent application document.

In 1896, many years before Dada artists began their rebellious art practice, Alfred Jarry performed his long-practiced play *Ubu Roi* at the Théâtre d'Art in Paris; it was his most significant work, and was an ongoing creation from his high school years. The play itself is a puppet show, but one that veers so violently from the comic to obnoxious it positively shocked the theater audiences of the time. Most shocking of all was Jarry's choice to use life-sized puppets, or performing objects, as his cast. These human-operated marionettes told the comical satire of Ma and Pa Ubu, a huge and aggressive, yet slapstick couple who plot to take over Poland in the manner of Shakespeare's *Macbeth*. The actors in the play wore masks, rode hobby-horses (a precursor for the term *Dada*),[56] and the entire drama occurred in a single mysterious landscape complete with a bed and fireplace that acted as conduits for character entrances and exits.[57] In Bell's account of the performance, Jarry is said to have announced to the audience that some of the performers in the two-evening run of the play had agreed to lose their personalities and play with masks over their faces to better "mirror the mind and soul of the man-sized marionettes you are about to see."[58] What is of note is that the objects on the stage were as important, perhaps *more* important, than the human actors to both the structure of the production and the intentions of its creator.

Abstract, found-object, and mechanized types of theater proved central to the course of development for performance arts in the twentieth century, and Jarry's work provided an important insight into the performing arts for radical theater makers.[59] Dada artist Sophie Taeuber (1889–1943) created a series of marionettes in 1918 for the play *König Hirsch* (*The King Stag*) by Carlo Gozzi, adapted by René Morax and Werner Wolff for the Swiss Marionette Theater in 1918.[60] These puppets were primarily constructed from painted, turned wood. They featured symmetrical bodies, metal joints, and abstract faces that resembled masks far more than traditional dolls. Some of the puppets were costumed in lace dresses and feather outfits. Historian Leah Dickerman argues that the fairy tale of the Stag was transformed into a modern allegory of psychological discourse, with characters named after Freud, Jung (Dr. Komplex), and the Jungian notion of "Urlibido"—for each have their effect on the king and his friends.[61] Taeuber also created a set of Dada performance masks resembling carvings from the African continent. Masks were made from found materials such as newspaper and cardboard. The masks represented to Dada artist Hugo Ball "not human characters and passions, but . . . passions that are larger than life. The horror of our time, the paralyzing background of events, is made visible."[62]

Photomontage artist Hannah Höch also exhibited *Dada Puppen* or *Dada Dolls* at the Dada Fair in 1916. These figures explored the social issues of the time, speaking with both their scale and their subject matter. In 1920, John Heartfield and Rudolf Schlichter created the *Prussian Archangel*, a life-sized human soldier with a pig head. In 1921, George Grosz and John Heartfield created *The Middle-Class Philistine Heartfield Gone Wild*, an electric light affixed to a headless tailor's dummy, with revolver, doorbell, and missing leg with a peg prosthesis attached. Upon returning home from World War I, Oskar Kokoschka created a life-sized doll to replicate his lost lover Alma Mahler, who left him to marry another man. Kokoschka escorted the doll to the opera and to parties, and hired servants to tend to it. This performative type of doll play, from make-believe social partner to rumored sex toy, relied heavily on notions of performance, sexual norms and fetishes, and socially acceptable behavior.[63] Dolls also appear in drawings. Max Ernst included doll-like diagrams and dressmaking patterns in his portfolio *Let There Be Fashion, Down with Art* (1919–1920). Dolls are also part of the painting *Water Babies* (1919) by John Covert, in which is painted as segmented parts in containers of water. Caught between a society that had initially sanctioned war and the horrors of military technology, Dadaists used dolls, puppets, dressmaker's dummies, and doll play as a means of fully exploring the impact of technological change on the body.

The Surrealists followed, bringing the doll further into the realm of the unconscious. Sharla Hutchinson notes that several of these artists used the creative method of "convulsive beauty," including depictions of violence, pornography, hysteria, and transgressive behavior to explore the psychological impact of restrictive social norms.[64] Man Ray's famous photograph *Coat Stand* (1920) showed a nude woman with a missing leg—in actuality, a hidden leg disguised with a dark sock—perched behind a doll-like cutout of a head and arms. Using both doll and dressmaker dummy as indexes, as well as a hand-drawn mask, the doll-as-woman-as-coat-rack stares ahead in silent shock, an expression of the horrors of war. Deleuze links artistic, fantasy worlds and the reality that generates such fantasy by noting, "A frightened countenance is the expression of a frightening possible world, or of something frightening in the world—something I do not yet see. Let it be understood that the possible is not here an abstract category designating something which does not exist: the expressed possible world certainly exists, but it does not exist (actually) outside of that which expresses it."[65]

From marionettes to life-sized artificial bodies, artists' dolls became more grotesque in the Surrealist period. Perhaps the best-known examples of this work were the headless, mutilated female dolls that emerged from German-born artist Hans Bellmer (1902–1975). Bellmer began working with dolls in Berlin in 1933. His papier-mâché, plaster, and tissue-paper bodies quickly became some of the most controversial artifacts of the entire Surrealist movement.[66] In a large portfolio of photographs, Bellmer staged scenes featuring these disturbing figures in both indoor and outdoor settings, sometimes with household props like carpet beaters (figure 2.13).[67]

The image of the doll is a complex site for the generation of meaning and, while problematic for reasons discussed later, Freud's useful description of the interesting tension between agency and pleasure his 1919 essay, "The Uncanny," helps ground an investigation into the human fascination with automata and life-like figurines. Using the term *unheimlich* (uncanny), which translates literally to "unhomelike," Freud described how the sense of the uncanny manifests when an otherwise normal situation reveals hidden abnormalities exposed by small shifts or derivations from normal, "lifelike" behavior. Linking the uncanny to desires repressed from infancy, and noting that this return to repressed desire is based on a desire for control, a viewer's or player's reaction to uncanny situations can create dread, fear, or fascination out of what on the surface appears to be an everyday circumstance.[68] While Bellmer's dolls have been criticized for their apparent sexist repulsion toward the female body, art historian and Surrealist scholar Hal Foster has argued that the dolls, fashioned during and

| Figure 2.13 |

Hans Bellmer (1902–1975), *Doll's Games* (*Les jeux de la poupée*), 1935–1938. 12.4 × 9.3 cm. AM1996-206(23). Musée National d'Art Moderne, Centre Georges Pompidou, Paris. Photo: Philippe Migeat. Photo credit: CNAC/MNAM/Dist. Réunion des Musées Nationaux/Art Resource, NY. © ARS, NY.

after Hitler's rise to power in Germany, mark an obsession with sexuality, death, and mental health that reflects much about the suffocation of a formerly liberal Weimar system of representation.

Therese Lichtenstein, a Bellmer scholar, delves further into the cultural context of Bellmer's work, noting that the National Socialist approach to the body, sexuality, and art was linked to the condemnation of modernist art as officially "degenerate" under Hitler (1937), and these themes are embedded in Bellmer's doll works.[69] Sue Taylor has observed that "Bellmer depicted female bodies reified, mutated, sodomized, bound, eviscerated."[70] His work *Doll's Games* (*Les jeux de la poupée*) (1935–1938) is a mild example of a typical Bellmer body (see figure 2.13). Bellmer bodies instead objectified, fetishized, and ultimately degraded the female body. In part these extreme and mutated bodies can also be read as a reaction to fascism.[71] Noting that World War I and the rise of fascist powers cultivated an ideology of the male body as a weapon, Foster suggests that the period's artists used dolls as a common ground for subversion, relating the violently deformed female form to real transgressions of the body, from the mutilations of the battlefield to the atrocities the Nazi regime inflicted on Jews, Communists, homosexuals, and the feminized "masses."[72] For reasons much debated in historical documents, most Surrealists avoided issues of homosexuality and the sexual liberation of women as "causes which the Surrealists were unwilling to support."[73] However, a few female artists were able to redirect Surrealist concerns to the female body. Based in New York, experimental writer Djuna Barnes created alternate narratives to defy societal norms, while photographer and self-portraitist Claude Cahun, also known as Lucy Schwob (1894–1954), played with gender stereotypes to criticize capitalist, fascist, and patriarchal ideologies. Their work will be explored in subsequent chapters.

Several contemporary artists are furthering this line of inquiry, taking the critical and reflective capacity inherent in the figure of the doll to fresh territories. The configuration of the body itself is called into question in the work of Jake and Dinos Chapman, artists and brothers who create grotesque, mutated groups of child-aged mannequins, frequently reconfiguring, removing, and repositioning a doll's genitalia to the face. The sneaker-wearing children tend to be arranged in playful groups as though engaged in a game, but the disturbing dislocation and relocation of the bodies in these works recalls Bellmer's grotesque and powerless females. In the Chapmans' installation of their work *Hell* (2000), nine miniature tableaus displayed in glass tanks feature distorted figurines that reference the apocalyptic and demon-and-machine-filled fifteenth-century images of Hieronymus Bosch. In *Hell*, the glass cases displaying the mangled figurines depict war and torture, presenting Nazis as both perpetrators and victims, all arranged in the shape of a swastika.[74]

While the Chapmans use dolls to reference war, violence, and public mutilation of the body, the married team of Bradley McCallum and Jacqueline Tarry uses dolls to critique historical notions of race relations in the United States. In their video installation *Topsy Turvy* (2006), McCallum, who is white, and Tarry, who is black, embodied their relationship in a "twinning doll," themselves portrayed as a nineteenth-century toy that is in reality two dolls joined at the torso with a skirt. Held vertically, one doll's face and body is hidden until the player flips the doll over to reveal the second aspect of the doll. In their video, dressed in nineteenth-century clothing, the two artists proceed to "flip" themselves down a long marble hallway. The white man flips to become a black woman, then the doll morphs to the figures of Thomas Jefferson and Sally Hemings. In installation, the video work is shown with doll artifacts and molded busts of the artists (figure 2.14).

The video and installation explores the experiences of a mixed-race couple by examining dualities: white and black, male and female. By referencing historical

| Figure 2.14 |
Bradley McCallum and Jacqueline Tarry, *Topsy Turvy* installation, 2006.

atrocities such as slavery and cultural challenges such as stereotypes, the artists both perform difference and document difference in a pseudoscientific display of performance artifacts. As the artists note, "The races are joined head to toe . . . continuously revealing and concealing one another."[75]

Australian artist Van Sowerwine (b. 1975) makes interactive dollhouses and films that depict girls in a contemporary state of crisis. Her work focuses on the confines of the house and on painful issues that affect young women: suburban isolation, abuse, teenage pregnancy, self-mutilation, and suicide. These reflect the historical conditions of girls' play in that they take on social issues already familiar to play over a century ago. In collaboration with animator Isobel Knowles, the interactive installation *Play with Me* (2002) engages viewers in play in order for them to experience these extremes of present-day girls' concerns.

In a gallery setting, participants approach, enter, and sit inside what is literally a children's playhouse in order to experience *Play with Me* (figure 2.15). In front of an embedded computer monitor, they can interact with an on-screen play world by using a mouse to make choices. A small doll appears in the scene using stop-motion animation, and gazes directly at the participant/player. *Play with Me* puts the player on edge:

| Figure 2.15 |
Van Sowerwine, *Play with Me* interactive installation, May 2002. Pine cubby, interactive stop-motion animation. Centre for Contemporary Photography, Melbourne.

the doll's direct gaze acknowledges the agency of the doll herself as she moves deliberately through the scene in her own time (figure 2.16). When the player directs the doll to play with items such as teapots and drawing implements, events quickly spiral away from the player's control. For example, if the player chooses for the doll to play with the teacup instead of playing the classic doll game of "tea," the doll "unplays" the expected by breaking her cup and sawing away at her bloodied arm, all the while staring uncannily at the player who is helpless to intervene. By giving the agency of subversion and criticality to the doll itself, Sowerwine and Knowles question the very notion of play while referencing the challenge of adult efficacy in real-world domestic crises.

Sowerwine's work *Sharper than a Serpent's Tooth* explores the difficult and violent world of childhood, and extends this in a large-scale photographic series. The title refers to this passage from Shakespeare's *King Lear* (1605):

If she must teem,
Create her child of spleen; that it may live,
And be a thwart disnatured torment to her!
Let it stamp wrinkles in her brow of youth;

| Figure 2.16 |
Van Sowerwine, *Play with Me* interactive installation.

With cadent tears fret channels in her cheeks;
Turn all her mother's pains and benefits
To laughter and contempt; that she may feel
How sharper than a serpent's tooth it is
To have a thankless child![76]

Printed as public billboards, doll images are scaled to be larger than life, subversively casting the child as loner, outside, or monster. The character Sophie, for example, sits alone, in an alienated state in one billboard (figure 2.17). This sense of loneliness and alienation is present among all of Sowerwine's doll works. In the recent short film *Clara*, Sowerwine again explores the trauma of adolescence in suburbia. Struggling with a massive change in her life, the twelve-year-old Clara character engages with her world as a disoriented and confused spectator. While playing in the yard of a suburban home, Clara finds that the flowers grab at her; when she enters a home, she finds it empty except for a coffin holding a small blonde girl. Ants flow around the perimeter. Clara moves about the scenes with a lumbering shuffle, clearly filled with sorrow, grief, and depression. Is this over the death of a friend, or life in an empty place? The girl enters the kitchen, where a boiling pot of

| Figure 2.17 |
Van Sowerwine, "Sophie #2," from *Sharper than a Serpent's Tooth*, 2005.

water tempts her to insert her finger and hold it there, then finally remove it blistered in pain. The lack of catharsis or resolution in Sowerwine's animated pieces work against the genre conventions of storytelling. Instead, Sowerwine is unplaying popular family narratives to create worlds that disclose the dark, helpless, and sinister lives many children face.

On a different mission, contemporary artists such as Martha Rosler (b. 1943) critique domestic space itself by simply playing house themselves. Rosler's important *Semiotics of the Kitchen* (1975) is an example of early performative video art (figure 2.18). Standing in a typical kitchen, Rosler recites the English alphabet, stopping only to seize the corresponding object as she says each letter and violently performing the stereotypic and repetitive action normally associated with the tool. Perhaps the most game-like of a group of early feminist technological works, the video twists the kitchen into an almost sideshow-like atmosphere. In her performance of otherwise unexamined domestic activities, Rosler unplays beliefs about domestic roles as well as the rules of television programming.[77]

Art and Popular Game Houses

The contemporary art practices of Rosler, McCallum and Tarry, the Chapmans, and Sowerwine are examples of the subversive tactics in use by artists today to use dolls in the exploration of social roles. The domestic space of the house, however, has also been the focus of contemporary as artists. Sculptor Rachel Whiteread's casting of interior household objects and spaces, as well as Gordon Matta Clark's literal deconstruction of houses

| Figure 2.18 |
Martha Rosler, still from *Semiotics of the Kitchen*, 1975. Courtesy of Electronic Arts Intermix (EAI), NY.

through cutting and moving them reflect upon the significance of domestic spaces. Since Activision's *Little Computer People* (1985), the house has served as both site and theme within computer games (see figure 2.19). Modern computer games invite both players and designers to draw on the domestic utopias of cultural imagination in a new embodiment of many of the same styles of criticality and subversion already documented. Gamers reskin, replay, unplay, and indeed, rewrite popular worlds all the while offering their own interpretations of play.

In the 2003 game *Neighbors from Hell*, players pull pranks on their neighbors in retaliation for suburban transgressions such as poor lawn care. In *Second Life*, players build businesses, homes, and entire islands. In the *Neopets* (1999) online world, players design pets to live in Neopia and keep their creations busy on quests, building homes as well as home pages. Players of *The Sims* build and maintain a consumer-driven suburban family or business. In a celebration of domesticity, games like these market their focus on ordinary activities such as care giving and emphasize their break from stereotypical, often violent, gaming models.[78] Instead of gangsters and guns, *The Sims* offers a virtual house, where players control characters known as Sims (derived from Maxis's early work creating simulation software such as *Sim City*) within an intelligent play space. Known also as the "dollhouse" game among parents, the space of *The Sims* is a

| Figure 2.19 |
Activision's *Little Computer People,* 1985.

site of negotiation between the real and the virtual domestic experience. The appeal of this approach is familiar. Both computer gaming and playing house are mechanisms of fantasy.[79] Both types of play involve role definitions, projection, and reversal. The fan culture surrounding contemporary virtual dolls and traditional doll play parallels the historic play patterns of the late twentieth century. In addition, play within a contemporary computer game like *The Sims* has distinct similarities to artist's use of domestic play.

In the last few years, well over half of the U.S. population has come to play video games.[80] The *Sims* series attracts both adults and children in all age groups. After purchasing the game, most new *Sims* players spend hours, usually days, in nonstop manipulation of their new, simulated house and the characters within it. The goal of the game is to keep one's *Sims* characters happy, fed, clean, and nurtured. *Sims* players work to make their initial prefabricated virtual home their own. Initially, players are given modest one-bedroom homes with simple yards, mailbox, and at times, flowers, shrubbery, and an outdoor patio. In *The Sims 2,* the array of standard houses offered to players is equal across player/character class, race, and ethnic lines. The initial houses themselves represent a particularly "Levittown" standard in domestic American architecture, yet simultaneously, they are intended to evolve to embody a player's individuality by presenting the opportunity to add on to and enlarge the house, purchase appropriate furniture, and take up a home-base pastime such as reading or watching television.

Players of *The Sims 2*, like players of the first version, have found that one of the most gratifying aspects of play is sharing unique objects with other players. For example, in just under four months (September 2004–February 2005), *Sims 2* players created and uploaded more than 125,000 characters and houses to share with others.[81] While point of view can change through player commands, the house remains the focus of interaction and play; the house structure is the only space players see. It is, as in paper playhouses, in the confines of the house that most *Sims* characters socialize, look for jobs, and study. While characters appear to have a life outside the home— most characters go to work, for example—player activity is focused on everyday happiness: cooking, reading, decorating, socializing. Players can design their ideal notions of domestic space. There are seldom markers of personal history, heirlooms, mementos, or baby pictures among any of the artifacts in the home, requiring users to create their own personal objects for importation into the game environment.

Players are offered start-up funding in order to purchase appliances, decorations, and essentials such as lamps, cooking utensils, and bookshelves, and are encouraged to purchase furniture for their new characters. Expensive furniture tends to "comfort" the simulated characters more; at least, they are programmed to derive greater happiness from sitting in an expensive, cushy chair, for example, than a plain wooden one. Once the player learns that caring for their *Sims* characters' happiness requires a bigger budget, they have characters look for an income that can then be used for further acquisition and shopping. Without an income or without new materials and spaces to augment their development, the Sims become unhappy and the game balance quite literally turns to chaos. Characters fall asleep or stop using the washroom for fundamental needs. As a result, a conception of character "happiness" decreases and filth accumulates unless funding and new items are continuously cycled through the experience. Without an income, the needs of a player's *Sims* characters escalate due to a lack of food and entertainment. Earning "Simoleans" is paramount to success in satisfying character necessities.[82] So in the very economic and personality models offered in *The Sims*, we see emergent themes of consumption and commerce-driven pleasure. As we shall see, players both use and challenge these values.[83]

Figures 2.20 and 2.21 are *Sims 2* showcase kitchen and bath designs. The kitchen allows the most opportunity for interaction as well as the introduction of new gadgetry; many items available to new players are kitchen appliances. The kitchen is also the default location characters use to enter and exit the home, marking this room as

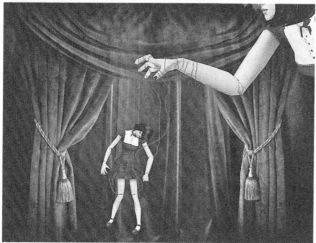

| Figure 2.20 |
A *Sims 2* household created with picture-perfect furnishings of the time. From *The Sims 2: Kitchen & Bath Interior Design Stuff* (2008), with which "your Sims" will have "the right attire and accessories to enjoy their brand-new kitchens and bathrooms," according to the packaging.

| Figure 2.21 |
An image from a *Sims 2* fan site, "I throw my threads" by violentdoll. Screenshot from http://www.koinup.com/violentdoll/work/38853/.May 31, 2008.

the permeable boundary between inside and outside space. This game-design element is in keeping with the trend of kitchens in contemporary American life. In her book *Geography of Home*, Akiko Busch notes that kitchens in modern American homes have expanded beyond the size of other rooms in the house, mostly to accommodate larger and more numerous appliances.[84] However, there is opportunity for experimentation with the system-set placement of material goods within the game. For example, if a player places a large chair and television in the kitchen, the *Sims* characters are just as happy as they would be if the same items were placed in the bedroom. This flexibility allows the player to change the stereotypical expectations of the home, the functions of rooms, and the layout of domestic space. While this and other examples allow for reworking, consumption (purchasing or collecting and placing items) remains one of the core game mechanics. The acquisition of goods and social interaction, however, remain the primary ways to affect a *Sims* character's well-being in the game.

Suburban Life

If the classic American player's physical home is a cul-de-sac "castle," then the player's *Sims* house and the surrounding *Sims* suburb can easily become a vision of utopia where each player's house is constructed as a world unto its own. While there are varying notions about spatial practices and particular urbanization models, suburbanization as phenomenon is central to the design of *Sims* experiences. Silverstone attributes the first suburb to London, where crowded conditions in the nineteenth-century city drove the middle class outside the city center.[85] Populations in London suburbs doubled in the second half of the nineteenth century, and other cities worldwide soon followed suit as transit systems such as commuter trains, freeways, and automobiles fostered suburban growth. The play environment of *The Sims* recreates these particular aspects of suburban design, especially those elements focusing on control over the environment and the idea of "safety." As architect Lars Lerup notes, the suburban dream extends even to the vehicles used by its inhabitants to go to work. More than transportation, the SUV is a now-classic icon that, at least metaphorically, extends the safety and shelter of the suburbs throughout the commute into the dangerous city. The larger the SUV, the better the control over one's environment. As players strive for consumer stardom by expanding their homes, accumulating luxury goods, and hosting unique social events, *The Sims* explores an almost infinite set of grandiose suburban control fantasies.

Sims homes are set in generic, suburban tracts outside the area where characters presumably work. As participants and voyeurs, players can zoom in or out and rotate the scene to get any view they prefer of their *Sims* surroundings. All *Sims* characters, even nearly penniless families, live along these pleasantly wide, blacktopped roads. In fact, Will Wright has noted that French audiences complained that the wide roads in the game felt "too American."[86] Meanwhile, Lyn Spiegel notes that in postwar America, the "new suburban family ideal was a consensus ideology, promising practical benefits like security and stability" to those who had lived through the deaths and rationing brought on by war.[87] After World War II, suburbia helped reinstate traditional roles within in the twentieth-century home. The suburbs were created in part as a response to the "swing shift," those women who worked outside the house for the war effort but who also contributed to the postwar perception of a collapse in traditional family roles. From the industrial revolution to World War II, the West has witnessed various liberations and subsequent "redomestications" of domestic space, and *The Sims* cannot be separated from these phases of the popular imagination. Real or virtual, suburbs embody particular kinds of architectural values and ideas about access, but more importantly, create a way of life that is the product of a set of cultural beliefs, economic forces, and expectations.

Around 2002, the year the first *Sims* game peaked in popularity, a significant shift in U.S. culture affected the balance between the physical and the virtual. Since the 1980s, there has been a growing U.S. trend to move to controllable spaces. The house has shifted from being a place of comfort to a site for defense. Unsurprisingly then, amid 1990s dot-com culture, *The Sims* embodied a period of great optimism, when a robust economy and low crime rates contributed to the utopian appeal of a new era. Software and hardware industries provided an almost mythic promise of a new, technology-infused lifestyle. Americans actively participated in both the consumption of household goods and virtual technologies.[88]

The collapse of the dot-com bubble was followed by a period of unusual economic decline and instability due to fears generated by the idea of impending terrorist threats. In the United States, old city neighborhoods are growing at the suburbs' expense.[89] With cities touted as terrorist targets, and U.S. Department of Homeland Security bulletins encouraging citizens to fortify their homes with plastic sheeting, stored water, and duct tape, digital entertainment sales simultaneously boomed. These practical everyday trends, combined with the increase in games' (especially *The Sims*) popularity, demonstrate that American consumers have retreated into their homes both physically and virtually to discover and enact their utopian ideals. In fact, the 2008 IKEA catalog slogan in the United States is "Home: The Most Important Place on Earth."

In reviewing play practices of nurturing, suburbanization, and home building, and in presenting consumption as a significant aspect of game play, *The Sims* does provide opportunity for a tongue-in-cheek reading that takes note of features like its "whimsical shopping Muzak" that accompanies the shopping interface used for purchasing objects for the home. By drawing attention to the boundary between consumption and desire, many of the goals in *The Sims* imply a critique of the mass-consumption playing the game requires. In some scenarios, the game might encourage players to question whether their characters would be happier with bigger, better items and houses, for the tasks necessary to acquire increase exponentially with possessions a character has. While goods and services are valued in this game, human interaction and compassion are also rewarded. The richer the characters become, the more they must work and the more effective their purchased items must be at delivering pleasure. Just as the first, post–World War II generation of U.S. suburbanites was conscious of the performative and artificial nature of the media depicting "consumer dreams" and suburban family life in the 1950s, *Sims* players are faced with paradoxes of pleasure, leisure, work, and consumption. While many *Sims* players play inside idyllic, virtual suburban homes, much research points to the social and collaborative nature of many of the game's play styles.[90] The majority of *Sims* players, then, may simply desire connections through play.

However, the positioning of consumption as an instrumental game goal is cause for further investigation, if only because it so closely resembles real-world corporate messages and the everyday practices of consumers. In *The Sims*, a typically "male" space of a video game has been integrated into both real (home) and virtual (game) domestic space. The argument offered by Ann Douglas in her groundbreaking writing on the "feminization" of the consumer provides a useful critique.[91] Dollhouses, real and virtual, use symbols to represent external reality.[92] Playing house can either reproduce the functional, such as building a kitchen and having dolls "cook," or it can adapt and assimilate symbols on a player's own terms. In the case of *The Sims*, a "feminization" of the player could logically represent the reclaiming of domestic space by the forces of capitalism. That the game is popular among women and girls may support this idea. The feminization of the player manifests through the design of the game space, game tasks, and game goals, and is reflected socially through the dominance of consumer culture. In playing *The Sims* or other contemporary dollhouse games, players encounter a fascination with household objects, with consumption, and with normative class values. Yet houses themselves function as institutions of domestic space and are situated as mechanisms for control, signifying traditional family roles, which inherently indicate traditional and limiting behavior by the rules they inherit.[93] Players, in their engagement with these domestic spaces, are fitted into these roles. If the definition of space in *The Sims*, and the way players control characters within the domestic sphere, becomes a process of domestication, a kind of *taming*, then the dollhouse is a metaphoric prison.

As many scholars have argued, domestic spaces continue to be associated with the feminine in television, film, and other media.[94] In further studying traditional dollhouses, Kuznets notes, "perhaps we should consider the longing for fixed familial roles a product of self-limiting nostalgia."[95] Earlier, normative behavior in domestic play practices was described as socially expected from nineteenth-century girls. If the fundamental role of suburbanized domestic space in *The Sims* seems to present players with economic, political, and ideological models that rely upon historically feminine associations to function, then the definition of space in *The Sims* is inextricably linked to a larger process involving the representation of such feminization and traditional conceptions of women's roles. If it is true (as Spiegel suggests) that domestic space has been historically linked to the feminine, players engaging in a game set in a dollhouse are in turn "feminized" in such roles and, just as playing house in miniature was a popular American pastime in the late nineteenth century, contemporary computer games may function quite similarly. In using the house and its immediate surroundings as a normative palette with which to create their own image of home and household relationships, game designers reinforce, though perhaps with a degree of self-awareness and irony, previously established ideas about domestic utopias, including those put forward by advertising and corporate marketing research.

Viewed another way, consumption could also represent "the great equalizer" among gender stereotypes, putting *The Sims* at the forefront of critically informed gaming. The fundamental role of suburbanized domestic space in *The Sims*, on the one hand, seems to be to present players with economic, political, and ideological norms, which rely upon a traditionally feminine role to function. On the other hand, using Sutton-Smith's ideas on play, if children learn adult roles, economic skills, and emotional behaviors through fantasy and imitative play, symbolic work and creativity not only mediate *The Sims* but also are simultaneously expanded and developed by the uses, meanings, and "effects" of cultural commodities.[96] In this view, consumerism has to be "understood as an active, not a passive, process—active, for it is a type of play which also includes work."[97]

Do screen-based interactive dollhouses simply manifest the material fantasies of capitalism? Are they a direct confrontation with Freudian notions of desire? Or, more intricately, are such games serving as essential opportunities for critical, subversive performance? Ultimately, the player decides which way he or she would like to read the game. Like the trend in capitalism toward globalization, games such as *The Sims* operate across cultural practices, offering an unadulterated model of American sub-urban living and capitalist desire.[98] *Sims* characters and neighborhoods are familiar to American audiences, and yet their nonrealistic language, their unpredictable reactions to change, and their autonomous behaviors offer surprise, and contribute to troubling questions of control and desire, important themes that can also be found in the artist-made games discussed earlier.

From Dolls to Desire

But how are games like *The Sims* pleasurable? Is it satisfying to complete tasks that maintain the status quo, or pleasurable to control characters and their environments, both playing within and pushing against the game's rules? Rarely if ever do players feel disempowered in domestic game scenarios, and this is essential to the wide appeal of these games. The player desires growth and achievement, but these accomplish-ments are secondary to pleasure derived from the assertion of the familiar. The fun of a virtual house is inextricably related to mastery of the household objects and the human-like dolls that are so very familiar. And no matter how much a player works to maintain the household or keep the pet happy and healthy, the desire to return to the place before desire, that is, the paradise that drives the fantasy play in the first place, always lingers. While toy and game theorist Lois Kuznets traces the complicated ways dolls and toys function as markers of culture, other scholars have explored issues of desire in doll play. Contemporary scholars such as Eva-Maria Simms describe the uncanny nature of dolls and the curious fact that Freud dismissed dolls from his his-tory of psychoanalysis and discussion of the uncanny since dolls "did not symbolize Oedipal issues very well."[99] Here, the work of philosopher Gilles Deleuze may shed light here on the complex play systems described so far.

Working from Freudian and Lacanian notions of the "other," Deleuze offers a compelling argument for the construction of the kinds of systems of desire that games may represent. He argues that, contrary to the theories of Freud and Lacan, the desire for the other is, in fact, a structure for the "*expression of a possible world:* it is the expressed, grasped, as not yet existing outside of that which expresses it."[100] Deleuze refutes the systems of desire offered by psychoanalytical frameworks of voyeurism, exhibitionism, and the various ways that the other is positioned visually in order to refrain from the binary oppositions so integral to psychoanalysis.[101] Instead, Deleuze claims interaction with the other depends on a desire for either the object the other represents, or the desire for other worlds the other expresses.[102] Currently, others have recognized that games, blogs, and various participant-driven systems function because there is a desire to produce meaningful interaction that motivates the creation of new worlds.[103] If this desire fills some kind of "lack" in the Lacanian sense, then the enthusiasm for intricate online games may imply a need for connectivity and for ways players might understand themselves within electronic culture.[104] Deleuze's postvisual look at systems of desire provides a valuable tool for examining online systems, where words and things, visual or nonvisual, are forever interchangeable, exchanged in an everyday framework.

No matter how much a player in a paper house or in an online world works to maintain his or her dolls, the desire to return to the place before desire—that is, the paradise that drives the fantasy play in its first impulse—always lingers. Freud's "lost object" may never be discovered through games in a literal sense, but it is sensible to note the ways so many games focus on finding, searching, and recognizing. Often, the simple wish to return carries users from one session of play to the next. Play objects have been used to make separation from parents easier with blankets, hats, and plush toys as transitional objects.[105] The imaginary nature of physical dollhouses and doll games could mean that players also imagine family relationships and social rituals as equally constructed. Ironically, while many players of *The Sims* work to subvert the game and project their unusual desires upon their *Sim* characters and houses, they do this from their own homes, keeping the order of traditional structures intact. Along these lines, it is worthwhile to note ways in which masculine roles are also constructed in the games. If consumption, interior design, and maintenance are traditionally feminizing roles, the masculine can be seen positioned as quest narratives involving the acquisition of money, status, and power, or, in technological games, figuring out how things work. Here, fun is negotiated by players through journeying and by pushing boundaries and limits, not in an arrival at a destination. With too much control, in other words, there is no point in play.

Subversive Play

Just as in the physical world, players of *The Sims* often encounter uncanny conditions or playfully create them by designing disturbing circumstances to intentionally undo the "expected" *Sims* play.[106] While players are instated into traditionally feminine roles when first playing, they are also encouraged to be critical players, creating miniature rebellions within these confines. In many games, this is possible through a variety of customization tools and reskinning. Reacting against the game goals—for example, consumerism—is another way players critically question the domestic scenarios.

In fact, some players are most satisfied when working against the safe, consumerist system they are supposed to support in the game.

Much player interest in *The Sims* is derived from subverting set norms and exploring the boundaries of what is, and is not, permissible. These modes of critical play are linked to historical models of playing with domestic situations: Victorian doll fiction has been replaced by fan fiction generated by *Sims* players. Victorian practices of doll funerals have translated into macabre *Sims* rituals where virtual dolls suffer, become malnourished, or burned within the normative suburban environment. This subversive desire must at once be compared to the domestic space and the degree of autonomy perceived to be inherent in a *Sims* character. In a game balanced on the edge of user control and system control, *The Sims* offers an *anxious* variety of game play, one that, strangely, might mirror a player's own suburban experiences or fantasies, and thus one that compels players to toy with possibilities. Invoking anxieties also evokes pleasure for a player if the player is put into a controlling position to manage and direct those anxieties.

Freud theorized the gaze as a phallic activity, an activity inextricably associated with the desire for mastery of the object, the voyeur's desire for power over the object. In this system of objectification, objects are rendered passive and gendered feminine. In many action and adventure games, one of the desired objects is the female body viewed primarily for pleasure, a relationship feminist film scholar Laura Mulvey also referred to as "the gaze" in the early years of film studies.[107] Using the gaze as a way of reading the pleasure in games, however, is inadequate for the complexity of analysis the domestic play environments require.

In *The Sims*, it is pleasurable to control characters in their daily routines and to see one's own influence upon the world. Yet it may also be the characters' autonomy that makes the gaze somehow more believable, interesting, and pleasurable for players. Recall Sowerwine's doll and her stare back at the viewer, or a *Second Life* avatar (figure 2.22). Much like Slavoj Žižek's interpretation of the gaze, players may identify with characters, but they recognize their own role as well: "The viewer is forced to face the desire at work in his/her seemingly neutral gaze."[108]

Žižek's ideas on photography, film, and image making transition remarkably well to game analysis, where an obvious break between player and characters at the interface is made apparent. This confrontation with desire is especially appropriate in systems fostered by doll play. Many artists' dolls, especially those created by Kokoschka, Bellmer, and the Chapmans, reinforce the connection between dolls and sex and pornography, whereby spectators and interactors are forced into a perverse position as

| Figure 2.22 |
Neferi Chajit, an avatar in *Second Life*. Interviewed June 10, 2008, at http://www.secondlifeherald.com/.

observers. This is particularly effective when the observation is made through the camera or the screen. The spectator identifies with and as a perpetrator. The gaze becomes, by default, the gaze of the other. "When I am looking at an object, the object is already gazing at me, and from a point at which I cannot see it."[109] For Žižek, the gaze "falls into ourselves, the spectators."[110] Because the player experiences a character's daily routine from a perspective divorced from lived experience, the virtual doll's human-like, autonomous gestures force the player to recognize that the "very procedure is, on a formal level, already 'perverse.'"[111]

The perverse and subversive elements of *The Sims* play are among the most powerful alternate play strategies available to computer game players. Some players subvert the game by purposely making life miserable for the little consumer characters. Players can download negative or subversive homes such as that of "Mr. Sadistic," a household where, instead of nurturing characters and getting them jobs, the *Sims* characters are tortured and frequently die. In *Second Life* or *The Sims Online* worlds, sadomasochism and sexual experimentation, such as that evidenced in the online sex industry, are notable extremes of doll play.[112] Games that involve domesticity are significant, then, because of the subtle yet powerful methods of enculturation occurring via game play and the way in which social values, interaction styles, and everyday activities are both practiced and challenged. The virtual household construction accomplished via shopping has a particularly loaded set of social meanings. Yet the normative play environments are designed specifically to be hacked and subverted, much like normative Hollywood films are meant to be "camped."

The critical practices in games like *The Sims*, in fact, clearly follow the Victorian play practices noted earlier:

Reskinning
Altering characters or objects. In *The Sims*, replacing the graphics of household object with other images, which could manifest different values or make no sense in the game;

Unplaying
Working or inventing scenarios to trap the characters, set them on fire, or otherwise abuse them;

Rewriting
Participation of a player to redefine play from within the writings of fan culture.

This fits computer games into the Deleuzian framework of wishing for, and creating, worlds. Game play within a system of desire is play within worlds of possibility where the players enjoy unexpected forms of satisfaction, including those created by disrupting or disobeying rule sets and experiencing the resulting emergent phenomena.

What can game designers take away from these historic and contemporary examples of domestic play? As evidenced by a long history of play and doll play, there are at least three forms of critical play that can be derived from prior play habits: reskinning, unplaying, and rewriting. Both doll play and playing house offer the interpretive space for the in-play critique embedded in social and cultural norms. Further, in the way these methods can be seen across a wide variety of making and playing practices, they point out commonalities for a "methodology of critical play"—the forms of criticality that players adopt as strategies for social resistance to normative roles have commonalities and move across technologies and time.

Critical play that takes on cultural patterns, such as gender roles in domestic space, functions within large cultural systems that are difficult to examine, and slow to change. The manipulation of characters and environments that many games offer is a complex means for negotiating player desire within game worlds. Care-giving games, from playing "house" to playing *The Sims*, maintain a tantalizing, rhythmic suspense related to the fundamental human desire to satisfy needs and connect with others.[113] This is not to say that this is the only motivating factor in domestic game play, but it is certainly a factor in the complex system a house game represents. Who we are when we play games and how we relate to the game world are important questions, for the pleasures of gaming derive from the structures of rules that define the game environments, and the rules range from specific internal game rules to more abstract social mores, commercial patterns, and gendered subject positions.[114]

A great deal of pleasure is derived from subverting online culture's norms of interaction and exploring the boundaries of what is permissible, and games are where people push these limits. By moving and playing within the structures of work and play systems, users interact and experience the pleasure of creating playculture. The digital "magic circle" that players enter is an open environment focused on experimentation and subversion.[115] Thus, such games reveal anxieties and uncertainties about domestic roles—uncertainties that manifest through the critical playing of games.

As Chris Crawford notes in *The Art of Computer Game Design*, games are closed systems, safe spaces in which one can enter into various kinds of conflict without risking comfort, enjoyment, or physical well-being. A good game must be safe and engaging, its elements must be cohesive and well integrated, and its interaction scenarios meaningful. Doll play, and computer games that take on characteristics of doll play, encourage critical play by providing environments for context perversion and emergent community formation, altering subjective lived experiences, the "hypocrisies of adult life," as noted by Sutton-Smith, who has argued that children's play offers narratives that negotiate the risks of the real world.[116] The relationship between dolls or avatars and players takes on a self-aware perversity that materializes in the interface. Victorian doll play, representations of the body, and political awareness in Bellmer's work demonstrate how voyeuristic transgressions can be used to draw awareness to normative social behavior.

Game makers, like any media makers, cannot simply step outside current contemporary social systems to write and think in ways completely "free of the rules." Rather, behavior, language, and discourse are themselves inscribed with those rules—both explicit and implicit, and as we have seen in doll play, these rules end up embedded in the play spaces created. Therefore, if game makers wish to encourage critical play, they must work like a virus from within to infect and radically change what is expected and what is possible when players play. Designers can specifically design to leave "open the possibility of a different language."[117] This different language may be a visual one, given the reliance in the West on visual culture (films, games, photography), or it may, perhaps more interestingly, be structural, linguistic, or procedural, as the digital games mentioned demonstrate.

BOARD GAMES

Chess is hand-to-hand combat
between two labyrinths.

—André Breton, *Free Rein (La Clé des champs)*

Some of the earliest evidence of human play can be found in the board games uncovered in ancient burial grounds or depicted in ancient drawings and carvings. Initially,
these games were simple folk objects made as needed out of earth, wood, or stone. But
as play became a larger part of culture, the ruling classes joined in play as well, and
extraordinary game sets for kings and pharaohs evolved. These boards were made of
ivory, faience, and other precious materials. Later, the mass printing techniques of the
industrial revolution enabled the huge variety of board games we know today.

Early game boards remain important to critical designers not only because they
reflect cultural notions of a given time but also because their play patterns continue to
influence contemporary design. Csikszentmihalyi and Bennett argue that play works
because the magic circle of a game defines its space and makes participation in the
action of a game voluntary. By convention, a game must limit the range of stimuli
players need to take in. Play fields or boards establish what space and what relevant
objects will be involved. "Within this limited spatio-temporal unit the player can
abandon himself to the process, acting without self-consciousness."[1] From the earliest
times, board games have incorporated Huizinga's "magic circle" as well as elements of
both strategy and chance in their design.

Yet board games embody fundamental differences in philosophy. Go and chess,
for example, are abstract strategy games that feature "perfect information"—that is,
all the information constituting the system of the game is visible on the game board
at all times. Play in an abstract strategy game often unfolds as players move pieces on
the board, creating a set of ongoing puzzles for other players to thwart. The earliest

board games, however, were based on an element of imperfect, or less than complete information. Many games incorporated chance. While we cannot delve into the complex nuances of the myriad game forms in existence, we can ascertain some archetypical features from prominent examples like mancala, Go, picture games, and, finally, chess.

The oldest games are found at sites of the world's ancient civilizations, Mesopotamia and Egypt, and in areas now known as Cyprus, Palestine, Iraq, Iran, and Jordan. These areas are the origin of a group of games known as *mancala*, or counting, sowing, and capture games. Other names for these kinds of games are awari, oware, warri, gebeta, qarqis, bao, and matara. Pallanguli,[2] or "many holes," is a South Indian version of the game.[3]

"Mancala" comes from the Arabic word *naqala*, literally "to move." The common Ghanian name *oware* comes from a Twi legend that describes a man and woman playing the game together endlessly. To someday end all of their various games they married, hence "oware," which means he or she marries or has a lifelong affair.[4] Originally, an oware or mancala "board" could be created from depressions in the earth. Later, stone benches and tablets were carved out. Moves in mancala are created as the player selects an indentation between the two rows of indentations, and, one by one, distributes a collection of beads, stones, or "seeds."[5] While mancala seems simple, there are many global and regional variations, and different mancala traditions feature different rules for movement, capture, and objective.

Game play in mancala is usually symmetric, meaning that players use the same strategy and play by the same rules in order to win. H. J. R. Murray (1952) and Russ (2000) categorize these mancala types by describing the board, the number of rows used in the game, and the particular rules for capture; for instance, one may continue around the board, or stop in the storehouse. The oldest Neolithic versions of mancala were unearthed in Jordan, from the Beidha discovery in 1966 (dating from approximately 6900 BC). Nearly as old, the 'Ain Ghazal excavation of 1989 dated a game board from approximately 5800 BC.[6] While the boards have subtle variations in their number of holes, they are all believed to be mancala-style games. Another ancient mancala game was found in Western Iran (dating from approximately 6300–5900 BC). Rollefson argues that these finds prove that Neolithic people had leisure time and an interest in games of chance. The Neolithic period was a revolutionary era in human evolution, during which humans became recognizable Homo sapiens and developed an agrarian culture capable of reflecting on the whims of nature and fate. That mancala style games involve an action modeled on planting seeds or sowing

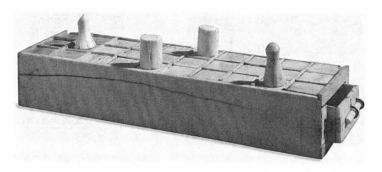

| Figure 3.1 |
Senet game, Egypt, New Kingdom, 1550–1069 BC. From the British Museum.

fields supports this claim. Mancala may be the most popular arithmetical game in the world.[7] In its simplest form, without counting the "seed" tokens, it can be played as a game of pure chance. Played along more complex lines, mancala is a game of strategy and, like chess and checkers, possesses "perfect information" in that all known pieces and options lie before the player.

Mancala, in being such early evidence of human play, resembles contemporary game boards by having territories (zones for play), actions (moving stones), rules (direction on board, number of tokens distributed), tokens (pieces that represent the player, the player's team, or other types of subject positions), and feedback (amounts collected). The fact that these early mancala boards were developed and customized speaks to the aesthetic importance of games and how the *play experience* has, for thousands of years, been intertwined with aesthetics.

Both chance operations and beautiful game boards were evidenced in the ancient games of the Middle East. The Egyptian game of Senet (figure 3.1), also known as Thirty Squares, was discovered in First Dynasty tombs at Abu Rawash, ca. 3050 BC; later boards became even more decorated and ornate. The Royal Game of Ur, also known as Twenty Squares, is also beautiful, with spaces on the board exceedingly decorative, even if the exact rules are a bit of a mystery. Do the abstract symbols represent something about time or space? In H. J. R. Murray's *A History of Board Games Other than Chess* (1952), Murray describes the Ur game found in a queen's grave dated ca. 2600 BC. The board apparently models a race, and includes seven pieces for each player and seven tetrahedral dice, four of which produce throws with low numbers from zero to four. The game appears to provide places for capturing an opponent's piece, as well as safe squares where players may avoid their opponents (see figure

| Figure 3.2 |
Royal Game of Ur, Ur, southern Iraq, ca. 2600–2400 BC. From the British Museum.

3.2). Squares seven and eight on the twenty-squared board are thought to represent a bridge, river, or canal that is a feature of ancient Akkadian and Egyptian game board designs.[8]

While Yale University archaeologist Robert S. Brumbaugh believed there to be too many "safe" spaces on this board to keep play exciting, he notes, "I have played the Ur game, and find it not too bad. (It seems to have been standard to gamble for a large stake, which of course would add some further interest to play.)"[9] A similar board was found in Knossos, Crete, and while Brumbaugh believed the game to be played for social and gambling purposes, Murray earlier had noted that Ur's purpose or function was unclear.[10] Indeed, it has never been universally established that gambling was associated with this game, but gambling is of course also intertwined with the history of play.

A board is mentioned in conjunction with the dice game to which the Roman Emperor Claudius was said to be addicted.[11] This game (and perhaps *all* board games) was referred to in Latin as *Alea*, and this is often mentioned in conjunction with *tabula*, hence, board game.[12] The material of Roman board games was usually stone or wood, or even ivory, depending on the wealth of the game owner. The Spanish documentarian Isidore also described a game called tabula as a Roman form of backgammon carrying the Arabic name of Nard.[13] Ovid described a board game, "distans," as based on what would now be described as geometry.[14] Interestingly, the play pieces of Roman games were never understood as figures—that is, they lacked representational qualities of earlier games like hounds and jackals and later games like chess.

The Maori game of Mu Torere, said to be at least generations old, was originally played on an eight-rayed star-shaped outline etched into a piece of wood or bark. Play moves forward in a fashion similar to the British draughts or American checkers. Two players each have four *perepere*, or persons, who start on the outside of the points, and attempt to cross to the opposite side. Best (1917) posed several questions of the game and its origins. If it is an original game, not much is known of its history; if it is a modification on draughts or checkers, why was the star shape added to the play?

The Spiritual Side of Board Games

While the focus of much humanities research in the late twentieth and early twenty-first centuries has shifted to popular culture and, in particular, the struggle to legitimize a study of everyday life—here de Certeau, Lefebvre, and, more recently, Highmore should be noted—the study of games has lagged behind. But games are legitimate forms of media, human expression, and cultural importance, and the ways games reflect the norms and beliefs of their surrounding cultures is essential to understanding both games themselves and the insights they may provide into human experience. In this playculture approach to media, board games become one of several artifacts of material culture used to trace social practices and beliefs. Game actions and rules can be characterized as principal play features, and these foci are not unique to games but are also shared across language systems, social orders, and ties of kinship, law, and ritual.

Scholars of game history, including Murray, Brumbaugh, and Austin, have researched some of the lineage of particular games. For example, backgammon could have been influenced by both the ancient Egyptian game Senet and Mesopotamian Ur. For those trying to record how these games functioned, the rules are traced, the game pieces are codified, and the documents that reference game play are collected. What tends to be overlooked by many current scholars of games is their purpose beyond the pastime; in some cases, scholars may lose sight of the fact that certain games were not intended as pastimes at all. Even Murray, the noted and prolific twentieth-century game scholar, avoids, and even at time disparages, games' spiritual connections, noting that "it is difficult to see how the private operations of the magician could be adopted by the secular members of a tribe. I think that we must look elsewhere for the origin of most board-games."[15]

In the 1970s, anthropologists and play scholars Csikszentmihalyi and Bennett noted that games of chance "seem to have emerged from the divinatory aspect of religious ceremonials."[16] Games of chance and divination were closely aligned for many thousands of years, for humans have long sought guidance from the changeable, powerful forces they believed may rule over one's destiny and control the probable outcomes for hunting, war, and successful harvests. Indeed, Csikszentmihalyi and Bennett argue that divination brings to those who seek it a sense of possibility. Furthermore, a "man who engages in divination as a consequence feels that his available projects are more nearly able to cope with the possibilities impinging on his everyday life and as a result his experience is closer to play than to worry."[17]

There is evidence that ancient games involving chance often held spiritual and ritualistic importance. Senet offered board designs for two players and rules incorporating chance. Hounds and Jackals, or Fifty-Eight Holes, appeared in Egypt in the Middle Kingdom around 2000 BC and consisted of two parallel tracks of twenty-nine holes assembled in groups of five. In Hounds and Jackals, the tracks of the two players were rather independent and the goal was to simply win the race, not capture the opponent's pieces.[18] In a late example of a fifth-century-BC version of the game, the board is created from a sculpture of a hippopotamus, perhaps Taueret, the goddess of maternity and childbirth. The pieces shown, though not originally from this board, are topped with god-headed figures representing Anubis and Horus, and other pieces, in a fashion similar to the modern game of cribbage.[19]

Antiquities specialists have reconstructed the rules of the game by examining other examples of Fifty-Eight Holes found in sites from the Egyptian Middle Kingdom (2040–1782 BC). To play this game, inset into the top of the hippopotamus figure in figure 3.3, players took turns moving their pin-shaped pieces forward along a path. At the tail and near the side, two special holes reversed the action, sending pieces backward on the board, and two holes at a hollow near the end offered the player an extra turn. This chance-based board game resembles games like *Snakes and Ladders* in that chance operations drive interaction, allowing fate to intervene in play.

The name of the Egyptian board game Senet (3500 BC) might also connote "passing" because it was to be played during the journey to the afterlife. The Senet board (with its metaphoric race against fate) was designed to involve chance. The examples all consist of rectangular boards of thirty squares with accompanying game pieces of clay and ivory. Two players toss wooden sticks to determine a number, and then move their game pieces around the long board in a snaking fashion.[20] While Senet is understood to be a social game, historical documents reveal its strong ties to rituals of Egyptian culture. Several paintings have been found that depict Senet players playing alone, or against a spirit opponent, suggesting that the game may have been played against Ra himself for the dead's fate. In this way, the game may have functioned as a spirit-medium connecting the living to the netherworld. Historians such as Piccione note that the game could be played recreationally or ritualistically.[21] Documentation from

| Figure 3.3 |

Senet game; Hippopotamus game, three jackal-headed batons (third intermediate period); Snake game (second dynasty). Wood, faience. Musée du Louvre, Paris. N1605; E2710; N3043; N4265; E29891. Photo credit: Réunion des Musées Nationaux/Art Resource, NY.

the Book of the Dead depicts the player navigating what may be interpreted as various levels of death in the game.[22] All along, play had magical and ritualistic elements.

Elsewhere, divination is linked to some histories of the Chinese game Wéiqí. Called Go in Japan, the game is believed to have developed from divination practiced by emperors and astrologers in Zhou culture. There has long been evidence that the Shang Dynasty leaders (sixteenth–eleventh century BC) used cracks on turtle shells and in animal bones to predict agricultural harvests and weather. Divination was associated with the legendary "Yellow River Diagram" and the "Luo Record," magic square diagrams said to have been fantastically revealed to the mythical ancestor Fu Xi while on the back of a dragon-horse and turtle.[23] The resemblance of these diagrams to a Go board is striking. According to game historian David Parlett in his *Oxford History of Board Games*, Go may be related "to a divinatory practice of casting black and white stones on a board representing the heavens, or earth and heaven, and interpreting the resulting patterns."[24] This is lent some weight by the cosmic terminology referred to by the board, which is defined along astrological or geomantic terms with the center called Tengen, or axis of heaven, the four quarters of the board surface related to cardinal directions, and some eight specially marked points are called Hoshi, or stars. Citing the "Wang You Qing Le Ji," or *The Carefree and Innocent Pastime Collection*, a Go manual from the early twelfth century, and one of the game's oldest surviving documents, Fairbairn notes: "The number of all things in Nature begins with one. The points on the go board number three hundred and sixty plus one. One is the first of all living numbers. It occupies the polar point of the board around which the four quarters revolve. The other three hundred and sixty points represent the number of days in a [lunar] year. They are divided into four quarters which represent the four seasons."[25]

The shift from Shang dynasty, during which divination diagrams were popular, to the Zhou dynasty, when yin and yang and other rational systems were emerging, may have helped shift an interpretation of the game from its roots in divination to its contemporary identity as a strategic game system.

If we situate the creation of early board games alongside the advent of other types of divination materials, the comparison points to a Neolithic shift in consciousness that agriculture brought to much of the world. For this generation of people, the shift was not only a technological change from food gathering to the sowing and planting of materials but also an intellectual shift, especially in the redefinition of space and time that this upheaval engendered. Agricultural planning, the saving of seeds, animal breeding and domestication, along with the abstraction of the heavens or rivers to create calendars all demonstrate new ways of understanding time. Separating hunting space into agricultural space, the division of land into fenced areas, and the invention of ploughs, irrigation, geometry, and mathematics made the abstraction of space a highly prized mental process. Board games appear to manifest these concepts and their effect on relationships, both social and physical, by presenting them in a safe, ritualized form. When encountered on a game board, challenge and competition are codified and explored within particularly strict bounds. So too were the functions of religious or spiritual rituals, including magic, shamanism, and divination. Scholars who have proposed this type of approach to the interpretation of ancient peoples and games include noted anthropologist Gary Rollefson.[26]

As game scholar H. J. R. Murray has noted, it was not until the early centuries AD that European scholars paid much attention to games, and not until the thirteenth century that European writers began to describe games as they were played in their respective countries.[27] In Europe, these activities generally date back to Roman or Celtic influences.[28] The most significant genre of historic European board games is

"Tafl" (table) games. Vikings considered the successful play of Tafl a valuable attribute and mention this as such in the Sagas. An abstract strategy game with perfect information, no chance, and multiple—though generally two—players, the Old Norse term *tafl* denotes a family of games usually played on a checkered or cross-shaped board. Tafl features teams of uneven strength and themes of surrounding, or seizing, the king and his army. Often thought of as precursors to chess, some examples of Tafl are the tenth-century Ballinderry game and the Brandub games of Ireland. The game Tawl-bwrrd, from Wales is documented in law as game play requires eight pieces on the king's team, but sixteen on the aggressor's. Tablut from Lapland[29] and Hnefatafl in Iceland were played across much of Northern Europe until chess supplanted them during the twelfth century.[30] Halatafl dates from the fourteenth century and is mentioned in the Icelandic poem the Grettis Saga.[31] The game is related to Fidchell in Ireland, Gwyddbwyll in Wales, Fox and Geese in Britain, Germany, and France, and Sheep and Wolf in Sweden. Believed to have been a game invented by the Celtic god Lugh, certain students of Celtic culture explain Fidchell as a demonstration of how one negotiates the wall between the physical world and the spiritual.[32] Meanwhile, there is evidence that Tafl was one of the first board-game genres important enough gain a place within the government and the church.

Evidence that the church in Europe had an interest in games is plentiful. In its time, tables, a game played with dice, was played on a backgammon board. While Europeans in the Middle Ages were captivated by the game, the church fought long and hard to forbid its play. In 1254, St. Louis IX of France forbade Tafl at court, calling the game "*inhonesti ludi.*"[33] Thus the battle between government or religious groups and games is at least as old as this event, if not much older. However, when faced with the uncontrolled popularity of Tafl-style games in Europe, the church finally decided to use the game to further its religious message. The twelfth-century Corpus Christi College Manuscript 122 housed in Cambridge describes a form of Hnefatafl called Alea Evangelii, or "The Board Game of the Gospel." According to game historian David Parlett, Alea Evangelii dates from the Anglo-Saxon days of England (see figure 3.4). Played on an eighteen-by-eighteen square board of nineteen-by-nineteen points, twenty-four guards are pitted against forty-eight attackers.[34] The manuscript describing the game from the reign of Athelstan (924–040) shows a game board arranged as a religious allegory.[35]

Alea Evangelii marks one of the first uses of a board game as an ideological tool. Overall, however, the Tafl games represented a significant break from other Near Eastern and Mesopotamian games in that these games emerged primarily as pure entertainment. Their links to the spiritual realm were less well documented, or were

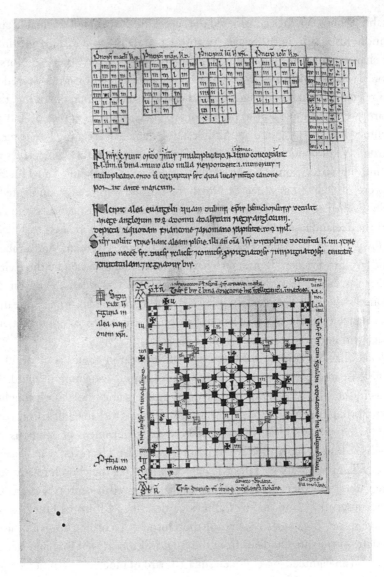

| Figure 3.4 |

A documented source for the game Alea Evangelii is in an Anglo Saxon–era manuscript at Corpus Christi College, Oxford, dating from 1140 AD. Corpus Christi College ms. 122 ("The Corpus gospels").

even purposely obscured. As chess emerged, new board games with different intentions developed and dominated cultural life.

Games of the Epic and the Everyday

At different stages of human history, then, games have played varying roles. From assisting in the development of conceptual processes, to invoking ritual, to forging a connection with time and the future, players throughout history have struggled to gain agency and understand uncertainty through game play. As the popularity of the Tafl board receded, European games other than chess evolved and flourished, some growing out of the most commonplace sort of play.

Successful post-Renaissance games built on Goose, an Italian chase or race-themed game that was invented in Florence under Francesco dei Medici in the sixteenth century. Under the Medici recommendation, Goose was adopted by Philip II of Spain and rapidly spread to other parts of Europe. Later, Goose became a model for early board games in the United States as well as other European games such as *Snakes and Ladders*. Fox and Geese—mentioned earlier as a game related to the Tafl games and their Celtic counterpart, Fidchell—was known to be a favorite of Edward IV of England (1461–1483) as well as the nineteenth century's Queen Victoria and Prince Albert.[36] In a category called "fox games," a group of board games featuring unequal opponents, one player is the fox, or aggressor. Other players control or play the numerous geese, sheep, or prey the fox tries to eat while the fox attempts to avoid the traps his opponents set all around him. Fox games are characterized by an unbalanced set of game goals and a rather abstract board. These "unbalanced games" paralleled the popularity of chess, Go, and backgammon, and their rules of play were relatively stable. Abstraction provided a universal quality to these play experiences while allowing the games to spread throughout various regions, religions, and cultures. Other board games evolved in specificity and content through the addition of detail. Some examined depicted large social concerns, others quite mundane events.

In China, games took on many forms. Printing was invented in Asia and mass-printed board games originated in China and Japan. Chinese playing cards, for example, are recorded from the year 1294 AD. Yet historian Andrew Lo has argued that card games as we know them actually emerged from the West, for they overwhelmingly share Western rule sets.[37] Cards used in conjunction with game boards, however, arose far earlier in Asia. Lo examines the game of "leaves" and has determined that early board games of the Tang and early Song periods incorporated both cards and dice into the play experience.[38] Some games, such as that depicted in figure 3.5, used more unusual elements than would a game today, such as incense.

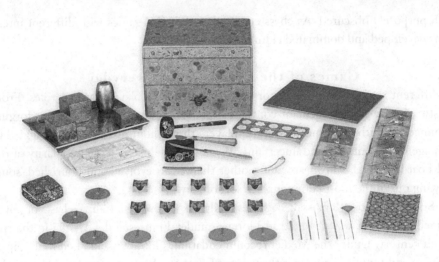

| Figure 3.5 |

Box with equipment for a Japanese incense game, eighteenth century, the British Museum.

Games were popular in Japan as well. Examples abound of games such as the complex eighteenth-century incense game from Japan. In addition to cards, Japanese nobility, in particular, women both designed and played *awase*, meaning "matchings" or "joinings."[39] These *E-awase*, or image-based games (as seen in figure 3.6) generally consisted of two alike, or related, images painted on shells. Players would then arrange the pictures in pairs or triplets, a pastime intended to be a casual, conversational game, suitable for debate, comparison, and judgment calls relying on the artistic and aesthetic sensibilities of those involved. In E-awase-style games, chance facilitates social exchange.

There are numerous examples of very old printed board games, or "Picture Sugoroku," from Japan. Sugoroku was a wooden board game played in Japan in the Middle Ages, but as printing technologies flourished, the games became narrative and portable. Early games were thematically Buddhist and featured religious doctrine. Papers were printed, then glued together in squares of six to eight sheets to form table-sized boards. The gameplay is similar to *Snakes and Ladders*. According to Kakuchi: "The player who advances through the labyrinth of adventure and mystery, often in the form of a map, and reaches the end first grabs the agari, or prize."[40] The image boards may have emerged as early as the thirteenth century via the woodblock-printing innovations of the Edo period. Like other board games, Sugoroku claims spiritual roots, and, while historical research on the game is limited in the West,

| Figure 3.6 |
Shell-matching game from the Heian period, 794–1192 AD, Tokyo National Museum.

image-based games such as Sugoroku may have been incorporated into the monastic life of Buddhist temples during the fifteenth century. There, priests used game boards to teach neophytes how the suffering that originated in human weakness could and must be conquered to reach purity and the higher goal of paradise.[41] Several hundred years later, religious versions of the game moved their focus to issues of everyday life, and travel to the famed city of Kyoto and other nations became game goals. Travel was a feature of *Famous Views of Edo* (1859), by the woodcut master Hiroshige II. The game depicts the city that would become known as Tokyo in beautiful miniature scenes. Game play is simple. Two or more players move counterclockwise around a picture game board to a final destination determined by a dice roll.[42] In another sugoroku, the player begins by leaving Japan on a journey to several Western cities, then returns to become a prominent official. In many nineteenth-century Japanese games, attaining the status of bureaucrat was a respected accomplishment.[43]

Noted Japanese artists of the time, including Utagawa, Hiroshige, and Hokusai, dealt with a range of topics and themes in these games, including fortune-telling.[44] These games remained popular during the Meiji period (1868–1912), often promoting educational themes such as world travel. Poetry served as subject matter in the board game *100 Poems by 100 Poets* (figure 3.7) by Utagawa Toyo Kuni, from the 1800s. Other game themes included religion, politics, actors, monsters, domestic life (figure 3.8), and even samurai accomplishments. In the nineteenth century, pornography

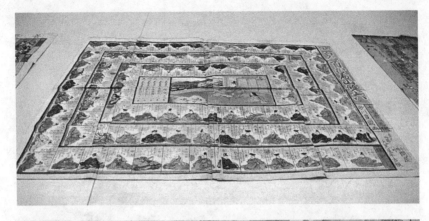

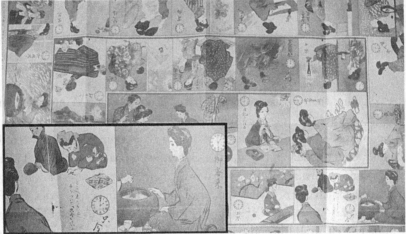

| **Figure 3.7** |
A Sugoroku featuring *100 Poems by 100 Poets* by Utagawa Toyo Kuni, from the Edo period, 1603–1868 AD, Tokyo National Museum.

| **Figure 3.8** |
A Sugoroku featuring everyday life, courtesy of the author.

and more found its way into *Board Game with Classification of Desirable and Undesirable Things* by Utagawa Fusatane.

Another game board depicts the *Process of Wearing Armor* by Utagawa Yoshikazu (Edo period, nineteenth century). In yet another sugoroku, the theme supports the idea of the *National Diet* (1852), and incorporated a board and cards that one draws along with the action of dice. The game of *Snow, Moon, and Flower* by Shosai Shugetsu (1885) depicts popular Kabuki actors with accompanying history and folklore scenes, while early twentieth-century examples depict naval officers and soldiers. According to curator Taro Nitta of Tokyo, the rewards displayed in sugoroku illustrate how a simple game becomes a tool for nationalist hopes: "The game is respected for its aesthetic beauty and also its historical value. For the Japanese, sugoroku, unlike most other board games, became a life experience because the game evoked national passions."[45] Even everyday living became a subject of Sugoroku (see figure 3.8).

That board games could arouse national passions, become sites for social critique, or provide platforms for religious instruction may seem surprising, but these uses were typical, and as the Japanese printing revolution showed, easily made portable through the development of mass production. In the United States and Europe, the mass production of games emerged in the nineteenth century, far later than in Asia. However, commercially produced games of the period provide a window on the values, hopes, and beliefs of a country facing immigration, urbanization, and the rise of industry. The middle class, with growing incomes and expanding leisure time, encouraged children to play games to develop thinking skills and for moral instruction.[46] Chess, which was often recommended, will be discussed later in this chapter.

American Games

In the United States, intact examples of nineteenth-century games are rare. The reasons for this vary, but include low print runs, wear and tear, and an unfortunate cultural devaluation that judged games as a toys and unworthy of preservation. Each of the three major North American board-game archives, the American Antiquarian Society in Worchester, Massachusetts, the New-York Historical Society, and the University of Waterloo, Ontario, contain only about two hundred games, a small sample of the rich diversity of game production in North America. In the United States, board games originally emerged from small companies or groups. Historian Margaret K. Hofer has noted in *The Games We Played: The Golden Age of Board and Table Games*: "The games that entertained Americans from the 1840s to the 1920s offer a fascinating window on the values, beliefs, and aspirations of a nation undergoing tremendous change."[47] Given American play history as sketched in the last chapter, it is no wonder that the first significant mass-produced board game in the United States also focused on domestic life. The earliest games created by the major game manufacturers focused on home and religious and moral instruction before moving on to economics, war, and the more abstract parlor and language games. The earliest nineteenth-century games, particularly games designed for children, were expected to have some instructional value and preferably some moral value as well.[48] As the country shifted from a rural to an urban industrial economy, the home was no longer a place of work, but the site for education, entertainment, and the instillation of values. The rise of new printing and shipping technologies made the mass production of games commercially viable. Most of the middle class could afford the games that typically ranged from twenty-five cents for small boxes of card games to as much as three dollars for games with boards and movable pieces.[49]

By the 1880s, the rise of game companies such as Parker Brothers, known for Tiddlywinks (1897), *Post Office Game* (1897), and *War at Sea* (1898), and the McLoughlin Brothers, which offered Pilgrim's Progress (1893) and *Soldier Ten Pins* (1890), made board games commonplace. Other popular games were *The Game of Playing Department Store* (1898), *Monopolist* (1885), *Mariner's Compass* and *Ten Up* (1885), *Advance and Retreat* (1900), *Game of the Little Volunteer* (1898), and the Grandmama's series of games including *The Sunday Game of Bible Questions* (1887). The Milton Bradley Company was known for *The Checkered Game of Life* (1860–1861), *Anagrams* (1910), and *Logomacy* (1889). J. Ottmann Lith. Co published *Jim Crow Ten Pins* (1910) and *Commerce* (1900). Selchow and Righter were the makers of Parcheesi and the maze game *Pigs in Clover* (1880).

Mansion of Happiness (figure 3.9), created in the 1830s and published in 1843 by the W. & S. B. Ives Company in Boston, was the first mass-market board game in the United States. According to game historians, it was developed by Anne W. Abbott, the daughter of a New England clergyman and a Salem, Massachusetts, native.[50] Abbott also invented the card game *Authors*.[51]

Mansion of Happiness was based on British, French, and Italian games like Goose.[52] However, the goal in the American version is distinct: players compete to be the first to reach "happiness," or heaven, a large square in the center of the board. Progress is attained through good moral conduct in the context of the home. Here, good deeds lead children and their play pieces down the path to "eternal happiness" and players must beware of landing on spaces that interject, albeit through chance, the setbacks of "vices" such as cruelty and ingratitude.[53] In other words, game rules dictated that the household was, at least at the metaphorical level, the battleground of good versus bad behavior. A player spins the spinner to move along a path where more than half

| Figure 3.9 |

Mansion of Happiness, 1843, 1864, print from W. & S. B. Ives Company. New York State Historical Society.

the spaces are illustrated with virtues and vices. According to the game rules, when a throw places the player in a space marked "idleness" he has to go back to "poverty." In like manner, "pride" throws the player back to "humility." In short, every vice is punished by an appropriate penalty and virtue is duly rewarded.[54] Success is attained through honesty and charity and players are wise to avoid idleness, breaking the Sabbath, and other lapses in judgment. The game's message is clearly laid out its directions:[55] "Whoever possesses PIETY, HONESTY, TEMPERANCE, GRATITUDE, PRUDENCE, TRUTH, CHASTITY, SINCERITY, HUMILITY, INDUSTRY, CHARITY, HUMANITY OR GENEROSITY, is entitled to advance . . . toward the Mansion of Happiness. Whoever possesses AUDACITY, CRUELTY, IMMODESTY, OR INGRATITUDE, must return to his former station and not even *think* of Happiness, much less partake of it."[56]

It was hoped that children would take these principles to heart and connect wholesome thoughts to the secular joys of competing for positions, projecting themselves into situations of good and evil, and enjoying the company of their playmates and family.[57] In reinforcing the high moral principles of its time, *Mansion of Happiness*, like many children's games, was played with a spinner or "teetotum," a type of top that, when spun, would "land" on imprinted numbers, to avoid associations with gambling that dice conveyed (see figure 3.10). The "boards," published in the same manner

| Figure 3.10 |
Various teetotum, and a rare alphabet die, New York State Historical Society.

as maps of the era, were flexible sheets of printed paper backed with glued linen for stiffness.[58]

It is interesting to note that when Parker Brothers republished *Mansion of Happiness* in 1894, when the game was sixty-four years old, they removed the vices and vice-related space labels of Immodesty, Passion, Ingratitude, Cheat, Robber, Perjurer, Road to Folly, and Summit of Dissipation. Parker Brothers also replaced the women pictured in the "house of correction" with men, removed illustrations of women practicing vice, and added poverty to the list of vices.[59]

In 1860–1861, Milton Bradley created the morality-based game *The Checkered Game of Life*, which likewise rewarded good deeds and punished bad ones. Where *Mansion of Happiness* explored virtues and vices exclusively, the player in *The Checkered Game of Life* was expected to collect points for achieving a variety of habits, including personal virtues and business sense, one goal being a "Happy Old Age," worth fifty points.[60] It took 100 points to win the game. Wealth, the second-highest point space, was worth ten points, Perseverance, Success, Happiness, Honor, College, and Fat Office brought five points, and Matrimony and Truth were pointless. Other notable board games from the period include *The Yankee Pedlar*, or *What Do You Buy?*, released by John McLoughlin in 1850 as the phenomenon of the department store rose to prominence. Parker Brothers' *The Game of Playing Department Store* (1898) asked players to purchase the most goods possible during a shopping trip.[61] Alongside dolls and paper playhouses, these mass-produced board games were played in a grass-roots or homespun fashion. Play for children centered on the home as the heart of both morality and economic consumption.[62]

Other early games used social interests and capitalist fable in their design. Take, for example, the McLoughlin Brothers' 1883 game, *Bulls and Bears: The Great Wall Street Game* (figure 3.11). As Hofer notes, "By the 1880s, wealth had emerged as the defining characteristic of success in American games, as in life."[63] Players took on the roles of speculators, bankers, and brokers and the game incorporated caricatures of railroad magnates William Henry Vanderbilt and Jay Gould as well as the investor Cyrus Field. Political cartoonists of the time lampooned the three as a critique against monopolistic railroad policies that prevented market competition and raised national costs for shipping.

While games in the United States were focused on morality and behavior, many European board games recounted folktales and historical events. Encounters with Cartaphilus or Ahasuerus, the mythological "Wandering Jew," were purported by Christians throughout the Middle Ages and beyond. According to a folk tale, this Ancient Mariner figure insulted Jesus on his way to the cross, and became an immortal due to a curse from Jesus. Sightings used to occur across Europe, particularly in the Middle Ages, with documented visits from Moscow and every Western European city, including London.[64] By the nineteenth century, most sightings of the Wandering Jew were associated with the mentally ill, but the legend became celebrated in cultural forms. Author Eugène Sue wrote his own version of the anti-Semitic tale, *Le Juif Errant*, which was serialized in 1844–1845. In his narrative, the Wandering Jew (whose name to Medieval Jews was a reference to a fool) and his sister are bound to protect the Rennepont family, for if this family leaves the earth, both the Wanderer and his sister will lose their immortality. The Jesuits have persecuted the family, which has grown and its members dispersed to become generals, an Indian prince, a workman, and even a Jesuit missionary in the Americas. Meanwhile, there is a large fortune to be gained by the remaining members of the family, and the Jesuits and their henchmen are hiding all around, attempting to acquire the funds. The immortal Wandering Jew and his sister help the family at crucial moments such as when they are about to be "scalped" by the Native Americans, or have been sentenced to prison. The serialized narrative has plenty of obstacles and adventure while reinforcing cultural biases.

Sue's sensationalist narrative was taken up in the game *Le Juif Errant*, or *The Wandering Jew* (1852–1858). Around the game board (figure 3.12), players encounter the Wandering Jew and events from the novel. This game is similar to "Round the World" games. In it, the Jew figure appears looking like stereotypical versions of Moses, with a

| Figure 3.11 |
Bulls and Bears: The Great Wall Street Game, 1883, from the McLoughlin Brothers. New York State Historical Society.

windswept cape and long hair. He appears like a ghost at castles, in the middle of a war zone, and other locations while the various nonwandering characters lounge about in classic French drawing rooms. The Wandering Jew also came to represent the cholera epidemic—wherever he goes, cholera comes in his wake, and this must have something to do with the design.

Similar in structure, the French game of *Jeu de la Révolution*, or *The French Revolution Game* (ca. 1850s), is a variation on the well-known *Jeu de l'Oie*, the French version of *Snakes and Ladders*. The players move along a path made of squares, and move ahead using a die thrown alternatively by each player (figure 3.13). The first player to reach the end of the path is the winner; on the way, if a player lands on the "jail" square, he or she must wait there until another player is jailed, replacing the player. In *Jeu de la Révolution*, the end of the path is the National Assembly.

The use of game design as critique took hold among game designers, though some of their productions would embarrass and offend audiences today. *Stanley's March Across the Dark Continent for the Relief of Emin Pasha* (1890) is a board game

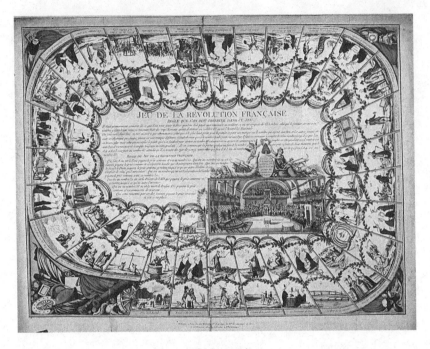

| Figure 3.13 |

The French Revolution Game, ca. 1850, Musée de la Ville de Paris, Musée Carnavalet, Paris. Photo: Agence Bulloz. Photo credit: Réunion des Musées Nationaux/Art Resource, NY.

that depicts the journey of British-born Henry Morton Stanley (1841–1904) down the Congo to Lake Victoria in Africa (figure 3.14). Stanley was known as a ruthless explorer who traversed Africa looking for ways Europe could pillage the continent during its colonial incursions.

The game box depicts Stanley with a chain of African people trailing behind him, carrying his bags, and includes playing pieces representing a white officer leading a group of black porters. Here the classic morality game or travel game has been reskinned to foster racist beliefs and a justification for colonialism. Contemporary journalists noted of the game: "Innocent fun when it was created, it is loaded with different meanings today."[65] But like most problematic media representing racial stereotypes, in fact the game was not innocent when it was released. Since the rise of pictorial board games, they have been used to educate and inform, from a particular point of view, through their play; game scholar Ian Bogost uses the term "persuasive" in this regard. Games clearly can embed racial and cultural bias under the guise

| Figure 3.14 |

The Conquest of Africa, board game based on the travels of Sir Henry Morton Stanley (1841–1904) and David Livingstone (1813–1873), color engraving by French School, nineteenth century. © Private Collection/Archives Charmet/The Bridgeman Art Library. Nationality/copyright status: French/out of copyright.

of innocent play, and they must be continually examined for this ugly tendency. Too often, play is used as a "loophole" for media, a place where racism, sexism, and classism appear in the hopes they will be tolerated as less problematic—since, after all, "it's only a game." Hopefully, a look at these historic examples sheds light on present-day, less-than-innocent representations in games.

The Landlord's Game was the first game to be granted a U.S. patent, in 1904, by Elizabeth (Lizzie) Magie, a Quaker woman from Virginia. Magie invented *The Landlord's Game* to promote the social ideas behind the Single Tax Movement (figure 3.15). Magie was a follower of political economist and San Francisco journalist Henry George. Disturbed by poverty in California in a time of otherwise economic prosperity, George wrote a book titled *Progress and Poverty* (1879), declaring the fundamental cause of poverty to be land monopoly. Instead of confiscating all land, George proposed a single, high, uniform tax be applied on all land, raw or developed. The belief

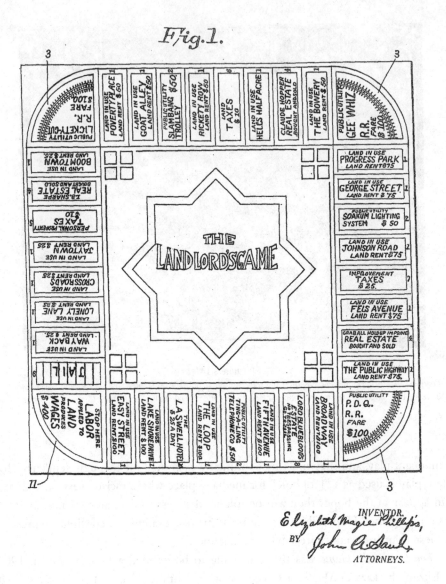

| **Figure 3.15** |

Elizabeth (Lizzie) Magie was issued a patent in 1904 for *The Landlord's Game*, the precursor to the later *Monopoly*. This is her September 23, 1924, patent drawing of the board, with improvements to the game. Photo: U.S. Patent and Trademark Office.

was that this "Single Tax" would discourage speculation, decrease land prices, and provide revenue for the state.[66] George positioned his system as a form of "pure capitalism" that would allow for free trade and fully and evenly competitive markets. The game based on George's principles and designed by Magie encouraged player modifications depending on their city or region, and became a success.

In 1924, Magie brought *The Landlord's Game* to a large commercial publisher, Parker Brothers game company, based in Salem, Massachusetts. But Parker was unimpressed, and told Magie her game was too complicated, too educational, and wasn't at all fun. Worse, the game was also political, which to Parker meant high risk in the commercial market. Thus, the game was rejected for publication. But locally, the game endured (in the Midwest, Pennsylvania, and Atlantic City, New Jersey), was used by college professors and their students, and took on a cult following during the 1920s and 1930s, particularly after the great stock market crash of 1929.

Charles Brace Darrow played the Atlantic City version, created his own version with new graphics, and by 1934, was selling his boxed game at Wanamaker's Department Store in Philadelphia. Darrow's game, entitled *Monopoly*, is enormously similar to *The Landlord's Game*. Each board offers a single path of forty spaces. Each has four railroads and two utilities, water and electric. Each offers rental properties whose values increase. Each board also includes a park space, a jail space, and a "go to jail" space. Darrow filed a patent on his modification, and sold his game to Parker Brothers, now under President Robert Barton. Later, Magie's patent was also purchased (albeit for a low price) to acknowledge her prior rights. Parker Brothers released the first version of the *Monopoly* game in 1933. By 1935, half a million copies had sold.

Monopoly as a framework seems to breed a sense of subversion, perhaps because of its original intention. Economics professor Ralph Anspach invented *Anti-Monopoly* in 1974, packaged in a way that bore a strong resemblance to the original *Monopoly*. Anspach had effectively reskinned the game with new language. One space, for example, instructs players to "Go to Price War," instead of jail. Rewritten, the game's goal is to challenge the concept of monopoly that underpins the game *Monopoly*.[67] "I tried to find a game which would be just as much fun as Monopoly but would show the dark side of monopolies," Anspach remembers. "After some students challenged me at my university, I decided to fill the gap by creating a game which is against monopolists."[68]

Anti-Monopoly reverses familiar conventions. The board starts in a state of monopoly and it is up to the players to compete in a style of free enterprise to return the game state back to a competitive, free-market system. When *Anti-Monopoly* appeared, Parker Brothers claimed trademark violation. In 1977, the district court ruled in favor of Parker Brothers, and a series of legal reinforcements and reversals continued.[69]

Finally, Anspach settled out of court and continued to sell his game, maintaining the tradition of game as protest, much as Lizzie Magie had done years ago. Another *Monopoly*-based game, *Class Struggle* by Bertell Ollman, was released in 1978 to help "prepare for life in capitalist America." In this game, Workers are those who produce (items such as shoes, cars, etc.) and Capitalists are the owners of the machines and factories with which these items are created. These two roles represent the Major Classes. As the Workers unite, they take power from other Capitalist players; if they do not unite, the Capitalist side wins. According to Ollman's rules, "'Class Struggle' reflects the real struggle between the classes in our society. THE OBJECT OF THE GAME IS TO WIN THE REVOLUTION . . . ULTIMATELY."[70]

Artists and Surreal Games

Let's get back to the early twentieth century. With the mass production of graphic materials, board games continued to grow in popularity. In the early part of the twentieth century, World War I, scientific developments, and the increasing influence of the writings of Sigmund Freud brought new interest in the unconscious and new experiments with play. Games became an important part of this exploration of the internal life, as games consistently reflect both the culture in which they were created and, through play, the present context as well. Artists have used game as a medium of exploration and expression for over one hundred years. Like art, games tend to reinforce larger cultural influences. Artists, especially those who followed the Surrealist and Fluxus movements, also tend to play games as a form of recreation and research. Furthermore, artists tend to be especially critical of the ways games are tied to social structures, economies, and ideas of their times.

In his mid-century study *Man, Play and Games*, the French theorist Roger Caillois lays the groundwork for the study of a range of play behaviors. Caillois argues that various play forms that emerged in the West have incorporated play qualities he describes as "a taste for gratuitous difficulty."[71] Here, Caillois addresses games designed for the mastery of a special skill or activity, typically leading to the discovery of some sort of satisfactory conclusion. Even when fictional or abstract, puzzles, math problems, wordplay, board games, and particularly games of strategy seem to point to the satisfaction inherent in successful completion of challenges. The more radical and political twentieth-century artists, such as the well-known Dada and Surrealist groups, balked at these challenges. Though only a few board games were formulated, Dada artists, brought together by the upheaval of the world war in Europe, were playful and absurd in their questioning of tradition, culture, and the role of art.

Surrealists, however, emerging under the leadership of writer, artist, and organizer André Breton and others during the 1920s, explored games through two prominent lines of inquiry. First, the Surrealists emphasized the playfulness of Dada through the use of chance and juxtaposition. But Surrealists were also concerned with the internal workings of the mind and encouraged a deep focus on the subconscious. Relying on the work of Sigmund Freud, and recognizing the importance of human perceptions of things and events, Breton, who had studied psychology and worked during part of World War I in a neurological ward, wrote the *Manifesto of Surrealism* (1924) and within four years published an unofficial case study of a mentally ill woman, titled *Nadja* (1928). After the now-famous inaugural manifestos of the early 1920s, several of the artists associated with Dada, among them the German-French sculptor Jean "Hans" Arp, moved on to participate in the Surrealist movement.[72]

In addition to writing *Nadja*, Breton worked with Philippe Soupault to coauthor the book *The Magnetic Fields* (1919), which some believe launched the Surrealist movement. With Louis Aragon, Breton and Soupault founded *Literature* (1919), the review that would become the standard forum for disillusioned intellectuals of the day. Within the pages of *Literature*, the Surrealists blamed the culture of the bourgeois as the primary cause of World War I.

Practices of automatic composition, game operations, and chance or aleatoric methods may have been used by artists before the 1920s; the Surrealists were aware of new trends in art and aesthetics like Futurism and Constructivism, but their focus on themes of the unconscious was novel, intense, and rooted in the budding field of psychoanalysis. In actuality, as organized civil society increases its "high" culture and sophisticated pleasures, the availability and intensity of daily pleasure appears to diminish. To twentieth-century critic Walter Benjamin, it is only through the intensification of everyday experiences that social change can occur. Play, in this case, could function not only to attract players from across the social spectrum but also to revolutionize culture by expressing what might otherwise manifest as dangerously repressed desires. It is precisely such psychic needs that were explored by the Surrealists through gaming operations and game methods. Surrealist art and literature stressed unconscious and irrational methods for creating art through processes of automatism, chance, and interruption. "Surrealism is not a poetic form," wrote the Surrealists in their manifesto. "It is a scream of the mind finding itself again and it intends to desperately crush its shackles with artificial hammers, if need be."[73] A fascination with play and how play invoked and evoked unconscious processes was the focus of much of Surrealist practice. In fact, members of the "Bureau of Surrealist Research" believed they could

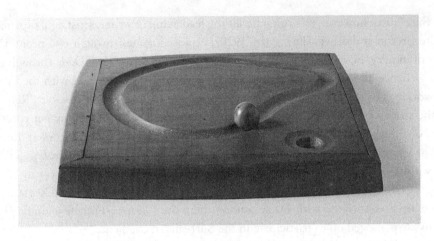

| Figure 3.16 |

Alberto Giacometti (1901–1966), *Circuit*, 1931. Wood, 4.5 × 48.5 × 47 cm. AM1987-557. Musée National d'Art Moderne, Centre Georges Pompidou, Paris. Photo: Adam Rzepka. Photo credit: CNAC/MNAM/Dist. Réunion des Musées Nationaux/Art Resource, NY. © ARS, NY.

achieve the "total liberation of the mind" through interactivity and multidisciplinary investigation.

Critical play, then, became the creative goal of diverse groups of artists and thinkers linked in the Surrealist artists' network.[74] Game-like images proliferated in Surrealist works. For example, in the paintings of Kay Sage, landscapes take on properties of board games as though alluding to chance and strategy as significant components in human nature.

With the goal of systematizing art in ways that psychoanalysis had achieved in science,[75] Surrealist artists sought to unite the worlds of fantasy and dream with that of everyday existence through an artistic interaction that was obsessed with music, film, and, in particular, games. Like the ancients, who saw games as a way to connect with the powers of fate, chance, and the afterlife, Surrealists believed that games might help everyone—artists, scientists, politician, even farmers, tap into the spiritual realm and the human unconscious. "I believe," Breton once said, "in the future resolution of the states of dream and reality—in appearance so contradictory—in a sort of absolute reality, or *surréalité*."[76]

Several artists engaged with Surrealism made artworks related to board games. Two prominent examples are Joseph Cornell's *Jouet surréaliste* (1932) and Charles Shaw's shadowbox game *Montage* (1935). *Montage* incorporated playing cards, clay pipes, and ivory discs, all housed in a wooden box.[77] In a series of game-board

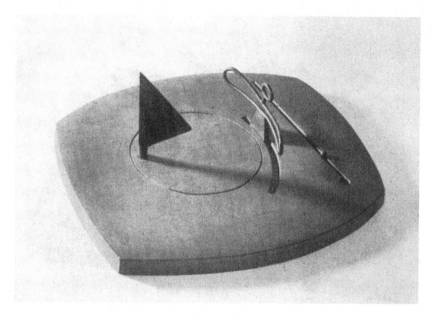

| Figure 3.17 |
Alberto Giacometti, *Man, Woman, Child*, 1931. © ARS, NY.

sculptures created at around the same time the portable pinball machine was developed, Alberto Giacometti showed an early kind of "conversation" between art and the popular culture's interest in play.

Giacometti's work *Circuit* (1931) was among the first of these board-game artworks (figure 3.16). The game board consists of a simple platform with an ellipse-shaped groove carved into it. A ball is placed on the groove, and can therefore roll continually around the path inscribed on the board. The board contains one more element, however: an indentation, or a possible goal, which is located outside the circuit the ball traverses. This possible end state, or destination, is alluded to, but designed to be physically unattainable. The ball's trajectory is endless and insatiable, operating within a closed system. Giacometti's *Man, Woman, and Child* (1931) can never be on the same interactive plane (figure 3.17); *Point to the Eye* (1931–1932) was another game-influenced work expressing ideas of frustration—in this case, the suspended state of near-torture. Permanently poised near a skull, pointing right to the eye, is a large, sharp spear.

Beginning in 1931, Giacometti wrote for Breton's Surrealist periodical, *Le Surrealisme au service de la revolution*. He, like other artists of the time, tested the ways in

| Figure 3.18 |
Alberto Giacometti, *No More Play* (*On ne Joue Plus*), 1932. © ARS, NY.

which games could access the nature of being human. His topographic boards, with their limited moving parts and constrained trajectories, can be read as statements on the closed system of art and on the closed nature of the larger system referred to as the human condition. The stunted possibilities and frustrating distances that frame these works cast the game concept of agency in a pessimistic light.

Through Giacometti, it is easy to see the dark and macabre side in play environments. In *No More Play* (1932), death is the theme, but this theme is played out in the landscape of the game board (figure 3.18). The title in French is *On ne Joue Plus*, which means that one is no longer playing.[78] Indeed, the board resembles more a war zone than a puzzle game. Thin human figures hover amid the larger of the holes on either combatant's side. *No More Play* (1932) goes far to juxtapose the whimsical board game and the macabre theme of war. The bombed-out "no man's land" dominating the center of the board opens to reveal human graves.

Museum of Modern Art (MoMA) curators have lauded Giacometti's *The Palace at 4AM* (1932) for its "cage-like" sculpture, and cite this piece as his most Surrealist work (figure 3.19). Not only does the sculpture step between actual space and the imagination, but the process Giacometti used in its creation was equally surreal. It was only

| Figure 3.19 |
Alberto Giacometti, *The Palace at 4AM*, 1932. © ARS, NY.

after the fact that works like *The Palace* represented "the tangled simultaneity of events in our memories."[79]

These game boards represent the last of Giacometti's Surrealist games. Beginning with his "disagreeable objects" in the 1920s, historian Christian Klemm and others suggest that the artist's playfulness gave way to darker and more sinister ideas. These later pieces become less abstract and focus instead on "real terms as sections of a board game or mechanical constructions."[80] These works use the idea of games as systems for critical thinking or as systems that explore the folly of human choice, incorporating friendly, childlike doll-play paradigms with war, imprisonment, and death. But Giacometti's game boards also reflect domestic play and the popular games of the time. The Surrealists' fondness for games could have, at least in part, been related to the long waiting periods experienced by European artists applying for visas to the United States, Canada, the United Kingdom, or Mexico in their flight from war. Improvising chess sets out of found materials, amusing themselves through language games—these activities recall the uncanny relationship of artist to prisoner during the early twentieth century. Surrealists took their play seriously, but their games could have been a means of survival from catastrophe.

Games and Hard Times

While Giacometti was developing his game boards, and the Surrealist artists were honing their play performances, the popularity of games continued to rise around the world. Part of what makes play meaningful is the social and cultural context in which a play takes place. In *Rules of Play*, Katie Salen and Eric Zimmerman state, "*Meaningful play* occurs when the relationships between actions and outcomes in a game are both *discernable* and *integrated* into the larger context of the game."[81] Therefore, changes in any larger social situation, such as a severe economic depression, may signal profound changes in games. Sales of board games such as *Monopoly* increased dramatically during the Great Depression in the United States, while the game pachinko was a favorite abroad in countries such as Japan during those same hard economic times. It seems the more that economies struggled, the more the sales of games increased.[82]

Pinball gained widespread popularity in the United States, United Kingdom, and France, mass-produced as a popular pastime for military men. Writes Roger C. Sharpe: "Pinball is like making love: It demands the complete concentration and total emotional involvement of the player. Nothing else will do."[83] The game was invented in the United Kingdom in 1871 by Montegue Redgrave, who added a coiled spring, plunger, and inclined play board to a game previously known as Bagatelle. After 1942, manufacturers such as Bally, Gottlieb, Genco, Exhibit, Keeney, and Stoner equipped their factories to create gun parts, communications technologies, and other defense products instead of producing pinball games. Existing game machines, however, were updated with paint and new graphics that reflected wartime themes. One example was Genco's conversion of *Ten Spot* (1941), where the company reskinned *Ten Spot* to become "*Smack the Japs*," a "Victory Game Conversion" (June 1943). There were several conversion units for sale for the Seeburg game company's shooting range games. Seeburg sold *Chicken Sam* and *Jailbird* gun games. These were shooting games that used a "ray-o-lite" from a toy rifle to "shoot" moving figures and targets, which were housed several feet away from the player. As seen in figure 3.20, the typical wildlife featured in the original game is replaced with a changeover unit to make the game politically relevant during the Second World War. Touted in advertising as "life-like" and "realistic," the buck-toothed toy figure that is supposed to look like the enemy moves back and forth, ready for participants to aim and fire through a glass lens that

CHICKEN SAM OPERATORS
"HIT THE DIRTY JAP"

Deluxe Change-Over Units Will Revive Your Chicken Sam and Jailbird Machines.
Unit consists of entirely new molded figures (not remolded or made of cardboard), flashy new sixteen color scenery processed on heavy cardboard—also streamer for top of machine, all units thoroughly checked — no unnecessary fitting to be done, may be installed in few minutes.

This Is Red Hot—
Order Now and Cash In

$15.00 Complete F. O. B. San Antonio, Texas. Terms: 50% with Order, Balance C.O.D. (Payment in full with order will save C.O.D. fee.)

HITLER UNITS SAME PRICE.

Samples Sold With Money Back Guarantee If Not Satisfied

BONA FIDE DISTRIBUTORS, WRITE.

Manufactured Exclusively By

HAROLD W. THOMPSON

(Seeburg Phonograph Distributor)
415 Carolina St., San Antonio, Tex.

| Figure 3.20 |

A game conversion for a Seeburg *Chicken Sam* game, 1940s. Various manufacturers jumped into the "game conversion" business during the war, for several types of arcade style games.

allows light to pass through the toy body. "This Jap is so mean looking you just can't help shooting at him," notes the advertising small print in one *Trap the Jap* conversion ad. Another of the changeover units is called *Keep Tokyo Bombed*.

As this conversion of *Chicken Sam* shows, even a simple, old fashioned arcade game—games that seem to focus far more on the mechanisms of play over any content—can in fact become political. This was true even for Parker Brothers, which released a series of reskinned board games such as *War at Sea* and *Little Soldier Boy*. Games often became political, some designed and even reskinned to reflect the necessary "patriotic" theme of the moment. As shown, in wartime, racial slurs are one of the commonplace ways a population articulated its fear of the other and its taking of sides.

Games and Contemporary Artists

Hundreds of artists of varying disciplines have appropriated board games in their work, finding the space of games and the game metaphor not only something accessible to audiences but also a disciplined frame for creation. In a further insight, the avant-garde artists of the Fluxus group in the 1960s to 1970s saw the forces of critical play—unplaying, reskinning, and rewriting—as the most urgent quality of art itself. Much like the earlier Dadaists, Fluxus represented an international web of artists who connected to each other and their followers through every type of medium and discipline imaginable. Games, bound by limited information, an emphasis on play, and a manifestation as either closed or open systems, struck Fluxus artists as a natural path for the creation of a vocabulary based on, or explicitly outside, popular cultural rules and expectations. Fluxus artists were quick to see that games lay between the rational and the absurd, between mobility and fixed trajectories, and between logic and chance. Furthermore, Fluxus artists understood games as processes as well as outcomes, capable of disseminating even the most elusive of Fluxus ideas. Opposed to seriousness and the ossification of art as object, Fluxus artists sought a new art practice, one that was open to humor, intimacy, player agency, and various aspects of performance. "Because games lend themselves to humor, often require physical participation, and undermine the seriousness of art that certain Fluxus artists opposed, they were a perfect medium for Fluxus expression and experimentation."[84]

Often, Fluxus games, and games by non-Fluxus contemporary artists, stemmed from performative events sometimes called "happenings" (discussed in chapter 5) or took the form of Fluxkits: boxes holding play items and, possibly, instructions. These were a range of inexpensive, even disposable, interactive game-like works, and Flux games were performed at Fluxus events. The Fluxkits offered players an assortment

| Figure 3.21 |

George Brecht (1926–2008), *Water Yam*, Fluxus No. C, 1963, wooden box containing paper cards. Hood Museum of Art, Dartmouth College, Hanover, NH; gift of Dr. Abraham M. Friedman.

of playing instructions that were often described as scores. Game pieces, everyday objects, and altered existing games such as new card decks, most of which are impossible to play in any predicted way, were other typical features.

Artist George Brecht made many collections of scores, instructions, and game boxes including his *Games and Puzzles—Swim Puzzle Box Game* (1965). Its instruction or score advised players to "arrange the beads in such a way the word CUAL never occurs." Paradoxically, the box contained no beads or letters, only a seashell, making the score impossible to execute. Either players cannot play this game, or they have already won this impossible challenge. One common Fluxus game form was the design of a rule set that left both the realization of a game and its outcome entirely up to its players.

Brecht's *Water Yam* box (1963–1969), one of the most famous of the Fluxkits, is another box filled with instructions and event scores that provided open-ended tasks and performances one can select and perform (figure 3.21). The success of each task or performance is really up to the performers, the group, and the intervention of chance. With about seventy event scores in the box, Brecht's Fluxkit provides another example

| **Figure 3.22a, b** |

George Maciunas, American (1931–1978); Eric Andersen, Danish (b. 1943); George Brecht, American (1926–2008); Ben Vautier, Swiss (b. 1935); John Cavanaugh (unknown, twentieth century); Willem de Ridder, Dutch (b. 1942); Robert Filliou, French (1926–1987); Vera Spoerri (unknown, twentieth century); Roland Topor, French (1938–1997); Albert M. Fine, American (1932–1987); Ken Friedman, American (b. 1949); Hi Red Center, Japanese, founded 1963; John Lennon, British (1940–1980); Frederic Lieberman (unknown, twentieth century); Claes Thure Oldenburg, American (b. 1929); Yoko Ono, American (b. 1933); James Riddle, American (b. 1933); Paul Jeffrey Sharits, American (1943–1993); Bob Sheff, American (twentieth century); Mieko (Chieko) Shiomi, Japanese (b. 1938); Stanley Vanderbeek, American (1927–1984); Wolf Vostell, German (1932–1998); Yoshimasa Wada, Japanese (b. 1943); Robert Watts, American (1923–1988), *Flux Year Box 2*, 1966. Five-compartment wood box with objects by various artists. Hood Museum of Art, Dartmouth College, Hanover, NH; purchased through the William S. Rubin Fund.

of how a Fluxus score creates a performance, an art object, and an evocative physical situation:

George Brecht: "AIR CONDITIONING" (from WATER YAM*)*

(move through the place).

George Brecht: "CHAIR EVENT" (from WATER YAM*)*

on a white chair
a grater
tape measure
alphabet
flag
black
  and spectral colors

| Figure 3.23 |

George Brecht (1926–2008), *Games and Puzzles–Swim Puzzle Box Game,* ca. 1965. Hood Museum of Art, Dartmouth College, Hanover, NH; gift of Dr. Abraham M. Friedman.

Water Yam contains other cards, like "Piano Piece," which tells players: "A vase of flowers on(to) a piano." On the card for "Two Vehicle Events," one can read "Start/ Stop." Brecht also contributed to international Fluxus group projects such as the *Flux Year Box 2* (as seen in figure 3.22), and created numerous other Fluxkits such as *Games and Puzzles* (figure 3.23).

The cards of Mieko (Chieko) Shiomi's *Events and Games* (created around 1964) contained "Music for Two Players II," which tells its participants: "In a closed room pass two hours in silence." Her work *Disappearing Music for Face* advises: "Smile/Stop to smile"; this was made into a slow motion black-and-white film as well. Similarly, Robert Watts's *Events* (ca. 1965) offers this: "Mailbox Event—open mailbox/close eyes/remove letter of choice/tear up letter/open eyes." In "Winter Event," we get: "Winter Event—snow."[85]

Fluxus artist Alison Knowles (b. 1933–), a painter by training and one of the founding members of the Fluxus movement, was a major force from its onset, collaborating with other Fluxus artists, documenting works by others, and performing in collective works. While also working in experimental book arts and printing, Knowles wrote Fluxus scores that focused on mundane, everyday objects and ordinary domestic events. Several Fluxus artists created games as interventions to open everyday life to more careful examination, rendering social moments as acts of exchange or opportunities to critique larger political situations. In fact, the Fluxus practice of making games or instruction cards to create situations that are indeed artworks is said to have originated with the American composer John Cage (1912–1992) in the courses he taught at The New School for Social Research in New York from 1956–1960. Play, to Fluxus artists, undermined the seriousness of high art, and pointed irreverently instead to intentionally creating everyday actions and experiences instead of sanctifying a pristine art object. Drawing inspiration from Cage and others, instead of producing the shocking spectacles her male counterparts were prone to create,[86] Alison Knowles's Fluxus events furthered the habitual investigation into everyday matters, championing the performative potential of everyday objects, foods, and organic products as Cage championed the operations of nature, "making my responsibility that of asking questions instead of making choices,"[87] Knowles said. She would frequently set up a table or situation in which to share food, a celebration on the pleasure of the mundane. In her *Events by Alison Knowles* (1962–1964), the following events were devised:

Proposition
Make a salad.
1962

Giveaway Construction
Find something you like in the street and give it away. Or find a variety of things, make something of them, and give it away.
1963

Variation #1 on Proposition
Make a soup.
1964

The work of Brecht, Shiomi, Watts, Knowles, and others was joined by the artists of "Fluxus West" (1966), formed on the West Coast of the United States, and responsible for games like Jack Coke's Farmers Cooperative's *Find the End/A Fluxgame* (ca. 1969). Shiomi's *Events and Games* was created with twenty event cards, half in Japanese, detailing game actions and offering performance instruction. Like other Flux game designers, Fluxus West encouraged audiences to unplay or rewrite these given scores in an "anyone can do it" attitude toward enactment. Most Fluxkits are impossible to play in any predictable way.

The approach of reconfigurability affects the work of Brazilian-born Swedish poet turned conceptualist, cartoonist, and theorist Oyvind Fahlström (1928–1976). Whether due to the toy-like nature of his work, or the line of politics, narrative, folk art, and humor included in his approach, until the recent surge in political game art, Fahlström's work was not celebrated for its innovation, or taken into the artistic canon. Critics considered Fahlström a "throwback to Surrealism or Agitprop at worst."[88] A more careful examination of images shows Fahlström's work goes further than mere confrontation in pieces ranging from dollar bills and pie charts to puzzles and games. Fahlström takes on politics with an intense, dark perspective. In *Notes 6 (Nixon's Dreams)* (1974), a drawing depicts a man, blue in the face, "counting panthers jumping over a police barrier and an electrified map of South Vietnam (and) lying on a cata-falque surrounded by gold bullion."[89] In the work *Notes 7 ("Gook"-masks)* (1971–1975), Fahlström draws on U.S. pop-culture references of the 1970s, sketching out the faces of Smokey the Bear, Angela Davis, and Uncle Sam, as well as referring to Hiroshima and South Africa.[90]

Fahlström's *Monopoly*-influenced "variable" paintings consist of over two hundred painted magnetic elements on a painted metal board, dealing with issues such as world trade, U.S. foreign policy, the CIA, and various world revolutions. They can all be played, according to the rules inscribed directly on the paintings, as variations of the game *Monopoly*, which is in turn described as "*the* game of capitalism: a simplified but precise presentation of the trading of surplus value for capital gains."[91] While acknowl-edging the simplification of very complex realities in his games, Fahlström notes that the works still emerge as basic game diagrams of political, social, and economic phe-nomena. By choosing sides and strategies, players become involved with miniature "political psychodramas." One of the variable paintings is *Indochina* (1971), a game whose various charts and graphs and *Monopoly*-like spaces bear labels like "Saigon/US Embassy," "Tiger Cages," and "Refugee Camps."[92] Since Fahlström wanted his reskin-ning to extend to his players, elements of these art games are fixed by magnets, allow-ing participants to "manipulate the world."[93]

Fahlström's performative objects and changeable paintings also invite viewers in to "choose strategies."[94] In addition to his *Monopoly* games, there is *Kidnapping Kissinger* (1972), in which game squares on a board are cut as though a silhouette had emerged from a part of the play area. Simple icons of people, machines, buildings, and cars are arranged on the board. Fahlström also made puzzle-style variable paintings, such as *Night Music 2: Cancer Epidemic Scenario* (1975) and *Night Music 4: Protein Race Scenario* (1976), and matching card-styled works, including *120 Improvisations (for Chile II)* between 1973 and 1974. These simple black-and-white pieces contained abstract shapes—states? territories?—that one could match. A significant part of Fahlström's work relates to the coup in Chile on September 11, 1973.

Like the Japanese Sugoroku games, Fahlström's pieces include a great deal of text, which can be read compulsively. Fahlström seems to understand the pleasure in this process of decoding, and looks at text as a way to play with and subvert notions of narrative suspense and structure, narrative resolution, and conflict. The eventual goal of the artist was to mass-produce the games, an aim yet to be realized.

Gabriel Orozco, the Veracruz-born Mexican artist (b. 1962) who has referenced games and recreated game artifacts, asks questions about play, games, and culture in his work. Initially, Orozco reframed obsolescence through found objects, such as an East German motor scooter or fruit. Several of his game-related works were produced for an installation called *Empty Club* (1996), commissioned by the British group Artangel. The exhibition, shown at a posh London men's club, critiqued the leisure lifestyle of the wealthy through sports photographs overlaid with geometry.[95] Orozco's work *Ping Pond Table* (1998) offered a reskinning of ping pong, asking: if the space of the ping pong net were to be reexplored, opened up, made multidimensional, would the shape of the board wind up being different? Circular? Square? Lotus-shaped? Orozco's *Ping Pond Table* emerges in its own space with its own dimensionality, with the net acting as a bridge between geometry and the physical world. The artist intends that the meaning of the work and its spatiality be infinitely interpretable when "put into play" by the viewer, so that the table opens up a new possibility for space:

The "Ping Pond Table" is connected to this idea of a new space, a new possible space. When you have a normal ping pong game you have a net which is enough space between two spaces. But when you multiply that space by four, instead of two people playing you have four people playing in four tables. You open that space so the net is also open. And what you have there is a new space because it didn't exist before . . . the net, that space in between two spaces—I opened it up. And I have a tri-dimensional space now in-between four spaces.

That is the space that I'm interested in, the in-between space. . . . To activate that space. To activate means to fill it with meaning and connections so that we can think about it. We can connect with it and make it happen as a space and time in between things.[96]

Art historian Jill Bennett has noted that that Orozco's interests in games, including sports, in his work can be read as "gestures."[97] These serve as an operative method rather than subject matter. The idea of gesture opens these works to the larger interests in play and in the way play is codified by culture. Orozco's photograph titled *Pinched Ball* depicts a soggy soccer ball filled with water. In his *Oval Billiard Table* (1996), also known as *Carambole with Pendulum*, Orozco created a curved linear object that acts more like a scientific instrument than a play space. The pocketless billiard table holds two white balls, while suspended above the table is a red ball that hangs like a pendulum, tempting the viewer to play. Pool cues are located nearby. But with the familiar pockets that one would expect from such a table absent, what might be the purpose of the board, and the goal of this game? The temptation to hit the hovering red ball is easy to give in to, and viewers pick up the pool cues close by to "see what happens." Hitting the white ball so that it collides with the red ball spurs on the larger geometric events of nature. Once hit, the red ball flies from the table on its own trajectory, acting as pendulum sometimes in sync with, and other times crossing over, the elliptical shape of the unique oval billiard table. Rather than a comment on the game of pool, the work looks at larger assumptions of movement, natural laws and physics, and the assumed agency in playing a game.

Orozco insists on a passion for political engagement in his work, even though the work tends to operate at a conceptual level. It seems clear, however, that he is concerned with chance encounter, physics, and agency. Art historian David Joselit has noted that Orozco's work has much in common with Paul Virilio's notion that contemporary politics, power, and collectivity must be understood not in terms of property but routes and vectors of circulation.[98] If not moving, Orozco's works infer movement and, often, play. To Joselit, Orozco's literal vectors—his pendulum and ovals, his inferences and actual movements—become tools for social critique and social imagining. Orozco's games reflect larger philosophical issues:

Probably they are more like philosophical games. I believe that philosophy has to be a practice. Practical philosophy. It's like the way the Greeks used to solve philosophical and mathematical problems, by walking. Not sitting. It's easier to solve problems moving— when you walk and you talk—probably because you have better irrigation in the brain or just because you are breathing better. Because you are moving you have better chances to solve complex problems. And also I think in a way it's an action thing. So I think philosophy is an action, it should be. And to play the games are part of it.[99]

The Most Popular Games Mirroring Conflict and War

The metaphor of war, of captured territory, and abstract personal combat, has served as a foundation for many of the most well-known board games from the Chinese game of Go to chess and checkers. Go, or Wéiqí, was noted earlier as a game having possible roots in divination practices. Wéiqí was exported to Japan sometime during the fifth through eighth centuries. One sandalwood game was discovered dating from the time of the Japanese Emperor Shomu (701–756 AD). The game became very popular within the court culture of Japan's Heian Period (794–1195 AD), and it is said that samurai appreciated the ancient game for its ability to shape strategic thinking. Military in its overall metaphor, the game involves the elements of defense, seizure, and capture. In the Japanese manifestation, Go was given as a special gift at weddings and was a documented pastime of Zen monks, shoguns, and tea ceremony masters. In its entanglement with ritual, the game itself reflects cultural and social characteristics of the times in which it developed and changed.

Go is played on a nineteen-by-nineteen square grid. Two players, black and white, take turns placing pieces on the empty starting board in an attempt to "capture" territory. The two players use their respective stones to capture points, or intersections of lines, and to lay out a continuous area for ownership. The opponent invariably tries to invade the free area to capture territory. Players who start the game at different skill levels can handicap the game by shrinking the board and by allowing the weaker player more moves or more pieces.

The Chinese poet Po Chü-i (772–846 AD) describes the special qualities of playing Wéiqí:

Mountain monks sit at the Wéiqí board
under the bamboo's semi-lucent shade.
No one sees them through the glittering leaves—
but now and then the click of a stone is heard.[100]

Here, a rare aesthetic is celebrated, and the game is identifiable through its noble sounds, its beautiful surroundings, and the engagement of ascetic men.

In a move toward critical play, several contemporary artists have used the game of Go to raise political and social questions. The artist Lilian Ball used the game as a template of sorts in order to foster collaboration and dialogue. Her interactive game

| Figure 3.24 |
Lilian Ball's *GO ECO*, 2007.

project *GO ECO* is intended to illuminate differing perspectives on an environmental conservation project on Long Island, New York. In the real-world situation, wetlands, wildlife, and rare plant species were endangered by politics and real estate interests. In response, the artist initiated a community project to help preserve a twelve-acre wetland in Southold, New York. Ball's concept revolves around using the game iconography and mechanics to generate new perspectives and points of view among players who are interested stakeholders in the conflict.

GO ECO (figure 3.24) helps enlist players to capture territories, but with a rule change, to make the player experience one of collaboration, not competition. The physical game pieces are accompanied by images, which represent viewpoints of biologists, landowners, government officials, and neighborhood residents. The images of the native cranberries, varied wildlife, and the endangered Iris prismatica are generated alongside the Go pieces moving on the game board and tracked by a camera.

Rather than the usual two players, Ball imagines that odd numbers of participants are preferable in her "zen" version of the game so that players' turns are never fixed. In this way, "cooperation is encouraged. One must see the other side's point of view since everyone occupies another side on the next turn.[101] The game is intended to encourage solutions in which all sides win or lose equally. Ball's intention for *GO ECO* is to help players of many ages to "be empowered and to learn about the issues through an art experience that maps paths of action."[102]

Like Go, the game of chess has influenced artists for centuries. Though historians disagree on the original details of the invention of the game, several well-regarded chess scholars have argued that texts in Pahlavi and Sanskrit support the idea that India was the site of development no later than the sixth century AD.[103] In Sanskrit, the game was called *Four Members* (*Chaturanga*), which referred to the four regimens of the Indian army (chariots, cavalry, elephants, and foot soldiers). The Indian version of the game was played with realistically rendered pieces meant to resemble human participants. The game was introduced to Europe around 1000 AD by Arabs, who had played since the seventh century.[104]

Arab scholars noted that the benefits of chess included diligence, thrift, and knowledge, one example of how the game has faithfully reflected cultural practices in the locations in which it has been played. For example, after death of the Muhammad in 642 AD, chess followed an edict of the Koran that forbids realistic human depiction. Game makers avoided representational models, opting instead for abstract pieces.[105]

Artists have depicted chess from its beginnings in drawings, paintings, and tapestries, including work in the influential document *Book of Chess*, written by King Alphonso in 1283 AD. The book served as both a textual and visual record of many chess-playing scenes in Europe.[106] Chess and backgammon dominated board-game pursuits in Europe until the Renaissance. There are numerous depictions of chess in artwork. Paintings such as Lucas van Leyden's *Chess Players* (ca. 1510 AD) or *A Game of Chess* (1906) by Bernard Louis Borione demonstrate that the game has frequently captivated artists in many everyday scenarios. Earlier, the Romanesque mosaic found in the choir of San Savino in Piacenza, Italy (dating from 1107 AD), included a floor mosaic that depicted both the playing of a dice game and a game of chess. Scholars now believe that the artist juxtaposed the two games to represent a polarity of two paths in life: man can either commit himself to the chance and the unstable forces of the world, allowing his life to become lawless, chaotic, and evil; or man may choose to live with virtue and intelligence, so that he may imbue to the world intelligence, law, and harmony.[107] The conflict between fortune and virtue was one that the medieval Catholic Church was ready to promote in favor of subjects' compliance with the rules of virtue espoused by doctrine. In contrast to the power of worldly "fortune," often personified as a woman, *Fortuna*, with the fortune wheel constantly changing, offered little opportunity for stability.[108] Church officials used this dichotomy to symbolically shape the choices of the player.

Of significance is the study conducted by Marilyn Yalom (2004), who detailed the generational—even epochal—changes in chess. Yalom's study of the queen piece in the game revealed that chess did not include a female figure on the board until the tenth century.[109] Even then, the queen was the weakest member of the cast, only able to move one square at a time. Yalom argues that the queen gained influence to become the most powerful piece on the board as cultural power for women gradually increased. A string of powerful queens in Europe during Medieval times, for example, influenced not only the piece's representation and gender (in earlier manifestations, the queen had been the king's vizier, a male figure) but also the piece's actions. Paralleling the rise of powerful female leaders in Europe, namely Eleanor of Aquitaine, Queen Ingeborg of Norway, and Queen Isabella of Castile, the piece moved from vizier to queen and was freed from the slow, one-square-at-a-time rule of movement to become the most powerful piece on the board. By the time of the famous Norweigan set, the Lewis chess set (1150 AD–1200 AD) (figure 3.25), the queen piece had an established place on the board.

While writing his treatise "The Morals of Chess," Benjamin Franklin notes that players of chess may learn foresight, circumspection, and caution, that is, a habit not entirely hasty:

We learn Chess by the habit of not being discouraged by present bad appearances in the state of our affairs, the habit of hoping for a favourable chance, and that of preserving in the search of resources. The game is so full of events, there is such a variety of turns in it, the fortune of it is so subject to vicissitudes, and one so frequently, after contemplation, discovers the means of extricating one's self from a supposed insurmountable difficulty, that one is encouraged to continue the contest to the last, in hopes of victory from our skill, or, at least, from the negligence of our adversary, and whoever considers, what in Chess he often sees instances of, that success is apt to produce presumption and its consequent inattention, by which more is afterwards lost than was gained by the preceding advantage, while misfortunes produce more care and attention, by which the loss may be recovered, will learn not to be too much discouraged by any present successes of his adversary, nor to despair of final good fortune upon every little check he receives in the pursuit of it.[110]

In their explorations of critical play, artists have been captivated by chess as a social system. The Surrealists Alberto Giacometti, Max Ernst, Man Ray, and Marcel Duchamp all referred to, or incorporated, chess into their work. Duchamp's love

| Figure 3.25 |
The Lewis Chessmen, 1150–1175 AD, included queens in its formation. The British Museum.

for chess, one of the games furthest removed from his well-known affection for chance and found objects, was established long before he moved to the United States. Duchamp had famously taken to playing chess as a form of art, even playing himself as chess-player in an experimental film directed by the American composer John Cage (1912–1992). In 1963, Duchamp played chess with nude challenger Eve Babitz at his first retrospective in Pasadena.[111] Duchamp's love affair with chess, according to many of his scholars, came from the beauty of the game and the "language" of chess. He played competitively in the 1920s, and certainly enjoyed winning.[112]

Chess is a compelling "experiential instrument" for artists like Duchamp (who drew the pieces in figure 3.26) for a number of reasons. First, it is a highly symbolic game, one in which pieces have extra meaning. Its hierarchic structure, resembling

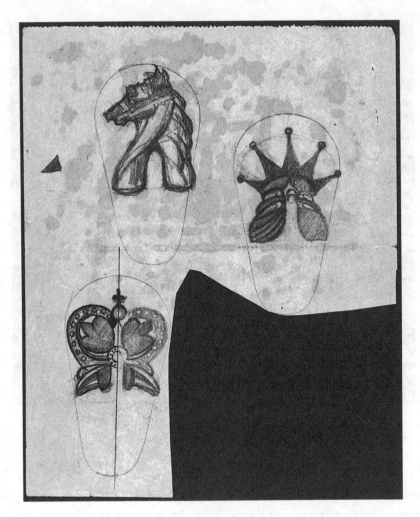

| Figure 3.26 |

Marcel Duchamp (1887–1968) autograph note for *Projects*: drawing of chess pieces (king, queen, knight), 1912–1968. Pencil, black ink, 19.8 × 16.2 cm. AM1997-98(205). Musée National d'Art Moderne, Centre Georges Pompidou, Paris. Photo: Jean-Claude Planchet. Photo credit: CNAC/MNAM/Dist. Réunion des Musées Nationaux/Art Resource, NY. © ARS, NY.

an army, a court, a rank and file with its rows of pawns, models nearly literally a state at war. It is generally believed the Greeks played the first war games where strategy is involved without the intervention of chance.[113] In one Greek game called *Polis* (the "town"), two opposing players maneuvered a large number of gaming counters on the squares of a game board, to trap an opponent's piece between two of one's own to capture it. This strategy replicates the battle strategy of the "phalanx" formation, where the strength of a given offense lies in cohesive, unidirectional attack, a literal lineup of rows of men with spears that is difficult or impossible for an opponent to penetrate. The strategy was broken in chess, where the example of the knight's move makes such a line less important.

This detail, the unique affordances of each game piece, calls to our attention the ways in which board games are taught, how expertise is passed down, and, most important, how the rules are interpreted and expressed. How does one, for example, explain how to play a complicated board game such as chess? First, there is the board itself, so familiar across cultures and used in many other types of games. This board provides a base understanding of "spaces" and "moves," though these could be altered and modified on a game-by-game basis. Second, one would explore the abilities of the pieces. In detailing the moves of a chess piece—for example, this is a pawn; it moves forward and can only capture other pieces on a diagonal—abilities are mapped to figures. These figures represent functionality and player agency. André Breton wrote, "Philosophical freedom is an illusion. In chess as in all other games, each move is loaded with the indefinite past of the universe."[114] Like other board games, if a chess set is missing a given piece, it is understood that something else may act in substitution for that piece. Thus, a lofty bishop might end up being played by an eraser or lipstick. In any event, the piece itself is viewed with its particular affordances and powers, having for both players all of the abilities and limitations of the rules that govern the piece. Using substitute objects in a game in this manner emphasizes that the transactions involved are so symbolically robust that the game's rules and processes can allow for pieces to stand in for one another, for games to forge their own control over temporality, and consensus to be reached among players about how to interact. With these abilities, games produce not only cohesive rule sets but also cohesive worlds, and worlds that express meaning.

The elements of engaging in battle—determining how to isolate the enemy, keep one's strongest pieces, make sacrifices, and identify and outthink the opposition—are abstracted and practiced in chess and are also the very elements that draw artists to use chess as a tool for social critique. The idea of battle formation and the conduct of conflict between opposing players characterizes much of the artistic intervention in the game. Between 1961 and 1970, Fluxus artist Takako Saito produced a number of chess modifications that were sold and distributed by George Maciunas's Fluxus Mail Order Warehouse. Saito's chess sets were Fluxus art staples and sold to collectors in the United States and Europe. *Grinder Chess* was an interesting "industrial" reduction of the game. *Jewel Chess*, with gems in small cases, was a pretty variation on the game. Other Saito chess sets included the use of senses other than vision. *Liquid Chess* (1975) was created from vials of liquids that also emitted smells. These vials could also be used to determine which piece was which (through smell) and use this knowledge so that players have rules for play. *Sound Chess* or *Weight Chess*, featured in the collective work *Flux Cabinet*, consisted of opaque, white plastic boxes containing items to be identified by weight or sound when shaking. *Spice Chess* appeared in several different iterations and featured corked tubes filled with spices in a rack. Game scholar Celia Pearce notes that Saito's chess sets offer a particularly beautiful take on the aesthetics of play, as the works take into account many senses, exploring the nuances of sensory difference and the malleability of rules.[115] Saito produced a score of chess sets, which, according to Yoshimoto, "became the embodiment of the Fluxus philosophy in their merging of strategy and humor."[116] Along these lines, Fluxus artists, particularly women artists, were attentive to senses other than vision; Alison Knowles, Takako Saito, and Yoko Ono all created smell- and touch-based artworks.[117] These too took on performative game qualities. Ono's *Touch Piece* (1963), for example, instructs performers to touch each other.

Ono, like Saito, found chess provided a cross-cultural vocabulary to apply in exploring play systems and larger social and political entities.

Play It by Trust (1997), a game in which the board and the chess pieces are all white, is one of a series of Ono's chess investigations. Chess-related artworks that Ono has exhibited range from her version of the game itself, *All White Chess Set* (1966), to installation versions of *Play It by Trust*. When *All White Chess Set* was first exhibited at the Indica Gallery in London, it was comprised of a wooden chess table, a chess set, and two chairs, all of which were painted white. A brass plate on the underside of the table read: CHESS SET FOR PLAYING AS LONG AS YOU CAN REMEMBER WHERE ALL YOUR PIECES ARE.[118] White, the color of surrender in war, essentially nullifies the competitive and confrontational aspects of the game.

Like several of her pieces examining themes of balance, Ono's approach to *Play It by Trust* (or the precious balance between the real world and the painted instructions in her *Instruction Paintings*, discussed later) may be read as an exploration into the art experience through scenarios which encourage cooperation and collaboration. Both *Cut Piece* and *Play It by Trust* interrogate human relationships, focusing on trust and the interdependency we all have with one another. Using everyday items like chess pieces, game boards, or scissors, Ono allows participants in the work to consider the marvelous nature of the everyday and engage with game-like concepts and processes in an endless queue of provocative situations. *Play It by Trust* emphasizes the ways in which serious issues might be tackled through games, and how multiple participants in games have equal opportunities and face equal stakes. Reskinning, or painting the work all white, eliminates the element of competition from the traditional form of the game.

One of the few Fluxus artists who used her whimsy and game-like constructions in the pursuit of political aims rather than merely challenging the predictable patterns of the art world, the stakes for Ono were clearly activist. Ono plays critically, using rules, symbolic meaning systems, the sociocultural context, and the inherent sense one has of game "time" to present pacifist aims.[119] This work goes beyond game to envision a "world-playground" and a wish for utopian solutions to social and political concerns.

Recent chess-based artwork compares favorably to Ono's use of the game. In 2003, UK artist Damien Hirst created *Mental Escapology*, a chess set featuring a glass-and-mirror board displaying a biohazard symbol with accompanying silver casts of medicine bottles and etched silver labels, all housed inside a glass medicine chest.[120] Jake and Dinos Chapman produced a set that includes "post- apocalyptic adolescent figures" of white children with phallic noses on one side, while the opposing pieces are black children with afro-styled hair, all on a board inlaid with double skulls and crossbones.[121] Perhaps one of the most significant sculptural pieces is by Gabriel Orozco, who delved heavily into chess with his work *Horses Running Endlessly* (1995) to examine the spatial materiality of the chessboard (figure 3.27). The result is a sculptural work comprised of an expanded chessboard—256 instead of 64 squares—and plethora of knights, also in four colors.

The configuration of the pieces in *Horses Running Endlessly* is exciting in that there are many potential positions and actions for the knight pieces. In a typical chessboard, the knight can in theory occupy all squares in sequence without repeating a position. There is something simultaneous happening among the knights on the board, as though all of the knights should be moving not in turn, but in formation. The result is a sense of infinite possibility. It is easy to imagine that a player or participant with this work would be free to modify the order of pieces as they wish. Like kinetic sculpture or a mobile by Xenia Cage or Calder, Orozco's horses could be activated. This is communicated through color, shape, and place.

The reconfiguration of chess continues in the digital versions of the game. Ruth Catlow's 2003 piece *Rethinking Wargames: A Chance to Remaster Conflict* was created in

| Figure 3.27 |
Gabriel Orozco (Mexican, b. 1962), *Horses Running Endlessly*, 1995, wood. Gift of Agnes Gund and Lewis B. Cullman in honor of Chess in the Schools. © 2008 Gabriel Orozco.

response to thinking about global conflict, and in particular, the context of the swift U.S. bombing of Afghanistan in response to the September 11 bombing of the World Trade Center in New York City in 2001. Catlow investigated ways that games could be used to express different kinds of aggression or to teach negotiation or nonviolent conflict resolution. If it were possible to teach these principles, she surmised, it should therefore also be possible to make these principles available to a wider audience, using the Internet as a vehicle of distribution. The result was the work *Rethinking Wargames*, a version of chess designed for three players representing white royalty, black royalty, and the united force of pawn. Players take turns making moves. White's goal is to eliminate the black royalty, black's goal is to eliminate white royalty, and the pawns place themselves as barriers to the aggression, trying to "slow down" the violence like virtual protestors, so that negotiation between the violent warring factions might possibly take place.

This version of chess is remarkable for how different it feels to play the game. Unlike typical chess, where one or the other opponent plays only to win, the experience of play is changed due to the possibility that the royals, with their powerful pieces, may not succeed. The action in *Rethinking Wargames* moves far faster; the resulting decisions by royalty are more aggressive and swift, and far less strategic, than in the usual version. The pawn player, knowing the pawns are relatively powerless except in sheer mass or numbers, intervenes by putting them on the line in the middle of violence, much as many protesters have done historically. The pawns act as "blocks," and after five turns, if neither royal side has taken a piece, a period of nonviolence is counted and a piece of metaphoric "grass" grows on the game board. After five turns of nonviolence, grass will have taken over the fighting field. By staving off the aggression and overcoming the "hotheaded" part of the conflict, the pawns win. The idea is to allow more time for negotiation, rather than immediate reactions and attacks.

It is important to remind ourselves that while pacifism and nonviolence in this game may emerge as a larger game goal, *Rethinking Wargames* itself is quite dependent on the premise that chess itself is founded on: conflict and the taking of pieces; in other words, violence. The viciousness of the royals is matched by the passion for peace from the pawns. For all sides, *play implies action*, and even if one is trying to accomplish an activist aim or a societal critique, the idea is that one takes action, as opposed to nonaction, even if the action results in a block. The game demonstrates that negotiation takes slowing down, that peace can only come with negotiation, not reaction and rhetoric. To rethink the current solution, one cannot be on the defense or the attack, but rather in a meta-state.

Chess is interesting precisely because it represents many ideologies, the first of which is an easy duality between opposing forces. This is apparent as early as Huizinga's critique of the political philosophy of Carl Schmitt, in *Homo Ludens* (1938, in Dutch). Huizinga notes that philosophies such as those purported by Schmitt provide a dangerous rationale for the oversimplified intellectual culture of fascism, in which social life is easily divided between "good" and "evil," "us" and "them," where nuance is dismissed and competition encouraged. Indeed, Huizinga argues this oversimplified line of thinking undermines the ethical workings, or "fair play" foundation of international law. Walter Benjamin also notes that competitive scenarios tended to oversimplify complex issues.[122] This critique is mirrored in Catlow's work, as she seeks to add nuance and multiple kinds of outcomes to the game.[123] Thus the aims of Catlow's project have much in common with many of the experiential chess games discussed in this chapter. *Rethinking Wargames* engages with the idea of choosing strategies. It interrogates the linear trajectory of time intrinsic to games, even with their interactive structure. It enhances the benefits of repetitive performance, mobility, and empowerment to make decisions through play. In these war games, players are empowered to make metaphorically large decisions through play.

Janet Murray defines agency as "the satisfying power to take meaningful action and see the results of our decisions and choices."[124] Artist-created board games use this theory to its fullest, providing table-based mini laboratories for the examination of choice, chance, and social interaction. Some works, such as Giacometti's board games, offer a critique of even the possibility of agency, implying that playing or enacting the sculptural game boards would be futile, cyclical, a trap. Games, such as Catlow's chess game, expose the possibilities of player agency in other ways: first, by empowering the pawns, thus imbuing traditionally conceived pieces/roles with new power; second, by opening up the possible outcomes of the game in terms of widening the possible win states, thus rewriting the original in visionary ways. Metaphorical or actual, the game design must embody action, and depending on how active a game feels, its critique may be more or less apparent. Artists may invoke game metaphors, as Giacometti did in his game boards, and as Ono did in *Play It by Trust*, or artists can produce contexts for play, empathy, and learning, as Ono does in *Cut Piece* and Catlow does in *Rethinking Wargames*. These are different types of experiences but all foster a critical type of play.

LANGUAGE GAMES

The only acceptable finality of human activity is the production of a subjectivity that is auto-enriching its relation to the world in a continuous fashion. The productive apparatuses of subjectivity can exist at the level of megapoles as easily as at the level of an individual's language games.

—Félix Guattari, *Chaosmosis: An Ethico-Aesthetic Paradigm*

Wordplay is fundamentally expressive and rich in critical play. Games involving language span across global linguistic systems, geographies, and cultures, and are vital for designers. Linguist David Crystal states that language games "cut across regional, social and professional background, age, sex, ethnicity, personality, intelligence and culture."[1] Rather than provide a comprehensive analysis of all language games, this survey is meant to uncover techniques of language play invoked by artists. What is most interesting for game designers is how certain forms of language invention can constitute a play space through the use of words themselves as a medium, placing critical language close by its own noncritical context. How are language games signaled? How do they subvert language itself? Exactly what kinds of language play can be unearthed from artists' practices?

Some subsets of linguistics refer specifically to language games as secret languages. These have been concocted around the world, passed down verbally in forms for use in ritual and everyday practices. These examples of transforming speech include at least some language play likely to be familiar to readers: pig latin, "formal" gibberish, the French Verlan, and hundreds of other invented language forms. Wordplay takes on many shapes: poetry, in word meaning and metric and shape; in symbolic and metaphoric language; in exchanges in fiction as practiced by Lewis Carroll or Dr. Seuss, word puzzles, word games, puns, limericks, riddles, and the unexpected use of language.

All are important sources for activist game designers.[2] Artists have used wordplay on various levels, from including text in paintings to affronting language performances. The absurdist theatrical work of Alfred Jarry (1873–1907), the poetry of Dada artists, and the "code" of Fluxus artists each provide critical exploration through play with words. Artists and writers aim for subversion of romanticized norms, of existing systems of power, of authority, and of aesthetic associations in each of these categories.

Even without representing text or pictographs, much ancient visual art incorporates subtle wordplay. Take, for example, a small Qing Dynasty sculpture of two carp, most likely a wedding gift, discussed by Chinese art historian Terese Tse Bartholomew in her 2006 book, *Hidden Meanings in Chinese Art*.[3] In Chinese tradition, such fish are believed to swim in pairs, and can symbolize marital commitment. Yet they also embody the type of linguistic pun quite common in Chinese: the characters for *fish* and for *abundance* are both pronounced the same way, "yu." There are multiple examples of double entendre produced through imagery and the significance of these fish in visual representation. The same linguistic device of the visual pun is also demonstrated in classic painting. Images of the Dutch masters are rife with humorous allusions to slippers. The Dutch *slippertje* can be used to denote a love affair into which a spouse falls, or "slips."[4] Here, and in other scenes, noticing the ways language plays with culture, especially language as used by artists, can help designers find methods of consciousness raising, or tools for social commentary.

Play, Form, and Theater

In the nineteenth century, writers like Rimbaud, Verlaine, Sand, Mallarmé, Baudelaire, and Poe experimented with language to voice criticisms about larger societal issues. The U.S. writer Edgar Allan Poe (1809–1849) and the French writer and playwright Alfred Jarry both pushed the boundaries of language use. It is likely that this obsession with wordplay was an international nineteenth-century phenomenon. In English, all types of wordplay appeared in the early nineteenth-century work of Emily Dickinson, Nathaniel Hawthorne, Washington Irving, and Henry David Thoreau.[5] Perhaps inspired by the twisty passages of other writers, or the mind-bending changes in French, and international, literature, especially poetry, writers accelerated their use of puns and palindromes at the turn of the nineteenth century. This is true particularly in France, where one could speculate that the roots of the avant-garde were possibly an accumulation of changes in the arts since Rousseau's innovative painting. Alfred Jarry made his mark in language circles with radical writing and theater projects. In his first publication (1893), Jarry used a near-pun to change "magnificent gesture" into "magnificent imposture" (in French, of course).[6] Afterward, Alfred Jarry "popularized" the use of nonsensical, rude, and abstract language in order to shock, creating scenes of monstrosity and controversy and focusing on language and performance as a means to achieve those effects. When Jarry staged his famous political satire, *Ubu Roi*, in Paris in 1896, it was met with almost violent protest and disdain.

Ubu Roi was conceived when Jarry was still in school, and was developed as an obsession over a number of years. The play uses farce, rudeness, and scatological jokes to rework the *Macbeth* narrative in a critique of art, politics, power, and the class system. In the plot, Mère Ubu lures an army officer into a plot to kill the "Polish King" Wenceslas, and supplant the royal throne with her abusive husband Père Ubu. Translated as "King Turd," Ubu Roi is a gluttonous man, whose buffoonery, greed, and lack of conscience make him an atrocious spectacle of power. The *Ubu* play faced a great deal of criticism, first and foremost for its language, which was described as comparable to an anarchist bomb. During the political turmoil of the 1890s, Paris railroad stations, cafés, and the national stock exchange were actual bombing targets.

PAPA TURD: Pshit !
MAMA TURD: Oh ! that's a fine thing. What a pig you are, Papa Turd !
PAPA TURD: Watch out I don't kill you, Mama Turd
MAMA TURD: It isn't me you ought to kill, Papa Turd, it's someone else.
PAPA TURD: Now by my green candle, I don't understand.[7]

The play's obscenity and its outlandish performances, centering on characters played by actors wearing massive, puppet-like outfits (these were sketched out on the original program; see figure 4.1) that brought the grotesque to life, were seen more as a hoax than an important artistic work.[8] In fact, in the preface Jarry used on stage to introduce the play to his 1896 audience, the author emphasized the point that the script was not written for puppets, but for actors pretending to be puppets.[9]

Jarry's *Ubu Roi*, *Ubu Rex*, *Ubu Cuckholded*, and *Ubu Enchained* are now counted among the earliest examples of "theater of the absurd,"[10] and Jarry's additions to critical play are several. First, he toyed with propriety in performance and in language, calling attention to social conventions, and consumerism, and making these points to the very group who might be the target of such criticism: the self-satisfied French theatergoers of the 1890s. In addition, Jarry wrote word puzzles at every turn, inviting audiences to piece together further criticism during his relentless assault on their good taste. Even the name of his most famous and abhorrent character, Ubu, is a palindrome, a word that reads the same forward as backward. Most of vulgar sayings that emerge from Ubu are palindromes, for example, MERDRE MERDRE MERDRE M.[11]

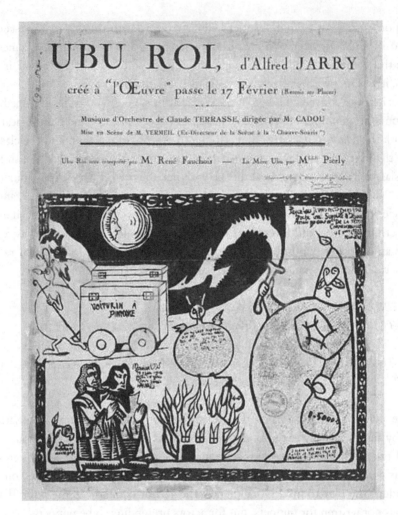

| Figure 4.1 |
Jarry's original announcement for *Ubu Roi*.

| Figure 4.2 |

The Sator-Rotas square is found over much of the Roman Empire; it contains a Latin palindrome. This square is from Tatti, Italy.
Photo by Marco Fedele.

While Jarry's scorn for his audience and society seems extreme, he drew on an established tradition of existentialism and nihilism in literature. Earlier writers involved in social critique also used clever turns of phrase or play to thrash out their points, including Dickens, Mallarmé, and Thackeray, the latter in his social satire *Vanity Fair* (1828).[12] Edgar Allan Poe, writing earlier than Jarry, was quite conscientious in the use and order of word patterns that played with contemporary literary conventions. Poe was particularly interested in the palindrome, perhaps due to his fascination with the arcane. Here, ancient word puzzles such as the Sator-Rotas rebus come to mind. Also known as the Templar Magic Square, the Sator-Rotas (an example of which is shown in figure 4.2) is one of the oldest unsolved word puzzles in the world. Some believe it was a secret code; others take it for a mark of the early Christians; still others believe the square is an ancient charm of great power and mystery.[13] When written out in the square, Sator-Rotas forms a palindrome that has been scrawled across five continents, including on a wall in the buried city of Pompeii, and among ruins discovered from Italy to the United Kingdom.[14]

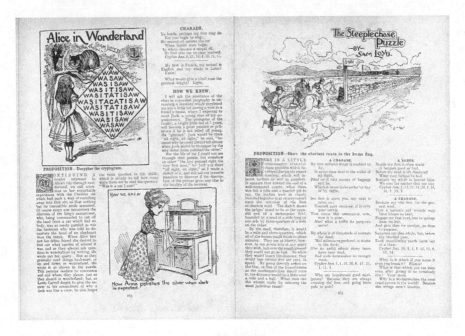

| Figure 4.3 |

The cultural prevalence of palindromes at the end of the nineteenth century was pervasive. Lewis Carroll's palindromic Cheshire cat from his 1866 *Alice's Adventures in Wonderland* is reworked by artist and puzzle maker Sam Loyd in his 1914 classic, *Sam Loyd's Cyclopedia of 5000 Puzzles, Tricks, and Conundrums (with Answers)*. Completely available at http://mathpuzzle.com/loyd/cop164-165.html.

Other palindromes are not as mysterious. See, for example, figure 4.3, a recreation of Alice in Wonderland's fantastic Cheshire cat moment, drawn as a palindrome. The contribution of Lewis Carroll (Charles Lutwidge Dodgson, 1832–1898) to the study of language cannot be denied; philosophers from George Pitcher (1965) to Leila Silvana May (2007) have explored Wittgenstein's concepts of language games through the complex work of Caroll. He specialized in the area of nonsense and the creation of language systems.[15] Most known for his children's books,[16] Dodgson was obsessed with logic, and published many games from 1860 to 1896. Some examples were *Puzzles from Wonderland* (1870), *Mischmasch* (1882), and *Circular Billiards* (1890).[17] He also created a huge set of ciphers and codes. One might argue that such play with language is not particularly critical, and with all liklihood does not in itself foster social critique. If Carroll's work remained outside political and social issues, however, he is interested in interrogating the structures around language itself.[18] His work offers a particularly abstract version of critical play, types of "allegories of philosophical systems" or in some interesting sense, an evolution of language.

The work of Edgar Allan Poe is more successful as a form of critique. In his 1837 story, "A Fable," Poe's obsession with repetition and palindromes is clear:

It was night, and the rain fell; and falling, it was rain, but, having fallen, it was blood. And I stood in the morass among the tall and the rain fell upon my head—and the lilies sighed one unto the other in the solemnity of their desolation. . . . And mine eyes fell upon a huge gray rock which stood by the shore of the river, and was lighted by the light of the moon. And the rock was gray, and ghastly, and tall,—and the rock was gray. Upon its front were characters engraven in the stone. . . . I turned and looked again upon the rock, and upon the characters;—and the characters were DESOLATION.[19]

Poe's allegorical means for critical wordplay takes the human condition as its project. By creating transcendent linguistic expressions that also speak to the structure of expression itself, Poe's language resembles secret, or nearly computational, codes whose rules of construction and operations are consistent and pervasive.

Puns

Known as the lowest form of humor, the pun is also one of the oldest and most typical modes of critical wordplay. Early writing systems, or protowriting, often contained a small number of signs in comparison to spoken communication. When a small number needs to be interpreted broadly, one sign can denote a range of possible meanings. Ancient literature in Mesopotamia, Egypt, Israel, and Greece demonstrate the importance of puns through historic examples. There is a transcription of a poem to a pharaoh's chariot, which is in some way translatable:

The *wheels* of thy chariot—
Thou *wieldest* thy battle-axe.
The *scythe* of thy chariot—
Draws *sighs* from all nations[20]

Nineteenth-century Egyptologist Adolph Erman was puzzled by the apparently significant amount of time spent on puns in the ancient world. More recent work by Scott Noegel, a specialist in ancient language play, notes that ancient cultures were fascinated by puns, but for reasons other than humor or rhetoric. Like early board games, most early examples of wordplay were used as a guide to divine questions.

| Figure 4.4 |

Duchamp viewed his creative work as "laboratory work." Shown here is his readymade *Apolinère Enameled*, 1916–1917. © 2000 Succession Marcel Duchamp ARS, NY/ADAGP, Paris.

Puns were used for both divination and dream analysis, and diviners would transcribe dreams looking for puns in the way words sounded as well as how they looked. Languages such as Sumerian or Chinese, with their large number of homophones, were rife with puns in everyday usage. The use of puns not only uncovered the meaning of dreams but also empowered the interpreter of the dream, and made the divination experience one of magical ritual.[21]

Twentieth-century avant-garde artist Marcel Duchamp understood the power of words in play, as well as the public's fascination with puzzles, which he tapped into in his work by using codes, puns, symbols, and allusions—even creating his own life as a puzzle. Duchamp was said to have "found" his readymade sculptures and visual works, called "readymades." Among these readymades was *Apolinère Enameled* (1916–1917) (figure 4.4), an advertisement (originally for Sapolin Paints) he altered with an intentionally misspelled homage to the poet Guillaume Apollinaire. His famous *Fountain* (1917) presented a urinal as a readymade art object that mocked art world conventions but also contained a play on language in the artist's signature, "R. Mutt."[22] Such games were essential to Duchamp's continual experimentation.

Duchamp's skill combined the visual and the verbal in "wildly free" episodes of "free visual verse."[23] Always calculating in his use of words, one of his most familiar works is a reproduction of Leonardo da Vinci's famous Mona Lisa, on which he inscribed a moustache, goatee, and the letters for which the work is known, *L.H.O.O.Q.* (1919). If pronounced in French, the initials are a risqué joke—L.H.O.O.Q. phonetically is *"elle a chaud au cul"* or "she has a hot ass." This use of language was a way of undermining, even poking fun at, his own experiments in form and content. His metaphors produce games of nonsense that raise compelling questions concerning his word games, such as: What point of view can the subject possibly take? Is it best to obscure meaning altogether with a sense of indifference? As Duchamp himself summarized in 1959: "Dada was an extreme protest . . . it was a sort of nihilism to which I am still very sympathetic. . . . Dada was very serviceable as a purative."[24]

The artist's famous *Anemic Cinema*, created with Man Ray in 1926, features seven minutes of rotating images intercut with spinning discs of words forming elaborate and nonsensical puns (see figure 4.5). Some of the humor of Duchamp's approach is due to the conventions of the time: intertitles were commonplace, and most moviegoers were quite used to reading while watching a film. Beginning with the title itself, *Anemic Cinema* includes near or spot-on palindromes as well as nine statements by Duchamp's female alter ego, Rrose Sélavy. Film scholar P. Adams Sitney notes the unique qualities of the work:

Anemic Cinema does not look like any film that had been made before it. The images are all disks of eccentric circles within circles and spiral lines. The words are nothing more than single sentences (in Rrose Sélavy's manner) printed spirally on disks, winding from outside in. The eye grasps the disks as wholes; their motion induces an optical illusion of three-dimensionality. Some seem to protrude from the flatness of the screen; others look like conical depressions. The viewer's response to this structure affirms the power of optical stimuli to create reflexes within a system of repetition.[25]

Kuenzli notes that the spiraling text and image in *Anemic Cinema* created a conceptual space between optical and linguistic play:[26] "The graphic alliteration and collapse of language of the rotoreliefs amplifies the effect of this 'fourth dimension' that is neither purely visual or discursive alone."[27] Duchamp's maniacal use of puns prevents any possible didactic relationship between text and image. Rather, the puns provide a multiplicity of meaning and room to interpret. Further, Kuenzli notes that the spiraling movement shifts in and out, alluding to the sex act, but not to one gender. Spirals might suggest breasts, but the "dart board" quality of the spinning discs alludes to

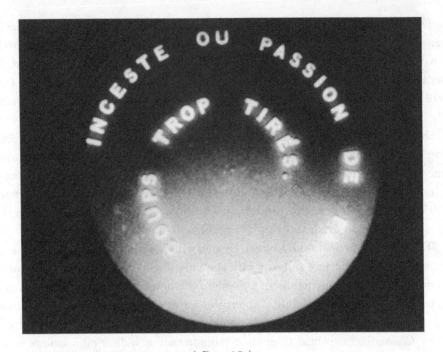

| Figure 4.5 |

Marcel Duchamp (1887–1968), frames from *Anemic Cinema (Anémic cinema)*, 1925, 35mm black-and-white film, silent, seven min. long. Technical assistance: Man Ray and Marc Allégret. AM1976-F0127. Musée National d'Art Moderne, Centre Georges Pompidou, Paris. Photo credit: CNAC/MNAM/Dist. Réunion des Musées Nationaux/Art Resource, NY. © ARS, NY.

objet d'art, or to Duchamp's *Objet-dard*, the "Dart-Object" of 1951, a pun on the word for an artwork and French slang for penis.

By continually working with double or triple entendres, and by inscribing objects with nonillustrative works, the function of both the visual representation and the semiotic function of the word is called into question and manipulated.

Duchamp's language moves beyond the word, much like Charles Dodgson's own puzzles that create new logic paths:

Prove PRISM to be ODEOUS PRISM

prismatic

dramatic

    melodrama

    melodious

ODIUS[28]

Like Dodgson, Duchamp's new words may have been invented along the same lines. Perhaps Duchamp created associative scientific "proofs" following language from places of high culture to those of low culture, from intensive scientific language to the language of entertainment. His own pseudonym, Rrose Sélavy, was a pun referencing he who takes what comes, or "c'est la vie."[29]

The Unconscious and Simultanism

Among other wordplay techniques that the West must credit to the French avant-garde is the free verse (*vers libre*) of Jules Laforgue (1860–1887), the symbolist poet and master of lyrical irony. Laforgue argued for the link between writing and the subconscious mind. The free-verse approach also influenced Mallarmé and his poem "Un coup des Dés jamais n'abolira le Hasard," or "One Toss of the Dice Never Will Abolish Chance" (1897). These lines were purposely unpunctuated and were spaced on the page in an expressive fashion.[30]

Avant-garde writer Guillaume Apollinaire (1880–1918) published innovative graphic poems in his books *Alcools* (1913) and *Calligrammes* (1918). Both contained unusual wordplay and served as inspiration to the Dada artists and Surrealists. Called the "impresario of the avant-garde," Apollinaire was committed to the discovery of the roots of narrative, or rather, "the opposite of narration," a way to work with language that reflected the author's notions in a kind of Cubist fragmentation. Apollinaire named this quality "Simultanism."[31] The technique represents "an effort to retain a moment of experience without sacrificing its logically unrelated variety. In poetry it also means an effort to neutralize the passage of time involved in the act of reading."[32] Apollonaire described his investigation of time as ontological, saying Simultanism means a telescoping of time. This led Apollinaire to practice "decoupage poetique."[33]

"Surprise," the category Apollinaire employed in his lectures to express all of the artistic innovations he advocated, describes only the surface aspect of his poems. "It is a secondary principle of a total freedom of invention, or plasticity, one that should lead to arbitrary constructions in no way imitating nature."[34]

The Rise of Automatism

Dada artifacts held by major museums or included in important books tend to be paintings, but the majority of Dada artwork took the form of reskinning or rewriting. Dada moved between the performance of, say, Duchamp costumed as his female alter ego Rrose Sélavy, to the production of texts that could fall anywhere within the range of demonstration, manifesto, declaration, or pamphleteering. Dada artists were experts at appropriating spaces, objects, and the language of sociocultural production. They achieved results through specific methods and procedures, many of their own invention. Dada techniques included juxtaposition and fragmentation, the incorporation of a play with materials, and a play with language.

Like Surrealism, Dada was also influenced by successful research processes of the past, especially *vers libre* and *Simultanism*, as well as by the intellectual upheavals initiated by Freudian psychology. In his wartime work at Nantes, André Breton attempted to use Freudian methods to psychoanalyze his patients. Many suffered from shell shock, and carried home the remarkable though disturbing images of war that captivated artists. Jacques Vaché, a wounded artist and soldier Breton met in the neurological ward, was one of many who concluded that war, culture, and art were all futile.[35] It is no wonder that many twentieth-century practices of the avant-garde signaled a belief that places outside conscious human decision—for example, chance or the unconscious—were of primary importance for a society recovering from the events and alleged rationality of a terrible and incomprehensible war. It is also worth noting that most Dadaists and Surrealists were directly involved in the world wars. Writers Apollinaire and Vaché and artist Max Ernst (1891–1976) all served in the armed regiments during World War I.

However, throughout Dada, what is prominent is a focus on language and the subversive powers of word games, randomness, and a sense of "natural order" acting in some ways as the "final frontier" and antidote to political prescriptions and announcements. In the fifth of his *Seven Dada Manifestos* (1916–1920), Tristan Tzara invited irrational and chaotic elements into his working process:

To make a dadaist poem
Take a newspaper.
Take a pair of scissors.
Choose an article as long as you are planning to make your poem.
Cut out the article.
     Then cut out each of the words that make up this article and put them in a bag.
Shake it gently.
     Then take out the scraps one after the other in the order in which they left the bag.

Copy conscientiously.
     The poem will be like you.

And here you are a writer, infinitely original and endowed with a sensibility that is charming though beyond the understanding of the vulgar.[36]

Dadaists were also influenced by the artists of the Futurist and Russian Constructivist movements, who opposed tradition and the state and who were adamant in taking an antiauthoritarian stance against preconceived notions of art. Artists like Tristan Tzara, Francis Picabia, Jean Arp, Hugo Ball, Marcel Duchamp, and Max Ernst were war resistors. They developed the idea that artistic groups could become social and political forces. They sought "the real" through the abolition of traditional culture and form. Dada involvement with play and chance was accompanied by a willingness to explore episodes of momentary madness through the use of found objects, abstract painting, sculpture, and drawing. They believed their social role was to balk and protest against trite narratives of "noble" politics and traditional art aesthetics, standing against the use of art for establishing propaganda. Instead, Dada wished art to speak for itself, connecting elements of the real world to the context of art and responding to war, technology, and shifts in social culture. Picabia's *L'Oeil cacodylate* (1921) (figure 4.6) is one visual example of collaging artifacts from culture with the fragmented images and language of the time. Many Dadaists intended to deconstruct all, *destroy everything*, especially the bourgeoisie that enabled and supported the war.

In many paintings and performances, Dadaist wordplay favored audience *interaction* and *chance*, new concepts in the arena of fine arts, and sought the brusque everyday quality of ordinary items. Tzara constructed cut-up poetry and manifestos from the newspaper. Picabia and others would create collage paintings that incorporated handwriting techniques alongside cut-ups and found materials painted into the canvas. As Apollonaire said: "Psychologically it is of no importance that this visible image be composed of fragments of spoken language, for the bond between these fragments is no longer the logic of grammar but an ideographic logic culminating in an order of spatial disposition totally opposed to discursive juxtaposition . . . it is the opposite of narration, narration is of all literary forms the one which most requires discursive logic."[37]

German Dada artist Raoul Hausmann, coinventor of the photo collage with Hannah Höch, wrote phonetic poetry during the year 1918, calling language "transactions within the mouth's chaotic cave" that guaranteed unique events and therefore a reassuring certainty in change. Hausmann, obsessed with the mechanized quality of contemporary living, chanted his poems, an attempt to embody popular notions of time in the act of breathing:

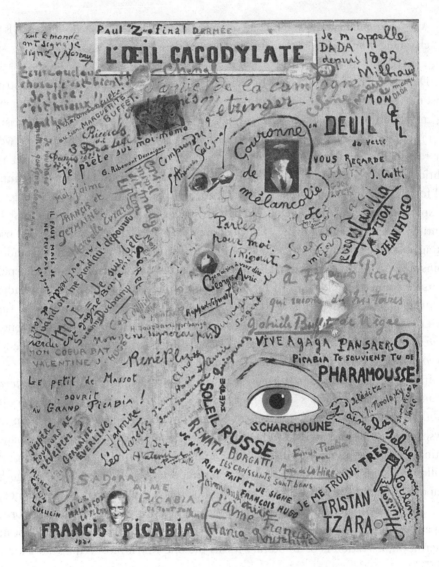

Solao Solaan Alamt
lanee laneao amamb
ambi ambCe enebemp
enepao kalopoo senou
seneakpooo sanakoumt
saddabt kadou koorou
korrokoum oumkpaal
lapidadkal adathoum
adaneop ealop noamth[38]

Hausmann was interested in the intersection between spirit and matter, a way to make concrete this relationship. In performance, he tried to assert the contradictory, coincidental, and "indifferent" in his works.[39] Later, working with Berlin colleagues Salomo Friedlander and Johannes Baader, he viewed his work in Dada as more magical than the work of other Dada artists; the Berlin group to which Hausmann belonged wanted to avoid works that had "the appearance of something entirely composed by a machine."[40]

Interestingly, Dada activities in the United States were largely promoted, performed, documented, financed, or even instigated by eccentric women.[41] Margaret Anderson and jane heap (sic), who ran the radical *The Little Review*, published James Joyce's *Ulysses*, as well as works by Ernest Hemingway, Ezra Pound, Aldous Huxley, T. S. Eliot, Wallace Stevens, and Amy Lowell.[42] In a review of a Whitney Museum of American Art exhibition, Robert Hughes noted that Manhattan Dada was comprised of "bizarre figures from the Greenwich Village avant-garde like Baroness Elsa von Freytag-Loringhoven, the first New York punkette, who made public appearances with her hair shaved off and her scalp dyed purple."[43]

The radical Baroness Elsa von Freytag-Loringhoven (1874–1927), whose absurdist performances predate most Dada events, took various guises: performer, poet, art model, and sculptor. She abided by rules that could not be accounted for under existing social conventions, and at times her behavior was more radical than that of the historically established Dada "founding fathers." These artists, she thought, were "all cowards who, while producing unconventional works, still insisted on a conventional lifestyle and traditional gender roles."[44] After a series of failed marriages, Freytag-Loringhoven moved to New York to pursue art in all of its forms. She began publishing poetry in 1918 in *The Little Review Anthology*, and her association with many of the famous artists of the period spoke to her acceptance by the Dada and literary circles.[45] Between 1913 and 1923, the German-born artist committed acts of gender bending, absurdist performance, experimental writing, and law breaking in an attempt to "live Dada"—that is, to embody the process of questioning and creation that Dada represented. Wandering the streets of New York with a shaved head, wearing mass-produced, everyday objects such as kitchen cutlery, automotive taillights, spoons, vegetables, and even a bra made of tomato cans, the baroness openly declared her actions and objects "works of art." In the estimation of jane heap, she was "America's first Dada artist, queen of international Dada, and the great-aunt of punk and of performance art."[46] In addition to jane heap, she befriended Man Ray, Margaret Anderson, Ezra Pound, William Carlos Williams, Hart Crane, Marcel Duchamp, Berenice Abbot, and Djuna Barnes: her eccentric behavior was an integral part of the Greenwich Village avant-garde community.[47] The baroness was known to have accosted William Carlos Williams and Wallace Stevens for promiscuous sex—she wished to "liberate them" to allow them to experience creativity to the fullest. Ezra Pound was inspired by the baroness to write about her in his *Canto XCV*, and Duchamp said of her, "she is the future." With Man Ray, Duchamp made a 1921 film, *Elsa, Baroness von Freytag-Loringhoven, Shaving Her Pubic Hair* (which now seems to be lost). Like other artists involved in challenging form and genre, the baroness was curiously less celebrated than Duchamp and the other male artists of the time, yet she was clearly engaged on with the Dada spirit well beyond her contemporaries in experimentation and creation.

Freytag-Loringhoven's process of working across performance, writing, and sculpture was very much aligned with Dada themes. Juxtaposition, chance, fragmentation, and the commodity were indispensable elements in her work. Unlike the readymades of Duchamp, Freytag-Loringhoven gathered material from the street, and materials particularly from domestic spaces were used to position the female body amid living social systems. Freytag-Loringhoven wrote incessantly; see figures 4.7 and 4.8 for examples of how she composed for the page. These "Ready-Made Poems," collaged from advertisements and automatic writing, were filled with sexual suggestion such as references to oral sex, and acted as a protest against America's conservative social mores and obsession with consumerism during the era:[48]

. . . Nothing so pepsodent—soothing
Pussywillow—kept clean
with Philadelphia Cream Cheese.
They satisfy the man of
Largest Mustard Underwear—
No dosing
lust rub it on[49]

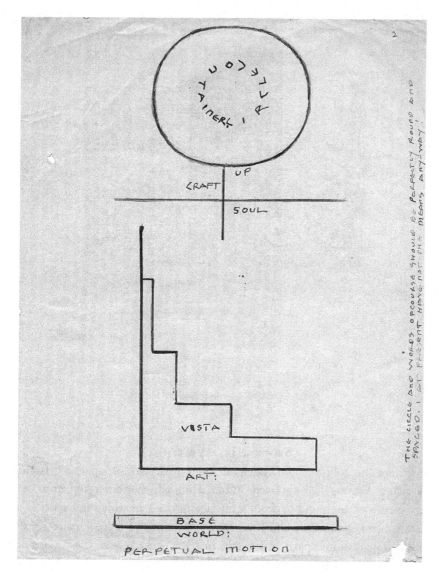

| Figure 4.7 |

Elsa von Freytag-Loringhoven's *Matter Level Perspective*, 1922–1923. Papers of Elsa von Freytag-Loringhoven, Special Collections, University of Maryland Libraries.

FOR DJUNA BARNES

| Figure 4.8 |

Elsa von Freytag-Loringhoven's *Wheels Are Growing on Rosebushes*, 1922–1923. Papers of Elsa von Freytag-Loringhoven, Special Collections, University of Maryland Libraries.

Surrealist Writing

Other writers also followed the systematic, automatic writing approach favored by figures such as Freytag-Loringhoven. Automatism, whether emerging from beyond-conscious levels of the mind or from a physical process in which the artist is not in complete control, is based on the absence of "conscious" design. Chance operations organize automatism into particular events or sequences. As noted historians of Surrealist processes, Broochie and Gooding describe automatism as follows: "Sit at a table with pen and paper, put yourself in a 'receptive' frame of mind, and start writing. Continue writing without thinking about what is appearing beneath your pen. Write as fast as you can. If, for some reason, the flow stops, leave a space and immediately begin again by writing down the first letter of the next sentence. Choose this letter at random before you begin, for instance, a 't,' and always begin this new sentence with a 't.'"[50] Broochie and Gooding also describe the work of the Surrealists in the vocabulary of gaming:

Surrealist games and procedures are intended to free words and images from the constraints of rational and discursive order, substituting chance and indeterminacy for premeditation and deliberation. . . . In one particular and important respect Surrealist play is more like a kind of provocative magic. This is in its irrepressible propensity to the *transformation* of objects, behaviors and ideas. In this aspect of its proceedings Surrealism makes manifest its underlying political program, its revolutionary intent.[51]

Many authors were acquainted with Apollinaire, who coined the term *surrealism* in the spring of 1917, as a subtitle to his play *Les Mamelles de Tirésias, or The Breasts of Tiresias: A Surrealist Drama*. The play shocked conventional Paris by proposing that men and women switch gender roles and men bear the children.

The work was an influence on fellow writers Breton and Soupault, who followed the path of other French literary investigators Rimbaud, Lautréamont, and Vaché, though without the assistance of the opium and absinthe available to the writers of that area. Their work, *The Magnetic Fields* (1920), was an early Surrealist text collaboratively created in 1919, just after the end of World War I. During 1919, Breton and Soupault would meet, sometimes for ten or twelve hours: "Soupault and I formed the intention of deliberately reproducing in ourselves the state out of which such (sentences) emerged. In order to do this all that was necessary was to disregard the context of the external world, and it was thus that they made their way to us, during a period of two months, soon following each other without interruption so rapidly that we had to resort to abbreviations in order to note them down."[52]

Automated drawing and writing were among several methods of automatism derived from, among other things, the Spiritualist movement in the United States. Spiritualists believed they contacted the dead with automatic writing. The late nineteenth-century Swiss psychic Hélène Smith, through automatic writing, claimed to have spoken with Martians and detailed her life as a fifteenth-century Indian princess.[53] Her story was a strong influence on the Surrealist movement members, and was especially appreciated by Breton. She and others such as the American Spiritualists used automatic processes to connect with the spirit world, but Breton and other Surrealist artists used the technique to understand the workings of the unconscious.

The Surrealists did not launch manifestos until five years later, but early on, participants still valued the objective nature of chance, automatic writing, and black humor.[54] Automatic processes proved to be essential to the Surrealist mission: "Beloved imagination," Breton wrote, "what I most like in you is your unsparing quality."[55] The discipline involved in automatic writing is to "vigilantly resist the temptation to interrupt the stream of consciousness, or rather that of the theoretically subjacent conscious-ness, or to interfere with or in any way alter post facto the results obtained 'with laud-able disdain as regards their literary quality."[56]

Surrealist word games also included the famous *cadavre exquis* ("exquisite corpse" in English). The classic example that gave this activity its name is the first sentence ever derived from the game: "Le cadavre—exquis—boira—le vin—nouveau." This simple language game can either be played by knowing only what the last person in a group work contributed, or by following a language pattern rule (such as adjective-noun-adverb-verb-adjective-noun). The order must be respected to produce grammat-ically correct sentences. The exercise, invented through inspiration from an existing parlor game at a gathering at a house shared by a group of Surrealists in Paris, was one of several language games and spontaneous group games created by the Surreal-ist artists.[57] In fact, Durozoi argued that Surrealism itself should be equated to pure psychic automatism in all actions—art, the spoken or written word, or any other act—and that these actions should be not subject to the dictation of thought or controlled by reason, outside factors, or aesthetic or moral concerns.[58] But here a criticism of the approach needs to enter into the picture.

Radical Surrealist writer Djuna Barnes (1892–1982) followed many of the game-like Surrealist research/creation methods put forward by the group. Barnes's avant-garde images and writing, including journalistic essays, were widely published from 1913 through the 1930s. Her works *The Book of Repulsive Women* (1915) and *Ryder* (1928) are destabilizing texts, which, much like the later work of Kathy Acker, incor-porated visual components to express feminist concerns. As scholar Irene Martyniuk has noted, "Just as in a patriarchal system women are conventionally perceived as 'handmaidens' to the male, so the visual component of a text has traditionally been viewed as an adjunct to the verbal component."[59] It is therefore an interesting feminist approach to take on male-female power relations through the struggle between image and text. Barnes created both the images and the text of her books (see her drawing in figure 4.9). As Irigaray noted, "Female sexuality has always been conceptualized on the basis of masculine parameters," and it is this construction Barnes examines in her intricate juxtapositions of image and text.[60]

The Book of Repulsive Women consists of eight poems about women in New York City, beginning with a woman who must expose her lesbian identity, one form of what some would term the "repulsive," and ending with a suicide, of a woman whose "exquisite corpse" is examined from two competing points of view, creating yet another instance of what some might deem a "repulsive" woman.[61]

| **Figure 4.9** |
One of Djuna Barnes's illustrations for her 1915 chapbook, *The Book of Repulsive Women*, which collects eight "rhythms" along with five drawings. Papers of Djuna Barnes, Special Collections, University of Maryland Libraries.

Those living dead up in their rooms
Must note how partial are the tombs,
That take men back into their wombs
    While theirs must fast.
And those who have their blooms in jars
No longer stare into the stars,
Instead, they watch the dinky cars—
    And live aghast.[62]

Barnes's women are unconventional and victimized by the culture they are forced to inhabit. They do not fit into social conventions of the author's time. In fact, one would question whether they could easily fit into twentieth-century New York. Barnes's marginalized, unstable characters and unfixed subjects lend themselves to representing women in Surrealism overall in their contradictory roles. Ironically, the author constrains the power of her women. In the end, these narratives are not about empowering the women; suicide or death are the means for the women's emotional, creative, or sexual freedom.

Other Surrealists told similar fables. Unica Zürn, whose relationship with Hans Bellmer introduced her to the automatic drawing and writing she would become known for, endured bouts of mental illness and died by her own hand, haunted by visions of the "Jasmine man" featured in her pages.[63]

From Art to Play

As the play anthropologist Brian Sutton-Smith notes, early twentieth-century art brought ideas from child's play and art together with ideas about the importance of imagination. Here, a child-like state is valued as primitive, innocent, original, and ultimately fresh and untouched.[64] However, Sutton-Smith argues that this view is simplistic and romantic, and leaves out other important aspects of play. For instance, play and art may share invention and personification, but not sensuality. Also, play constitutes a system of symbolic forms that may carry their own objective codes.

Howard Gardner sees play as a way to master anxiety, the self, and the world, while art might be more about the mastery of symbolic systems.[65] Whatever the subtle and not so subtle differences between art and play may be, the examples presented here conceptually engage with economies of exchange and social order, the nature of art and play as conceptual and fluid spaces, and the role of chance and intervention in creative events and works.[66] The fluctuating social networks produced in these interactive art forms can be described in Deleuzian terms as sites of becoming.

In his essay "What Is Becoming?" Gilles Deleuze describes a state of event-centered being that is a fundamental way of experiencing play and interactive artworks.[67] Most important, these works create a context for the production and reception of radical versions of social order through their emphasis on shifting the authority of the artist.

Historical foundations for playculture—creative social networks and the combination of art, play, and subversion, must be examined for histories of play within "analog" twentieth-century art movements, especially histories demonstrating a significant interrogation of authority in artistic systems, an ability to empower users through participation, and dedicated questioning of normative behavior.

Dada's subversive practices in its reworking of authority and authorship were one way social norms were pushed and literally "at play." The Dadaist critiques discussed here used participatory play, gaming as practice research, and interactivity to reflect everyday concerns and to unplay, reskin, rewrite, and, in some cases, actively redefine culture. The artistic experiments with games described in this chapter should serve as a provocative look at how artists can challenge objects, behaviors, and ideas and subsequently transform them.

Fluxus Language Play

As noted earlier, like the Dadaists and Surrealists, Fluxus artists relied on humor, instructions, impermanence, and interactivity in a practice where the permanence of the object is trumped by the moment of experience. Created by a group of artists in the 1960s, Fluxus and its related magazine of the same name revolved around the artist-organizer George Maciunas (1931–1978), its name emphasizing both change and flow in the artists' play, games, and "disposable" work. Fluxus broke from its Dada origins, shifting focus from the importance of the individual artist toward celebrating collective identities and alternate venues for artwork.[68] For many of the Fluxus artists, play and "the joke" evolved as a methodology, moving interaction and audience participation away from galleries and traditional theater environments and creating for the first time a kind of multiplayer artistic play space and environment. The approach of Fluxus artists seems much like the best creative works functioning on the Internet in the twenty-first century, or the work of emerging twenty-first century media collectives in that "Fluxus objectives are social (not aesthetic). They are connected to the group . . . Fluxus is definitely against art-objects . . . Fluxus therefore should tend towards collective spirit, anonymity and ANTI-INDIVIDUALISM."[69]

Several Fluxus artists created games as interventions that could work to open everyday life to more careful examination, rendering social moments as acts of exchange or opportunities to critique larger political situations. The Fluxus practice of making games

or instruction cards to create situations that are indeed artworks is said to have originated with John Cage in the courses he taught at The New School for Social Research
in New York City from 1956 to 1960. Cage, in his focus on creating everyday actions as
art actions, draws Huizinga's magic circle around the activity, making it a game, placing it
into fantasy.[70] Philosopher Herbert Spencer notes that in actions like these "play and art
are the same activity because neither subserves, in any direct way, the processes conductive to life and neither refers to ulterior benefits, the proximate ends are the only ends."[71]

The work of these artists demonstrates a particular potency in subversive acts
through participatory play. Several Fluxus artists engaged with language games,
but these often relied on performance to be realized. Nevertheless, some should be
included here. Ono's series of *Instruction Paintings* are among the most important art
artifacts from the twentieth century, for they take conceptual art to a new level by
refusing the evidence of the art object itself. Often distributed on throwaway cards
in the gallery, Ono gave participants instructions on how to create the artwork themselves. Investigating the medium of painting and the act of image making, Ono's ulti-
mate goal was participatory art. Her work *Painting to Be Stepped On* (1960) includes
instructions that makers should "Leave a piece of canvas or finished painting on the
floor or in the street." In 1961, Ono exhibited the *Instruction Paintings* at George Maciunas's AG gallery in New York City, inviting visitors to drip water on the *Waterdrop
Painting*, or walk by the *Shadow Painting*, a blank canvas hung on a gallery wall, its
fleeting images merely created by the shadows of the visitors.[72]

Painting to See the Skies (1961) is one of Ono's many *Instruction Paintings*. These
paintings may be read in the tradition of Fluxus works, or scores, that position the
viewer as the "fuser" or creator of the work merely by putting an image, thought, or
sound together in the viewer's head. In *Painting to See the Skies*, Ono encourages the
visitor to merely view the sky. Ono's model of instruction making was later used by
other conceptual artists such as Allan Kaprow and George Shaw in their performance
and performance documentation work.[73] The instruction poems read as little "programs" directing the viewer to more consciously become a participant:

SUN PIECE
Watch the sun until it becomes square.
1962 winter

TOUCH POEM FOR A GROUP OF PEOPLE
Touch each other.
1963 winter[74]

Fluxus games stemmed from performative event-like happenings, or took the form of Fluxkits and boxes with play items enclosed within.

In her work *Finger Book of Ancient Languages* (1982), Alison Knowles created a hybrid board game/pop-up book/sculpture featuring "tactile" languages (figure 4.10). The work, which consists of seven eleven-inch-high pages, is in part written in Braille. The work also contains a message in Kifu, a bead language. Carved Chinese glyphs expressing a Tang dynasty battle cry are inscribed in the standing "pages."

Stitched into a length of cloth are twenty-six objects that represent each letter of the English alphabet. A sewn-in pin might stand for the letter *p*, a feather, for *f* (figure 4.11). To discern the alphabet, "readers" touch each alphabetic zone and can, in effect, spell out words through touching objects. The consequence of Knowles's treatment of objects-as-letters is that the everyday objects transition from being insubstantial objects to becoming monumental sign systems. This "book" was shown at the Lighthouse for the Blind in New York among other venues. "Because the books engage a person in exploration without awareness of time or place, their performativity is simultaneously conceptual and Event-like."[75] *Finger Book of Ancient Languages* offers "a sensory alternative to the purely cerebral, or disembodied, definition of language in the idealist sense."[76]

Making Words Material

Artists using text during the 1960s and 1970s had a great impact on contemporary art practices. Especially relevant are those artists who either used technology in their own projects or who critiqued technology amid larger cultural analyses. Women artists of the late 1960s and early 1970s faced a hostile and male-centered art world, and some turned to nontraditional media such as posters, video, and performance to work against art steeped in the traditions and themes of masculine-focused modernism.

Other artists of the 1970s were simultaneously involved in the political actions of the time. Jenny Holzer, with her pro-woman, political poster brigades, stickers, and electronic LED messaging displays, is a noteworthy example of an activist artist using various forms of technology to confront pedestrians, techniques common to Situationist intervention in the decade before. Aiming to jar the public to reflect on the conditions of the consumer culture in which they lived, Holzer began creating language-based works in 1977 as a student. From 1978 through 1987, she distributed one-line phrases, or "truisms," as posters or stickers. Taking this work to public venues, she produced *The Survival Series* in 1983, which incorporated these aphorisms (such as, "a strong sense of duty imprisons you; absolute submission can be a form of freedom; abstraction is a type of decadence; abuse of power comes as no surprise" in various delivery forms, including signage and park benches (see figure 4.12).

| Figure 4.10 |
Alison Knowles, *Finger Book of Ancient Languages*, 1982. Photograph by Christian Farnsworth.

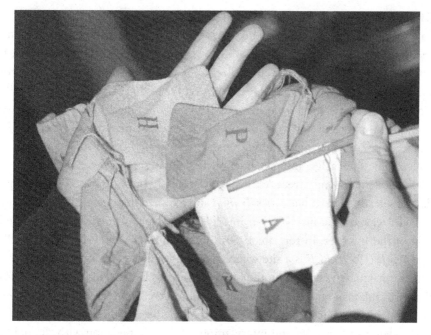

| Figure 4.11 |

Alison Knowles, *Finger Book of Ancient Languages*, 1982. Photograph by Christian Farnsworth.

| Figure 4.12 |

One of Jenny Holzer's Walker benches, fabricated at Cold Spring Granite. Photograph courtesy of Ted Sher.

Holzer's text interventions addressed consumerism, gender roles at work, and media representations of women and rape. Many were likely to appear in public spaces, disrupting the traditional space of the gallery, though Holzer is shown frequently in traditional venues as well. Holzer's older works harbor an accusatory tone, provoking the reader to react. "YOU ARE A VICTIM OF THE RULES YOU LIVE BY," claims one of her lines from her 1989 show at the Guggenheim Museum. The interventionist nature of her work means Holzer's texts can surprise, often catching the reader unaware. Her pieces range in size from ephemera as small as stickers to large electronic spectacles, and take both analog and digital forms. For example, during Creative Time's 42nd Street Art Project (1993–1994), Holzer used city marquees displaying selections from her series *Truisms* and *Survival* that seeped into the viewer's reality. Holzer's artistic intervention into place also spread to the emerging public domain of the Internet. In the late 1990s, she produced the web-based work, *Please Change Beliefs* (1999). *PCB* is a site where Internet users can participate in the artist's "statement making" by uploading their own new "truisms" to a list of truisms already databased in the program.[77] Texts pass at timed intervals, but are open to change by users. Though not explicitly a game, participation by the audience and a sense of social concern relate to protest art and intervention. Here, a connection with the public is not a mere preference of the artist, but essential to the practice.[78] Her texts foreshadow techniques used by locative game designs (see chapter 6).

For the last decade, Holzer has been undertaking interventions with light projections. Early street-based interventionist practices are clearly linked to this new interrogation of media and tactics, the approaches of advertising, and news broadcasting. These texts are projected, interrupting the lives of passersby to form a community of ephemeral experience in public. Her work *For the City* (2005), in figure 4.13, illuminated New York with both political poetry and declassified documents that were projected across city landmarks. Her texts are serious, but coming upon one creates a temporary magic circle, a play space for reading, thinking, and conversation in the community.

Using the terminology of subversion, Holzer both rewrites advertising slogans for political ends and reskins public surfaces through signage and stickers. The contemporary art practices of Holzer represent merely a few of many examples of artists working against dominant norms using subversive tactics (figure 4.14).

A final example to establish context for exploring linguistic artistic intervention is the work of the group known as the Guerrilla Girls, formed in the mid-1980s to critique cultural institutions such as the Metropolitan Musem of Art (see figure 4.15), the Whitney Museum of American Art and the Museum of Modern Art in New York.[79]

| Figure 4.13 |

Jenny Holzer's *For the City* project, 2005, light projections of poetry and declassified documents to illuminate landmark New York City buildings.

The Girls' members are completely anonymous and have staged art events, performative actions, and ad campaigns that spark dialogue about the status of women in the arts.

While language play has the capacity to engage the mind, the contemporary artists are seeking to "reembody" that mind in their play. Through their use of text within software systems, language becomes part of animation, audio, video, and physical installation spaces. Installation artist Camille Utterback (1970–) creates immersive video installations that incorporate the whole body of the participant. She writes, "As we create new interfaces between our bodies and our symbolic systems we are in an unusual position to rethink and re-embody this relationship."[80] Like Duchamp's collision of text and image, Utterback and Romy Achitiv achieve a unique remapping of the relationship between text and the body of the player/participant in their projection work *Text Rain* (1999) (figure 4.16).

In this highly playful work, letters from a previously written poem drift, or "rain" down a screen located across from participants. A camera is trained on the participants,

| Figure 4.14 |

New York City skywriting—"Who Is?"—over Greenwich Village, 2006, by unknown artist, courtesy of the author.

| Figure 4.15 |

Guerrilla Girls, *Do Women Have to Be Naked?*, 1989, from the portfolio "Guerrilla Girls' Most Wanted: 1985–2006," 11 1/16 × 27 1/8 in. (28 × 68.7 cm). Hood Museum of Art, Dartmouth College, Hanover, NH; purchased through the Anonymous Fund #144.

| **Figure 4.16** |
Camille Utterback and Romy Achituv, *Text Rain*, 1999. Image by Kenneth Hayden, 2007.

tracking their movement so their silhouettes may be composited into the program and their shadows may "interact" with the letters. As they play, participants can "catch" letters as they fall, or hold them on a silhouette-shape such as an arm or other object. Participants gather the letters and phrases together, finding the poem to be about bodies and language.[81]

The ideas of modern artists open up the possibilities of using games as a way to move against power and oppression.[82] Rosi Braidotti notes that knowledge functions to "consequently mark radical forms of re-embodiment," and needs to be dynamic, or nomadic, to allow for shifts of location and multiplicity.[83] This shift is more than just "playing with letters"; *Text Rain* infers Apollinaire's Simultanism, and a present in which a system of multiple truths in the form of puns, collisions of text and image, or collision of body and text can flourish. *Text Rain* can provide an emotionally complex slice of experience, an embodied notion of procedural play for the participant.

It is appropriate, in conclusion, to return to Guattari's notion that opened this chapter. The works discussed here reshape subjectivity through their own rules—and, in particular, such language games become as political acts from the very top of "high culture" circles, down to the trenches of everyday experience. As Félix Guattari has noted, "The only acceptable finality of human activity is the production of a subjectivity that is auto-enriching its relation to the world in a continuous fashion. The productive apparatuses of subjectivity can exist at the level of megapoles as easily as at the level of an individual's language games."[84] Artists' language games are thus frameworks for an opening up of subject positions, a liberation of what it means to make rules, share them, and play.

The artists mentioned in this chapter who engaged in language play have demonstrated innovation through obnoxious position, such as Jarry's assault on taste, and through palindromes and puns, such as those so favored by Duchamp. Apollinaire's ontology of Simultanism provides another example of the powers of language, the unconscious, chance, and invention. Automatism, long explored under various terms, including Mallarmé's *vers libre*, shifted notions of subjectivity, form, and function, and invoked play methods that allowed significant shifts in authorship. Together these artists present a form of practical, location-specific critique in physical space. Such artists' critiques can be traced to the rough categories of reskinning, unplaying, and rewriting, as can Holzer's challenge to contemporary information systems and advertising. Holzer's turn toward performative texts, social awareness, and possible activism continues in the Guerrilla Girls, who literally reskin themselves as jungle creatures to desexualize or oversexualize and complicate their female identities. Utterback reintroduces the body to language, and in the space in between offers something to be learned. As the connection between art and critical play continues, artists will further explore embodied play and situations in and efforts to "unplay" preconceived notions of the body, computers, and everyday living, and rework them into radical maps and written documents. While these works are not necessarily games in a strict sense, they are heavily engaged with the theme of participatory play and are part of the lineage of the contemporary playculture forms, subverting dominant notions in popular culture and media, as well as the "traditions" ensconced in the contemporary art institutions.

PERFORMATIVE GAMES AND OBJECTS

Playful procedures and systematic stratagems provided keys to unlock the door to the unconscious and to release the visual and verbal poetry of collective creativity.

—Alastair Brotchie and Mel Gooding, *A Book of Surrealist Games*

To Johan Huizinga, play incorporates a myriad of games: "games of strength and skill, inventing games, guessing games, games of chance, exhibitions and performances of all kinds."[1] In this chapter, we explore the last type of games Huizinga describes: *performative games*, or games that achieve critical play through a significant sense of performance in their attempt to influence society, or to provide utopian and playful visions and revisions of the world. Their history is as rich and deep as that of the game forms already noted. Throughout the past century, various art and social movements have engaged in staging forms of participation and creating interactive events, playful subversions, disruptions, and interventions. In the broadest sense, the performance of critical play includes historic games and performative objects, performances themselves, and mediated performance.[2]

In some sense, all games are performative, requiring some negotiation of action—thinking, guessing, running, or tossing—for play. Performance, when understood as context, constitutes a spectrum of cultural practices including theater, dance, music, event making, ritual, and spectacle, and could just as easily be studied by anthropologists as art historians. By calling attention to intercultural relationships, social inequity, cultural processes, the role of the body, and the use of language, performance comes with a particular history, and a set of strategies, some of which automatically infer *play*. Theater, for example, presents actors, or players, who invoke make-believe and imaginative worlds just as children do when playing with a playhouse or dollhouse. Such actions may or may not use props or follow instructions or scripts. In other cases, performances may be constructed around particular objects that are typically used in games—for example, a chess piece or a shoe both denote other specific uses and other contexts when they became elements of a game.

Performance and play are intrinsically linked to the artist's intervention.[3] In her book *Bodies that Matter* (1993), philosopher Judith Butler puts forward a theory of performativity, noting that the identity of the performing subject is a creation not of a body per se, but of a type of performance. Butler has observed that social norms such as gender are sites of negotiation for subjects who must choose from unrealistic or exaggerated binaries of gender identity. According to Butler, performance locates a point of resistance for those wishing to oppose narrow social categorizations. Some 1990s technology theorists like Sandy Stone, who saw a need to separate bodies from personae as Internet technologies entered the culture, also adopted this form of resistance.[4] Butler's break between the biology of sex and the performative nature of the gendered self resulted in the opening up of new ways gender and other social realities could be embodied and interpreted.

Performance can also incorporate improvisation or "flow," a common studio-art methodology. Flow is the state of consciousness in which one is so completely absorbed in an activity that even the ego falls away, letting creative urges shape direction.[5] Similar to Butler's alternate performances, practice researchers Cole and Knowles suggest that "whether it is through poetry, prose, movement, drama, mime, meditation, painting, drawing, sculpture or any other non-traditional linguistic or non-linguistic form, the important thing is to find a way or ways that will allow us to follow the natural internal flow of our inquiry. In a sense this is an essential element for researching through artistic expression."[6] Marcel Duchamp's "laboratory work" is another example of practice-based artistic research that incorporates multiple methods and concepts similar to flow.[7]

If historic avant-garde practices are consistently focused on decentering authority, game projects based on performance have created critical alternatives not only to other games, but to street culture as well. Important to this exploration is the role of rules in games and in art. Glimcher has argued that in helping to establish Russian Constructivism, Alexander Rodchenko founded one of the first "systematized" approaches to art making. In Constructivism, elements of an artwork would be assembled and then followed by a "laboratory" where the work was analyzed and perhaps iterated.[8] Others might argue that art has a long history of composition by some type of principle or schema. Commissioned portraits of the Renaissance, for example, contained rules that might have been seen as just as prohibitive in the composition of works. The difference, however, may be in the choice of content matter and in the formation of new stylistic formulae—for instance, a game dealing with the constructed nature of architecture, or the expressive compositional nature of other forms of art.

Performative Objects

How did a broad range of artist-performers create a context for critical play in their painting, photography, installation, and scenarios? As with technological change, shifts in playculture parallel the upheaval of world events like economic depression, world war, or cultural and social movements. Cinema had a great effect on twentieth-century art movements, though historical accounts of art history generally downplay film's contributions as "low art." Nevertheless, while Marcel Duchamp was asking his audience to make its own decisions about the nature of art, American cinema fans were doing just that through the development of fan culture.[9] Film fans, usually avid consumers of popular culture as well as members of the working class, were more than passive viewers, even in the early years of Hollywood. Women were a major creative force from the 1910s on.[10] During the 1930s, in what is now a clear illustration of fans interacting with larger cinema culture, Louis B. Mayer, MGM studio head, initiated a fan-magazine contest to rename actress Lucille LeSueur. One fan submitted the name "Joan Crawford."[11] Popular magazines like *Look* (1937–1971) offered many opportunities for fans to interact with each other and with cinematic culture. Games, contests, and fabulous giveaway schemes were routinely planted in the popular press to excite the discussion surrounding movie stars. After all, audience participation, from viewing the artistic productions (the film), to gathering about red carpet showcases or forming audience-created fan clubs, helped create the media spectacle that has become integral to the entertainment industry.[12] This popular blend of spectator and media object, and of mediated and cultural participation, is not only facilitated by games, today it is also a hallmark of games themselves.

The themes Hollywood relied on to launch a new movie or the latest star personalities were also reflected in the twentieth-century works of art, though perhaps for different reasons. Here, it is important to note the very divergent approaches to "art" and art practice at the start of the twentieth century. The fine arts had become a profitable business with collectors acting as "buyers" and artists playing the role of "independent contractors" who provided "products"—generally in the form of paintings. This business necessitated, and still necessitates, a set of narratives about what that product might represent. While political art groups such as the Futurists and Dadaists were shocking the adherents to the status quo by shouting "Down with art!," part of their motivation was a desire to counteract the mainstream artists, such as Henri

Matisse. Matisse and other traditional artists had long promoted the self-absorbed and now classic positionality of the "great artist." Matisse wrote that his goal was "an art of balance, of purity and serenity, devoid of troubling or depressing" subjects; an art that possessed a "soothing quality, a calming influence." These "classic" artists established the notion of aesthetic purity and beauty and the artist's obligation to these expressions. They also promoted the belief that an artist's style of expression always will emerge from the artist's temperament.[13]

Painting and Performance

Other artists rejected the idea that art existed merely for self-expression and longed for larger truths. Painter Wassily Kandinsky's (1866–1944) theoretical treatise *Über das Geistige in der Kunst* (*Concerning the Spiritual in Art*) (1912) moved away from a self-absorbed idea of purity and balance. Instead, Kandinsky discussed the idea of "inner necessity," and searched for ways of revealing the spirit in a utopian, transcendent, automatic process.

With these ideas in mind, radical artists of the twentieth century subverted art practices and the art world itself in both the forms and delivery of their works. Photography and film, for example, had altered the way Western twentieth-century artists conceived the world.[14] In France, George Braque and Pablo Picasso developed Cubism as the logical next step in visual art representation. Their experiment was due to in part to notions of play and what it could produce in response to industrialization, war, and emerging technology. Manifestations of this media-rich world view can be found in Giacomo Balla's *Dynamism of Dog on a Leash* (1912) and Duchamp's famous Cubist painting, *Nude Descending a Staircase* (1919). These works built on other avant-garde practices—notably, those of the Futurists—who rallied around F. T. Marinetti's *Futurist Manifesto* (1909). The mechanization of the image in Duchamp and Balla's paintings demonstrates the effect new paradigms of time, consciousness, and production had on artists' perception. Old methods of representations had been mastered and were sometimes judged inadequate by artists looking to express concerns of the day. This thinking set the stage for a series of radical shifts in creative work. The particular pieces by Duchamp and Balla also mark a significant shift toward abstraction and help lay the groundwork for conceptual art. It is the way play, rules, and motion are inextricably intertwined in their creation that sets these images apart from others as they are establishing a new symbiosis between technological change and play. When World War I unleashed terrible examples of the destructive powers of technology, the everyday perceptual and social disruptions caused by new technologies in art were just as profound.

Performing Dada

While several scholars and curators have noted the Dada movement's influence on interactive art, its influence on *gaming*, especially in relation to the notion of performance, needs further exploration.[15] First, and foremost, Dada concerns and interests do not appear intrinsically "fun." From the point of view of European artist-refugees escaping the turmoil of World War I, Dada was not only a creative approach but also a *reaction* that valued creativity over violence and social upheaval. Jean Arp, one of the central Dada practitioners, noted, "In Zurich in 1915, lacking interest in the slaughterhouses of the war, we devoted ourselves to the fine arts."[16] Dada arose in the midst of war-torn Europe, which was still reeling from the shock of combat methods that had grown more horrifying from new technologies such as the first machine gun and the first military bombing run. Dada artists formed a belief, and a dread: A culture that had produced the horrors of a world war could not appreciate, indeed, did not deserve, art. Therefore, a complete break with tradition was necessary—a break that had to extend beyond art itself to the myths surrounding the artist. Only then would it be possible to create art without continuing political evils like fascism. The result was a blunt rejection of hierarchy, craft, and aesthetics.

Dada artists in New York City gathered at Gallery 291 run by Alfred Stieglitz. Man Ray and Marcel Duchamp participated there. Francis Picabia moved between groups in Barcelona, New York, Zürich, and Paris. This was the time Duchamp was concocting his readymade sculptures, and Elsa von Freytag-Loringhoven was taking the streets of New York by storm.[17] Other artists of the time also manifested concerns regarding aesthetics, taste, form, and other art styles co-opted by totalitarianism. As noted in the previous chapter, automatism was popular, as was the use of chance to compose images. Chance helped artists avoid the lure of the aesthetic formation of images and their resulting romantic expressions.

Arp's *Collage Arranged According to the Laws of Chance* (1916–1917) is one example of a Dada work that was created through automatism. In his automatic processes, Arp would draw, rip the drawings into pieces, allow the pieces to fall where they may, and then affix them where they lay as a memento of the operation. Arp, and artists like him, viewed chance not merely as accident, but as a *systematic approach*, and a means of access through the unconscious to the basic ordering processes of the natural world.[18] By 1915, Arp was creating chance works that avoided the artistic ego to claim a place closer to nature. Hence, he declared that "these works, like nature, were ordered 'according to the law of chance,'" "removing the artist's will from the creative act, "by arranging the pieces automatically, without will."[19]

Hanna Höch (1879–1978), an imaging pioneer from Berlin, engaged in both social interrogation and rethinking of materials, composition, and cultural investigation to create the "reordered reality" of her series of found-object and photo collages.[20] Inspired by folk practices popular during World War I, lithographs were distributed to Germans of a soldier at a barracks, and family members would supplant the generic face of the soldier with a print of their own relative's face. Höch and her partner, Raoul Hausmann, developed a technique now called "photo collage." Höch and Hausmann often created compositions that featured human figures or bodies in fragments along with machine parts and recognizable brands as mechanization and advertising endlessly reproduced across the global landscape.[21]

These artists also examined the expansion of traditional gender roles in relationship to technology in works of a reordered reality that the collages create.[22] The early collages are visual works that demonstrate critical play through their spatial relationships and the quirky engagement with the body. The photo collages of Höch, like the performances or cut-up poetry of Freytag-Loringhoven, are products of deconstructive processes that reveal that systems of representation of the body, specifically of women's bodies, are not only problematic but also are as equally constructed, as is collage. Found object collages like Höch's *Das Schone Madchen* (*Pretty Girl*) (1920) and *Dada-Ernst* (1920–1921) (figure 5.1) eschew the traditional representation of woman and the body, the authority of the artist, and ideas of originality. Höch's collage provided "another way of refusing the image of woman as a transcendent object of art and the male gaze, generator of a string of similarly depoliticized art objects."[23]

Like other performative objects, such as the Surrealist Meret Oppenheim's *Breakfast in Fur* (1936), photo collage possesses two qualities. The first is a sense of "liveness"—a "wanted to be acted with" visually or tactically. These performative objects show evidence of collision, evidence of particular rules that govern how an artwork functions. The second quality is its "intended use," or how the object's affordance is displayed through its shape and texture. This invitation to act, joined with shape, forms the rules that govern the object, how it can be played with, how it can function in the imagination.

Photo collage can also be read as a technique mirroring the political interrogation of gender stereotypes and imaging of the body, reinforcing the uncomfortable relationships between commercialization, machinery, and the physical self. In her use of juxtaposition and body image, Höch's work has been compared to that of feminist media artists Cindy Sherman and Barbara Kruger. But it is also worth noting the role of technology in Höch's work. Not only are machines depicted alongside, with, or as

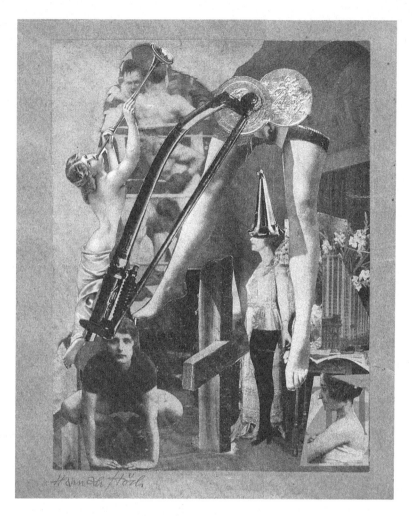

| **Figure 5.1** |

Hannah Höch, *Dada-Ernst*, 1920–1921, photomontage and collage on paper 18.6 × 16.6 cm (7 5/16 × 6 9/16 in.). The Vera and Arturo Schwarz Collection of Dada and Surrealist Art at The Israel Museum. © Israel Museum, Jerusalem. Photo by Avshalom Avital.

bodies, but also the reproducible nature of the work's fundamental basis and its novel technological form contribute to the confusing between-world-wars status of both female artists and the representation of female bodies. This type of collage became an important means of expression in Dada and continues to function as a critical medium. Given the era and the Dada movement's limited access to institutions, this type of critical play demanded a complete break with political and cultural concerns.

Surrealists and Performance

As we have seen, the trend for artists and game makers involved in critical play is to start with the workings of the human mind, the same human mind that had conceived and enacted the monstrosity of war. Most Surrealist games were based on activities as familiar as Victorian-era parlor games—group games played indoors to amuse the members of the upper and middle classes during their newfound leisure time.[24] But the Surrealists pushed activity into an exploration. Max Ernst's writings show one element of his investigation of everyday space during leisure time:

The 10th of August 1925
Raining day in a seaside inn found me gazing at the floorboards of my room. My gaze became excited, then obsessed by the sight of the boards. There were 1000 rubbings set deep into the grooves. I decided to then investigate the meaning of this obsession, and to have my meditative and hallucinatory faculties; I made a series of drawings by placing on the boards sheets of paper which I rubbed with black lead. I gazed at the drawings and surprisingly a hallucinatory series of contradictory images rose before my eyes. Superposing themselves one upon the other.[25]

Like Ernst, the writer André Breton searched for procedures and methods to match his process techniques. Breton's 1921 meeting with Freud in Vienna solidified his commitment to exploring theories of the unconscious, and through time Breton continued to develop methods inspired by psychoanalysis.

But whether examining the mind or the machine, the Surrealist definition of a game, and the route to the discovery of a game, differs significantly from the rigorous frameworks put forth by recent games scholars, particularly the frameworks offered by the study of computer games. Surrealists were, above all, sensitive to method, to technique, to a process that is as fundamental to an art practice as its outcome. Games generated from Surrealist experiments were themselves cultural methods that brought meaning to the everyday by altering participant relationships to the world through rule-based systems. Surrealists believed that as the seat of imagination, the unconscious could be accessed through organized procedures—for example, in consciously performing or collaborating on "unconscious acts." Through these methods, artists could connect with what they believed was the source of creativity. This structure of critical play, open experimentation, and rule-based systems emphasizes the social and intellectual role of the artistic community. The Surrealists' experiment and their use, at times, of violence and surprise were a vital part of understanding the larger questions of consciousness and culture.[26] Therefore, in looking at critical play, Surrealist games—as documented in Brotchie and Gooding's small *A Book of Surrealist Games* (1995) as well as in Rosemont's 1998 text *Surrealist Women*—warrant careful examination. These include games based on existing parlor games, spiritual practice, automatic writing, and the growing genre of board games. The techniques that follow are culled from historic accounts of Surrealist practice.

Automatism

Spontaneous writing or drawing without any conscious interference in the results. Most automatism was textual, but similar themes emerge in Surrealist's use of automated drawing, which was conceived as an accelerated or intensified sketch process where surprises and unpredictable images would appear. The technique was also used by early followers of Freud as a way to understand the unconscious through the writer's subconscious word choices.

Cut-Up Technique

As previously discussed in relation to some of Tzara's Dada writings, including his various manifestos, "cut-ups" are texts derived from existing writing or printed sheets that are then dissembled or cut up at random and reassembled to create a new text. Cutting and pasting readymade material was a subversive and creative Surrealist strategy that had aesthetic, poetic, and political implications.[27] This technique has been used by countless language players, including the American novelists Kathy Acker and William Burroughs.

Reassembly

This technique is visual in nature and uses fragments of found images in collages that are then reassembled into a completed work. The technique of decollage was used to disassemble images from their original state. Because collage originated from a Dada-inspired critique, it has remained a strategy of alterity, or otherness, for other marginalized groups as well. Today, it is a staple of political and outsider art such as zine culture. Höch and Hausmann were the primary instigators of this form.

Exquisite Corpse

One of the most famous participatory Surrealist art activities is known by the French name *cadavre exquis*, or "exquisite corpse," after the first sentence it produced: "*Le cadavre exquis boira le vin nouveau*" ("The exquisite corpse shall drink the new wine"). Exquisite corpse is a multiplayer game in which players decide to create an image or text together. Each player either creates words along a pattern (such as the example of the corpse consuming the new wine) or draws on a folded section of a paper, so that when other players receive their section of the paper, it is folded so that the other players cannot see what has been drawn before. Some variations are to leave small link lines from one section to the next, so a drawing can continue, or give one word to the next player, so that the composition becomes seamless. Figure 5.2 offers an example of such a collaborative drawing from leading artists of the 1930s. Some scholars offer an analysis of exquisite corpse through a feminist lens, examining the constructed and mysterious nature of the "body" (or the artwork) of the exquisite corpse as a location of distress, both physically and psychically. As collaborative works, these images might be interpreted as a manifestation of Jungian "collective unconscious."

Fumage

In this technique, impressions are made by the smoke of a lamp or candle on paper or canvas. Fumage is similar to fortune-telling activities such as the reading of tea leaves and Hermann Rorschach's inkblot tests developed for psychological research in 1921.

Movement of Liquid Down a Vertical Surface

This is an abstract technique that creates images by allowing liquid to flow down a surface. While drip-paintings were not yet imaginable themselves as "art" products in fine arts circles even during the rebellious Dada and Surrealist periods, they could be valuable process works to tap the unconscious.

Would You Open the Door

If there were a knock at the door, and you saw . . . a famous historical figure—an artist, for example, or a politician—would you let him or her in? Would You Open the Door was a Surrealist parlor game of question posing. If Guillaume Apollinaire came to the door, would you let him in? How about Joan of Arc? Instant-decision activities such as this prompted discussion in the group about politics, aesthetics, and ethics, and revealed the inner workings of the participants. The Would You Open the Door game is nearly identical to a popular French parlor game of the time, but it is focused on personalities of interest to the group of Surrealist artists, or those visitors deemed especially absurd.

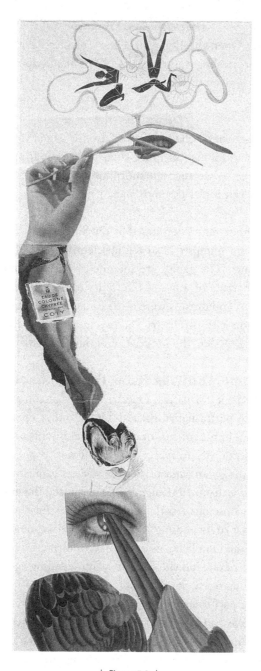

| Figure 5.2 |

Jean (Hans) Arp (1888–1966) with Oscar Dominguez, Sophie Taeuber-Arp, and Marcel Jean, *Exquisite Cadaver*, 1937, collage and pencil on paper, 61.6 × 23.6 cm. AM1973-20. Musée National d'Art Moderne, Centre Georges Pompidou, Paris. Photo credit: CNAC/MNAM/Dist. Réunion des Musées Nationaux/Art Resource, NY. © ARS, NY.

Time-Travelers' Potlatch

Related to Would You Open the Door, in Time-Travelers' Potlatch players collectively come up with historical figures to discuss and think of gifts that they would offer these historical figures if given the chance.

Dessin Successif

Dessin successif translates into "chain drawing." In this game, each player studies the previous player's drawing for five seconds, then redraws it from memory, with the point of the game being to see the metamorphoses from the first, middle, and last drawings in the chains as it passes through many hands.

These and numerous other games developed by the Surrealists are collective methods, each of which provides a glimpse, however unscientific, into the unconscious processes of the participants. The games are intended to critique rationalism, possibly in recognition of the horrors of war and the frailty of human understanding. Again, unconscious motivations and dreams were areas of deep engagement for the Surrealists, and their fascination with psychiatry and psychoanalysis helped focus the artists' play on the abstract, the sudden, the intuitive, and the instinctual.[28]

Opportunities from Performance

How are these processes performative, exactly? And what can game designers learn from these examples of performative games? Unlike other creative methodologies, the specific use of games in the process of creativity represents a significant shift. The Surrealists *made games* in order to *make art*. Games were a *process*—an integral part of *their research*—not merely an *outcome*. Games such as exquisite corpse (see the example of *Exquisite Cadaver* from 1931, figure 5.3) harnessed the notions of chance and automatism, a set of unconscious acts that emerged possessing the unusual "possibility of thought, which is that of its pooling."[29] This pooling of thought, its collective distribution among artists and intellectuals of the day, in turn created an effort that went beyond the perceptions of one individual author, transcending ego and self-interest to create an artifact of group research.

In critical play, the performance of games can foster creativity, and further, produce new art forms, styles, and genres. Performance might reveal particular connections between subjects or shapes previously unknown. It might help the designer, for example, explore questions of permutation, repetition, and repeatability. The sense of subjectivity and the role of the player are additionally questioned and repositioned in these games. And, furthermore, "winning" might mean to experience or make

| Figure 5.3 |

Nusch Eluard (1907–1946), with Eugène Grindel, Paul Eluard, and Valentine (Gross) Hugo, *Exquisite Cadaver*, 1931, colored pencil on black paper, 31 × 24 cm. AM1980-20. Musée National d'Art Moderne, Centre Georges Pompidou, Paris. Photo: Philippe Migeat. Photo credit: CNAC/MNAM/Dist. Réunion des Musées Nationaux/Art Resource, NY.

something new, beautiful, puzzling, or surprising, or to touch on an artifact or process that helps one experience the artistic process or the mysterious mind. At other times, performance is pure amusement. As Breton reflected in the 1950s:

If there is one activity in Surrealism which has most invited the derision of imbeciles, it is our persistent playing of games, which can be found throughout most of our publications over the last thirty-five years . . . right from the start it proved useful for strengthening the bonds that united us, and for encouraging sudden awarenesses of our desires whenever these were held in common. Furthermore, the urgent need we felt to do away with the old antinomies that dominate work and leisure, "wisdom" and "folly," etc.—such as action and dream, past and future, sanity and madness, high and low, and so on—disposed us not to spare that of the serious and the non-serious (games).[30]

Performance can also be of use to push through expected cultural norms. Dali adopted the methodological approach of "paranoia criticism" in 1929 with a proposal to discredit reality and break with the external world so that *irrational knowledge based on the interpretive critical association of delirious phenomena* could result.[31] After deciding to be one of the enlightened "confusionists," Dali supported anything that could question, even ruin, the core ideas of family, homeland, and religion through "systematized confusion."[32] To Dali and others, the paranoiac mind perceives signs, but creates extra, new, unexpected, or deluded instantaneous links, making new relationships of meaning by playing with the signifier-signified relationship. This procedure, along with the other gaming methods described earlier, may be considered one of Surrealism's central contributions to modern art.

Writer and photographer Claude Cahun (1894–1954) worked along similar lines. Cahun met André Breton in 1932. Like other women artists, she was an outsider to a movement that had problems negotiating the complex state of gender and, as a lesbian, she had little chance to be defined in relationship to other men, issues not unknown to other women in the Surrealist movement.[33] In her practice, Cahun investigated power and personal/social identity, applying Dali's strategy of "the paranoiac-critical method" to photography and mixed-media object collages. In her writing, Cahun was political, espousing a "theory/practice" approach to equalize and integrate the making of things and the research about them; Cahun sought to understand how objects functioned, and how worker relations functioned in systems such as capitalism or communism. Of *Objet* (1938), a table-top-sized assembly of design elements set into wood, Harris notes the investigating, gesturing hand motioning toward an open eye, set on its edge, referencing female genitalia.[34] Gender and sexuality were significant themes in Cahun's work. In many projects she questioned binary categorization, playing with the notions of sexual difference, high and low art, and the mind/body separation. Like many Surrealists, Cahun used photography to "render the surface of the world *palpable* and render it marvelous."[35] Later recognized for their resistance to the Nazis, both she and her partner, Marcel Moore (Suzanne Malherbe), shared a commitment to identity play through the act of role-playing. Their related use of pseudonyms further demonstrated how representation in the "true eye" of the photograph could be problematized.

Cahun used costumes ranging from monsters and vampires to sailors and masked, alien figures to foreground female transgression and desire, for her various self-portraits. These images do not merely present a play-act, however, or "portray" something. "*They look back*."[36] They have the indexical qualities of a photograph, the connection to the subject through light, the real "writing itself," and the iconic reference to a problematically gendered body, providing surreal "counter archives" of the female body.[37] Cahun's interest in gender and power led to her investigation of opposites—Buddah, to a school girl, geisha to weightlifter, Cahun's exploration pushed at the edges of these opposites, exposing them as ineffective and artificial through her shifts in costume (see figure 5.4). On her photographic self-portrait collage titled "Claude Cahun and Marcel Moore," an illustration for her book *Aveux non Avenus* (*Cancelled [or Unavowed] Confessions*, 1930), Cahun wrote, "Under this mask another mask. I shall never finish stripping away all these faces. And underneath all these masks, there is no 'real' identity."

These complex images explore social codes and mimic standard tropes of identity. They reveal less a desire to become "other" and more a movement toward dissolving distinctions by presenting oppositions, by erasing boundaries between genders. By mixing the costume that might typically comprise a gendered performance, she merges opposites and renders them nonoppositional.[38] Cahun's combining, juxtaposing, and blurring of male/female form exhibit an unsettling voice of the double, the uncanny, and raise questions about the conscious performance of sexuality that other Surrealist work misses.[39] Importantly, Cahun demonstrates through her "charades-like" guessing game of self-portraits the ways in which gender identity itself is constructed much like a performative game, a sentiment mirrored in Judith Butler's later texts on performativity, and also in the work of Félix Guattari.

Postwar Artists and Play

Innovation and intervention continued as mainstays among artists of the mid-twentieth century. Instead of a focus on unconscious processes, postwar artists sought engagement beyond the parlor game and outside the gallery. Their particular focus on social

| **Figure 5.4** |
Claude Cahun (born Lucy Schwob) (1894–1954), *Self-Portrait with Mask*, ca. 1928, gelatin silver print, 11.7 × 9 cm. INV996-3-2PH; INV9101. Musée des Beaux-Arts, Nantes, France. Photo: Gérard Blot. Photo credit: Réunion des Musées Nationaux/Art Resource, NY.

intervention had significant impact on contemporary art and on social changes, such as the May 1968 movement in France and the antiwar protests in the United States during the conflict in Vietnam. These artists again turned to nontraditional media, using posters, video, and performance to unplay traditional art and its traditions, the themes of "highbrow" modernism, and the power and politics of the state. Games demonstrate particular reflections on technology, and as new technologies swept the globe the widescale effects of war—especially the Holocaust in Europe and the dropping of the atomic bomb in Japan—the promises of science and the possibilities (and dangers) of machines gripped those in the art world and beyond. Artists searching for meaningful relationships between lived experience and culture once again turned to extreme situations and the performance of artistic interventions or "art actions" that took artworks out of the gallery and into untraditional territory.

Japanese artists were particular proponents of such actions. The Gutai movement, assembled in post-Hiroshima Japan, originated a particularly intimate set of responses to twentieth-century concerns about technology and the "new society" it heralded. Gutai were conceptual artists, incorporating novel materials and media of the day as a way to break the boundaries between the artistic forms of sculpture or painting and the forms of events. With events culminating in art actions, scenes and tableaus of performance, creative outdoor events and camping, or interruptions of popular culture, the artists were interested in creating difficult-to-categorize phenomenon. In 1955, Gutai's founders conducted a two-week performative event in the suburbs outside Osaka. This rigorous artistic experiment was designed to take art out of the hallowed hall and expose artworks to the outside elements—in this case, literally. Young artists took over a pine grove and staged a thirteen-day exhibition of paintings, gigantic sculptures created from abandoned machinery and other unusual objects, and performances, in the face of sun and rain. Atsuko Tanaka (1932–2005), one of Japan's most important avant-garde figures, put out a large pink-bubble-gum-colored vinyl sheet to ripple in the wind.[40] Another Gutai member, Saburo Murakami, took a ball, dipped it in ink, and tossed it against a wall repeatedly, trying to invent a "new painting" using the "feel" of velocity through chance operations and random play. According to Alexandra Munroe, Gutai means "tool and body"—thus elements of performance and technology are intertwined in many of the works.[41]

In fact, Gutai produced a very early strain of conceptualism, one specifically influenced by both the shock of the annihilated Hiroshima and Nagasaki and by the 1950s utopian visions of technological change and science. Atsuko Tanaka is known for creating playful clothing works. Inspired by a drugstore sign in the Osaka train station, Tanaka appropriated the medium of electricity to create a changing, technology-driven garment. Her outfit, known as *The Electric Dress* (1956), was composed from flashing neon tubes. From objects to installation to drawing, her work was influenced by technology and includes schematic drawings and electric cables as a comment on the rapid industrialization of postwar Japan. *Bell* (1955) was a sound installation that defined architectural boundaries through a row of progressively ringing bells. Tanaka also engaged consumer culture through the use of fashion and clothing, especially her "clothing that evolved." Evolving clothing is an interactive and open-ended game structured within "boundaries" of infinite change. As the garments change over time, they suggest the everyday as a new play arrangement, one that critiques the fashion industry, its attitudes toward women's bodies, the top-down nature of its designs, and its drive for ever-increasing sales, not necessarily to the benefit of the consumer.[42] Tanaka's ouevre included paintings, sculptures, performances, and installations. Tanaka's paintings often were created by painting as the canvas lay on the floor with gestural movements typical of Gutai artists (Gutai means "embodiment"). Her interest in the ring shapes (see figure 5.5) is said to be a continuation of her interest manifest in *Electric Dress*. These bulbs were covered in primary colors, and the paintings also typify colorful, concentric circles, as though bulbs are hanging down to the canvas.

Gutai's play with materials, location, and embodiment, as well as concerns about the appropriate role of formal exhibitions, took the Surrealist concept of process-based exploration into the actual product of the work itself. Rather than use games behind the scenes to develop fixed artworks, the Gutai artists created events and objects that were *games in their entirety*. Neither high art nor costume, nor merely invention, Gutai artists pushed the critical capacity of the arts through an investment in performance and performative objects in a global context, where war on an immense scale had echoed earlier wars.

Again, their motivation was lived experience. The Japanese role in World War II left Gutai with a specific set of questions. Rather than investigate the unconscious, the Gutai were closer to Dada artists in that the horrors of war brought traditional authority and an entire way of living into question. In Japan, social organization and cultural norms had been shaken to the ground by fascism, war, and modernization. Gutai artists felt a particular conviction to recovering or instilling childlike wonder and openness to equitable social structures. These artists commented on emerging commercialism and capitalism and allowed themselves to be obsessed with innovation and newness. According to one writer: "Gutai was not just an art-world strategy, but a way to be reborn."[43] Viewed this way, Tanaka's light dress was "a symbol of the modern Asian city."[44] In the tradition of critical play, it was also a site of transformation.[45]

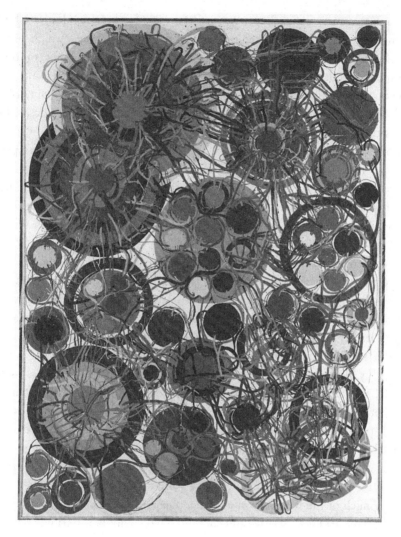

| Figure 5.5 |
Atsuko Tanaka (Japanese, twentieth century), *Wor*, 1966, oil on canvas. Hood Museum of Art, Dartmouth College, Hanover, NH; purchased through the Julia L. Whittier Fund.

Akira Kanayama, Tanaka's partner, is often credited as the leader of Gutai. Kanayama created a robot, "the remote control painting machine," which automatically discharged paint so that he could make artwork even while absent, on the busy days he spent outside his studio organizing Gutai. The artist wittily recounts the first experiment the machine produced, a gooey mess turned black from hours of labor. Created while Kanayama napped, it was the highest-selling work he had created at the time.[46] As the 1950s promised an automated domestic lifestyle complete with washing machines, automobiles, and the new, self-cleaning range, Kanayama's painting machine playfully reduced the act of creating "high art" to a task for an appliance.[47] Kanayama moved beyond the concerns of Abstract Expressionism and even beyond Jackson Pollack's dependence on bodily gesture by replacing the body entirely with a machine. As an automated work bound by rules, Kanayama in effect set up a game space for producing art.

Among Japanese creative movements, those of manga and anime continue to affect international art and culture. These forms emerged in 1945, when Dr. Osamu Tezuka was inspired by the influx of Western—particularly American—films such as those produced by Walt Disney Productions. Tezuka adopted a Disney-like art style, creating character faces that had exaggerated eyes, small mouths, and tiny noses. The only text in Tezuka's comics appeared as character dialogue, giving his pages a "cinematic" quality. The style became incredibly popular. Today, anime films, using the same style, are incredibly popular internationally; and the manga market in Japan grosses approximately $4.7 billion each year, with advertising and games following the successful style.[48] Artist Takashi Murakami (b. 1963), who creates sculptures, comics, and inflatables, holds this view of popular playful cultural icons and manga: "When I consider what Japanese culture is like, the answer is that it all is subculture. Therefore, art is unnecessary"[49] In acknowledging games and popular culture, Murakami admits the much of the work becomes static, objectified. He notes, "I express hopelessness . . . if my art looks positive and cheerful, I would doubt my art was accepted in the contemporary art scene." Also: "My art is not Pop art. It is a record of the struggle of the discriminated people."[50] In this way, Murakami, like many contemporary artists emerging from tumultuous historical sites and situations, shows how the politics of play, technology, and swift cultural change are interrogated by artists. With Japan the primary producer of manga game art, and a prolific generator of computer games overall, the critical nature of Japanese art styles should be noted, though it is impossible to do them justice. Suffice it to say that while manga can be read as highly gender-biased and merges sites of difference in radical ways (for example, human/machine characters, human/animal identities), the system of fantasy that manga draws upon generates a dizzying form of critical play. Mamoru Oshii's famous *Ghost in the Shell* film series (1995, 2004) is one good example, examining the "human" boundaries of body augmentation. *Paprika* (2006) is another work that looks at the uploading of consciousness.[51] Outside film, however, manga and anime styles have proven to be critical as well as playful, as in the work of Yoshimoto Nara.

Play in the United States

In the United States, conceptual artists of the 1960s were, on several levels, engaged with the idea of process as a way to rethink issues of authority, politics, and the notion of a cultural status quo. Artists created "situations" and performed art actions complete with instructions. Like games, many of these events featured precise and unalterable rules players had to accept in order to engage work.[52] Alan Kaprow (1927–2006) made rules into Happening scores (or instructions), while artist Sol Lewitt (1928–2007) created "plans" for works that in fact constituted those works.[53] Lewitt's plans were often a basic rule set for an artwork such as a wall drawing. As noted in his writings, while conceptual art uses its own logical strategies for execution, "conceptual art is not necessarily logical":[54] "To work with a plan that is preset is one way of avoiding subjectivity. It also obviates the necessity of designing each work in turn. The plan would design the work. Some plans would require millions of variations, and some a limited number, but both are finite."

For Lewitt, art making-as-instruction was a performative game with concrete rules and outcomes. While Lewitt did not call his work games, his rule sets, processes, and rewards played out much as a game might. Like the other methods discussed for critical play, Lewitt's plans for various projects worked against ideas of subjectivity and manipulation, running to their own logical conclusion as the work manifested. The constant drive to eliminate the subjective is interesting because in many ways, games thrive by creating subjectivities. There is also the reminder of Félix Guattari's call for a "refoundation of the problematic of subjectivity" and even a collection of "partial" subjectivities. Whatever their persuasion, those interested in critical play began to create subjectivities that are "pre-personal, polyphonic, collective, and machinic."[55] By doing so they also commented on larger ideologies and political situations. As technology became a more and more integral and bombastic element of contemporary life in postwar U.S. culture, artists tested the new boundaries through their playful interest in writing new rules for everyday living.

Along with sculptor and performer Claes Oldenburg (1929–), the conceptual artist Allan Kaprow staged events or "happenings" that mixed everyday reality and artwork with multiple participants. Dick Higgins (1938–1998) wrote of the media convergence in the art world and the event in his "Statement on Intermedia" (1966), in which he argued that an "intermedia" of blended forms represented an essential trend in popular culture that incorporated liveness and promised to revolutionize art and life. As a case in point, in his *18 Happenings in Six Parts* (1959), Kaprow involved "participants" rather than merely "spectators." Guests were given instructions similar to game rules on how to interact with the environment, often moving from room to room and bending into uncomfortable positions to experience a particular place or event differently. Later that year, artist Red Grooms staged *The Burning Building* at his studio, the Delancey Street Museum. In this ten-minute piece Grooms played "Pasty Man," a pyromaniac on the run from firemen.[56] The stagings were quite successful. The happenings themselves were detailed by Kaprow in his missive, "Untitled Guidelines for Happenings" (1966), which held that happenings allowed art to manifest as a continuous work in progress. Kaprow's guidelines reflected the desire to prompt an artistic and critical engagement with the public, to acknowledge the social role of art, and indeed emphasize that idea that artistic practice and artistic consumption can and should be brought closer together. The collaboration of semi-anonymous artists and "the masses" as participants was especially important in the happenings and participatory performances staged in the 1960s and 1970s.

Happenings also were a precursor to other art movements that featured the dissolution of the active and passive dichotomy of the art world, as well as an aestheticization of the everyday. The importance of the everyday object continued to grow with this new emphasis on play. German sculptor and performer Joseph Beuys (1921–1986) used little clown drummers set on a piano in one of his works, marking a shift through both the use of everyday objects and non-art performance situations.[57] With events organized by Lithuanian born George Maciunas, Fluxus artists bypassed the museum and gallery circuit in favor of flexible performances, films, readymade-style kits, and publishing. Like the postwar groups Gutai, Cobra, and the Situationist International, Fluxus was a reactionary group, combining historical aspects of Futurist and absurdist theater, Dada irrationality, and the interest in chance and games purported by composer John Cage. Fluxus work was ephemeral, engaged in everyday actions, and above all, funny. In one of the Fluxus manifestos from the mid-1960s, Maciunas stated: "Fluxus art-amusement is the rear-guard without any pretension or urge to participate in the competition of 'one-upmanship' with the avant-garde. It strives for the monostructural and nontheatrical qualities of simple natural events, a game or a gag. It is the fusion of Spike Jones Vaudeville, gags, children's games and Duchamp."[58]

Maciunas's goal was for a "nonprofessional, nonparasitic, nonelite" art in which anything could be art, and anyone could make it. In the 1965 manifesto, Maciunas went on to declare: "This substitute art-amusement must be simple, amusing, concerned with insignificances, have no commodity or institutional value." Maciunas experimented continually with "gag" events. For example, he composed a musical score that called for hammering nails into each key of a piano.[59] In 1961, he began organizing makeshift performances and concerts at an important New York gallery—his studio. These quickly developed into larger-scale international art festivals of absurdist performance. At one of the festivals, Korean-born artist Nam June Paik (1932–2006) performed another artist's score, by dipping his hair in a bowl of ink and painting with his hair until the performance was complete:

Draw a straight line and follow it.[60]

Takehisa Kosugi (b. 1938), a Tokyo-born composer, used daily materials in his event pieces; in 1969, he cofounded the musical group Taj Mahal Travellers, which played around the world. He was invited to perform at Fluxus events in Europe in 1972, as was Japanese-born artist Mieko (Chieko) Shiomi. As noted earlier, from the 1960s on, Fluxus artists created hundreds of games in the form of events and as Fluxkits or objects (see Saito's *Heart Box*, figure 5.6). Fluxus artists also gathered at "Flux-Festivals,"or Fluxfests, initiated by Maciunas in 1962, beginning with concerts at the Wiesbaden state museum, six concerts in Copenhagen, seven in Paris. These performances were primarily musical compositions, some scored by animals. There was Fluxus music for lips, mud, bottles, pebbles, balloons, ladders, and violin, and piano pieces requiring twelve pianos. The next year (1963), the festivals expanded to Dusseldorf, Amsterdam, The Hague, and Nice and grew to incorporate street events. Games and game-like artifacts followed. In 1964, Fluxus events incorporated ping-pong and badminton and, in 1966, adhesive nets were dropped over dancing guests. One Fluxfest, held at Douglass College in New Jersey in 1970, featured physical games like soccer on stilts, balloon javelin, and table tennis played with paddles that featured large holes at their centers.[61] The Handicap Run game encouraged players to run while drinking vodka, eating oatmeal and ice cream, grinding coffee, shouting, counting, writing, and playing instruments.[62] Such absurd events are aligned with the perennial Fluxus emphasis on insignificant activities, games, or gags.

Unlike Duchamp, who signed anything, from an ink sample to an advertisement to call it "art," Fluxus artists collected ordinary objects and left them "around" as mere clutter, sometimes recontextualizing these objects in the middle of a street or sidewalk as a means of social engagement. Other items found their way to the middle of galleries where they could act as a playful surprise.[63]

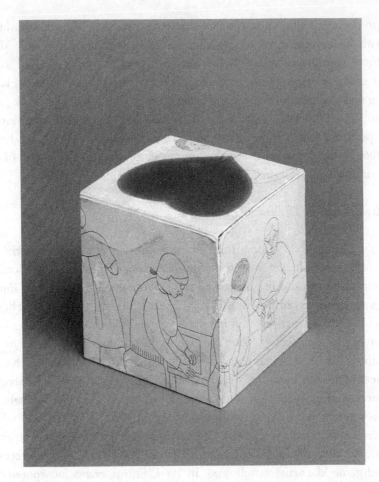

| **Figure 5.6** |
Takako Saito (Japanese, b. 1929), *Heart Box*, 1965, paper. Hood Museum of Art, Dartmouth College, Hanover, NH; gift of Alison Knowles.

The American composer John Cage had been investigating the dialogue between rules and aesthetics since the 1930s. On August 29, 1952, Cage continued this investigation by initiating a now-famous dialogue between the audience and the rules that guide aesthetic experience. For the premiere performance of *4'33"* (*4 minutes, 33 seconds*), David Tudor sat at the piano and, when the piece began, played nothing, closing the keyboard lid at the proper moment to signal each of the "silent" movements in *4'33"*. In the act of depriving the audience of "music," the works asks the audience to listen, transforming the listening experience to one in which listeners actively create their own composition through the live sounds and noises around them. This work, like other Cage compositions, involves chance operations and redirects the authority of the creative process to the participant, completely altering the social roles of composer and listener. In a keynote address, Cage said: "My *Music of Changes*, composed by means of *I Ching* chance operations, I was to move from structure to process, from music as an object having parts, to music without beginning, middle, or end, music as weather . . . choreographies are not supported by my musical accompaniments. Music and dance are independent but coexistent."[64]

The openness of Cage's process surfaced in many Fluxus artists' philosophies. "I don't ever want the art to be still, finished," states Alison Knowles. "I want it to be available for somebody to do something else with it . . . [something] that I wouldn't have thought of."[65] The use of the scores or instructions emphasizes the profoundly boring activities in Fluxus games. But merely drawing a Huizingian magic circle around an everyday action transforms it into an art action, a game, and places it in an area of fantasy.[66] Knowles's performances involving ordinary activities became a hallmark of 1960s and 1970s performance art. One of her most well known works, *Identical Lunch* (1971), is a performance of eating a sandwich. Documented in the *Journal of the Identical Lunch* (figure 5.7), the work consisted of a series of performances that actually constitute the piece. The identical lunch was a tunafish sandwich on wheat toast with lettuce and butter (no mayo) and a large glass of buttermilk or a cup of soup. The lunch was eaten many days of the week, by different people but at the same place and around the same time (lunchtime). Documentation of each lunch was provided in a variety of formats. This work succeeds in breaking down the distinctions between audience, artist, artwork, and everyday life.

Spencer noted that "play and art are the same activity because neither subserves, in any direct way, the processes conductive to life and neither refers to ulterior benefits, the proximate ends are the only ends."[67] The work of these artists demonstrates a particular potency in subversive acts through participatory play. Though her work has been discussed earlier in this book, it is worthwhile to note here that Knowles pursues

| Figure 5.7 |

Alison Knowles (American, b. 1933), *The Identical Lunch with George Maciunas*, 1963, screenprint on canvas. Hood Museum of Art, Dartmouth College, Hanover, NH; gift of the artist.

a vein of research into randomness and chance as they affect ordinary, some might say, banal objects. In her documentation of a project titled *Bread and Water*, Knowles analyzed the cracks in homemade bread and mapped them to rivers in atlases, creating prints of these congruencies. Knowles brings geographic and ecological information to these works, juxtaposing it with poems that interplay with the drawings.[68]

Again, what is important to note in these examples are the ways in which Knowles's poems and other writings elevate process over other aspects of the work or, in other words, constitute a form of critical play. As French theorist Henri Lefebvre asks, "Are not the surreal, the extraordinary, the surprising, even the magical, also part of the real? Why wouldn't the concept of everydayness reveal the extraordinary in the ordinary?"[69] The magical transformation of ordinary materials such as beans or bread speaks to conceptualizations of time and to the transformative act that a playful repositioning of the everyday might accomplish. The way in which it restores time and labor to our experience of objects—be they shoe soles or beans and paper—is partly captured by Knowles's statement: "As we know, time spent on shoes is never wasted"; while simultaneously divesting the objects of their original function, it playfully transmigrates the object to its own magic circle.[70] Knowles's work, like that of other Fluxus artists, becomes fundamentally political, and surprisingly subtle. While Dada and other groups interrogated social norms, politics, and art practices, focusing on an "antiart" antiaesthetic, Fluxus emerged as a practice of process and aesthetic, themes that ultimately reflected core Fluxus ideologies on time and being.

The New Rules

Game designers might be familiar with Salen and Zimmerman's theory of explicit and implicit rules of play.[71] In much of the Fluxus artists' work, we can derive a critical version of these two concepts. Explicit rules are those given by exposition in the instructions or scores—for instance, "Make a Sandwich." Explicit rules are obvious, or written down, in the rule set. The explicit rule "Follow a Line" is a direct command: an explicit rule. The beauty of a Fluxus work, however, lies in the implicit rules surrounding the explicit. The player might ask: "Follow a line to where? Whose line is it? Where did it come from? Why should I follow that line?" Or even: "That line is ugly" or "I don't like where that line goes." The resolution of these questions requires implicit rule making. Implicit rules take into account how the game is really played: do players shake hands after a game? Does the winner refrain from gloating, or revealing that he or she had been bluffing? Implicit rules arise at those points where the player of a Fluxus game must negotiate the jump from an everyday action into play, into the magic circle where, hopefully, the player will go along with the joke and truly have a new, unusual, or delightful "sense-heightening" experience. Fluxus embodies the shift in consciousness that defines the magic circle so central to Huizinga's *Homo Ludens*, particularly because it incorporates so much of the everyday.

One of the masters of the implicit rule set, Yoko Ono set up her magic circles very carefully, playing with danger and risk in her many of her performances. Like her *Instruction Paintings* discussed in chapter 4, Ono's performances were well-staged and required audience participation.

Her work *Cut Piece* was originally performed in 1964 in Japan. Ono performed it again at New York's Carnegie Hall in 1965. In the work, Ono sits still on the stage with scissors nearby. The members of the audience approach the artist, one by one, and snip off a piece of her clothing. Here, we might recall Gutai artist Tanaka's reconfigured clothing work. The degree of audience participation in Ono's *Cut Piece* varied widely. Some audiences mobbed the artist in a frenzy of cutting. Others were hesitant and respectful in their approach. Whatever the style of response, interaction in such an open, game-like system reveals compelling aspects of human behavior. "I'm just part of the participation," Ono noted in a 1968 interview. "So what I'm trying to do is make something happen by throwing a pebble into the water and creating ripples. It's like starting a good motion. I don't want to control the ripples."[72] The artist explicitly designed her work to create situations of participation. Ono's commitment to a lack of control by the artist is a particularly activist stance, for it challenges the traditional notion of the artist as genius. As Linda Nochlin observed in the 1980s, the idea of artistic "genius" is thought to be an inevitable, mysterious power embedded into the very fabric of the great artist.[73]

By calling attention to the pleasure of everyday play, the construction of rules, and the very logic behind games, a shift in consciousness is required for most of the public to perceive action as "art." However, critical play opens up an obvious free space for player subversion. While related to other activist art in the 1960s and 1970s that took a more serious turn, Fluxus kept critical play as a central tenet of event design. In the years that followed, critical performance remained central to artist/ activist events, from the street theater performances of the guerilla group El Teatro Campesino, to the Farmworkers' theater, The Black Revolutionary Theatre (BRT) led by Amiri Baraka,[74] to media interventions such as *Paper Tiger TV*.[75] The forms of critical play continue to have the power to disrupt everyday activities.

Further Enactments

Working primarily in Paris, Polish artist André Cadere (1934–1978) used game methods to create one hundred and eighty "performative" sculptures, or wood staffs, called "Barres de Bois." From a distance, these hand-painted individual spindles, sitting on a pole, appear to be striped. The bars reference games, in part, as they were produced mathematically and constitute a type of language in their manipulation and arrangement of color. Their special, coded instructions seem to invoke strategy. James Hyde, a scholar of Cadere's work, notes: "Cadere valued his works as conversation starters— props for opening dialogue."[76] This intention is aligned with the formal patterns of the bars: As Daniel Birnbaum has noted, the "color schemes of his signature barres de bois rond (bars of round wood) are based on a code derived from mathematical permutations, into which Cadere introduced a single error in each case."[77]

Cadere not only made rules for his work but also included in them subversion and deviation from his own system. Playing a game of mismatch and error, Cadere tempted participants to notice, recognize, and either subvert or disrupt the system that appears to the naked eye as evenly colored, but at a distance seems erratic. The mix of exactness and error, according to critic James Hyde, "tempts one to decipher its logic, but even with this simple piece it is virtually impossible to grasp the pattern. In the process of trying, however, the viewer opens a dialogue with the work."[78]

The bars were primarily used in performances. Cadere would take these spindles, which looked like traditional staffs or even wands, to events and art galleries, documenting every occurrence that unfolded. His typewritten records include time, date, and place of appearance. Performance was integral to Cadere's work and as he wandered from event to event his interventions were carefully planned. He announced his walks in advance, and even conducted disruptive visits to other artists' openings. There is evidence that occasionally Cadere's staffs were confiscated. To guard against repeated impediments to his work, he took to carrying miniature rods in his pocket. At times, these "parasites" would mysteriously appear on gallery floors.[79] When interviewed, Cadere deflected economic or political critique: "I am not interested in the reaction of people and I do not need their reactions." In this way, his work effaced the actual performance or intervention to focus instead on the process of the work "becoming visible."[80] It is as though Cadere brought the game goal, or the safe zone, and interactors had to figure out the game from there. There are then several levels of critical play demonstrated here. Cadere's intention was to encourage viewers to choose approaches to interact with him, the artist whose opening he disrupted, and with others. Surprise appearances of a staff, and the conversations that ensued, created game-like interactions in public spaces with the general public and the arts establishment.

Other performative works are more closely tied to the role games play in popular culture. One example is based on the Japanese game *shougi* (shogi), a version of chess. The board, or *shougi ban*, is made up of a nine-by-nine grid and includes twenty game pieces. Shogi is not as popular in the West as it is in Japan, but the game is particularly significant to theorizing critical play because of the way it is *replayed*.

On certain holidays or festivals, it is a custom to play human-sized or *ningen* shogi, especially in the city of Tendo, where the greatest number of boards and pieces are fabricated (see figure 5.8). Contemporary cos-play, or costume play, takes place at many events around the world and include human shogi; cos-play participants dress up as their favorite cartoon characters, game objects, or avatars. Many of these festivals feature shogi cos-play as well. The anime convention *Youmacon* in the United States is one well-known site for annual cos-play shogi game.

Moving a game like shogi to the physical world does two things: first, it turns what was a traditional board game into an act of performance. Second, the game becomes a social event, one with multiple participants, facilitators, and spectators. These aspects

| Figure 5.8 |
Ningen-Shogi (Human Shogi) in Yamagata during the Traditional History Tea Festival, with black and pink cherry blossoms in spring. © Yamagata Prefecture/© JNTO.

of the translation of the shogi game board to include human involvement, which along the way involves reskinning, replaying, and rewriting all at once, might inspire a designer to create a replay scenario of a game in real life, or even produce a game that has more interventionist power or agency.

Tactics and Intervention

Anne-Marie Schleiner's computer-based projects allow users to see that the design of computer-based communities and games are of political consequence. Schleiner reveals how the structures imposed by systems, and what users are allowed to do within these systems, are significant conceptual constructions that require critique. In her creative pieces she spends much of her energies exploring online characters, reworking first-person shooter-style games such as *Counter Strike*, and responding to or undermining networked computer gaming experiences such as *America's Army*.

| Figure 5.9 |
OUT by Anne-Marie Schleiner.

Schleiner's 2004 work, *Operation Urban Terrain (OUT): A Live Action Wireless Gaming Urban Intervention*, used as a site for performance the preexisting game environment of *America's Army*, commissioned by the U.S. military as a way to entice young American men to enlist.[81] *America's Army* functions as an ideological tool, as a social software environment, and as a mean for marketing recruitment materials in electronic and paper form to players. The game costs nothing to download and play. It has a strong following of primarily male players, including a large right-wing Christian contingency.

The artistic intervention *OUT* takes its title from "MOUT," a term for "Military Operations in Urban Terrain." Choosing not to play the game, but to play *with* the game (figure 5.9), Schleiner armed herself with a mobile Internet connection, a bicycle, a battery-powered video projector, a team of players and technicians, and a laptop. Moving from site to site, Schleiner and her team played *America's Army* as a live urban performace, projecting the onscreen action onto the buildings and streets of New York during the 2004 Republican National Convention. The group intervened in the online gatherings of regular *America's Army* players, and discussed antiwar and antimilitary beliefs both in game space and in physical urban space. The performers consider Schleiner's *OUT* to be an artistic intervention in the "public" space of online games and cities, working to keep, as Schleiner writes: "Republicans OUT of New York. The United States OUT of Iraq and the Middle East. Escalating worldwide Militarism and Violence, from whatever source (right wing oil hungry U.S. capitalists or wealthy Islamic fundamentalists), OUT of Civilian Life. The U.S. Army and Pentagon computer game developers OUT of the minds of prebuscent [sic] gamers."[82]

Performative games can function as critical frameworks. As interventions, they are an active process, a scenario of a situation that produces more than an "active reader." The effect is akin to Barthes's notion of the writer, or what he terms, the scriptor: "the modern scriptor is born simultaneously with the text, is in no way equipped with a being preceding or exceeding the writing, is not the subject with the book as predicate; there is no other time than that of the enunciation and every text is eternally written here and now."[83] Games represent such a performative text, blurring authorship and the creation of meaning as they unfold. Additionally, the fluidity of performance and simultaneous reading and authoring of texts has deep ties to interventionist feminist art practices.

Schleiner argues in her curatorial essay, "Cracking the Maze": "Many artists, art critics, new media critics and theoreticians have expressed a disdain for games and game style interactivity, in fact, to describe an interactive computer art piece as 'too game-like' is a common pejorative. But considering the increasing popularity of computer games with younger generations, even at the expense of television, it seems perilous to ignore the spread of gaming culture."[84] The tension between popular culture, specifically games, and art is an important yet perhaps passing phenomenon, as museums and galleries from the Barbican Gallery in London to the Whitney Museum of American Art have shown artist-created computer games in the twenty-first century.[85] Artists' appropriation of games as an expressive performance genre can allow for a critical take on popular forms of entertainment and propaganda. Schleiner's commitment to activism through games and her use of games in large-scale, public spaces present a potent approach to social change.

Acting Out Resistance

Tanja Ostojic (1972–) is a Croatian artist whose diverse performances have included *Personal Space* (1996), which explores the perceptual states of the body, and *Black Square on White* (2001), in which the artist shaved her body hair to match the composition of the Russian Suprematist Kazimir Malevich's 1915 painting, *Black Square*. In 2001, the performative work *I'll Be Your Angel* (2001) called attention to the workings of the art world. In this piece, the artist shadowed the curator of the 2001 Venice Biennale, smiling pleasingly at him throughout. In this work, as in others, Ostojic uses her body to place herself among power relations, from dominant male figures of the art world to international citizenship, calling into question public, social hierarchies, the age-old consumption of women's bodies in art, and the complex relationship between the public and the artist.

Her most significant performative game work, *Looking for a Husband with an EU Passport*, ongoing from 2000 to 2005, began with an online advertisement—Ostojic literally advertised for a husband with an EU passport. Being Croatian, and investigating boundary crossing between European nations, Ostojic attempted to transgress the limitations inherent in a non-EU passport. She then postulated that people who belong to the EU discriminate against those in non-EU nations, particularly the Balkan states and Eastern Europe. Ostojic described the timeline of the work as follows:

I arranged our first meeting as a public performance in the field in front of the Museum of Contemporary Art in Belgrade in 2001. One month later we officially married in New Belgrade. With the international marriage certificate and other required documents, I applied for a visa. After two months I got one entrance family unification visa for Germany, limited to three months, so I moved to Düsseldorf, where I lived officially for three and a half years. In spring 2005 my three-year permit expired, and instead of granting me a permanent residence permit, the authorities granted me only a two-year visa. After that, K. G. and I got divorced, and on the occasion of the opening of my Integration Project Office installation at Gallery 35 in Berlin, on July 1, 2005, I organized a "Divorce Party."[86]

There is a game-like quality to this work, whereby rules were established, conditions met, and challenges overcome. Ostojic met the chosen respondent, German artist Klemens Golf, and their interactions led to personal exchanges, and ultimately, to their wedding. The work explores, through role-play, the details of immigration and the development of heterosexual, intimate relationships. In the work, Ostojic repositioned the "physical" body and its engagement in a social milieu, challenging public and private hierarchies in the complex world of identity politics.

Ostojic's critical exploration of borders, materialism, nationality, and intimacy push toward an understanding of activist principles as well as the impact of globalization and individuals' experiences of it. As the noted feminist scholar María Fernández argues in her extensive critique of Eurocentric political art practices, many involved in critical approaches, such as the cyberfeminist movement, have simply avoided issues of race, language, and other historical and material specificities in this discourse. If international work like Ostojic's means that collective action emerges as a tactic in global activism, the original aims of artistic intervention are more readily met.

In a world increasingly framed by borders, immigration, and migration, critical play has taken on an important role in performance and performative media in general. The strong political and utopian aspects of event-based, performative, and rule-based works are well suited for addressing the concerns of marginalized groups.[87] Critical play strategies also figure prominently in the methods of tactical media groups. Contemporary political art practice continually renews itself and emerges from a combination of interventionist theories and practices. The radical art and technology collective Critical Art Ensemble (CAE) is one such group. CAE uses everyday tactics of resistance similar to those described by the twentieth-century French theoretician Michel de Certeau to review and rework consumer culture.[88] CAE consists of both anonymous and known members and stages interventions and disruptions at various sites internationally. The group primarily relies on Situationist-styled interactions valued for their anonymity, surprise, mixed authorship, and brevity.[89] CAE practitioners startle their audiences in order to foster massive critiques of biotechnology, new media, and aspects of computer culture. Most of the work is staged in public at city squares, conferences, and street corners. These artists engage public interaction through the use of new technologies such as biometric equipment and computational systems.

The two partners in the activist arts pair known as The Yes Men claim to "agree their way into the fortified compounds of commerce, ask questions, and then smuggle out the stories of 'their hijinks' to provide a public glimpse at the behind-the-scenes world of business, also engage in political subversion and disruption. In other words, The Yes Men are team players . . . but they play for the opposing team."[90] Put another way, The Yes Men impersonate corporate and political leaders, those individuals or groups they believe to be criminals, in order to openly humiliate them.[91] Operating under the names Mike Bonanno and Andy Bichelbaum, the duo is famous for masquerading as representatives of Exxon Mobil, Dow Chemical, and the World Trade Organization. After gaining access to corporate events, The Yes Men disrupt annual meetings, shareholder speeches, and television appearances, producing media spectacles that critique the very seat of corporate and political power. For example, in 2006, the pair posed as WTO representatives to propose "Slavery for Africa." In 2004, The Yes Men posed as Dow Chemical representatives for a live BBC television interview. Once on the air, Bichelbaum announced Dow would claim full responsibility for the 1984 chemical disaster in Bhopal, India. The statement was accepted as genuine and triggered a storm of media inquiry that forced Dow to state again and again that, despite the massive destruction unleashed by the accident in Bhopal, the company had no such plan for taking responsibility or for making reparations. The Yes Men target those "leaders and big corporations who put profits ahead of everything else."[92] In their 2007 prank on Exxon, the speakers proposed that while oil excavation practices are becoming more harmful to the environment, increasing the chances of global calamity, the oil industry could "keep fuel flowing" by transforming the billions of people who die into oil. The representative "Shepard Wolff," played by Andy Bichelbaum, described a new technology that could be used to render the thousands of bodies about to die from climate disasters into a new Exxon oil product called "Vivoleum." 3D animations of the process made the joke of Vivoleum credible. Exxon representative "Florian Osenberg"—in fact, The Yes Man Mike Bonanno—noted, "With more fossil fuels comes a greater chance of disaster, but that means more feedstock for Vivoleum," for fuel from the bodies "will continue to flow for those of us left."[93]

As critical play, these performances offer challenging readings of existing systems of representation, politics, and power. This shift also provides a new working model for activists who would like to lose what Fernández terms as "colorblindness." Beyond mere exhortation or critique, the contributors encourage experimentation with communication systems, using the Internet as a tool of collaboration and social change.

A New Way to Play

An earlier and influential precursor to performance and play is the New Games Movement of the 1970s. Founders included Stewart Brand, creator of the *Whole Earth Catalog* (a late 1960s countercultural resource guide), and many designers, writers, and theorists who based their practice on an ethos inherited from the counterculture of 1960s California. These activists investigated ecological issues, sustainable design, and approaches to peace during the tumultuous Vietnam War era. No matter how carefree their pose and demeanor, members of the Whole Earth movement were quite serious in their belief that the types of games people play, as well as the way they play them, was culturally significant and could produce real behavioral and philosophical change.

In 1974, Brand and his collaborators organized a "New Games Tournament" where people could play large-scale, physical games. Play hard, play fair, nobody hurt—those were the three principles central to the design of any New Games spectacle.[94] The games were intended to alter the way people interacted with each other, especially in interactions that crossed perceived limitations of age, ethnicity, gender, and economic background. The New Games Foundation also published *The New Games Book* (1976), which became an influential text in experiential education and utopian thinking. In his introduction to the book, Andrew Fluegelman positions games as a way of getting people such as war protestors and activists to engage in new types of play. Here, Fluegelman also noted a concept from Stewart Brand termed *the softwar*, or the idea that "people could design their conflict forms to suit everyone's needs," as "conflict which is regionalized (to prevent injury to the uninterested), refereed (to permit fairness and certainty of a win-lose outcome), and cushioned (weaponry regulated for maximum contact and minimum permanent disability)."[95] In his "Theory of Game Change," Brand himself argued that one cannot alter a game by winning it, judging it, or watching it: "You change a game by leaving it, going somewhere else and starting a new game. If it works, it will in time alter or replace the old game."[96] As an example, the New Games organizers held a physical game called "Slaughter," whereby forty players competed for four balls and moving baskets. Instead of fighting people off the territory from within, in this case, pushing players from the mat, players pulled each other from one area to another. Part of the New Games Movement, then, was a shift away from game content to a new focus on game actions. Designers did not make games specifically based on the war in Vietnam, for example, or games about gentrification or racism, but turned instead to an emphasis on what players were actually doing in a game as the vehicle for change.

This focus on the player's action as a translation of political and social intent was far ahead of its time. The idea that player actions have real meaning will be explored more fully, but suffice to say that such subtle changes in game play, or game goals, can have larger ramifications when it comes to activist design. Designers might ask: what themes from the New Games Foundation have stuck? But to shift design concerns from content to mechanics reveals a fundamental epistemological change behind the idea of games. Knowledge in games is typically generated through doing. In this way, games are fundamentally experiential.

Critical "Doing"

By acting through a game's given "verbs," players are at work with two fundamental aspects of play: limits and agency. One cannot overestimate the effectiveness of what is actually done during game play, the expressive actions of a player. Janet Murray aptly describes agency as "the satisfying power to take meaningful action and see the results of our decisions and choices." Agency is fundamental to critical play precisely because doing and action, essential to performance, constitute knowledge.[97] Along similar lines, French theorist Jean-Francois Lyotard focused on the idea of the event and the use of performativity as a working principle of knowledge. According to Lyotard, performance can be seen to represent a form of knowledge: "No single instance of narrative can exert a claim to dominate narratives standing beyond it."[98]

The acts of navigating a game space, picking up items, reaching goals, interacting, or evading are distinctly linked to the concerns of performance. Game designers enact conflict and larger human themes, but what one is doing in a game matters significantly not only to the meaning of the game but also to players' understanding of their own actions. As Félix Guattari might say, game actions are machines of materiality, expression, desire, and politics.[99] In this way, a game's mechanic is its message.

The experiments by 1960s and 1970s video artists are also related to participatory history. Drawing from the work of the cinematic avant-garde, video artists used the popular, almost "crass" material of television to invoke a critique on consumption. Joan Jonas's *Vertical Roll* (1972) used out-of-sync video frequencies to produce optical illusions instead of understandable television narratives. Paper Tiger TV, an activist video art collective, expanded the reception of lesser-known video artwork through the development of an artists' television network. Like the New Games Foundation, a new kind of video art aimed to subvert the mass media format, playing "pranks" with the very medium of video itself.

Criticism of Game Methods

As shown, artists have long questioned many aspects of institutionalized art practice, as well as the role of the object. Through methods of critical play, they have problematized the product or outcome of artistic processes. Happenings and other instruction-based performances along with the rule-driven visual works of artists like Sol Lewitt now invest in the script or score as much as, or perhaps even more than, the traditional artifact or art performance. In fact, the goal of many conceptual artists was the elimination of a product altogether in favor of the system of creation itself.

But while artists critique others, they are also a self-critical group. Some Surrealists believed that paranoia-criticism (recall the method espoused by Salvador Dali and utilized by Claude Cahun and others) could help intervene in the physical world, yet earlier artists cautioned against the overuse of gaming methods. Tristan Tzara became disillusioned with automatism, saying it resided too close to fascism's "cultivation of unreason" to continue to work with it.[100]

The impossibilities within most Fluxus games hint at an inherent dichotomy: an art object is only useful if it invokes action. For Fluxus artists, a foundational truth is that art is found *in the action*. This makes games a sound strategy, for Fluxus rules invite action. But the rules of a game call attention to the process of creating that action in the first place. The impossibility of realizing many of the Fluxus games easily moves beyond the strategy of the joke, even if Maciunas distinguished on a 1965 Fluxus broadside between "ART" and "FLUXUS ART-AMUSEMENT," stating that

Fluxus aimed "for the monostructural and non-theatrical qualities of a simple natural event, a game or a gag."[101] Artists with Fluxus tendencies called attention to social rules of buying, selling, collecting, and canonizing in their own rule making. They also questioned the practices of the art world and of society through illogic, repetition, humor, and irony. Fluxus games culminate as complexities that, when taken to their end, unplay their own apparently simple themes and rules. Participant players become artists themselves, and formulate the opportunity for others to set individual goals during a Fluxus activity. Even at its most abstract, playful level, for the player-participant-artist, this activity is transformed into a game.

The philosophy behind much of conceptual art, then, is closely aligned with fundamental aspects of play. Game theorist Roger Caillois, who consistently argues that "unproductivity" is an essential aspect of play, reinforces this: "Property is exchanged, but no goods are produced."[102] Caillois goes on to argue that: "characteristic of play, in fact, is that it creates no wealth or goods, thus differing from work or art. . . . Nothing has been harvested or manufactured, no masterpiece has been created, no capital has accrued. Play is an occasion of pure waste; waste of time, energy, ingenuity, skill, and often money."[103] If in its noncommercial form conceptual art has historically been bound with behavior, patterns, and the processes of product, the works of conceptual artists are far more like play than anything else. Viewed this way, conceptual art and games are parallel worlds and perhaps it is due to this parallelism that they are able to offer alternate cultural theories, even utopian promises for living.

At the same time, while gaming and play function in particular roles in the work of contemporary artists, the participatory nature of certain gaming methods, such as those of the Surrealists and Fluxus artists, undermine how games are traditionally defined.[104] Dada activities, Surrealist games and play, and Fluxus antics all incorporate play, and sometimes these activities constitute games, especially in the case of certain Surrealist procedures. Such games encourage game scholars Salen and Zimmerman, Crawford, and others to point to these activities as play, for games, they would argue, must at the very least have a winner or loser. Critical artist's games, however, tend to be abstract or open. There are abstract games that incorporate "quantifiable outcomes," if one takes into account the prose of an automatic writing exercise, the Fluxus experience of art as *action*, or the finished "product" of a multiperson exquisite cadaver exercise. Yet games, even when played within particular economies and ideologies, capitalism or communism, for example, can embody their own system of exchange and function from a potent critical distance. The critical procedures and strategies of performative player-artists is a significant aspect of innovative, critical gaming practice.

As a cautionary note, however, it must be admitted that political and social climates make critical play, especially in the form of performance, unavailable to a significant percentage of the population. What would happen if The Yes Men were, say, immigrant women, or African American men? We can only speculate. But in the first part of the twenty-first century, minority artists would likely have difficulty entering venues and staking their claims. This is why radical groups such as the Guerrilla Girls use costume, or artists such as Keith and Mendi Obadike use online venues as an arena. If artists of color did manage to infiltrate certain places of power, the result might be deportation or prison rather than acclaim. What does this say about critical play's efficacy regarding real-world issues? How probable is it that everyday people may playfully intervene? In the final analysis, a critique of performance practices must ask: Who gets to play? For all its delights and wonders, twentieth-century art includes very few documented examples from women and people of color and despite the age of global communication it remains difficult to survey trends particular to marginalized artists. The history of art has not reflected these artists' accomplishments, and until the latter half of the twentieth century, most were simply ignored. Only a few writers, such as Linda Nochlin (1971), incorporate a critique of the elitism of the "high art" arena into their analysis of political and social movements.[105]

Another area of concern is the artistic use of technology. Alone this might lead to an inherent bias toward the status quo. This is noted in various research projects on emerging media technologies in developing areas. Leslie Shade Regan, for example, notes that those corporate interests that introduce new technologies foster consumption, rather than production or critical analysis.[106] This critique can easily extend to the play and consumption of even the most radical situations. The tight link between new technology and consumer culture is a major cause of concern. Shade Regan is quick to analyze ways the Internet can be said to be "feminized" as a site for popular content and consumption.[107]

Each of the art movements discussed in this book used participatory play, gaming as research method, art experience, and social tool to reflect upon everyday culture, often with the aim of actively redefining it. From Dadaist culture jammers and Surrealist gamers to Fluxus and beyond, each offered new perspectives on how to subvert and inform the creative process. Finally, as a form of critical play, performance elevates the role of the player and the aura of artworks shifts to the public.[108]

ARTISTS' LOCATIVE GAMES

The study of everyday life would be a completely absurd undertaking, unable even to grasp anything of its object, if this study was not explicitly for the purpose of transforming everyday life.

—Guy Debord, "Perspectives for Conscious Alterations in Everyday Life"

Introducing Contemporary Game Interventions

In earlier chapters,[1] forms of player subversion were observed in games ranging from Victorian era girls' play to board-game play to *Sims* play. Reskinning, unplaying, and rewriting formed the basis of some of this interventionist play. Physical movement, however, and the active use of space are frequently used as interventionist tactics as well, and location-based games are also often designed to unplay the dominant systems of control.

As early as World War I, Dada artists staged a number of interventionist street events, moving performance into public locations and engaging a mass public audience. Public game projects create critical alternatives not only to other games, but to street culture as well. Artists of the 1960s and 1970s, facing an art world still ensconced in tradition, specifically and playfully disrupted public space, often using nontraditional media like posters, video, and performance in reaction to a culture steeped in the themes of modernism and focused on masculinity.

Today, artists borrow freely from mapping and location technologies for creative purposes.[2] Groups like Blast Theory and Glowlab bring a new physicality to play. Many performative projects require mass participation, occur in cities, and are designed more or less as games. There is much contemporary interest in locative media and in particular, locative games that occur in forms of the public sphere such as news broadcasts, movies, parks, street corners, and in any form of advertising including graffiti, clothing, game characters, and music. At the same time, the use of certain technologies, some of which may be overly reliant on a compromised communication model or a Cartesian worldview can, by extension, reinscribe a power structure's implicit mechanisms of social control.[3] There have been several recent papers focused on the critique of a locative media that lies perilously close to industry and the military. Network theorists like Andreas Broeckmann note projects that might be the "avant-garde of the 'society of control.'"[4] Others ask whether, given the ubiquity of media and messages, and the collective privatization of the public sphere, play and games are emerging as instruments of protest, or as misguided specters of agency. Some investigators question the role of city space in these activities. Here, and with respect to historical movements, the work of the Situationists is particularly relevant.

Therefore, while examining locative games and spatial interventions, further questions arise, including: How might location-based play environments be presumed to hold problematic assumptions about space and the city? Why are urban locative media games emerging at this particular point in history? In what ways are the works emerging as political artifacts? Who is left out of these games? Finally, if technology is used, what are its effects? Can industrial systems reflect the contested nature of lived reality, space, and place? As will be shown, the current social and technological landscape presents certain peculiar characteristics and challenges to locative media works.

Toward an Interventionist Space

In discussing the uses of space and the tactics ordinary people deploy as a means of resistance, the transdisciplinary work of French historian and philosopher Michel de Certeau offers significant insight. As de Certeau noted, "Many everyday practices (talking, reading, moving about, shopping, cooking, etc.) are tactical in character if they become independent from the rhetoric of power. And so are, more generally, many 'ways of operating.'"[5] In other words, one's daily decisions can affect the hegemonic power structures that oppress. De Certeau wrote primarily in a historiographic mode, describing how gestures of resistance among the "disenfranchised" or "the other" give the powerless a way to survive and, at times, even thrive within or against dominant cultures. In particular, he examines the act of consumption, noting that consumers, instead of being passive and malleable, are in fact deploying "tactics" that operate within and against power systems such as capitalism.[6] Going further, de Certeau then describes his resuscitation of historical accounts as interventionist and, like Foucault, works to outline the dynamics of power that lie hidden in the very act of recording such marginalized histories. In turn, the attention de Certeau pays to everyday acts of resistance provides the evidence needed to question the prior, totalizing narratives fashioned by historians.

With his emphasis on the ordinary tactics of workers and artists who are "making do" with the fragments collected from power to support the individual, de Certeau's ideas can be used to argue for the effectiveness of subtle interventionist tactics on small, everyday levels.[7] For example, his observations on resistance tactics in consumer culture are well matched to behavior in games, especially when one examines the ways players determine their behavior. Player actions in video games frequently include tricking authority figures such as game administrators, using codes to comment upon, alter, or invert game play, and reskinning characters to introduce humor or absurdist readings in a game. In the online environments of the "digital vernacular," these tactics become de Certeau's "art of the weak."[8]

Mobile Media

Within this breadth of thinking about play on location, we should now move to an example of a work that has been described by its maker as a communicative game. Steve Symons's *Aura* (2004) is an interactive sound installation based on GPS, augmenting a particular participant's experience of a real space with three-dimensional sound environments. To engage with the work, participants wear backpacks containing small computers or PDAs (personal digital assistants) and walk around an outdoor space whose coordinates have been preprogrammed with sound clips—specifically, musical sounds and beats. As participants move to various positions, a particular sound mix is created based on the location and direction of movement, providing "full spatial listening that blurs the real world and artistic intervention. Sound takes on a physical quality in *Aura*, thereby encouraging the creation of 'sculptures of the mind.'"[9] The sounds stay fixed in terms of location, but the participants move from sound node to sound node. Therefore, space can be "mapped" by participants in terms of the sound they hear in a particular location.

Symons's project has been staged throughout various public squares in Europe and North America.[10] Noting that interaction between participants becomes "a communicative game based on aesthetic cooperation," the intention is for participants to somehow communicate and engage with each other to enhance or alter their own sonic experience of the space.[11] In *Aura*, sounds are assigned not only to spatial coordinates but also to interactors. Each participant, and his or her movement in relationship to other participants, creates sounds shared by several in the vicinity. When in proximity to each other, participants listen to the "collision" of sound as it is processed in real time, becoming, in effect, a sonic encounter. In this way, Symons compares the work to a multiuser computer game, in which such collisions can create a cooperative sonic game.

As much as the project creatively engages with participants as they encounter space, and each other, in the field of listening, the use of various latitudinal and longitudinal coordinates is not assigned particular meaning in the work. That is, the emphasis is on a music-like soundtrack, mixed live, and based on the relative positions of participants rather than on the space of encounter. On the one hand, this means that a public space, such as a square, is an entirely appropriate site to experience the work, for these are indeed sites for engagement and congregation. The work can be shifted to nearly any location and stay relatively the same in terms of audio location, proximity. On the other hand, the emphasis on the mix over the place infers that this work, like games to be discussed later in this chapter, is "location free," even though it has tended to take place in urban locations of historic and social relevance. Here, the issue of locality, of the embedded meaning of space, is a strategy calling for further development, even though Symons notes that *Aura* "is site specific work."[12]

It is useful to reflect on location and its relationship to play. Play, in its Huizingian magic circle, is not an activity that stays purely in the realm of the physical, but is also a *mental* construct, one in which participants might experience human values like beauty, goodness, justice, fairness. Even when crossing into taboo subjects, or resorting to extreme physical actions such as tackling in field sport, play possesses for Huizinga that "well-defined quality of action which is different from 'ordinary life.'"[13] Play is possible only when players *decide* it is possible. This involves permission, an agreement between players, and also between spectators or passersby.

On the first page of *Homo Ludens*, Huizinga asserts that play—whether it is among dogs, lions, or people—always has *meaning*. It is more than a mere physiological or psychological phenomenon, but a process of *signification*. Regardless of the specific definitions of play offered earlier in this chapter, one commonality figures into most scholarly interpretations of both games and play: the *significance of* signification. As a process of signification, play traverses ordinary life and allows players to take on difficult issues from an insulated position. From games to humor, from role-playing to the arts, from wordplay and poetry to gambling to festival, these activities are only *play* in context. What is play in one location, in one language, in one public space, may or may not be recognized as play in an entirely different context. With only a few exceptions, one can conclude that the phenomenon of play is *local*: that is, while the phenomenon of play is universal, the experience of play is intrinsically tied to location and culture.[14] Therefore, when examining locative media projects, one must interrogate the role of the *site*. Spaces have histories, social relationships, associated languages, customs, flora, and fauna. The importance of the site in terms of one or more cultural aspects is a frequent consideration in site-specific work. It is useful to ground the issue of locality and mobile artworks within earlier practices, such as that of urban engagement through the figure of the *flâneur*—that European detached pedestrian, the stroller/observer among city streets.

Much recent cultural studies scholarship has focused on *flânerie*, from its historical origins in early nineteenth-century Paris, to its promotion by Western thinkers such as Charles Baudelaire, Walter Benjamin, and a host of critics throughout the twentieth century.[15] Eighteenth-century flâneurs across Europe walked both to see and to be seen, committing to an urban engagement for social and aesthetic reasons (see an eighteenth-century painting depicting such strolling along a Venetian promenade in figure 6.1, and a nineteenth-century depiction of a Belgian promenade in figure 6.2).

In the twentieth century, flânerie slowly but surely transformed into the far more psychically grounded experiments of psychogeography, a discipline or method to study and experience the effects of environment and geography on emotions, thinking

| Figure 6.1 |

Giovanni Battista Tiepolo (1696–1770), *Venetian Promenade*, ca. 1750–1760. Image courtesy of the Art Renewal Center.

| Figure 6.2 |

Baron Jan August Hendrik Leys (1815–1869), *Promenade hors les murs* (*Walk out by the walls*), 1854. Image is courtesy of the Art Renewal Center.

processes, and behavior. Built largely on the writings and practices of a loosely associated group of writers, anarchists, and artists who formed the Situationist International (SI) movement, the group worked in and around Paris in the mid-twentieth century.

Situationists

Perhaps most well known of the activist-artists were the members of the Situationist International movement, a movement that described both a philosophy of space as well as political action. Formed in Italy (1957) by thinkers and artists of diverse practices, the various factions of the group were a force in political art until the 1970s. Whether it was the writing of philosophers Guy Debord, Michel de Certeau, and Henri Lefebvre that stimulated artists and students to carry out protests, actions, and art works in urban city centers, or whether these philosophers were inspired by students and artists already taking the streets by storm, the Situationist group emerged in the 1950s and grew to become influential for over a decade with projects aimed at everyday consciousness. 1968, members of the SI were involved in the May student revolution in France and in the occupation of French universities.

Drawing inspiration from Dada and Surrealism, the Situationists were interested in the banal, everyday acts of urban life that could be subverted in a radical redefinition of everyday experience. The first issue of the journal *Internationale Situationniste* (1959) defined "situationist" as "having to do with the theory or practical activity of constructing situations. One who engages in the construction of situations." Henri Lefebvre was closely involved in the group's early activities. Guy Debord (1931–1994), also known as the founder of the Letterist movement, and famed for his later ideas that society has now become a society based entirely on shock and grandiose display, called for the practice of "psychogeography" to consciously document the experience of environment and geography on emotions, thinking processes, and behavior. One of the significant intentions behind psychogeography, as Debord described it, was to be *mindful* of space in the method's open-ended, deliberately vague mission of encouraging people to explore their environment, usually the streets of the city. Psychogeography provided a means for participants to open themselves up to play and chance in context. It was a method of studying the world, combining compelling, inventive proposals with "the long-term aim of transforming 'the whole of life into an exciting game'—the play principle before the work principle."[16]

Through their manifestos, publications, and other writings, the Situationist International members detailed specific strategies to help achieve their critical purpose: to examine the psychological ramifications of the urban landscape: "We now have to undertake an organized collective work aimed at a unitary use of all the means of revolutionizing everyday life."[17] This revolution would occur through the creation of temporary *situations* that would offer a brief moment of transcendence from boredom, thought to be a counter-revolutionary state. Using what they referred to as the *dérive* (derive), or "drift," Situationists explored the urban terrain by enacting derives or drifts—migrations undertaken with the intention of discovering new perspectives on city life[18]—and practiced an active type of *flâneurship* whereby the formerly aristocratic walker was transformed into a conscious, political actor. According to Debord: "Our central idea is that of the construction of situations, that is to say, the concrete construction of momentary ambiances of life and their transformations into a superior passional quality. We must develop a methodical intervention based on the complex factors of two components in perpetual interaction: the material environment of life and the comportments which it gives rise to and which radically transform it."[19]

Obviously, this view was based on particular assumptions about statehood and human rights. As theorists, Situationists were bound by their time, place, class, language, and ethnicity, and may have failed to understand the *dérive* as an activity with

| Figure 6.3 |
Jean-François Millet (1814–1875), *The Walk to Work*, 1851. Image courtesy of the Art Renewal Center.

race, class, gender, and ethnic implications. Theirs was also a class-specific view, in that they prioritized the autonomy of the individual who has unrestricted movement. The flâneur was a figure possessing independence due to the celebration of freedom that walking intrinsically confers. They had the power to stroll at their leisure.

On the other hand, walking for most individuals was still a necessity. The majority of nineteenth-century workers made their way on foot over long roads; see figure 6.3 for a romantic view of this walk from painter Jean-François Millet from 1851. This image might serve as a reminder that much of this ideology speaks from a white, educated, and privileged middle-class specificity. Who after all really has unrestricted movement on roads, or in large cities? Which members of society have the time to follow whatever direction their curiosity takes? Who is really able to wander and drift?

While these limitations do detract from the potential of the SI members' efforts toward radical social and political change, theirs was still a movement founded in

Marxist ideology, serving to critique a commodity-driven culture and a growing bourgeoisie that allowed the consumption of both space and objects by a voracious cultural and economic machine. Inspiration was sought elsewhere with situations and experience elevated through playful, intuitive methods. The participant became the artist, constructing the art experience and using urban walking as a reflective, and critical, tool. On the surface, locative projects like Symons's *Aura* seem to be a type of sonic *dérive* created to both offer a heightened sense of space and forge social instances of cooperation and community. If it is indeed a site-specific work, the issue of locality, of the embedded meaning of space, is an aspect of the work that appears far less relevant to the intention of the piece than the facilitation of social interaction.

"Locative Media"

Play's ability to empower, build community, and foster collaboration and cultural change has been cited as a significant motivating factor in many location-based media projects. Intel researchers of ubiquitous computing recently helped organize the Inter-Society for Electronic Arts festival in 2006, noting that "the contemporary city is weighted down. We can no longer technologically or socially be constrained by something planned and canned, like another confectionary spectacle. We dream of something more, something that can respond to our dreams. Something that will transform with us."[20]

As a genre of projects and set of tools and technologies involving computing, mobile technologies, physicality, and location, *locative media* is asked to speak to those dreams through playful scenarios, interactive events, or actual games with rules and win states. Artists in this field are repurposing GIS/GPS, communications, and mapping technologies to create experiences labeled as diversely as "Urban Games," "Locative Art/Games," "Massive Games," "Flashmob Art," "Ubiquitous Games," "Hybrid Games," "Alternate Reality Games," and "Pervasive Games." Locative games offer an ambiguous or ambient game experience. Players explore ideas of participation and space, particularly the space of the city, by combining physical and technological play.[21] In most locative games, players also experience the game as belonging to the realm of ordinary life, since the events or play sessions often occur in recognizable places and situations. In many of these projects, themes of mobility and play are touted as liberatory, opportunities for interactions of scale and in environments where play has not been experienced. Here, play emerges as fabricated or designed phenomena in various locations. Commercial games, which already exploit locative media technology or pervasive play styles, include *The Beast, La Fuga, I Love Bees, Mogi, ConQuest, Numb3rs,* and *Crossroads*.[22] Locative games can have fixed play lengths or offer a scenario for play until a winner, or winning team, emerges.

In major cities such as New York, London, Sydney, Amsterdam, Minneapolis, and Tokyo, urban games and locative media have steadily increased in popularity. New York has hosted *Noderunner* (2002), a game in which players race to particular location nodes defined by the urban Wi-Fi grid.[23] Another game, called *PacManhattan*, led by Frank Lantz and a team of New York University students, enacted a locative performance of the *PacMan* game in Washington Square Park and its environs.[24] Asphalt Games used street corners as territory for players to capture.[25]

Outside New York, the Design Institute of the University of Minnesota commissioned *Big Urban Game* (2003), also known as the *B.U.G.* project, as a part of its Twin Cities Design Celebration. In this game, participants moved large-scale game pieces around the city in coordination with online voting on city maps.[26] Megan Heyward's *traces* (2005) explored locations in Sydney, Australia, and the relationships of these locations to people, place, and narrative. Australian based *Snap-Shot-City* (2006) is an ongoing international locative photography game. Blast Theory's *Can You See Me Now?* (*CYSMN*) (2001), *Uncle Roy All Around You* (2003), and *I Like Frank* (2004) enacted tag-like play patterns to merge offline and online play.[27]

Internationally, there have been a significant number of location-based media events held in the twenty-first century media arts arena. These share an acclaimed history with other city-based research initiatives.[28] In 2006, the Inter-Society of Electronic Arts held a conference in San Jose, California, centering on the theme of an "Interactive City." The conference focused on interactive systems and games based in urban terrains for "passers-by participants." Some of these games add participants until they are quite large play groups, potentially approaching the size of social smart mobs.[29] The Come Out and Play event, held annually in New York City, is another instance of the convergence of game design, art, and the use of technology. The appeal of urban play events and festivals demonstrates the increasing interest in urban play through locative media. In fact, media scholars have long linked psychogeography to games: "Psychogeography provided a means for participants to open themselves up to play and chance in context. It was a method of studying the world, combining compelling, off-the-wall proposals with the long-term aim of transforming, as film theorist Peter Wollen has suggested, 'the whole of life into an exciting game'—the play principle before the work principle."[30]

With aims similar to, though perhaps not as far-reaching as, this particular claim, the UK arts group Blast Theory's work is among the best-known collections of locative gaming projects in the world. Blast Theory makes interactive performances, installations, video, and urban-based mixed reality projects. Based in Manchester, England, the group combines research and development with games, narrative, and new technologies. The group's project *Can You See Me Now?* is a locative media game that has been performed in Sheffield, Rotterdam, Oldenburg, Köln, Brighton, and Tokyo. In this game, players around the world can challenge the members of the Blast Theory group online in a virtual city. Blast Theory runners, mapped via satellite, appear on a city map. Carrying handheld computers that track and transmit their location, the runners can also communicate with each other via walkie-talkie interaction, which in turn is broadcast to online users via streaming audio on the web. Allowing for up to twenty players at any given time, the game explores the ubiquity of handheld communications technology in the city. Noting that "some research has suggested that there is a higher usage of mobile phones among the homeless than among the general population," the group explores the mobile device as a common denominator for urban experience.

In Blast Theory's work, technology is thought to be normative.[31] According to Kate Richards, the stance is significant, and Blast Theory projects "extend user and audience affect outside the game—rather than delimiting our consciousness to the stereotypical and virtual, the game play pushes us to understand aspects of communities, our social responsibility and ourselves. This is partially achieved by the very visceral game play—in *CUSMN?* the players and gameplay self-generate affects of pursuers and pursued. . . . It was encouraging to see Blast Theory awarded the Prix Ars Electronica Golden Nica, which has in the past lauded some commercial, apolitical projects."[32]

Here, with the acquiescence of the participants, the city is transformed to playscape and city landmarks and streets become mere spaces on an existing game board, without meaning or history in their own right. An appropriation of the city as enacted by Blast Theory and other locative media groups means that space has been abstracted and decontextualized, in part because, as theorists such as Lefebvre have pointed out, the abstraction of space is in certain ways a capitalist strategy of power. According to Lefebvre, it is through everyday habits, and through the body, that people experience urban space.[33] One's personal preferences, identity, language, and social group or status all have a significant effect on urban experience. As Lefebvre notes in *The Production of Space* (1991), spaces that are defined in the abstract—that is, those aspects of space that can be installed anywhere, can be configured and reconfigured—become manifestations of a way of thinking produced entirely by capitalism. This is significant since capitalist spaces, to Lefebvre, are systems of property relations, surveillance, and consumption. Certainly most of the urban games discussed here, and the type of space these games typically produce, rely on an abstracted, loose relationship to the location in which they are played, thereby commodifying the urban landscape.

In this sense, urban critic Dennis Judd might be close to the heart of the matter when he argues that major urban centers have become spectacles of tourism and entertainment, and that these spectacles no longer serve residents, but have become tourist destinations in their own right. Cities attract a new form of tourist, a "post-tourist" and "unlike ordinary tourists, post-tourists do not wish to gaze upon officially sanctioned tourist sites," argues Judd. Framed this way, one can imagine ways in which locative media may remind us of an emerging industry that offers middle-class capitalist entertainment for the twenty-first century.[34]

In addition, questions that applied to Situationist efforts must also be asked of locative games: Who has time to engage in "alternate playgrounds?" Who has the freedom to explore those urban spaces in which designers should "create new sand-boxes in the metapolis" and promote playful encounters?[35] Some artists and designers certainly have answered the call to create such works at numerous events, but, objectively speaking, their efforts may need to better address real-world disparities.

Located Media: Organizing Tactics and Resistance

While international arts organizations and artists are beginning to explore the use of game-like projects in terms of space, this is still largely an emerging field outside wealthy Western nations. Therefore, the ways in which critical play manifests itself outside games and game scenarios in larger critical networks should also be noted here. In other words, there is another point of focus here, and having noted the popular new methods of locative media, it is instructive to turn to the everyday realities of "located media." This fledgling field, commendable for its plurality and transnational reach, as well as for its ability to build on both intellectual and grassroots contributions, crosses into powerful new territories. In doing so, located media provide a unique way to link institutions, such as galleries and universities, to the social and cultural organizations working with the ordinary issues of embodiment, play, and social interconnectedness. What is recognized in this practice is the need for further experimentation with play embodied in a location and the possible benefits of newer and more inclusive models of collaboration and social change.

For example, one way to access larger societal issues is via [mapscotch] (2007), a locative game that focuses on play and the interpretation of the environment in terms of mapping (figure 6.4).[36] Players are asked through small provocative cards to draw out hopscotch patterns on the pavement, addressing themes of displacement, translation, cultural negotiation, language, class, food, and power. For example, participants may be asked to construct a "laborscotch," or even a "humanrightscotch." All maps represent priorities and interests, embedding in their design philosophies about the environment and the way in which it is experienced. [mapscotch] translates the experiences of the city into *playable maps*, with the goal of instigating some kind of social change, or

| Figure 6.4 |
Conflux *[mapscotch]*, 2007, locative game. Photo by Doris Cacoilo.

at least conversation about social change. Using the old street game of hopscotch as a tool to explore and critique existing issues in social, preferably public spaces, *[mapscotch]* builds a counter-image of possible urban futures. Hopscotch works best with simple rules, but simple rules can generate complex, emergent, and intelligent systems.

To understand the importance of this shift to a focus on the spatial ramifications of a site, the history of site-specific art is particularly revealing. Long before contemporary art began to engage locative media, earthworks, architecture, and rituals were intrinsically bound to particular geographies. More recently, artists such as Sol Lewitt, Maya Lin, Daniel Buren, Christo, Nancy Hoyt, Robert Smithson, and Michael Heizer have created work that formed "an inextricable, indivisible relationship between the work and its site, and demanded the physical presence of the viewer for the work's completion."[37] The site can be a political cause or social issue, as much as a street corner, but it nonetheless engages with geographical relativity. Artists who worked at particular sites, as well as those artists who take the idea of site to the very material of the location and create earthworks (Smithson and Goldsworthy are two examples), were in part influenced by 1960s politics. In many respects, their motives in moving away from the traditional art systems of the museum, the gallery, and the collector were similar to the impulses of artists involved in Situationist International, Fluxus, Letterist, and performance art.[38] By making art that was anticommodity, that seemed impossible to collect, and was bound to location and social or spatial resonances of place, site-specific artists activated and politicized public arenas in their creative work.[39]

Play Actions vs. Spaces

Though historically artists have carefully involved the site in prior work, there are numerous examples of recent media-rich experiences, which refer to and appropriate space while divorcing it from its meaning, history, and significance. In September 2006, Eyebeam in New York City hosted Come Out and Play, a festival dedicated to street games. The festival offered three days of talks, parties, and events, all focused on "new types of games and play."[40] Some games did not refer to specific spaces, preferring to imply the use of space. In one example, Frank Lantz's *Identity Game* could have been played in a large house, conference center, or school instead of the urban street. Other games specifically took on street themes in their design.

In the locative media game *Cruel 2 B Kind* (*C2BK*), initial teams of two players act as assassins, stalking other teams and "killing" them with acts of kindness. These acts

| Figure 6.5 |
Come Out and Play 2006, *Cruel 2 B Kind* game in Manhattan. Photo courtesy of Tracy Fullerton.

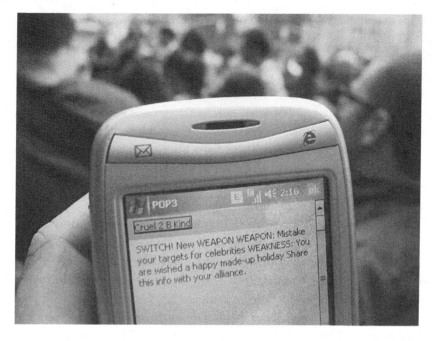

| Figure 6.6 |

Come Out and Play 2006, *Cruel 2 B Kind* game text instructions. Photo courtesy of Tracy Fullerton.

could be anything from a compliment to helping someone cross the street. Because play takes place in urban environments amid the general public, *C2BK* players cannot easily identify who is a player/actor and who is a bystander. In order to use a weapon of kindness, a player might, for example, try to compliment the shoes of a target from the other team to "kill" them. Players may, however, compliment a complete stranger in determining who is a player and who is not. Yet this compliment might also "kill" a target from the other team (figure 6.5). As a team-based mobile game, the assassination targets from the other team are successfully "picked off" the game board of the city, and those now "dead" join their killer's team and continue to play. The teams grow larger and larger in this manner until the climax, which features a showdown of two mobs descending upon each other for a "spectacular, climactic kill."[41] As the game rules note: "Will innocents be caught in the cross-fire? Oh, yes. But when your secret weapon is a random act of kindness, it's only cruel to be kind to other players."[42]

With *Cruel 2 B Kind* (figure 6.6), the use of "random acts of kindness" to dismantle the opposing teams involves, at times, unwitting participation of passersby, and

thus seeps over into an appropriation of passersby as game objects or nonplayer characters (NPCs). Interaction is motivated by the personal gains garnered in the game,
not by kindness in general.[43]

At a time when the gap between the richest and the poorest Americans is wider
than it has been since the end of World War II, and the gap between the richest and
the poorest in Manhattan is surpassed only in the disparities among a group of seventy households near a former leper colony in Hawaii, it seems as though the transformations of the city as a game board have been destined for the enjoyment of
the privileged.[44] Therefore, the audience for locative games could be expanded and the
concerns the games address could be more inclusive.[45] Many more examples of locative play could also be analyzed for their appropriation of space.[46]

Large-scale, mob-like games like *C2BK* offer a new type of human-centric, technologically mediated spectacle. Perhaps it is the contemporary conditions of labor, or
the role of mobile technology and media, which contribute to resurgence in Situationist thinking in relation to urban games.[47] Historian Adam Barnard theorizes: "People
have become divorced from authentic experience, are passive spectators of their own
lives and no longer communicate or participate in the society of the spectacle. The
dominant form of spectacular commodity production and consumption ensures that
people do not engage in self-directed or autonomous activity, but answer the needs
of the spectacle."[48] Once again, the question of empowerment must be noted in contemporary locative media examples.

Questions of Empowerment

As the work of Augusto Boal, the Situationists, and others have shown, subtle changes
in art and game play may have larger ramifications when it comes to social change and
activism.[49] Historical evidence proves these techniques can work. The resurgence in Situationist rhetoric in locative play projects is infused with a critique of consumerism, and
offers the promise of locative play that leads to a form of empowerment for participants.
Some proponents note, "Locative media strives, at least rhetorically, to reach a mass
audience by attempting to engage consumer technologies and redirect their power."[50]

Yet there are reasons to tread carefully through the space of locative games. It
is useful to recall Brian Sutton-Smith's assertion that "play is never innocent."[51]
While play has long functioned as a tool for cultural transmission, and as a forum for
empowerment and cultural change, it has also been ascribed a number of other functions. Ideas about the cultural role of play are at times conflicting.[52] Scholars frequently
use terms involving choice, need, practice, and the like. To consider the idea of possibilities of liberation inherent in play, Sutton-Smith notes that play is fun, voluntary,

intrinsically motivated; incorporates free choices or free will; offers escape; and is fundamentally exciting.[53] Linking play with taboo and survival issues,[54] Sutton-Smith holds out a wide net for what play can be, including gambling, children's play, festival, sport, creative activities, and nonsense. Some of these have already been explored at length.[55] But the question remains: Can locative play reflect the contested nature of lived space? If technology is used, can it too reflect the realities bound to space? Is locative media work mistakenly aligned with the principles of psychogeography, which, by its very nature, is distinctly political? Few of the projects in this medium address key concerns like biotechnology, consumption, war, identity, militarization, or terrorism. These are certainly central aspects of the contemporary interactive city. Are locative media events billed as artworks merely a new form of entertainment, a new spectacle? Are city spaces, as theorist Dennis Judd might argue in relation to new urban renewal projects, merely building a tourist city, one that chooses not to engage with local residents?[56] If artists' goals are to transform cities such as New York into game boards prompting play, what does it mean to "conquer turf" or "take out opponents" without regard for the city as a lived, social space? Is the city an impoverished space? An incredibly wealthy space?[57] As discussed earlier, Judd notes that cities are evolving to provide spectacle in the service of tourists, rather than of residents.

With this in mind, is locative play merely another problematic appropriation of space and custom, a form of entertainment "colonization"? In prior work, I noted the particularly problematic mythos of "frontierism" in some new media works and commercial software development. Many games nurture themes of conquest, individuality, survival, and dominance over the local inhabitants and natural landscape, a recurring trope in 3D gaming and in particular virtual reality (VR) work.[58] The use of location is a delicate matter, and artists making locative work need to recognize the prevalence of site as a social, discursive category. Scholars and artists must beware of a discussion of locative media that is ensconced in an unexamined rhetoric of innovation, liberation, and possibility. Indeed, for the Inter-Society for Electronic Arts (ISEA)'s call for participation in Interactive City 2006, questions included "What spaces could be accessed, created or re-imagined by a massively-scaled intervention?"[59] If play and interaction in the streets are to be empowering, exactly *who is to be empowered?*

Finally, artists and designers must take into account ideas about *who* plays in general. In their recent study of pervasive games, Swedish games researchers Montola and Waern note that in two case study games, each of the games raised ethical questions about the role of the "unaware" player in such experiences. In the game *Vem Grater* staged at Götland University, Sweden, players provided public clues by leaving notes, rearranging objects around the university, and making graffiti for gaming purposes. These acts were considered, at best, instances of vandalism by the university staff. And, for some, the use of an actor in the game in the role of occult investigator posed a danger to the academic community.[60] In *Vem Grater*, the custodial staff members were unfortunately the losers, as they had to undo the clues, graffiti, and what had been moved. In a look at another game, the Stockholm-based *Prosopopeia*, Montola and Waern note that the community protested the game on the grounds that people should not play pranks on others without their consent; *Prosopopeia* involved explicit tasks that fundamentally required participation by outsiders, such a priest.[61] In this game, most participants are not players; the NPCs are unaware that there is a game going on, and unwillingly commodified by the players.

In major cities throughout the world, the homeless, prostitutes, and domestic workers possess the streets in a way that speaks to economic and social *disempowerment*. Their "drift" is not one of exploration or privilege, but a search for a place to sleep or for labor. In the digital age, with economic, intellectual, and cultural divides both effective and prevalent, some artists and theorists may have grave doubts about following in the footsteps of creators of an urban game or locative media event whose premise of "interventionist" work actually manifests as an entertainment spectacle for an advantaged audience. While individual freedom and rights can construct subjectivity from looking and experience, some participants still emerge more empowered than others. Few location-based art projects are nuanced enough to address these kinds of issues.

When artists and designers set about to create an environment for play, the rhetoric surrounding the role of play, and the rhetoric of power, are consistently intertwined. Players have abilities. In games, players are agents of action and change. In the mere act of deciding to play, an understanding of the shift in potential occurs among players, for in games, rules set up novel frameworks for action and agency. Artists have long been critical users and consumers of play systems, and in addition to its role in entertainment culture, play has long been used as a tool for practice, education, and therapy. From war games, in which troops sharpen their skills before battle, to games involving learning about science, to games that help one tease out reactions to phobic scenarios, these "uses" of play are thought to lead to a kind of rehearsal, a practice, a type of empowerment. When taken to the streets, this empowerment can be transformed into a reengagement with the city and thus reclamation of that space. But if this is a goal, it must be integrated into the mechanic and the setting of the game system developed. Taking play onto the pavement, in this light, cannot be seen as a de facto act of empowerment in and of itself.

To return to Lefebvre once again, the appropriation of the city has meaning beyond the urban grid or its buildings. One can divide space into categories of spatial practices, for example, perceived space, routes, and patterns of interaction. Divided in terms of representations, space can be a cultural and social order organized by scientists, planners, and so on. Space can furthermore be tied to maintaining the public good, or to knowledge. Lived space and lived experiences constitute the space of everyday life. Such space is not cohesive or consistent, but is embedded in a history of a group of people, or a history of a site. Lefebvre argues that much of urban space is dominated by the powerful through architecture and urban or town planning, while representational space is a living, emergent practice, linked to encounter, art, or community. Representational spaces "need obey no rules of consistency or cohesiveness."[62] Therefore, while many locative media games are designed around particular representations of space, a public square, or a pattern of streets, the games designed for these spaces often omit the emergent qualities of lived representational space.

This distinction is essential to understanding both the strengths and the shortcomings of the social and political power of locative games. If Lefebvre is correct in his belief that the creation of new spaces has the ability to change social relations, locative games must address history, lived experience, and site in order for both participant and designers to learn how to produce something better—another city, another space, a space for and of social equity and change.

Revisiting Huizinga and play's signification function, if play is local, then play within those spaces cannot help but refer to, rework, or, conversely, avoid history, social relationships, and customs of a play site. Inventing new and conscientious forms of play requires also inventing a context for that play, one that inclusively examines empowerment, location, and the specificity of culture at that location. This does not mean that the games cannot be fun, but rather, that this type of design practice be reflective and sensitive in its design.

While art must indeed break borders, there are many instances where the borders broken are misguided and actually reinforce existing class, ethnic, and other power structures. Australian writer Danny Butt, for one, calls for a "'new media' in which the technologically augmented experience of location is inseparable from a philosophy of land and belonging."[63] Critiquing what he calls new media's overly abstract, modernist stance,[64] Butt asks artists to reground their work with sensitivity so that novelty is not the only motivating force behind the work.

Offline Locational Gaming

Since locative media projects borrow heavily from both the language and philosophy of the Situationist International, one cannot avoid interrogating the role of situation as well as location in urban play-based projects. The flâneur, the new drifter, held for members of SI the possibility of subversive transgression.[65] International artists, technologists, urban adventurers, and the public celebrated these principles at the Glowlab's Conflux event in New York in 2006.[66] Many of the events at the Conflux, the annual festival for contemporary psychogeography, sent participants out in playful drifts to explore the ramifications of everyday city life. From the very beginning, ideas about psychogeography were bound to the creation of situations, but the concept of situations expanded over time to take on not only the urban walk but also the entirety of space of the city and beyond. The idea was to propose delirious experiences that would not only seduce citizens to become partipants, but that would end up "transforming the whole of life into an exciting game'—the play principle before the work principle, homo ludens, in Huizinga's words, before man as thinker or worker."[67]

Debord suggested, for example, that all the equestrian statues in Paris should be taken down and reassembled somewhere in the middle of the Sahara desert, arranged in the formation of "an artificial cavalry charge." He added: "Not just all the statues in Paris, in fact, but all the statues 'in all the cities of the world'! The new ensemble should be 'dedicated to the memory of the greatest massacres of history, from Tamburlaine to General Ridgway.'"[68]

In was in this spirit that one group of Conflux festival artists attempted to engage locational specificity in their project. Other projects use the drift to create situations that span borders and interrogate international policy, but *You Are Not Here* (*YANH*) by Thomas Duc, Kati London, Dan Phiffer, Andrew Schneider, Ran Tao, and Mushon Zer-Aviv is a self-proclaimed "urban tourism" game that takes place in the streets of New York City and invites participants to become metatourists on an excursion through the city of Baghdad (figure 6.7).[69]

Supplied with a map of both cities printed back to back, players of *YANH* were provided with a tourist map of Baghdad to guide them through a walk down the streets of New York. Participants navigate to sites posted on lamps, signs, and buildings, which mark various Iraqi landmarks within the spatial bounds of the American city. Offering a tourist hotline, participants could listen to a *YANH* audio guide to the Iraqi site. At the point designated to represent central Baghdad's Firdos Square, participants received a voiceover recording about the toppling of the statue of Saddam Hussein. In addition to the facts, the voiceover noted that the event might have been staged as a spectacle for U.S. journalists and military personnel. Here, location is a contested concept, for the two cities, both the subject of U.S.–Middle East hostilities, are inextricably intertwined though physical alignment in the project. In this way, the meaning of *YANH*, contrary to many other location-based projects discussed in this chapter, lies directly in each site "visited," and uses technology to explore the

| Figure 6.7 |
You Are Not Here (.org) participant, September 2006, Conflux Festival, Brooklyn, NY.

| Figure 6.8 |
You Are Not Here (.org) in July 2007, Rabin Square, Tel Aviv (or, alternatively, The National Palestinian Football Stadium, Gaza).

| Box 6.1 |
Transition Algorithm by Suyin Looui, 2006

The Rules

1. Visit a neighborhood in transition.
2. Take a photograph(s). This photograph documents physical changes to the neighborhood and street life, whether they are juxtapositions; conflicts; changes in language, ideals and politics; interactions between people, old and young, rich and poor.
3. Take home a souvenir. This item cannot be something purchased but should mark the changes taking place in the neighborhood. The souvenir can also be a memory of an overheard conversation or observed interaction.

---

relationship between sites (see figure 6.8). *You Are Not Here*, then, engages the issue of locality and mobile artworks within its very premise, linking locations and therefore histories metaphorically and physically.

The transitional aspects of an urban environment are manifest in the work of new media artist Suyin Looui. Looui's *Transition Algorithm* (2006) (box 6.1) presents itself as a set of instructions with an identifiable outcome, and leads players through the streets of New York City, documenting neighborhoods characterized by cultural fractures and collisions (figure 6.9). Looui chose to design an experience focused on neighborhoods under the threat of gentrification, places where racial and cultural communities exist and overlap and come into conflict. Her urban algorithm, designed to position players at points where there are such conflicts, explicitly plays with and uses a tourist's lens as a way to investigate and document places in transition. Participants take home photographs and souvenirs of their "travels" from New York City neighborhoods as diverse as Jackson Heights, Williamsburg, Lower East Side, and others.

Likewise, the sound artist and locative media practitioner Samara Smith designed *Chain Reaction* (2006), a locative game with the goal of sensitizing players to the disappearance of independent enterprises in New York City (figure 6.10). To align her project with other performative action projects, Smith looked to Boal's idea of action and the individual's state in such action: "Theatre—or theatricality—is the capacity, this human property which allows man to observe himself in action, in activity. . . . Man can see himself in the act of seeing, in the act of acting, in the act of feeling, the act of thinking. Feel himself feeling, think himself thinking."[70] This urban game requires the participants to change direction each time they encounter a pedestrian

| Figure 6.9 |

From Suyin Looui's *Transition Algorithm*, Les Enfants Terrible French restaurant amid Chinatown stores, 2006.

carrying a particular consumer item. For example, one rule set requires that the players change directions each time they see a Starbucks coffee cup or Barnes and Noble bag. Participants are released and allowed to walk in any direction they choose only when they encounter an independent bookstore or music seller. Maps of each walk reveal differences in various neighborhoods around New York. A fun and participatory way to explore and map urban space, this game's type of investigative rule set holds interesting potential for community-based documentary projects (instructions are detailed in box 6.2).

Media artist Ariana Souzis' *Cell Phone-Free Temporary Autonomous Zone* (2006) (*CFTAZ*) is inspired by Augusto Boal's community theater exercises and Hakim Bey's concept of the Temporary Autonomous Zone (TAZ). Bey's theory, based on his research of pirate utopias, islands where pirates of the eighteenth century formed communities outside the law, is clearly influenced by the Situationists' notion of constructed situations.[71] In his elaboration of these concepts, Bey claimed that the way to revolt against modern life was through the creation of temporary autonomous zones that enable "socio-political tactics of creating temporary spaces that elude formal structures of control."[72] As Bey notes, "Like festivals, uprisings cannot happen every

Chapter 6

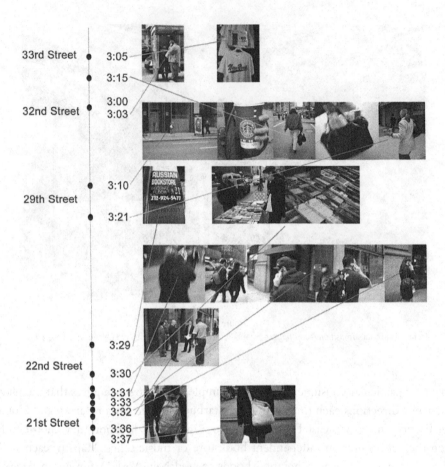

33rd Street   3:05

              3:15

              3:00
32nd Street   3:03

29th Street   3:10

              3:21

              3:29
22nd Street   3:30

              3:31
              3:33
21st Street   3:32

              3:36
              3:37

| Figure 6.10 |
A diagram of one session of Samara Smith's *Chain Reaction*, 2006.

| Figure 6.11 |

Cell Phone-Free Temporary Autonomous Zone participants, organized by Ariana Souzis, 2006.

day—otherwise they would not be 'nonordinary.' But such moments of intensity give shape and meaning to the entirety of a life. The shaman returns—you can't stay up on the roof forever—but things have changed, shifts and integrations have occurred—a *difference* is made."[73]

Along these lines, Souzis designed and implemented a TAZ where participants would agree to not use their cell phones, in order to liberate participants from what she saw as a demanding, and at times oppressive, technology (figure 6.11). In this game, also conducted in New York City, Souzis required participants in a specific space and time to follow a set of rules—which, ideally, they determine themselves.

Participants wear "cell-phone free" badges to mark themselves as nodes in the zone, and move through space wearing them. This zone explores a simple way participants can transform their experience of public space both individually and collaboratively and with or without technology. *CFTAZ* also provides liberation from the demands of time and communications technologies, the goal being a transformative

| Box 6.2 |
Chain Reaction by Samara Smith, 2006

The Rules
1. Choose from one of the following sets:

SET ONE

Lead Objects:
a. a Macy's bag
b. a Bloomingdales bag
c. a Duane Reade bag
d. a Gap bag

Release Objects:
a. a homemade sign
b. graffiti/street art

SET TWO

Lead Objects:
a. a Barnes and Noble bag
b. a Starbucks cup

Release Objects:
a. an independent book or music store
b. a street vendor selling books or music

SET THREE

Lead Objects:
a. people wearing white headphones
b. people talking on cell phones

Release Objects:
a. street musicians
b. anyone singing or dancing
c. two or more people stopped on the street having a conversation

SET FOUR

Noticing what you see and don't see, create your own set of lead and release objects and follow your own rules. If you want to keep going after set four you may return to set one and repeat the process.

2. Beginning near a subway stop, stand on any Manhattan street corner.
3. Wait until you see someone pass with any of the lead objects. Once you see the first lead object, begin that set.
4. Each time you see someone with one of the lead objects, begin walking in that direction. Continue only in that direction until you see another lead object. At that point, continue in the direction of the new lead object.*
5. When you see one of your set of release objects, you may stop and do whatever you like until you see one of the other sets' lead objects.
6. Once you see one of the remaining sets' lead objects, return to step three and repeat the process with the new set of objects.
7. Keep a tally of the lead and release objects you see and the times you spend in each phase.
8. At each release moment, stop to document your walk thus far. Map where you walked, and note what you saw. You may also want to document the lead and release objects as you go.
9. If time is an issue, you may shorten the process by releasing yourself from any one step after fifteen minutes should you have not progressed to the next set in that time.

*Participants do not have to follow the lead objects, just begin walking in the direction they are being carried. They may only change direction with each new lead object that passes in a new direction or upon seeing the release objects. For example, is the first person you see carrying a Gap bag and walking east? Then you must keep walking east until you see another of the lead objects or a release object in that set.

space that encourages participants to envision a different experience outside that with which they might be familiar.

Readers may notice that many of the projects discussed in this chapter that appear most sensitive to issues of space, location, and place *also* happen to be those that involve minimal technologies or remove technologies altogether. Here, I would like to suggest that it is not due to some inherent bias against technologies, but rather, that the design of locative play and games might evolve to take into account the lived experience of those spaces, and the mediated experience of such spaces as a secondary issue. While inhabitants of cities often experience these phenomena as one and the same thing, this is not typically the central or unifying feature of the locative media projects previously critiqued. These "low-tech" experiences also closely match the ethos of Situationist exploration, spending less time on the technological means for creating a project and choosing instead to interrogate the conceptual concerns surrounding their staging.

This type of interrogation is key to developing ethical media projects that can also challenge, inquire, and empower. As geographer Don Mitchell notes, social change continues to entail a street-centered reclamation of public space by creating disorder where there was once order, or by challenging a particular way a space has in the past been experienced.[74] While there is opportunity for protest and empowerment through play, play also must be carefully organized to have a lasting and meaningful impact. Space must be understood, ordered, and reexamined, and, where technology is used in a project design, that technology must begin to reflect the contested nature of the lived reality of such spaces.

Hybrid Play?

What happens when game makers and players begin to blend spaces such as public urban space and online game space? These instances of play bounded by space offer yet another social critique of the influence of electronic games. Computer games especially can be seen as critical frameworks that engage space and, when used in the context of artistic practice, become environments in which player-participants can make meaning that directly relates to urban spaces. There are additional deep ties to interventionist art practices in viewing the fluidity of performance, the city, and the simultaneous reading and authoring of social interaction in electronic game worlds. In turn, artists' appropriation of games in large-scale, public spaces presents a potent approach to social change.

Here, the projects of game designer Katie Salen are useful for thinking about performance and games. Her *Big Urban Game*, mentioned earlier in this chapter, was designed by Salen, Nick Fortuno, and Frank Lantz to call attention to urban planning and involves massive, local participation. The *B.U.G.* project served as an innovative way to investigate social change through urban space and participatory play. The game was a race between three teams—red, yellow, and blue—each composed of Twin Cities residents, who try to move their own twenty-five-foot-high, inflatable colored game piece through different neighborhood checkpoints in the shortest time with the common goal of reaching the Lake Street Bridge. The progress of the three teams was tracked electronically each day, and shown in the local newspapers and on TV news. The public could participate with the players to choose the fastest route to the next point by voting online or calling the *B.U.G.* 800 number. The players, volunteers from the community, raced their pieces through the city following the path that earned the most votes.

The most interesting part of *B.U.G.* is the emphasis on watching the game pieces crossing neighborhoods, sometimes quite disparate neighborhoods, and the resulting tendency groups of residents had to mingle and play together. *Big Urban Game*, which not only took the city of Minneapolis by storm but represented an adventurous experiment in urban design research, led to *Karaoke Ice*, a project that also explores the realm of the participatory public work (figure 6.12). Like an earlier political work by *Tactical Ice Cream Unit* (2005) by the Center for Tactical Magic, this entertaining project, which centers on a karaoke-rigged ice cream truck, was a collaboration by Nancy Nowacek, Katie Salen, and Marina Zurkow, with help from students and graduates of

| Figure 6.12 |

Nowacek, Salen, and Zurkow, *Karaoke Ice*, 2006, is spotted in Santa Monica, CA, 2007. Photo courtesy of the author.

| Figure 6.13 |

Nowacek, Salen, and Zurkow, *Karaoke Ice*, 2006, in Santa Monica, 2007. Photo courtesy of the author.

the CADRE Laboratory for New Media, with music produced and arranged by Lem Jay Ignacio in 2006. *Karaoke Ice* first took place in the city of San Jose during the ISEA digital arts conference in 2006 and continues to operate.[75]

In *Karaoke Ice*, the truck, named "Lucci," is staffed by a master-of-ceremony character (in actuality, a person in a computer graphics–inspired squirrel outfit) named Remedios who hands out ice pops to the public. At certain intervals, the rear of the truck becomes a stage, opening to reveal space for two singers complete with a revolving disco ball. The designers believe the truck can be used to unite people in a collective mission to perform and document community character, as it did in the 2006 ISEA Interactive City events. As the truck moves from neighborhood to neighborhood, new groups form to sing and play together. The truck, stopping in parking lots and on street corners, automatically attracts a crowd whose busy trajectory is interrupted by a participatory, musical interlude.

Any passersby may climb into the truck, choose from a menu of "interpreted pop," or familiar songs morphed to match the ice cream bell–style theme of music, and perform for the audience (figure 6.13). The play space generates player pleasure and engagement, and this understanding translates to light-hearted, collaborative play experiences. An entertaining form of social intervention emerges commercial-free from the spectacle, fostering new experiences of community and fifteen seconds of neighborhood fame for those willing to sing.

| Figure 6.14 |
Ricardo Miranda Zúñiga, *Vagamundo: A Migrant's Tale*, on the road.

In a similar manner, Ricardo Miranda Zúñiga's *Vagamundo: A Migrant's Tale* highlights the experiences of illegal Mexican immigrants in New York City through a transportable arcade-style interaction. The artist describes the game as a "mobile public art" project. Using a battery-powered ice cream cart containing a computer, joystick, and monitor, he takes the immigration game into the urban neighborhoods.

In *Vagamundo*, players stand alongside the cart (figure 6.14), looking down at the computer screen as they control and play the role of the central game character called "Cantinflas." Cantinflas, a character from classic Mexican cinema, engages in slapstick humor while attempting to overcome obstacles to get ahead in the game. After sneaking across the border in a standard arcade style, the player must avoid flying liquor bottles in order to get a job. Evoking the serious underlying themes of this game, Miranda Zúñiga notes: "Since 9/11, the Bush administration has added 100 million

| Figure 6.15 |
Ricardo Miranda Zúñiga, *Vagamundo: A Migrant's Tale*, level one.

dollars to border patrol, increasing the annual tab to 2.5 billion dollars. However the number of people crossing the border has not decreased, though the number of mortalities along the trek across the border has increased, perhaps this is the point."[76]

Vagamundo is constructed with three levels of play, each intended to represent a "move up" the social scale and, therefore, an assimilation into U.S. culture (figure 6.15). Between levels, grave facts about immigration, border crossing, and immigrant life inform the players that while the game may appear simple and fun, the situation for most immigrants is a dire one. In level two, Cantinflas arrive at a New York corner store, where cockroaches emerge and wander towards our hero while mutating into huge, threatening thugs (figure 6.16).

While the graphics in the game cross into the ridiculous—for example, players can guide Cantinflas into a knockdown fistfight against a gigantic cockroach in order to learn English—the immigrant *Vagamundo* poses some of the same questions and concerns that propelled Victorian doll play. As a framework for "home," *Vagamundo* engages questions of assimilation and the process of fitting into cultural norms, albeit lightly through its arcade-style game play.[77] Other similarities to Victorian doll play are highlighted in the ways in which players are confronted with information about

| Figure 6.16 |
Ricardo Miranda Zúñiga, *Vagamundo: A Migrant's Tale*, level two.

the death rates of immigrants attempting to cross the border. The macabre, violent play of flying liquor bottles and disturbing insects exposes the dark side of custom and culture.

The work of cultural theorist Homi Bhabha addresses the issues surrounding migration and the complex relationships among community and kinship, language, and the concept of nation, by arguing that the loss produced by migration translates into a metaphor of home that makes the meaning of belonging manifest. In this time of unprecedented human movement, is there something about the metaphor of home that works to unify a sense of place in the liminality of digital environments? Games may be apt vehicles to explore the complexities of migration if only because they emphasize the problematic boundaries of modernity and enact the "ambivalent temporalities of the nation-space."[78] If, as Bhabha argues, "the 'unhomely' is a paradigmatic colonial and post-colonial condition," what does it mean in play spaces to "write home" in such contexts?[79] That domestic play here can be read within the larger manifestation of the idea of home, a theme that becomes a site of international political and social importance explored in critical play.

Creating meaningful social change with artists' games has larger implications for activists. Theorists of activism such as Michel de Certeau note that power must be changed in fundamental, internal ways. Tactics such as bartering, trading, *la perruque* (meaning to work for oneself while "on the clock" for another), and the use of discarded materials undermine the rules of the larger social game one is bound within.[80] Judith Butler has also offered a critique of contemporary activist strategies. Along with other theorists, Butler argues that it is not enough to present a simple subversion of a stereotypical norm, such as the strategy I've identified as reskinning might imply. Rather, it is only through changing the *logic* of traditional relationships and categories—in Butler's specific case, categories such as gender—that larger systemic changes can be effected. Positions such as Butler's recognize the fact that social systems hold many fixed categories from gender to class, race, and economies and that these systems can only be challenged by examining the categorizations that sustain them.[81] Players in these locative game systems also become players outside the system. In the next chapter, we will see further work in activist use of computer game systems. We will also look at ways in which some artists keep their messages on the screen to say what they need to say.

CRITICAL COMPUTER GAMES

Since the 1990s, the extraordinary impact of individuals affiliated with the arts starting "grassroots wildfires" and "building guerilla technologies" in their quest for creative intervention has flourished onscreen. That context is important for this phenomenon is obvious. Computer games are more profitable and popular than ever before and have become a major cultural medium crossing a wide range of social, economic, age, and gender categories. Indeed, from casual games played on the Internet to large-scale stand-alone games like *The Sims*, *Metal Gear*, *Bioshock*, or *Grand Theft Auto*, or the millions of players in massively multiplayer online role-playing games (MMORPGs), the popularity of computer games suggests a "revolution" measurable in terms of financial, social, and cultural impact.[1] As a cultural medium, games carry embedded beliefs within their systems of representation and their structures, whether game designers intend these ideologies or not. In media effects research, this is referred to as "incidental learning" from media messages. For example, *The Sims* computer game is said to teach consumer consumption, a fundamental value of capitalism. *Sims* players are encouraged, even required, to earn money so they can spend and acquire goods. *Grand Theft Auto* was not created as an educational game, but nonetheless does impart a world view, and while the game portrays its world as *physically similar to our own*—setting one of its stories and action in the city of Miami, for example, and presenting humanoid avatars as characters—the game world's value system is put forward as one of success achieved through violence, rewarding criminal behavior and reinforcing racial and gender stereotypes. Many scholars, game makers, and consumers observe that computer games can embody antagonistic and antisocial themes including theft, violence and gore, cruelty, problematic representations of the body in terms of gender and race, and even viciously competitive approaches to winning as a primary game goal.[2] While these practices are, of course, not the case for all games, related issues arise in a significant number of popular games and frequently overwhelm other, subtler interactions and representations. At the same time, artists continue to use games to take on social and cultural issues. Although much of contemporary play takes place online and onscreen in commercial environments, an exploration of computer-based artists' games is essential to understanding the complete picture of contemporary critical play.

As mentioned earlier, the popularity of online networks, peer-to-peer exchange, and games have made playculture itself into a type of revolution. However, as formative cultural artifacts, games and game cultures are problematic. First, the computer games industry around the world is not inherently diverse. In the United States, for instance, the statistics in the game industry mirror those in other computer-related fields, and the demographic of the games workforce—the people who make the games—reflects the overall, limited expertise of the general public in computer languages and technologies. The number of women enrolled in computer science degrees has, surprisingly, declined considerably in the last twenty years.[3] Black and Hispanic Americans represent a small percentage of all computer systems analysts and computer scientists working in the field, and well under 10 percent of programmers.[4] The inequities that result are troubling, especially at a time when computers have become central to most disciplines and when computer games are emerging as a dominant medium. Researchers have described the dearth of diversity in technology professions as a social justice issue.[5] As noted by many industry insiders, the vast majority of technology companies that produce games do not target women or people of color as players.[6] Therefore, as gaming drives the development of new technology, and new technologies are made by a consistently similar demographic, the cycle of technological innovation and games entertainment remains fairly consistent. This has the unfortunate affect of keeping high-tech domains primarily white, primarily male, and primarily profit driven.

Therefore, commercial, masculine computer artifacts have taken pride of place in contemporary culture, whereas noncommercial technology tools, including artistic games, are relatively rare. Artist Martha Rosler argues, "Art with a political face typically gains visibility during periods of social upheaval."[7] The information revolution continues to be a disruption of older, more traditional modes of production and labor. With this change have come both an inscription of new technologies across more traditional roles, and also a significant movement towards the monitoring and control of the individual. This technological adoption and *adaptation* creates a continued disparity in working conditions, privacy, privileges, and wages, even in Western high tech arenas.[8] The computer is a portal to digital culture; however, it is more than a tool. Technological literacy and competence are essential to disadvantaged groups, which are once again in an unequal position in terms of experience and ranking in key fields. Artists and activists tend to be the ones who uncover such realities experientially, sometimes by playfully making work that comments on technology itself.

At the same time, within the culture of computer games, race, ethnicity, language, and identity relations including gender emerge as complex and contradictory. According to a recent Pew Research study, game playing is universal among young people.[9] Women also do play games, yet this play emerges differently than the play of their male counterparts. Women are perceived to be the primary audience for casual games, for example. In Western countries, computer games are still perceived as an arena created by and for white men, with women comprising approximately 10 percent of the game development workforce in the United States.[10] Current trends indicate that those who label themselves as gamers are moving out of the PC game market and onto consoles, while female players and those new to gaming, such as older age groups, may be migrating to the PC for casual games, to cell phones, Wii-style sytems, and handheld devices for play across mobile technologies.[11] An entirely new group of adult female gamers emerged to play online social games such as *The Sims Online, EverQuest, Uru,* and *World of Warcraft.*[12] Games that depict everyday activities such as communication, social negotiation, caring for elements or characters that are part of a game world, or stabilizing precarious situations have become extremely popular with female players. In 2003, for example, it was a novelty to have more than one hundred thousand simultaneous players in an online game, but this happened in the game *EverQuest*; subsequently, the massive multiplayer *World of Warcraft* claimed a total of ten million users signed on in 2008 and broke *EverQuest's* simultaneous player records.[13] Despite contradictions in data, there is evidence that women constitute either the largest, or second-largest, group of online gamers. The largest group has been cited as women aged thirty-five to forty-nine.[14] Games journalist Kris Oser notes that women players, however, are still almost an invisible constituency to advertisers and game designers. While the statistics show us that women are increasingly playing games, few are envisioning and constructing these software environments.[15] On top of these industry figures, few contemporary artists engaged with games are women.

Despite the probable social benefits that could result, game designers have yet to grapple with the full range of inequities ingrained in the player categories and game models exhibited in most of today's games. Possible overcategorization or reductionism from such classifications—for example, which designers are included under the rubric of "activist games"—is worth risking should such research provide for useful discussions, the design of alternate subject positions, new possibilities of agency, a revitalization of authorship, the promotion of equity, or other redefinitions of the cultural constructs currently embedded in digital environments.

In a further complication, the lack of diversity in the creative documentation by those at work in these movements makes it challenging to trace any historical practices that lie on the fringes of the accepted art world. Other than Alison Knowles's *House of Dust* (1967), for example, there may be no earlier accounts of the development of full-blown computer games by women until *Mystery House*, an interactive narrative game by Roberta and Ken Williams and the first computer game to incorporate graphics of any kind (1980).[16] In addition, there is poor representation of artists of color in these art movements, and a lack of designers, scientists, and others of color in contemporary gaming culture.[17] Female artists and scientists, as well as artists and scientists of color, have certainly been involved in the major art and technology movements in the twentieth century—or have worked in parallel to them. More documentation and inspection is needed to broaden the way in which their recorded histories are shaped. The dearth of women and people of color represented in art history needs to become part of the investigation in critical practice.

Given the limitations outlined, the artists' work explored here, historic and contemporary, responds to the commercial ubiquity of play. At the moment, computer and locative games are especially prominent aspects of playculture. From war simulations to Bulletin Board System style chess to 3D computer games, digital technology has been inherently bound with interactivity and diversion, and artists who engage in computer-based creation and critique represent the majority of contemporary examples of critical play. Questions surrounding participatory play and multiuser participation within the creation and reception of artistic, game-related works should, therefore, at least be introduced. Players of popular games may reskin, redesign, and indeed, reissue scenarios in online game environments such as *Second Life*. Music fans may download, upload, mix, and remix popular and independent music. The web can continue to provide a unique space where mainstream meets cult interests, creating subspecializations and massively multiplayer environs numbering in the millions of players. But, are artist-produced computer games, as systems, reinventing how these practices and their artifacts, how the culture, are constituted? What are the social ramifications of artist-produced computer games? How are these ramifications playing out? Above all, by what means do such works achieve in terms of critical discussion, dialogue, or interaction?

First, artists' games by definition take an "outsider" stance in relation to a popular, commercial games culture. This position itself suggests alternate readings of contemporary issues in electronic media and offers the possibility of commentary on social experiences such as discrimination, violence, and aging that traditional gaming culture either avoids or unabashedly marks with stereotypes.[18] With her low-tech

| Figure 7.1 |
Natalie Bookchin, *The Intruder*, 1998–1999.

game projects, California artist Natalie Bookchin uses humor, low-tech graphics, and juxtaposition to place the player in various difficult, challenging, or paradoxical situations. Bookchin's use of both political and personal stories emphasizes ideas about the exterior and interior worlds of a game.

Best known of Bookchin's gaming works is her influential narrative project *The Intruder* (1998–1999).[19] Working from a short story by Jorge Luis Borges, "La intrusa," the game takes the participant through ten arcade-style games as a means of interactively conveying the narrative. Readers or "players" interact with the simple arcade puzzles to advance the plot. Text and spoken-word narration, of a sort, emerge as players engage in what presents itself as a classic arcade system.

"La intrusa" was first printed in the third edition of *El Aleph* (1966) and was later included the volume *El informe de Brodie* (1970). As in the original Borges story, the game too is set in the 1890s. Cristián and Eduardo Nilsen, two close brothers known for their fierce behavior, both fall in love with the same woman, and decide to share their intimate relationship with her. The woman, named Juliana, is later perceived to come between the violent brothers, causing emotional conflict. The narrative is distributed across a series of mini-games. Encountering and defeating, or outthinking, the small games that lie along the narrative path enables the player to move the story forward (figure 7.1). With each game move, the player earns a sentence or phrase. Players learn about the brothers' relationship, their history, and their fights over Juliana. As the narrative progresses, things become more complicated. When the brothers

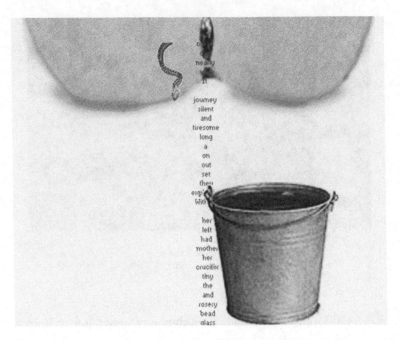

| Figure 7.2 |
Natalie Bookchin, *The Intruder* trinkets collection game, 1998–1999.

decide that Juliana is getting in the way of their close relationship, they have her pack up her meager belongings in a bucket and sell her to a whorehouse.

This part of *The Intruder* may help game designers explore levels of abstraction and narrative that become a part of any critical game. Rather than set the game in the whorehouse, or depict the two brothers with Juliana's belongings, the image onscreen is abstracted in space and situation to feature simple elements of the narrative like the text, the belongings of the character, the props from the story, and the upfront images of a nude woman.

As *The Intruder* begins, players are presented with the image of a woman's bare underside situated over a bucket (figure 7.2). In this game, it is the woman's body that literally produces the story, as though the story was a kind of birth. The female body also produces trinkets the player must catch while maneuvering the bucket. This loaded image represents several narrative layers: Juliana's meager possessions, her own status as a possession of men, and the value of the woman's body as replacable in the narrative, to be exchanged for her sales price to the whorehouse.

Rather than a celebration of the brothers' fraternity, or an inscription of a "cult of masculinity," a growing feeling of helplessness engulfs players of *The Intruder*. The narrative is dark, brutal, and compelling, but Juliana, so important to the story, is rife with mystery. She cannot speak. Who is she? What does she look like? Bookchin removes the character's last name to further impersonalize her in the telling.

In another mini-game in the same story collection, Juliana emerges as a silent, pixilated figure. Players immediately know this figure to be Juliana, yet she is never given dialogue or a voice. As the story unfolds around her, the Juliana character becomes a mere blocky shadow produced by the men's desire. The game's aesthetic further supports this narrative evolution. While the background graphic is somewhat detailed, in a high-contrast photograph of a rustic street, the closer human figure is obliterated in chunky pixels. Game players maneuver Juliana down the street, causing her to run or jump, and eventually advancing the narrative when the character falls into the traps set for her. These are inevitable. Juliana's possible actions and the meaningful choices that players make along with this character are irrelevant. Participants must oblige this framework to continue the narrative.

The story and the interaction in *The Intruder* may appear at odds with each other until the players understand the futility of Juliana's agency. The set of games are designed to establish a gap between successfully advancing the story and compromising the safety and well-being of the character. The disjunction between interaction and narrative is deliberate, a gap that could be a site for critique or irony. To activist designers, irony is one of many strategies of critical play.

In *The Intruder*, Bookchin's low-tech graphic style and her narrator's solemn reading ironically subvert the arcade-game art concept. While the story itself is written by a Latino, the pieces excerpted into the games are narrated, when there is voice at all, by a Latina. Since the narrative involves the control of a Latina character, having a Latina both participate in the narrative and refute, or at least cause us to reflect upon the issue of voice by reading the text aloud, is an important aspect of the artwork. Here, Bookchin not only unplays game conventions—for example, the narrative advances when Juliana falls into the hole, which, in other games, would represent failure or restarting—she also rewrites questions of authority, identity, and representation in games through the confusion of narrative voice. This rewriting is particularly evident in the position of a game player versus that of a reader. Game players participate in the construction and evolution of narrative in different ways than in traditional textual forms. *The Intruder* narrative grows to become particularly effective and poignant because players, the once-"innocent" (perhaps) readers of text, now find themselves actually *participating* in the abuse of Juliana in the interactive format of the game.

What is most striking about *The Intruder* as an interactive work is not the assembly of cute, fun games and their blatant, funny sound effects, but rather how those cute, fun games implicate the participant within what is actually a very dark narrative. The full implications of game interaction style in relation to the narrative become stronger when one takes an actual player into account. *The Intruder* positions users in a precarious and uncomfortable place, rather than the typical "command post" position of power most computer gaming examples provide for players. Software theorist Chris Chesher (2003) explores this unquestioned positioning of power in his work on game interfaces: "The cursor is not telling me something, but indicating that it is listening for my command."[20] Players are almost always constructed as powerful agents, super-heroes, or even gods. Additional implications of this positioning for the male player or, at least, a male gaze come to the fore given the current focus of much of the games industry. "Control," Chesher notes, "undermines the liberal notions of privacy based on the inviolability of the subject. It changes what a subject is."[21]

The complication of Borges's text and the critique of woman's position emerge from the "overpowering" control a player must enact to win in this system. The final game in the set transforms the implications of all of the previous games into an indictment. The player takes part in a "fugitive"-style scenario in which he or she guides crosshairs over a pixilated, natural landscape graphic (figure 7.3). The point of view from the crosshairs and the sound of a helicopter let us know we are indeed the hunters and that there is also someone or something to be hunted, in other words, a victim. To complete *The Intruder*'s disturbing narrative, we must aim and "shoot at" a fugitive figure below who, metaphorically at least, must be Juliana. In return, players earn their "reward," the story's end. Bookchin's *Intruder* design invokes violence against the lone female character.[22] Perhaps this paradoxical involvement is a stronger indictment of violence in computer games, or perhaps it should be read as a metaphorical critique of the larger technologically influenced culture to which women do not yet substantially contribute.

Bookchin's next game, *Metapet* (2002), is an online simulation game that examines the line between work and play (figure 7.4). In the *Metapet* simulation, players create virtual workers of the future in biotech corporations, specifically one fictional company called STAR DNA. The player's task is to try to help employee characters, who are seated at their desks in a work environment no doubt familiar to many of the game's players. Employees who can be trained to work more efficiently are

yoking the oxen.Cristián said, "We have to

| Figure 7.3 |
Players hunt Juliana in Natalie Bookchin's *The Intruder*, 1998–1999.

| Figure 7.4 |
Natalie Bookchin, *Metapet*, 2002.

allowed to climb the corporate ladder. As a tongue-in-cheek critique, this game allows users to examine worker roles within corporate hierarchies. The game also touches on the constant presence of the network, and the addiction to maintenance brought forth by email, online dating, blogging, social networks, instant messages, voicemail, news feeds, and games like *The Sims*. Activities in *Metapet* include the workers' constant checking, tweaking, and maintenance tasks as they care for workplace systems. These matters reflect the themes of networked culture inherited from both domestic practices and from the daily grind among the lower echelons of the information technology workplace. In *Metapet*, players are constantly reminded of the ubiquitous presence of the network and of the constant upkeep they themselves do at terminals throughout the day.

Manuel Castells, in his book *The Rise of the Network Society* (1996), notes that the change in the ways technological processes have become organized originates at the shift from surplus value and economic growth to data and knowledge economies. Bookchin's work makes apparent this economic flow, and goes on to ask, "But at what cost?" The workers at STAR DNA are themselves products of genetic manipulation, optimized for multitasking performance. The network as a conceptual structure plays a vital role in the formation of Bookchin's work and in many other kinds of Internet art, engaging with systems of information and communication and allowing us to examine links and structures that shape our experience of computer-mediated culture.

In other examples of critical play, computer-based gaming projects may delve into the meaning of identity in culture or more concrete subthemes, such as "woman in games" or "human versus machine." The issues brought forth by the duality between body and mind are in some ways celebrated by games, where the agency of the physical body only now is beginning to approximate the agency of the virtual. Human computer-interface designer Joy Mountford observed that as "the computer stares back at you, it sees you as one eye and one finger."[23] In other words, computer interfaces are still designed as if players and users themselves are only partly bodied, or even disembodied. The relationship of the body to the mind, and now to the network, must be better articulated beyond various forms of utopian rhetoric, particularly in the era of the "social networks" frenzy, where ranges of intimacy and knowledge are set computationally, and often by systems designers, rather than by participants. Here, it is worthwhile to remind ourselves that, as architect Karen Franck notes, we "construct what we know, and these constructions are deeply influenced by our earlyexperiences and by the nature of our underlying relationship to the world."[24] This is true for purely digital experiences as well as for hybrid or physical manifestations of play.

Games that Play Themselves

The computer game is the paradigm for the critical play of other artists as well. Eddo Stern's work flourishes at the intersection of game-related art and technology works. Dealing with system-on-system interactions and game-related interactions, Stern's remarkable range of projects has helped define the field of new media art, and larger art and technology practices. His *Dark Game* (2006) is a videogame prototype in which two rivals are deprived of their sight. Like his *Tekken Torture Tournament* (2001), where the injuries of the virtual characters are translated to the physical players, *Dark Game* demonstrates the link between virtual actions and the players' own bodies. *Cockfight Arena* (2001), perhaps the most whimsical of Stern's works, consisted of a performance in which players work to control their avatar on the screen while wearing feathered chicken suits embedded with sensors. When Stern's work borders, or crosses into, the absurd, the resulting players' actions are most pleasing. The work unabashedly explores masculinity and power issues within commercial games, taking the manifestation of machismo posturing and "the fight" among players to their extremes.

In *Best . . . Flame War . . . Ever* (2007), Stern documented and interpreted heated online arguments as animated collaged characters speaking the dialog. In *RUNNERS: Wolfenstein* (2002), Stern inverted the destruction of World War II by allowing Israeli players to invade Nazi Germany. In addition to large-scale political issues, Stern investigates the mundane everyday experiences of his players. *Fort Paladin: America's Army* (2003) is a Fisher Price–styled castle that houses the game *America's Army* (figure 7.5). Robotic "fingers" play the game maniacally and repeatedly, like a human player might have to do to stay on top of the game. The game's play features a repetitive scene: the same character launches the same grenade attack on the same nonplayer characters, or NPCs, and then spawns the same new NPC soldiers to kill again, in an endless loop.[25] By letting the game play itself, Stern's theories on play and his practice highlight the futility of agency in closed systems. Stern also exposes the iconography of games as fetish items and as forms of cultural shorthand. Demonstrating technical, conceptual, and aesthetic aspects of the work at all times, Stern questions what it means to play critically, opting at times for a system to play itself, as it understands its own rules best.

A Race of Races

In a comment on scientific perspectives and categorization, games and play are also used in the work of Paul Vanouse. One Vanouse work in particular, *The Relative Velocity*

Inscription Device (RVID) (2002) is particularly important (figure 7.6). In this installation, which consists of a computer-controlled separation gel and DNA and displays, Vanouse runs a live scientific experiment wherein four separate DNA samples from each member of his multiracial Jamaican American family are literally raced in a portable lab. The family members' DNA samples travel slowly, and in addition to the race action, viewers can read a eugenics treatise that explores the historic positioning of racial identification practices. Vanouse posits, "In 1960, my 'brown' mother emigrated to the US from Jamaica, and met my 'white' father. Why is my skin color lighter than my sister's?"[26] With this simple demonstration, Vanouse's project critically examines the genetics behind even small variations in skin color and the ways in which those variations are transmitted.[27] Vanouse's intention is not to literalize the genetic variations among mother, father, sister and brother, but to question the validity of such choice in what he calls "scientific spectacles." The project also brings forward our unease as spectators with regard to our own genetic and racial identity.

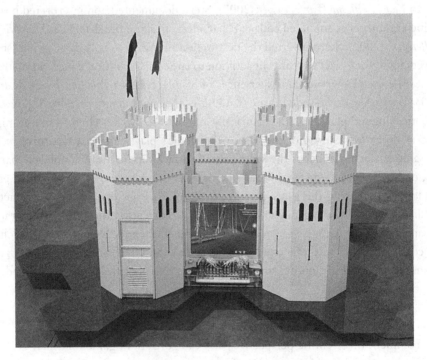

| Figure 7.5 |
Eddo Stern's castle-like *Fort Paladin*.

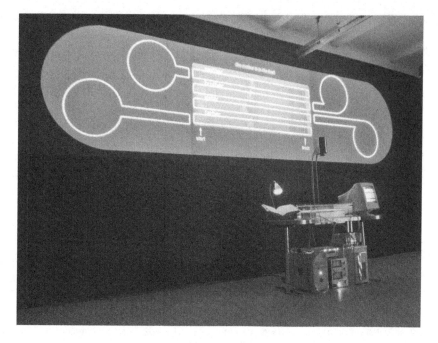

| Figure 7.6 |

Projection from Paul Vanouse's *The Relative Velocity Inscription Device* (*RVID*), 2002, which displays a closeup of the live video image of the electrophoresis gel holding the individual DNA samples, with graphical overlays.

Citing the ambitious Human Genome project in his work, as well as past research artifacts like the 1929 tract "Race Crossing in Jamaica," a three-year study exploring the "problem of race crossing" during a time of racial separatist doctrines, Vanouse is keen to problematize the scientific process on a fundamental level. Vanouse's work then embodies critiques of science first launched by the Austrian philosopher Ludwig Wittgenstein in his depiction of language as a game capable of representing a system of knowledge, which was later more specifically developed by the American Thomas Kuhn, whose ideas about the nature of the social knowledge produced by science, including the theory that science is inherently political, are well documented. Kuhn's belief is that science is a game, or is at least modeled on a game metaphor, and that this game, like other social practices, constitutes primarily a language game of power, legibility, and control in the Wittgensteinian sense.[28] If the very working of society is a network of language games, science, with its hyperspecialized language, its particular knowledge, and specific community of authority, must therefore be a subset of such a game, where truth is relative, and where what constitutes fact is instead relative to

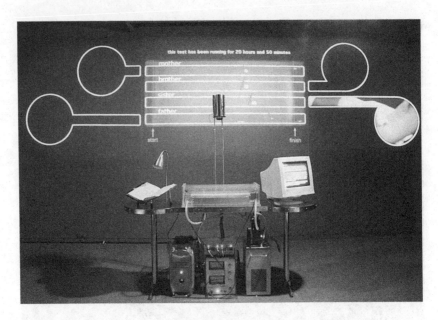

| Figure 7.7 |

Projection from Paul Vanouse's *The Relative Velocity Inscription Device* (*RVID*), 2002. The samples glow because of the UV light irradiation below the gel.

one's subjectivity. Kuhn's creation of the concept of the "paradigm shift," a dynamic that models how scientists move from doubt, or even disdain, to consideration and finally acceptance and enthusiasm for new theories reveals the rules by which science operates and delineates how as a system of knowledge, science relies on social and psychological factors.

In terms of critical play, Vanouse reskins the simple interactive display of the race much like a game show from the 1970s invites players to guess the prices of goods or to wager on the success of randomly playable elements (figure 7.7). Even a scientific visualization would both simplify and posit as incorrect assumptions about content. He also unplays the "game" of science, questioning its validity.

Social and psychological factors are key to the work of Wafaa Bilal, an Iraqi-born American artist and U.S. citizen. Bilal's work explores the position of the Iraqi civilian through technologically mediated games. In May 2007, Bilal confined himself in the Flatfile Galleries in Chicago for thirty days under twenty-four-hour webcam surveillance to raise awareness about the everyday life of Iraqi citizens and the home confinement they face on a daily basis due to violence and surveillance in their cities

| Figure 7.8 |

Wafaa Bilal, *Domestic Tension*, 2007. Photo from http://media3.washingtonpost.com/wp-dyn/content/photo/2007/05/28/
PH2007052801232.jpg.

and towns. Titled *Domestic Tension*, this work allowed members of the public to visit Bilal's project website, watch him via webcam, and shoot him with a remote-controlled paintball gun (figure 7.8).

The work is one of the strongest anti–Iraq war statements made during the conflict, and was followed in over one hundred and thirty countries around the globe. During the month-long exhibition, the site received eighty million hits, and sixty thousand paintballs were shot. The work also featured various forms of player subversion, such as the ability to "unplay" the scenario overall. Several viewers acted by forming "protective groups like the VIRTUAL human shield [sic] SHIELD, who take turns aiming the gun away from Bilal around the clock."[29] Anonymous comments on popular aggregate sites such as Digg.com noted during the event that the exhibition was "one step closer to stabbing people in the face over the internet." Another commenter said: "I think the most disturbing part of this exhibit is one of the comments in the chat room. 'Do we get to shoot more if we donate?'"[30]

Bilal's incorporation of a mediated-game interface provoked viewers to interaction, encouraging participants to "Shoot an Iraqi." Bilal, who left Iraq due to imprisonment and torture during the last Iraq regime because he himself had made anti-Hussein art-works, would conceivably be the last person to face U.S. censorship due to questions of political loyalty. But this was not the case. In 2007, Bilal decided to recreate the 2003 game *Quest for Saddam* as a way to voice a critique of U.S. policies in the Middle East. The original game, using the *Duke Nukem* 3D game engine, asked players to fight generic "Iraqi" soldiers, and to find and kill Saddam Hussein, Iraq's leader from 1979 to 2003. The game was created by United American Committee Chairman Jesse Petrilla. This first *Quest for Saddam* was reskinned as a "hunt" for George H. W. Bush by the Global Islamic Media Front, a group said to be related to Al Qaeda.[31] Their game, *The Night of Bush Capturing* was hacked by Bilal so that the artist could put his own, more nuanced spin on this epic conflict, in terms of both the actual war and the video game battle.

In *The Night of Bush Capturing: A Virtual Jihadi*, Bilal places himself as a character in the hacked Al Qaeda version of the Petrilla game. The Bilal game narrative is part autobiographical and part fiction: after learning of the real-life death of his brother in the Iraq war, Bilal is recruited by Al Qaeda to join the hunt for Bush. Bilal intends for the work to communicate both the racism and hatred embedded in U.S. games such as *Quest for Saddam* or *America's Army*. He also aims to demonstrate the difficulty Iraqi citizens face and their vulnerability during recruitment for violent groups such as Al Qaeda, maintaining that ordinary Iraqis have little to show for their "freedom" but incredible loss and violence. "This artwork is meant to bring attention to the vulnerability of Iraqi civilians, to the travesties of the current war, and to expose racist generalizations and profiling. Similar games such as 'Quest for Saddam' or 'America's Army' promote stereotypical, singular perspectives. My artwork inverts these assumptions, and ultimately demonstrates the vulnerability to recruitment by violent groups like Al Qaeda because of the U.S. occupation of Iraq."[32]

Bilal undertook the game modification while a resident visiting artist at Rensselaer Polytechnic Institute in Troy, New York. But close to the time of the scheduled exhibition opening, the school shut down the show. It moved to an alternate art space, and this too was shut down, by representatives of the city government for "code violations." Although Bilal's presence was welcome on campus, and his exhibition themes well known, suddenly the artist's work was perceived as too controversial to support. Bilal believes that during "these difficult times, when we are at war with another nation, it is our duty as artists and citizens to improvise strategies of engagement for dialogue."[33]

September 12th

In 2003, the NewsGaming.com team lead by Gonzalo Frasca launched *September 12th: A Toy World* as a reaction to, and criticism of, U.S. policies in the fight on global terrorism (figure 7.9). Named to invoke the World Trade Center bombings of 2001, *September 12th* is a simulation that uses video game technology to model the obvious paradox in the American–Middle East conflict: the problematic inevitability of collateral damage suffered in the standard "combat models" of fighting terrorism. *September 12th* is an interactive toy world that provides "a simple model" players can use "to explore some aspects of the war on terror."[34] In some ways, the experience is a reskinned version of a classic *SimCity* game, with a highly reduced set of player options.

In *September 12th*, players are presented an isometric view of a bustling town and market, where terrorists and civilians intermingle, and a simple choice: fire or don't fire. The view offers a "big picture" of a presumably Middle Eastern city. The player's only available action is to manipulate crosshairs over the view, clicking to fire missiles from far away onto the village. If a player chooses to fire her missiles at the terrorists in the

| Figure 7.9 |
Gonzalo Frasca and Newsgaming.com, *September 12th: A Toy World,* 2003.

market, she will quickly find that it is nearly impossible to hit them. The missile will, however, destroy buildings and kill innocent civilians. Shooting again and again is permitted in intervals and only generates more rubble, more mayhem in the village, and more suffering. Civilians left alive after each missile attack weep and mourn the loss of the dead. Soon after, the embittered survivors become terrorists themselves through a shift in animation. If the player keeps firing, in just a few minutes the marketplace will be destroyed and only terrorists will be left to run through the ruins. Described as a simulation on its start page, *September 12th* has no win-or-lose state. Since there is no goal, there can be no obstacles to that goal and so the game has no inherent conflict, except that which might arise in players themselves. Even a simple illusion of a win state cannot be maintained in a game that openly declares it has no end and can't be won. The lack of an opponent makes conflict or balance irrelevant. The game does not involve any form of progression. There is no learning curve. However, *September 12th* possesses many qualities of both a game and an artwork: it has a clearly defined set of cause-and-effect actions the player can choose to pursue, and the world thoughtfully models a problematic situation that might also classify it as a game for social change. It is also successful at providing a safe way to experience reality, or in this case, a possible playing out of choices which might create a reality. Since the results of the simulation are less harsh than the real situation the game is modeling, with no actual lives lost and no actual terrorists created, the overall effect is what game scholar Chris Crawford labels emotional content: "A game creates a subjective and deliberately simplified representation of emotional reality,"[35] something easily accomplished in a simulation that draws its content from a current situation in the real world.

To game designer Frasca, the task was to demonstrate that destruction of cities and high civilian casualties can only cultivate a climate of resentment, vengeance, and hatred that can spawn new enemies. In short, violence breeds violence.[36] In this way, the *Sims* aspect of the work is rewritten into a futile cycle: players do not work for character happiness and can do nothing to make the lives of the characters better or more productive. Frasca explored different techniques to convey the act of turning regular villagers into terrorists. "What I wanted to show is simply this circle of terror that seems to not have an ending. We tried a traditional morph between the two characters, but we felt it was not clear enough. The technique that we ended up with flashes back and forth between the two characters, and I think it works pretty well."[37] Frasca noted that all the responses to the game were positive, even among Arabs in the United States.[38] Is the *September 12th* simulation a comment on the term "terrorism" itself? Absolutely. However, in *September 12th*, the message is not only that violence produces more violence but also that the work behind developing the software allows those who engage with the simple simulation to actively participate in creating meaning. This act, to players, is fundamentally different from reading a static text or visual representation.[39]

Another project, Frasca's game *Madrid*, is a response to the Madrid bombings of 2004. During the rush-hour peak on March 11, three days before a Spanish general election, ten coordinated explosions went off on Madrid's commuter train lines, killing one hundred and ninety-one people and wounding over seventeen hundred and fifty-five others; responsibility for the event was attributed to an Al Qaeda–style terrorist group. Working as a memorial, Frasca's *Madrid* is subtle, using suggestion and simple design to attract players and open up the tragedy of the bombings for remembrance and dialogue. The instructions and the game play are simple: the player only needs to maintain the light of the candles held by drawn characters in an act of remembrance. *Madrid* includes a light meter that tracks player process, but, ultimately, the player cannot move back and forth quickly enough to keep all of the candles lit. In many ways the game starts off as a work of mourning, but works to question the very act of staging a memorial for a tragedy, as well as to comment on human memory itself. The game also serves the needs of an activist community around the world.

Jamie Antonisse, Devon Johnson, Chris Baily, Joey Orton, and Brittany Pirello created the game *Hush* in 2008 to explore the 1994 civil war and genocide in Rwanda. Called a rhythm game by bloggers, and a concentration game by players, *Hush* uses the 1994 Rwandan civil war as the setting for a challenging scenario. Players play as Liliane and the goal is to keep Liliane's baby quiet in order to prevent mother and child from being captured by the Hutu patrol (figure 7.10). The "lullaby" is appealing, consisting of falling letters of words related to the calming of the child. The letters of the word appear quietly on the screen, and must be matched on the keyboard by the player precisely at the point they appear their brightest.

The initial concept for the game was created in a critical play brainstorming exercise for the Values at Play project, an effort of artists and humanists to reflect further on human values in games. Antonisse and Johnson state: "The idea for Hush was actually born out of a Values at Play exercise:[40]

We had to create a game from a randomly chosen game mechanic and game theme, and we drew "Singing" and "Human Rights." The contrast between these two cards posed a challenge and yielded many unconventional ideas, including the core concept for *Hush*. One of the things that attracted us to the concept is that the player isn't viewing this horrific event from a distance and attempting to "solve the problem"; they are immersed in the moment, experiencing the terror of a Hutu raid. It's also important that even though the player is not in a position of power, the player still has the noble goal of saving a child.[41]

| Figure 7.10 |
Jamie Antonisse, Devon Johnson, and USC team, *Hush*, 2008.

Game play in *Hush* is quick, but the experience is immersive, with the matching, timed game mechanic requiring full concentration. The game soundtrack convincingly conveys the conflict between staying calm and a surrounding world of mayhem and violence. To game scholar Ian Bogost, "*Hush* offers a glimpse, as it were, of how vignette might be used successfully in games . . . as a vignette of a situation in mid-90s civil war-torn Rwanda, the game is compelling," for the "anxiety of literal death contradicts the core mechanic's demand for calm, but in a surprising and satisfying way, like chili in chocolate. The increasingly harsh sound of a baby's cry that comes with failure attenuates the player's anxiety, further underscoring the tension at work in this grave scenario."[42]

Most important, *Hush* explores subjectivity. It is the strength of the belief in a position, from which an experiential "truth" emerges, that helps this game move from a broad statement to a personally moving experience. We can look to the ideas behind standpoint epistemology that open up the possibilities to use games as an approach against power and oppression.[43] Here, Braidotti's notion of radical forms of reembodiment can work in a game; even though the body is not visibly acting a scene to an observer, the participant is bodily engaged.[44] While lived experiences culminate in a variety of complex physical, social, and philosophical realities, even simple games such as *Hush* can provide an emotionally complex slice of an experience, and present a layered, "nomadic" perspective by shifting from player, to character, to world citizen and more.

The Rise of Serious Games

Artistic interventions in the form of games arise from a number of intentions, including social critique, a need for solidarity and action among participants, and the impulse to stage large-scale games in order to disrupt political scenarios or daily life. Some of those making video games, as we have seen, can be identified as artists. Bookchin, Stern, Vanouse, Bilal, and Schleiner have provided compelling activist models. Bookchin reskins games in light of critique by using existing narrative. Stern rewrites how games work and adds to their complexity. Vanouse brings in a critique of larger epistemological concerns through a look at scientific discourse and classically styled games. Bilal changes the stakes of a game, crossing lines not only in representation but also in national and international comfort levels, ethnic stereotypes, and the power of institutions and the state. Even earlier examples such as Schleiner offer historical precedents for projects that move primarily into the realm of activism. In all cases, digital worlds are enormous sites for the import of content from the real world. These can include social interactions and social constructions like racism and sexism, which can prevail inside particular types of game frameworks.

The examples discussed in the rest of this chapter are described by the terms *serious games*, *games for change*, or *social impact games*. The debate regarding the general use of these terms must be noted. Different groups favor different categorical labels. Games scholar Woods argues that serious games are the goal of those within the game industry for the future of games, noting that many developers wish to create "serious" content or experiences that are typically represented within traditional narrative forms such as books or film.[45] Though these lines are not fixed and easily definable, most in the community understand serious games to be those primarily within the domain of education or military applications. Such games might focus on training for service, disaster relief, hazardous occupations, crime, the redesign of public spaces such as transit systems and parks, or the creation of frameworks for team building.

On the other hand, games for change or social impact games are understood as those that address social concerns more broadly. These might include poverty, racism, bias and discrimination, war and peace, or human rights through education and outreach. There is a fast-growing collection of computer-based games designed to educate on matters relating to environmental concerns, human rights abuse, worker's issues, land use, and other social ills. These games are often created to address real-world issues or to raise awareness and foster critical thinking. Both categories of games integrate real-world data and stories, focus on education and public opinion, and aim to provide an alternative to existing media on such issues.[46]

Many social impact games use video game technology in innovative and novel ways in order to convey their messages, but in the end bear little resemblance to existing mainstream video games. This relationship is an interesting one to explore. In his 1984 book, *The Art of Computer Game Design*, Chris Crawford, perhaps prematurely, provided a definition of what games are and how they should be designed. He identifies four elements common to all games: representation, interaction, conflict, and safety. Of the four, the ideas of conflict and safety are the most useful in distinguishing a game from a simulation or other interactive media forms. To Crawford and other game designers, even a social impact game would require conflict:

Conflict arises naturally from the interaction in a game. The player is actively pursuing some goal. Obstacles prevent him from easily achieving this goal. If the obstacles are passive or static, the challenge is a puzzle or athletic challenge. If they are active or dynamic, if they purposefully respond to the player, the challenge is a game. However, active, responsive, purposeful obstacles require an intelligent agent. If that intelligent agent actively blocks the player's attempts to reach his goals, conflict between the player and the agent is inevitable. Thus, conflict is fundamental to all games.[47]

The absolute insistence on conflict can emerge to be more interesting and subtle. The conflict in *Madrid*, for example, lies in the player's abilities given an impossible task. In *September 12*, conflict is in the player choice itself. Primarily in reference to social activist games, game scholar Shuen-shing Lee refers to these as "you-never-win" games. Lee's theory would be extraordinary familiar to a Fluxus game maker, for art games have a long history of circumventing win and loss states for other themes. Yet in games that attempt to appeal to the vast majority of conventional game players, or those interested in activism without a radical edge, Lee builds on notions from scholars like Janet Murray and offers literature for a model, connecting games for change to the dramatic form of tragedy, where the player is not meant to win because that is what maintains the tragic form.[48] This idea builds on Frasca's approach. In his now classic "Video Games of the Oppressed," Frasca points to the playwright Bertolt Brecht's critical play with Aristotelian drama, insisting that actors and audiences remain aware that what they see and engage in is a simulation and that they are present to provide a critical view. Frasca also mentions Augusto Boal's "Theatre of the Oppressed," which strove to tear or break down the fourth wall between subject and viewer.

These theories are important to understanding the strategies behind social impact games. The simulative nature of a game creates an environment where a game becomes a venue for those otherwise uninterested in experimental art per se to think through and challenge the heady ideas of society and culture.

In 2006, MIT and other organizations launched a nationwide student competition with the goal of linking technology to the genocide in Darfur, Sudan. The winning entry, *Darfur Is Dying*, was conceived and developed by a group of students from the University of Southern California and was launched to critical acclaim. *Darfur Is Dying* is an online game designed to raise awareness of the three million people in refugee camps. The game is intended to function as a call for aid, intervention, and progressive legislation. The game is also designed to empower students and others to become involved in actions that could stop an international crisis.[49] Players in the game, described by the makers as "a window" onto the experience of the refugees, must keep their refugee camp functioning in light of the danger of invasion by Sudanese government-backed militia, the Janjaweed.

A simulation-style game, *Darfur Is Dying* places the player in the perspective of a displaced Darfurian refugee. Initially, players each choose a character from a wide range of age and gender, and then begin to forage. The first goal is to leave camp and fetch water. But it is a long run to get water in the barren desert—five kilometers— and the magnitude of the mission soon becomes clear to the player. Armed militia groups patrol the land, and players must guide their game characters to hide when appropriate behind scrub or boulders. If the character is caught, a text screen ends the play and makes a point on the crisis: "You will likely become one of the hundreds of thousands of people already lost to the humanitarian crisis" or "Girls in Darfur face abuse, rape, and kidnapping by the Janjaweed. If she succeeds in fetching water, the girl can bring more water back than a smaller boy, but less than an adult."[50] If the players' characters survive this game level, they move on to help the camp manage small plots of land and gardens by collecting water, building shelters, and harvesting food.

Darfur Is Dying plays much like a traditional action game. The refugee characters negotiate danger, forage for water, and rebuild their village in order to accomplish a clearly defined goal: survival for one week. The game's players become steadily more skillful at guiding their characters to avoid and prevent danger as time progresses, so the game has a smooth learning curve. The challenges that are presented entail relatively simple navigation and limited artificial intelligence. Game enemies exist in endless numbers and will deliberately move toward their intended targets via the shortest possible route. Conflict emerges as the player's Darfurian refugee struggles to avoid capture or murder by the Janjaweed militia. The game maintains the illusion of winnability by defining a reasonable win state and providing a means to this end.

The complication comes in when the camp is successfully established, for a healthy camp attracts raiders. Given this event, the player must pay for her own success, rebuilding the village after attacks, and continuing to collect water, harvest gardens for food, and stave off disease by visiting the clinic when it receives new supplies. Exploring the village reveals information about the general state of the Darfurian people and the tragic events that lead a refugee to the camp in the first place. While *Darfur Is Dying* allows players to safely experience the trauma of being a displaced Darfurian refugee, the game is so closely tied to real people and events that it unsettles the player and disturbs her sense of comfort. Hovering over huts in the refugee camp, text reveals chilling personal accounts of real refugees. The *Take Action Now* button on the interface has a real-world effect by offering players the chance to write or email the U.S. president, petition Congress to support the Darfur Peace and Accountability Act, or email the game to others to spread information about the Darfur situation.

Unlike mainstream games, *Darfur Is Dying* sobers feelings of accomplishment, and allows players to feel the distance between a game and the real-world situation. It can be argued that *Darfur Is Dying* is another "you-never-win" game, for surviving for one week does not resolve the conflict in the game or in the world around us. If one survives the game in character, he or she will succeed in the digital version of the Darfur universe, but no further. Games that inform do not end the real conflict. Perhaps, however, we may design games that have more and more global influence or even enact changes in education, fundraising, or work through play.

Other artists and activists have looked to games as a means to building support for a cause. The *Peter Packet* game was created by NetAid, a nonprofit organization whose aim is to eliminate poverty, and by Cisco, a technology company (figure 7.11). NetAid designed *Peter Packet* so that U.S. players could learn about children in less developed countries, and send superhero Peter Packet to move messages on the Internet to those in need. The game explores issues of education, clean drinking water, and AIDS in Haiti, India, and Zimbabwe through the use of computers and specifically, the Internet. Players help Peter Packet dodge viruses and hackers in order to help in-game characters communicate with international contacts such as teacher organizations. By

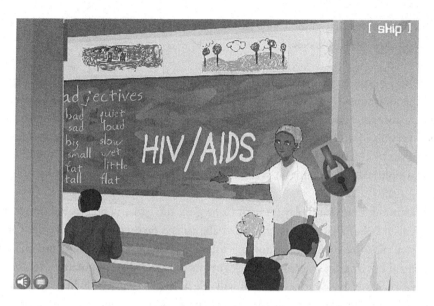

| Figure 7.11 |
A scene from NetAid and Cisco's *Peter Packet* game.

interacting, these players not only learn about computer networking such as rout-
ing messages but also gain awareness about contemporary situations regarding technology, education, health, and poverty around the world. The game also offers players
and their friends a chance to learn more about fundraising and taking action to help
in the related causes.[51]

If games are supposed to be a source of entertainment, should they also attempt
to enhance critical thinking as well as address social and political issues? *Peter Packet*
has critical content, with relatively straightforward arcade game play, but games such
as *Darfur Is Dying* and *September 12th* appropriate or alter established gaming models
in an effort to send a message or affect change.[52] These games are infused with socio-
political criticism in their quest for digital activism.[53] They challenge the notion that
games must be only entertaining and fun, and offer alternative goals such as meditative play or, as in the case of these two examples, out-of-game engagement, with
or without the often trivial pleasures offered by industry standards.[54] In his article
"Videogames of the Oppressed," Frasca writes, "The goal of these games is not to find
appropriate solutions, but rather to trigger discussions. . . . It would not matter if the
games could not simulate the situation with realistic accuracy. Instead, games would

work as metonyms that could guide discussions and serve to explore alternative ways of dealing with real life issues."[55]

Along these lines, Persuasive Games created the "game for change" or a game engaged in raising awareness about social or political issues titled *Oil God*, which puts the player in the position of a god, complete with a moveable "God-hand" as the cursor, in a simplified version of the popular PC game *Black and White*. Players attempt to raise the price of oil to a certain level by starting wars, causing natural disasters, and altering national political and economic systems through political change and civil war (see figure 7.12).

Presuming that many players wish to be god, the game is predicated on the perhaps cynical belief that players will subscribe to the favored game strategies for the subversive pleasure of profit, endorsing military coups for financial game, and even directing aliens to kill and probe large segments of the civilian population. In *Oil God*, information about how various stimuli will affect oil prices is withheld, and it appears impossible for the player to discern which nasty actions benefit prices more than others. Starting wars usually seems to increase oil prices, and it is clear that directing damage at regions and nations with oil seems to keep oil prices at a premium. While Persuasive Games calls this work a "news" game, *Oil God* in fact abstracts the factors

| Figure 7.12 |
Persuasive Games, *Oil God*, 2006.

that influence oil prices in order to make critical comments on the potentially devious strategies of oil cartels and corporations. *Oil God* aims to educate players about complex economic systems through simulation, fantasy, and humor, and while it succeeds in fulfilling fantasy and providing humor, it is not the equivalent of a "news" game, where at least factual elements or systems would function, and while *September 12th* is an example of Lee's "you-never-win" concept, *Oil God* is a cynical "you-always-win" game, proving games for change can relate closely to artists' game work, while strategies among artists and activists can diverge dramatically.

Whatever their message, serious games are among the most challenging games to design. These play spaces must retain all the elements that make a game enjoyable while effectively communicating their message. Either component can be lost in the attempt to manifest the other, resulting is a game that is dull and didactic, or entertaining but hollow. In the worst case, the results are both dull and hollow. Games are frameworks that designers can use to model the complexity of the problems that face the world and make them easier for the players to comprehend. By creating a simulated environment, the player is able to step away and think critically about those problems. Frasca refers to these games as a "trigger of discussion," and existing social activist games work largely on that level. They are not necessarily meant to be fun, though fun may be a side effect, and are rather meant to make people think. Like other designers of critical play, social activist designers can approach serious issues through games. In some cases, a game may provide the safest outlet available for exploring devastating problems and conflicts.

DESIGNING FOR CRITICAL PLAY

Play is grounded in the concept of possibility.

—Mihaly Csikszentmihalyi and Stith Bennett, "An Exploratory Model of Play"

Whether it is their capacity to stimulate participation in an Internet-connected age or their role as a platform for entertainment, intervention, authorship, and subversion, computer games—indeed, all games—are highly relevant to the twenty-first-century imagination. Games have also constituted a significant component of arts practice for almost a century. While the central parts of this book engaged with historical questions surrounding critical play and artistic approaches to play and game design, an investigation of the design methodologies informing critical play should begin by defining the context in which many games are now made.

If, as according to Bennett and Csikszentmihalyi, "Play is grounded in the concept of possibility,"[1] then critical play is the avant-garde of games as a medium. But *where* is play critical? When assessed in terms of criticality, a wealth of questions arises concerning the way games actually function. The last chapters have provided theories, approaches, and examples to help address some important questions: Can games be activist? Does play raise critical awareness or does it minimize its effects? What is the role of the arts in games, and can methods derived from artists make a difference? Can the various methods of creation followed by the artists discussed in prior chapters offer novel approaches to actively reshaping everyday playculture?

Marshall McLuhan was ahead of his time in understanding that "Art, like games or popular arts, and like media of communication, has the power to impose its own assumptions by setting the human community into new relationships and postures."[2] From doll play to wordplay, from Simultanism to various Surrealist games, there is a good deal of evidence that the processes of artists in pursuit of critical play can offer research methods, actions, and play situations, whether sites or collections of one of more actions, that are adaptable to present concerns. The critical play method I propose here should provide an effective model for designers and artists to use to engage in, and encourage, critical play in both game making and game playing. Critical play can and should be included in the traditional game design process. By proposing this design model and creating games with this set of strategies, it is hoped that other practitioners, artists, designers, scientists, and researchers will be able to question and elucidate many of the so-called "norms" embedded in our current play frameworks and technology practices, ultimately including a more diverse set of voices in the game design community and a wider spectrum of game experiences.

Why Care about Methods?

On first glance, it can be difficult to see how artists working in a very different place and time would have significant manners, modes, and processes that inform game making today. Computer games are often discussed as an exciting new medium, but its ties to prior forms of play are not automatic. To the typical gamer, computer games are not obviously aligned with such concerns as ancient divination, psychoanalysis, utopian tax laws, environmentalism, or social protest. In the case of activist gaming, perhaps it is thought that the goals of the designer are "real," and therefore can be best achieved with more direct approaches to the making. For example, a designer may wish to make a project concerning a local food bank. Typical disciplinary research would encounter particular truths and strands of information, rather than an artistic aesthetic.

However, if we look to the fundamental reasons for *why we play*, the connection between artistic methods, activism, and game design becomes clear. There is something about designing play, especially the process of conceptualizing and making games, that requires an attention to possibility. As in art, the creation of play and games necessitates rule making at a fundamental level. Even simple role-playing activities, or playing house, both seemingly limitless open-play scenarios, include implicit or explicit rules that establish behavior, possible actions, environments, and the safe zone for play itself. Due to the systemic nature of both the product and the process, game makers use particular repeatable processes, or methods. Like activists, game designers also follow an overall scheme of investigation or research, creating processes to address specific concerns and ideas. In addition, the creation of rules of operation makes interesting constraints to provoke innovation in both the designer's process and the player's role.

As game design matures, and as games themselves become more ubiquitous and more meaningful to culture, there is a growing need for designers to approach the creative process with increased awareness and responsibility to be inclusive, fair, and cater to a variety of play styles. Computer games, especially networked computer games, have become often-used and "public" social spaces. As such, they must be seen as spaces of translation, already transformed by game designers and the growing numbers of game players: international, transbordered, fluid. However, this international significance brings ever more importance to what those games are designed to be, what one does in them, and how play is constructed within them. Political change once occurred in the public space of the street, town square, and the plaza. Many games, some of the type geographer Gillian Rose labels "non-real," are significant because now, more than ever, electronic games constitute cultural spaces.

Furthermore, as a site for production and consumption of culture, community, language, commerce, work, and leisure, playculture is what can be termed a "thirdspace," which Homi Bhabha in *The Location of Culture* calls the space of subversion, hybridity, and blasphemy. In fact, Bhabha argues that hybridity and cultural translation are in themselves subversive ideas, and therefore must be the place where binary divisions are challenged.[3] Urban planner Edward Soja argues that all spaces are "thirdspaces" which are lived and imagined spaces in between empirical or the previously understood geographies and physical forms of "firstspace" and the conceptual, ideological, or semiotic spaces of representation and mental forms of "secondspace." Thirdspace is the site for play and struggle. Players may eschew binary oppositions and allow for the possibility of a subject to be simultaneously in several spatialities. As Soja points out, spaces are socially produced (1996) and thirdspaces are the only sites that contain the possibility for social and political transformation (1999). As Anne-Marie Schleiner notes, "Instead of replicating the binary logic of the shooter genre, of Cowboys and Indians, of the football game, if the US government borrowed tactics from real time strategy gamers or RPGers, we might be looking at a different global response."[4]

If we think of games as presenting the possibility of the thirdspace, a social space with its own social relations, struggles, and symbolic boundaries, it is within this thirdspace that we must envision the more diverse and equity-promoting style of activity I call critical play. Following the line of work inspired by Langdon Winner's well-known assertion that artifacts "have" politics, and building on my own theory-practice research in this area, I've come to realize that the methods followed by practitioners, whether consciously evaluated or not, are key to the meaning emerging from a game.[5] Researchers studying social and philosophical dimensions of technologies have used a variety of terms to label and extend Winner's ideas, such as the "embeddedness" of values in technology, or the "play" of the values in a game.[6] Systems other than games are influenced by ideology as well: technologies such as search engines, medical systems, and file-sharing software are designed with different models of human behavior, motivation, privacy of information, and the like. Perhaps even more than these "tools," games are simultaneously systems of information, cultural products, and manifestations of cultural practice. On some level, systems such as games must, due to the conditions of their creation, represent cultural norms and biases in their realization. These results can go, and have gone, completely unacknowledged. Game makers and artists work in a certain time, place, and situation. Many work in a particular medium and genre. Others must contend with definite pressures and practical realities. In a further complication of these realities, what is distinctive about play is that one cannot always easily see that a clear boundary exists between it and social reality, or rather, see that play uses the tools of everyday reality in its construction.

Although artists' play continues to create new meaning, to challenge existing power relations, and to align with activist/interventionist strategies, postmodern culture and the technological revolution may have changed histories, social relations, markets, and home life in deep and profound ways. Globalization and its effects may produce or reinscribe problematic ideologies into technological artifacts such as computer games.[7] Given these conditions, along with the fact that any creative act is complex and usually generates unintended consequences, the game creation process must mature to allow constant review and much more "reflection."

The Critical Play Method

Based on the needs of game design and the importance of iteration, the ideas from over a century of artists' games can prove useful to making radically different games. But first, it is important to see how designers are making games today. Here are the rough steps in the cyclical development process called "iterative" design:[8]

- *Set a design goal (also known as a mission statement).* The designer sets the goals necessary for the project.
- *Develop the minimum rules and assets necessary for the goal.* The game designers rough out a framework for play, including the types of tokens, characters, props, and so on.
- *Develop a playable prototype.* The game idea is mocked up. This is most efficiently done on paper or by acting it out during the early stages of design.
- *Play test.* Various players try the game and evaluate it, finding dead ends and boring sections, and exploring the types of difficulty associated with the various tasks.

- *Revise.* Revising or elaborating on the goal, the players offer feedback, and the designers revamp the game system to improve it.
- *Repeat.* The preceding steps in the process are repeated to make sure the game is engrossing and playable before it "ships" or is posted to a website.

The traditional model contains concrete steps toward realizing a particular design by iterating it until core elements and concepts have been adequately matched by game elements and mechanics. Generally, a designer or a design team may choose to iterate one small design goal, a subset of a particular game, or they may choose to iterate the entire game system in some skeletal form (see figure 8.1). The model is scalable to many types of play and development.

I wish to appraise this process in light of the myriad critical approaches to projects included in this book. Part of this process is a constant reflection on the humanistic themes, or values, during design. At least one designer, Donald Schön, refers to a "reflective practice" as a methodology and encourages makers to step outside their processes to "see the big picture." For Schön, it is important that the experiments do

| Figure 8.1 |
Mary Flanagan, model of iterative design process.

not "confirm" an "answer" to a challenge, but affirm that challenge instead. Schön's approach avoids the traditional goal of a final, or definitive, resolution and involves shaping and altering priorities as a result of findings. Schön notes, "It is the logic of affirmation which sets the boundaries of experimental rigor."[9] Other reflective frameworks, such as the "critical technical practice," which is advanced primarily by computer science practitioners working on artificial intelligence, have similar aims. A growing number of designers are committing to the notion of a continuing dialogue between values and practice.[10] In sum, reflective practice encourages designers and technologists to verify that both their design goals and their values goals are supported.

Any game design heuristic, however, would be ill conceived without either accompanying an existing creative process or being able to conceivably work in an existing design context. If many game designers practice an iterative model of design, then these ideas must integrate. The critical play process might therefore look like this:

The iterative cycle would do better to become more open, more reflective at this point in the evolution of playculture, given the long history of the technical benefits, increases in inclusion, and widening of social discourse achieved by alternate design methods. For example, in my own research into play systems, I have noted a number of ways in which girls participating in play environments, such as their long history of doll play, worked against these systems, and how players in popular computer culture use intervention or subversion in games as a play method. Feminist criticism and practice has played an important role in informing such disruptions with technology, as well as examining how power relationships are upheld and how intervention is orchestrated. Leading technologist and game designer Brenda Laurel has noted, "Culture workers at their best make just such conscious interventions—mindfully creating technologies that cause us to produce new myths, and mindfully making art that influences the shape of technology."[11] The disruption of contemporary games, whether through play, or preferably, through original designs that eschew the embedded interaction styles of current computer games may offer models for other emerging practices in playculture. Designer actions are powerful sites of empowerment for giving a voice to marginalized groups.

But a critical design methodology requires the shifting of authority and power relations more toward a nonhierarchical, participatory exchange. While the games made might disrupt the existing social realities offered by most popular games, they also disrupt the design process itself. Instead of compliance to a pattern whereby the usual designers develop the usual ideas through the usual stages for the usual players, what is needed now is a model that will augment these practical but limited stages of the design process in a way that addresses intervention, disruption, and social issues

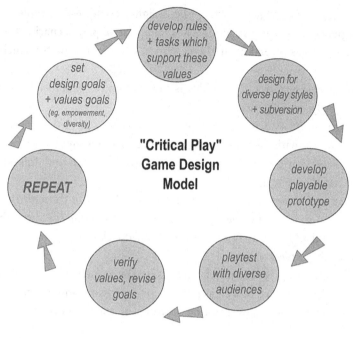

| Figure 8.2 |
Mary Flanagan, model of critical play method.

and goals alongside of, or even *as*, design goals embedded into the mechanic and game elements.

Here I would like to propose a different model, one that approaches critical play. The critical play method (figure 8.2) introduces several crucial elements into the iterative model.[12] Human concerns, identifiable as principles, values, or concepts, become a fundamental part of the process. While moving through the stages of the Critical Play Method, the artist, activist, or designer can reflect upon the state of his project and see if the design continues to meet the base goals set initially for the research:

- *Set a design goal/mission statement and values goals.* The designer sets the goals necessary for the project to create meaningful play, and sets one or more equally weighted values goals.
- *Develop rules and constraints that support values.* The game designers rough out a framework for play, including the types of tokens, characters, props, etc. necessary to support the game's values and play.

- *Design for many different play styles.* The designer could, for example, provide for a noncompetitive type of play alongside a competitive play scenario. The designer should design for subversion of the system and other means by which play can emerge.
- *Develop a playable prototype.* The idea is mocked up on paper or by acting it out during the early stages of design.
- *Play test with diverse audiences.* Designers need to get out of the studio or laboratory and play test with a wide-ranging audience, making sure to play with nontraditional gamers. Various players test the game for dead ends and dull sections, and types and levels of task difficulty.
- *Verify values and revise goals.* Designers evaluate the game through the play tests and player comments. They verify that the values goals emerge through play, and revise goals and add or drop options based on feedback to ensure an engaging game and support the project values.
- *Repeat.* This process is repeated to make sure the game supports the values it set out to frame and support, as well as provide an engrossing and playable experience. These two criteria for success must be measured in each iterative cycle.

Within the critical play method, difference and value are fundamental concerns. Testing with paper, performance, or electronic prototypes should prove to be an especially important means of verifying that design decisions agreed upon during the process, such as equity in power relations or enhancing diversity; the system should adequately handle the complexities of critical play principles. In such testing, it is necessary to determine not only that a particular feature or idea was successfully implemented in a technical component but also that its implementation did not detract from prior decisions that were functional, interactive, or conceptual in nature.

The iterative design process is well known; research has shown that iterative cycles can help designers facilitate feedback, including the discussion and evaluation of embedded social issues, while keeping the creation of a game more dynamic.[13] For artists making games, this approach is useful too. The cyclical nature of the creative process can serve as a parallel studio practice and involve the community with which the artist wishes to engage. After all, games are dynamic systems.

In making anything, however, there tends to be a gap between what was intended and what actually is created. Here, a critical play perspective engages a diverse audience of testers to ensure that the particular aspects of the project that are informed by conceptual, thematic, and technological factors continue to "say the same thing" once the project is finished. This agreement to examine the "doing" of "practice" can be of use in the laboratories of artists as well as those of independent designers interested in politics or social justice.

The critical play method may also assist those in mainstream game development innovate by suggesting radical, fresh ways of playing. Significant innovations in the design of games can be made by changing design and development methodologies currently used by companies, teams, and individuals and by incorporating artists' and activist approaches along with methods such as iterative design. Games are artifacts of historic and cultural importance, but they are also something *beyond artifact* in that games also function as a set of activities that carry conventions like audience role, interaction, currency, and exchange. There are systematic causal correspondences between particular design features in games that indicate specific social conceptualizations and outcomes.

Design Actions and Design Methods

Deleuze argues that as people, we "normally perceive only clichés. But, if our sensory-motor schemata jam or break, then a different type of image can appear: a pure optical-sound image, the whole image without metaphor, brings out the thing in itself, literally, in its excess of horror or beauty, in its radical or unjustifiable character."[14] For art to move beyond cliché, Deleuze believes it must engage with a set of strategies "to show how and in what sense" an image means x or y to wrest the image away from the danger of cliché.[15] Therefore, one of the most important frameworks critical play can provide is a range of examples that show what artists have done in their creation of games and play. Throughout this book, I've examined the ways artists have used doll play, instructions, obnoxious language, tactile letters, street text, and maps in their games to pose questions. Other practices, like Boal's "Theater of the Oppressed," offer further insights on ways to move both the game developer and the game player beyond "normalcy." Each chapter of this book can be used to generate strategies meant to inspire other artists, designers, and innovators. From chapter 4 alone, the tactics include:

- writing commands or instructions
- using obnoxious language
- making humans into puppets
- making computer programs that write poems
- making words tactile
- creating instruction paintings
- making palindromes

- shifting points of view
- creating sound poetry
- making text that is a street intervention
- skywriting

I also have explored some noteworthy methods for the production of games. These have included:

- Simultanism, a method defined as a telescoping of time
- free verse/free visual verse
- automatism
- the drift, derive, detournement, and psychogeography

These methods preserve what has been accomplished in critical play and will, in turn, help designers examine "what's out there" in contemporary circles, providing a vocabulary for existent techniques that risk going unnoticed. But while play, art, and politics are intertwined, the ways in which designers and artists can intervene currently remain in the affordances of these fields. As Jacques Rancière notes, "The arts only ever lend to projects of domination or emancipation what they are able to lend to them, that is to say, quite simply, what they have in common with them: bodily positions and movements, functions of speech, the parceling out of the visible and invisible."[16]

Shifts in Play

In addition, criticality in play can be fostered in order to question certain aspects of game content, or certain aspects of play's scenario function, many of which might otherwise be simply assumed necessary. Guattari, for one, calls on the arts to produce a "refoundation of the problematic of subjectivity," wanting to bring to forward "a partial subjectivity—pre-personal, polyphonic, collective, and machinic."[17] In a similar vein, Yale professor James C. Scott writes about subjugated persons and how the subjugated public resists power (1990). He examines the spaces where those dominated can express their "hidden transcript," or offset narrative, one that serves to critique those in power.[18] It is easy to see that games provide one such outlet. An effort to reveal or make visible these "hidden transcripts" that often lie among the "official transcripts" of power relations parallels the investigations of many players and artists in a variety of milieus. Is this not the essence of unplaying? If Sutton-Smith is correct in asserting that much of what children do in play serves as compensation for their general life conditions, then the hidden transcript played by those who are far from empowered can perhaps communicate to game designers important strategies through which games can expose, validate, or celebrate these equally valid modes of discourse.[19] In turn, players may use this information and their experiences to alter the social institutions we live by. Using the critical play method, the role of the designer can widen to include an analytical framework for comprehension or analysis, characterized by a careful examination of social, cultural, political, or even personal themes that function as alternates to popular play spaces.

The challenge, then, is to find ways to make interesting, complex play environments using the intricacies of critical thinking and to encourage designers to offer many possibilities in games, for a wide range of players, with a wide range of interests and social roles. We can manifest a different future. It is not enough to simply call for change and then hope for the best; we need interventions at the level of popular culture.[20]

Too often social challenges are presented in overwhelming or depressing ways. Most players are not attracted to overly didactic communication. After all, play occurs only when players feel comfortable. Play is, by definition, a safety space. If a designer or artist can make safe spaces that allow the negotiation of real-world concepts, issues, and ideas, then a game can be successful in facilitating the exploration of innovative solutions for apparently intractable problems. Play offers a way to capture player interest without sacrificing the process of thinking through problems that are organized subjectively. Games engineer subjectivity because they create, or rather they are, both affective and relational systems, both for the designer and for the player. Critical play is not about making experts, but about designing spaces where diverse minds feel comfortable enough to take part in the discovery of solutions. Derived from artists' creative processes, investigations, and practical work, critical play is to popular computer games what performance art once was to the traditional, well-made stage play. As in that earlier shift, critical play demands a new awareness of design values and power relations, a recognition of audience and player diversities, a refocusing on the relational and performative as opposed to the object, and a continued and sustained appreciation of the subversive. Critical play is also a new discipline of theory and practice that embodies a set of methods and actions. The critical play method is intended as a tool for future game makers, play designers, and scholars. The desired results are new games that innovate due to their critical approach, games that instill the ability to think critically during and after play.

Just as artists have long experimented with such transcripts and have worked to integrate social concerns in their work, game designers have the option to open up, experiment with, unplay, reskin, and rewrite the hidden transcripts so tenaciously rooted in the systems of our world. As we have seen, social climates and technological changes have greatly affected play environments on an everyday level. Shifts in play have historically mirrored shifts in technology and these shifts in technology signal shifts in societal norms. With groups tired of isolation and longing for community, the rise of massively multiplayer online role-playing games and social networks have provided a few ways to relink communities. The continuing popularity of Come Out and Play events in major global cities demonstrates that the public wants to play, and play outside, because of what games are: creative, collective, and social reactions to the dominant practices and beliefs of any culture.[21] From these simple examples, it is possible to see how games in and of themselves function as a *social technology*. Games distill or abstract the everyday actions of players. Games also imprint our culture with the motives and values of their designers. Above all, a game is an opportunity, an easy-to-understand instrument by which context is defamiliarized just enough to allow what Huizinga famously refers to as his "a magic circle" of play to occur.

Notes

1 Introduction to Critical Play

1. Computer games constitute a massive cultural form internationally, have special relevance in the United States: retail sales of video games in the United States in 2004, for example, exceeded $6.2 billion, not including hardware, peripherals, and related products, on par with much-studied and theorized media such as film.
2. Duchamp, *The Writings of Marcel Duchamp*, 123.
3. This phrase being of course a play on John Cage's famous saying, "I have nothing to say and I am saying it." Even if Cage refused the idea of the lone expressive artist expressing himself to the masses, his framework of chance operations and contextual participatory art expresses and values a different system of creativity, and thus a game-like system of priorities and values.
4. Sutton-Smith, *The Ambiguity of Play*, 174.
5. Pellegrini, *The Future of Play Theory*.
6. Sutton-Smith, *The Ambiguity of Play*, 87, 107, 107, 50, and 49, respectively.
7. Huizinga, *Homo Ludens*; Csikszentihalyi, "Some Paradoxes in the Definition of Play"; Sutton-Smith, *The Ambiguity of Play*; Salen and Zimmerman, *Rules of Play*.
8. Sutton-Smith, *The Ambiguity of Play*, 91.
9. Sutton-Smith, interview by E. Zimmerman.
10. Huizinga, *Homo Ludens*, 25.
11. Ibid., 32.
12. Ibid., 36.
13. Ibid., 38–39.
14. Blanchard and Cheska, *The Anthropology of Sport*; Sutton-Smith, *The Ambiguity of Play*; Pellegrini, *School Recess and Playground Behavior*; Pelligrini, *The Future of Play Theory: A Multidisciplinary Enquiry*; and Pellegrini and Smith, *The Nature of Play*.
15. Huizinga, *Homo Ludens*, 39.
16. Costikyan, "I Have No Words," par. 28.
17. Ibid., par. 15–16.
18. Ibid., par. 20.

19. Salen and Zimmerman, *Rules of Play*, 80.

20. Ibid.

21. Formanek-Brunell, *Made to Play House*.

22. Ollman, *Class Struggle Is the Name of the Game*.

23. McLuhan, *Understanding Media*, 238.

24. Judovitz, "Rendezvous with Marcel Duchamp," 184–202.

25. Dean, "Claude Cahun's Double," 71–92.

26. Fer, *Realism, Rationalism, Surrealism*.

27. *Oxford English Dictionary*, 88.

28. Gramsci and Williams describe subversion as behavior that works against the mono-lithic structures of "culture" and "state"; these structures Gramsci grouped under the concept of hegemony—the dominance of one group over other groups. Subversion is offered as a way to undermine such powers. However, the monolithic powers in technoculture do not directly correspond with the structures Gramsci was working against. Computer culture, and the widespread availability of information, for instance, makes it impossible to homogenize the different kinds of structures in operation. Jameson's concept of late capitalism, whereby capitalism co-opts any possibility of change or dissent back into its own matrix, is slightly more useful to extend this definition, for in this way we can better analyze the hegemony of cultural imperialism we see in globalization practices. See: Jameson, *Postmodernism*; Gramsci, *Modern Prince and Other Writings*; Gramsci, *Selections from the Prison Notebooks*; Gramsci, *Prison Notebooks, Volume 1*; Williams, *Culture and Society 1780–1960*; Williams, *Television*; and Williams, *The Country and the City*.

29. Foucault also extends the definition of subversion through his work on nineteenth-century industrial revolution and the contemporary formation of Western nations and statehood. Foucault's *History of Sexuality*, for instance, details the discourse of regulation in the nineteenth-century, and its sites for subversion of this regulation. Contrary to Freud, who developed the idea that the unconscious regulated dark matters, that sexuality, death, repression of desires were all linked within a framework to the workings of the mind, Foucault challenges the direct equation between personal "regulation" and the hegemonic state. Certainly the state, he argued, had a direct, vested interest in the control of the population's repressed desire and sexual urges. See Foucault's "Intellectuals and Power"; *Discipline and Punish*; *Language, Counter-Memory, Practice*; and *Politics, Philosophy and Culture*.

30. Butler, *Gender Trouble*; contemporary philosophers such as Judith Butler define subversion broadly, discussing the performative nature of subversion as a potential site for transgression.

31. In the twenty-first century, the division of power changes and becomes much murkier. In terms of subversion, things have shifted from Gramsci's ideas of hegemony to more distributed hegemony; there is no one medium. Dick Hebdige in his book

Subculture noted the tendency to celebrate moments of resistance amid mass cultural forms from music to television; in his research he noted ironically, however, that "power breeds resistance": as power structures exist in order to simultaneously contain these subversions, there is no real way to escape power. Williamson, "The Problems of Being Popular," and Morris, "Banality in Cultural Studies," also criticized academics that had spent their time finding subversion in any media form and through any kind of action.

32. Such as subRosa, the artists group that creates installation and media works. In the context of technological experiences, feminist scholarship has been particularly focused on ideas of subversion.

33. Hardt and Negri, *Empire*.

34. *Oxford English Dictionary*, vol. 8, 1989, 3.

35. For over a century, artists have utilized the "manifesto" to communicate their ideology and group goals (such as the Futurists' declaration of 1909, or the many Dada and Surrealist manifestos by Tzara and Breton).

36. Goodman, *Contemporary Feminist Theatres*.

37. For El Theatro or BRT, see Elam, *Taking It to the Streets*; for feminist film and video, see Mellencamp, *Indiscretions*; and Echols, *Daring to Be Bad*.

38. Whiteread is an artist who creates reverse sculptures of everyday space; see, for example, Townsend, *The Art of Rachel Whiteread*.

39. Wark, "Suck on this, Planet of Noise!"

40. Christensen, *The Innovator's Dilemma*.

41. Anthony and Christensen, *Seeing What's Next*.

42. Compelling accounts of cheating in computer games have been examined by Consalvo, *Cheating*.

43. Jenkins, "Complete Freedom of Movement." The field of game studies has been slow to open itself to activist, social, racial, or activist critique. In fact, as computer gaming has grown into a major industry, and as computer game studies emerges as a respected focus of academic study, the parallel example of artists working in critical play is not as visible. For artists who examine gender relations in terms of power, digital culture can be particularly frustrating; aspects critiqued by scholars include violence in games, online harassment, the representation of the human/machine "cyborg" woman, and the ways in which digital products represent desire, commerce, race, and gender. See Haraway, *Simians, Cyborgs, and Women*; Sutton, "Cocktails and Thumbtacks in the Old West"; and Flanagan, "Hyperbodies, Hyperknowledge." All of these writers problematize the relationship among gender and computer games. "Other" in "cyberculture," from the representation of women in games to the creation of technologies that help run, for example, activist websites, leaves the disenfranchised less and less interested in cyberculture's artifacts. The representation and experiences of "other" in cyberculture are connected to structures that

epistemologically shape those experiences. By these I mean the types of representation in digital cultural artifacts (from texts, such as cyberpunk fiction, to net games, to high-technology films such as *The Matrix*), the point of view and styles of game play/interaction roles that are offered to players or participants in various media forms, and the structure of the relationship of the user to the media experience.

44. Important critiques of patriarchy from Irigaray, *This Sex Which Is Not One*, and technology, science, and scientific processes from Fox Keller, *Reflections on Gender and Science*; Haraway, *Simians, Cyborgs, and Women*; and Rose, *Feminism and Geography*, equipped scholars to do further activist research in gender and technology areas, and the theories generated by cultural critics of gender and visual culture have been used to develop larger critical discourses on cinema, architecture, the visual arts, and popular culture. Gayatri Chakravorty Spivak, for example, a noteworthy scholar in the activist movement, proposed building upon existing research methodologies to render visible the unheard voices of the oppressed; see Spivak, *In Other Worlds*.

2 Playing House

1. Sports offer fascinating examples that blend information in the form of scores, logging names, and bets with social event and game. People attended the races to see and be seen, and cocktails and parlor-style games such as cards extended onto the booths near the track, making the race track a site for an early gaming network that changed with cultural and industrial shifts.

2. In writing about play and the view many citizens and scholars hold of play as a type of frivolity, Brian Sutton-Smith has noted that play, often considered inconsequential or mere whimsy in more traditionally austere areas, has historically been controversial, shocking, or dismissed by the ruling class (*The Ambiguity of Play*, 205). This is indeed the case for traditional forms of art, such as painting, in an era when a fascination with the playful rendering of everyday life among the "high arts" was incorporated into a body of work.

3. Hindman, "Pieter Bruegel's Children's Games, Folly, and Chance," 455.

4. Ibid.

5. Sutton-Smith, in *The Ambiguity of Play*, discusses the high-art and low-art aspects of play in culture and the class bias inherent in distinctions about play. See also Ollman, *Class Struggle Rules*.

6. Brusati, *Artifice and Illusion*.

7. Van Hoogstraten's peepshow boxes are held in collections around the world. *The Perspective Box of a Dutch Interior* (1663), for example, is held at The Detroit Institute of Arts.

8. Arnheim, "Brunelleschi's Peepshow."

9. Armstrong, "The Dollhouse as a Ludic Space."

10. Caillois, *Man, Play and Games*, 66.

11. Milam, *Fragonard's Playful Paintings*.
12. Sutton-Smith, *Toys as Culture*.
13. Milam, "Playful Constructions and Fragonard's Swinging Scenes," 549.
14. Ibid.
15. Lefebvre, *The Production of Space*.
16. Piaget, *Play, Dreams, and Imitation in Childhood*; Vygotsky, "Play and Its Role in the Mental Development of the Child"; Bruner, "Play, Thought, and Language"; Bergen, *Play as a Medium*.
17. Bredekamp, *Developmentally Appropriate Practice*, 3.
18. Slavin, *Educational Psychology*, 72.
19. Bettelheim, "Play and Education," 2.
20. Veblen, *The Theory of the Leisure Class*.
21. Sutton-Smith, *The Ambigiuty of Play*, 116.
22. Some material in this chapter is derived from the prior research publication, Flanagan, "SIMple & Personal."
23. Formanek-Brunell, *Made to Play House*.
24. This moment is particularly relevant to digital culture, given that the majority of computer games and network-based artworks on the Internet also moved from the space of spectacle and privileged distribution (i.e., science labs, arcades) to situations in which the consumption of these experiences takes place in domestic environments.
25. Cross, *Kids' Stuff*.
26. Kuznets, "Taking Over the Dollhouse.
27. Foucault, *The History of Sexuality*.
28. Formanek-Brunell, *Made to Play House*, 22.
29. Lefebvre, *The Production of Space*, 121.
30. Armstrong, "The Dollhouse as a Ludic Space, 1690–1920," 23.
31. Many feminist scholars have noted that the space of the domicile is thought to be a traditional space, limiting to women and nurturing to men, clearly centered inside patriarchal structures. If it is as Lyn Spiegel, *Make Room for TV*, suggests that domestic space has been historically linked to the feminine, players engaging in a game set in a dollhouse are in turn "feminized" in such roles. Daphne Spain, in her book *Gendered Spaces*, looks at domestic spaces cross-culturally and at the influence of gender associations in particular rooms. In dollhouse games, players encounter a fascination with household objects, with consumption, and with normative class values. The feminization of the player manifests through the design of the game space, game tasks, and game goals, and is reflected socially through the dominance of consumer culture.
32. Roth, "Scrapbook Houses," 308.
33. Ibid., 302.

34. Formanek-Brunell, *Made to Play House.*
35. Campbell dolls were manufactured by the Horsman Doll Company in 1910 and sold for one dollar. The original dolls were stuffed with cloth and cork and covered with linen muslin. Clothing for the dolls was most frequently a simple coverall and pinafore. Both Campbell dolls and Dolly Dingle were created by artist Grace G. Drayton.
36. Sutton-Smith, *The Ambiguity of Play*, 295.
37. Formanek-Brunell, *Made to Play House*, 8.
38. Formanek-Brunell, *Made to Play House*; Flanagan 2003
39. Formanek-Brunell, *Made to Play House*, 32.
40. Turner, "Body, Brain, and Culture."
41. Formanek-Brunell, *Made to Play House*, 20.
42. Ibid., 22.
43. Ibid., 23.
44. Ibid.
45. Kahn, "Murder is Merely Child's Play," 8EB, par. 16.
46. Formanek-Brunell, *Made to Play House.*
47. Ibid.
48. Hillier, *Automata and Mechanical Toys.*
49. Formanek-Brunell, *Made to Play House*, 41.
50. Wood, *Edison's Eve*, 111.
51. Formanek-Brunell, *Made to Play House*, 42.
52. Hillier, *Automata and Mechanical Toys*, 93–94.
53. Formanek-Brunell, *Made to Play House.*
54. Powell, Lowry, and Racine, "Forward," xi.
55. Bezolla, *André Breton*, 14.
56. Dadaists' social role was to balk and protest, "hobby horse" to and fro against trite narratives of noble politics and traditional art aesthetics. The name of the movement, "dada," is said to be a translation of "hobby horse."
57. Bell, "Puppets and Performing Objects in the Twentieth Century," 30.
58. Ibid.
59. Ibid., 28.
60. Dickerman, "Zurich," 74.
61. Ibid., 30.
62. Ball, *Flight Out of Time*, 64.
63. Roos, "Oskar Kokoschka's Sex Toy."
64. Hutchison, "Convulsive Beauty."
65. Deleuze, *The Logic of Sense*, 307.
66. Taylor, *Hans Bellmer.*
67. Webb and Short, *Hans Bellmer.*

68. Freud, "The Uncanny."

69. Lichtenstein, *Behind Closed Doors.*

70. Taylor, *Hans Bellmer*, 2.

71. Foster, *Compulsive Beauty.*

72. Ibid., 66.

73. Haslam, *The Real World of the Surrealists*, 99.

74. *Hell* by the Chapmans, and other works in the Saatchi collection, were destroyed in a Leyton, UK fire in 2004.

75. Williams, "L'Étranger," 11.

76. Passage from William Shakespeare's *King Lear* at I, iv.

77. In recent writing Rosler is ambivalent about "political art," noting that often, political art may not necessarily lead to good art, but that it can. In a 2004 *Artforum International* essay, Rosler notes, "At its best, Conceptual and other post-Pop forms of art led to a tremendously productive encounter between artists and the 'life world,' providing a space for deduction, exposition, and insight, as well as self-revelation and play" ("Out of the Vox," par. 7). For future work, however, Rosler suggests interactive work and computer games as a direction for interventionist artists.

78. In March 2002, Electronic Arts announced that *The Sims* was not only the best-selling game in 2000 and 2001, but also had become the best-selling PC game of all time, selling over 6.3 million copies worldwide. Translated into fourteen different languages, the game also appeals to women: in 2002 almost half of the players were women (in later games, this percentage rose) (Business Wire, "*The Sims* Becomes the Best Selling PC Game of All Time," par. 1).

79. Crawford, *The Art of Computer Game Design*; Formanek-Brunell, *Made to Play House.*

80. Half of all Americans age six and older played computer and video games in 2003, while the average age of a game player hovers at around twenty-nine. In fact, the demographics of game players are almost evenly split into thirds between the categories "under 18," "18–35," and "over 36." See Interactive Digital Software Association (2003) "Games are positive addition to children's lives, parents say—Data from the IDSA's 2003 computer survey."

81. Business Wire, "*The Sims* Becomes the Best Selling PC Game of All Time."

82. There are many ways in the game to garner more money through "cheat keys" as well as labor.

83. Bittanti and Flanagan, *Similitudini. Simboli. Simulacri.*

84. Busch, *Geography of Home*, 45.

85. Silverstone, *Visions of Suburbia*, 3.

86. Boal, "Three Days in the Most Surreal Game on Earth," par. 13.

87. Spiegel, *Make Room for TV*, 2.

88. After the crash of the dot-com economic boom, spending in the United States on durable goods dropped significantly, though it was still higher than pre-dot-com

indices—in fact, since September 11, 2001, spending on durable consumer goods such as appliances and furniture has increased more than ten points, especially on kitchen appliances, alarm systems, and home technologies.

89. *Tomorrow's Cities, Tomorrow's Suburbs*, by Lucy and Phillips, analyzed U.S. metro areas and found that by 2000, older neighborhoods (pre-1940s) have made comebacks, while many suburbs have sunk lower in relative income. This is true for cities such as Detriot, Atlanta, Baltimore, Chicago, and San Francisco.

90. Graner Ray, *Gender Inclusive Game Design*.

91. Douglas, *The Feminization of American Culture*.

92. Huizinga, *Homo Ludens*.

93. Spain, *Gendered Spaces*; Silverstone, *Visions of Suburbia*.

94. Examples such as the film *Fight Club* (1999) show how consumption and domestic interests are literally feminized and therefore literally "fought against" by the development of the male-only fight club spaces.

95. Kuznets, "Taking Over the Dollhouse," 152.

96. Sutton-Smith, *Toys as Culture*.

97. Willis, "Symbolic Creativity," 287.

98. Jameson, *Postmodernism*.

99. Simms, "Uncanny Dolls," 663.

100. Deleuze, *The Logic of Sense*, 307.

101. Psychoanalytic discourse organizes human experience in sweeping binarisms, such as nature/culture, passive/active, woman/man, and posits much of lived experience in terms of transference between these binary states. Famous critics, from Irigaray to Derrida, have found various flaws with many of Freudian and Lacanian models of desire. Thus psychoanalysis has fostered a problematic binary extremism that refuses to take into account multiplicities of desire and lived experience.

102. Deleuze, *The Logic of Sense*, 307.

103. Juul, "Games Telling Stories?"; Salen and Zimmerman, *Rules of Play*.

104. Kiplinger's Personal Finance Magazine. "Women Play More Games Online," 9.

105. Winnicott, *Playing and Reality*.

106. This research appeared in Flanagan, "SIMple & Personal.

107. Mulvey, "Visual Pleasure and Narrative Cinema."

108. Žižek, *Everything You Always Wanted to Know about Lacan*, 223.

109. Žižek, "Looking Awry," 35.

110. Ibid., 37.

111. Ibid.

112. Urizenus (user name), "Maxis Is Deleting In-Game References."

113. Kuznets 1994, 10.

114. Ibid.

115. Huizinga, *Homo Ludens*.

| 271 |

Notes to Pages 61–69

116. Sutton-Smith, "Interview."
117. Irigaray, *This Sex Which Is Not One*, 80.

3 Board Games

1. Csikszentmihalyi and Bennett, "An Exploratory Model of Play," 46.
2. The game was determined to be a women's game by Western anthropologists in the early twentieth century, but its original purpose remains unclear in Western texts.
3. Some of the mancala boards in evidence today appear portable; examples even include animal-shaped and fish-shaped board cases; See: Durai, "Pallanguli."
4. Agudoawu, *Rules for Playing Oware*.
5. H. J. R. Murray, *A History of Board Games other than Chess*; Russ, *The Complete Mancala Games Book*.
6. Rollefson, "A Neolithic Game Board," 1–3.
7. Agudoawu, *Rules for Playing Oware*.
8. Brumbaugh, "The Knossos Game Board," 136.
9. Documentation of stakes play and gambling in these ancient games is extremely limited. Ibid., 137.
10. H. J. R. Murray, *A History of Board Games Other than Chess*, 1978, 23.
11. Austin, "Roman Board Games II," 76.
12. Ibid., 77.
13. Ibid., 78.
14. Ibid., 79.
15. Murray, *A History of Board Games other than Chess*, 1978, 233(f).
16. Csikszentmihalyi and Bennett cite Huizinga and others in this argument in "An Exploratory Model of Play," 47.
17. Csikszentmihalyi and Bennett, "An Exploratory Model of Play," 47.
18. Brumbaugh, "The Knossos Game Board," 137. The ends of the lengthwise board were used to store the pieces.
19. Cribbage was said to have been invented by Sir John Suckling in the 1600s in England.
20. Over one hundred Senet boards exist in museums and collections, having been found in a number of tombs. A painting in the Third Dynasty tomb of Hesy holds the oldest-known painting of Senet (ca. 2686–2613 BC) in which two people play against each other. The boards generally consist of three identical tracks for game markers divided into thirty squares.
21. Piccione, *Senet, Gaming with the Gods*.
22. Over one hundred Egyptian Senet boards are currently housed in the ancient civilization collections of institutions around the world, with the oldest at the Musée du Cinquantenaires in Brussels, Belgium; see Costell, *The Greatest Games of All Time*.

23. Fairbairn, "Go in Ancient China," par. 13.
24. Parlett, *The Oxford History of Board Games*, 168.
25. Fairbairn, "Go in Ancient China," par. 16. See also Fairbairn's classic, *Invitation to Go*.
26. Rollefson, "A Neolithic Game Board," 1–3.
27. Murray, *A History of Board Games other than chess*, 1978, 2.
28. Austin, "Roman Board Games I."
29. First documented by Carolus Linnaeus in 1732 during his travels through Lapland, where he observed the game having eight blonde Swedish soldiers and a king, and eight dark Muscovites and a king. Cited in Bell and Cornelius, *Board Games Round the World*, 4.
30. Murray, *A History of Board Games other than Chess*, 1978, 56.
31. Ibid., 101.
32. Hamilton, *The Celtic Book of Seasonal Meditations*, 237.
33. Murray, *A History of Board Games other than Chess*, 1978, 119.
34. Parlett, *The Oxford History of Board Games*, 202.
35. Ibid.
36. Provenzo and Provenzo, *Favorite Board Games*, 168.
37. Ibid.
38. Lo, "The Game of Leaves."
39. Ito, "The Muse in Competition," 201.
40. Kakuchi, "Tokyo Treasure Hunt," 56.
41. Ibid.
42. Eskin, "Pass Go."
43. Kakuchi, "Tokyo Treasure Hunt," 56.
44. Ibid.
45. Ibid.
46. Jackson in Hofer, *The Games We Played*, 14.
47. Hofer, *The Games We Played*, 13.
48. Turim, "American His-toy-ry."
49. Hofer, *The Games We Played*, 14.
50. Jensen, "Teaching Success through Play"; O'Brien, *The Story of American Toys*.
51. Orbanes, *Game Makers*, 15.
52. Jensen, "Teaching Success through Play," 812–819.
53. Bowdidge, "Toys and Sporting Goods"; Turim, "American His-toy-ry."
54. Bolton, "The Game of Goose," 146.
55. Jensen, "Teaching Success through Play."
56. Stevens Heininger, *A Century of Childhood*, 8.
57. Goodfellow, *A Collector's Guide*, 53.
58. Ibid.

59. Wallace Adams and Edmonds, "Making Your Move," 372.
60. Ibid., 373.
61. Jensen, "Teaching Success through Play," 812–819.
62. Games have continued to reflect popular interests; significant changes in finances and an interest in investing, for example, mirrored the rise of board games such as *Monopoly* in the 1930s.
63. Hofer, *The Games We Played*, 82.
64. In Spanish writings, the Wandering Jew is called "Juan Espera en Dios," which is a hopeful term for the one who apparently retained in his personal memory the details of Christ's crucifixion.
65. Jenkins, "Reviews," par. 5.
66. Candeloro, "The Single Tax Movement and Progressivism," 114.
67. Anspach, *Anti Monopoly*.
68. Williams, "Monopoly."
69. Zeisel, "The Surveys that Broke Monopoly."
70. Ollman, *Class Struggle Rules*.
71. Caillois, *Man, Play, Games*, 29.
72. Aragon et al., "The Surrealist Manifesto."
73. Ibid.
74. André Breton and fellow surrealists in "A Surrealist Manifesto, The Declaration of January 27, 1925," as printed in Nadeau, *The History of Surrealism* 240–241.
75. Conley, *Automatic Woman*, 5.
76. Breton, par. 30.
77. Both the Cornell and Shaw works are housed at the Smithsonian American Art Museum, Washington DC.
78. Lord, 138.
79. Klemm, 100.
80. Klemm, 104.
81. Salen and Zimmerman, *Rules of Play*, 34.
82. Michael Colmer (1976), among other historians of the pinball machine and the arcade, notes that pinball, the most popular game of the 1930s, has its origins in the nickelodeons and penny arcades of the early twentieth century, which used kinetoscope machines and other visual entertainment machines to attract visitors. Where board games had primarily been games of domestic space, these games were public. In addition, while many board games had been suitable for children, and a not insignificant number designed by women, the arcade became quickly defined as a place featuring games popular with men, conducted in masculine spaces. Bagatelle was a pastime imported along with French soldiers who assisted the United States in the Revolutionary War. Over time, pinball machines evolved from primitive mechanical contraptions to devices with levels, narratives, and even more mechanical features

(Hoffman 1993, 96). In fact, both the Japanese form of the game (pachinko) and the U.S. form (pinball) developed from these simpler wooden parlor games, aided by the 1870 patent awarded to Montague Redgrave for a spring-loading plunger to launch the ball in Bagatelle. Such an invention set the stage for development of the game (Howell 1986, 94).

The aura of "seediness" with pachinko parlors and pinball arcades, mostly male environments, has been an artifact of the early development of public game spaces. Pachinko parlors in Japan were historically located in *doya-gai* (flophouse) neighborhoods and historically these parlors attracted primarily male customers for gambling. Because women in both the West and the East rarely went unescorted to entertainment establishments like arcades or theaters, available subject matter followed this trend, and even the earliest kinetoscope film arcades depicted the working of machines, bawdy humorous skits, or dancing women (Musser 1991). Bally founder Ray Moloney distributed his pin-based ball game in the early 1930s, spawning a group of pinball manufacturing companies to fill burgeoning arcades.

Cited as the most popular activity among mid-century poor urban Japanese men, "Pachinko is therefore genuine gambling and is the preferred activity of laborers on rainy days when they cannot work and do not have any other hope of getting hold of money except by chance" (Caldarola 1968, 521). Contemporary game parlors are more similar to casinos, with attendance in the tens of millions, some offering childcare facilities and restaurants as well (Fawcett 1983, 41).

83. Sharpe 1977, 19.
84. Absolute Arts, "Fluxus Games Exhibition," par. 3.
85. Cook. "What? Institutional? Us?," par. 5.
86. Here I have in mind Fluxus works such as the *Licking Piece* (1964) performance by Ben Patterson (1934–), in which Fluxus members covered shapely women with whipped cream in order to lick it off at a public exhibition.
87. Cage, "An Autobiographical Statement," par. 17.
88. Kelley, "Myth Science," 1.
89. Richard, "Oyvind Fahlstrom," 167.
90. Ibid.
91. Fahlström, "On Monopoly Games," 82.
92. Moore College of Art Gallery, *Öyvind Fahlström*.
93. Arnold Herstand & Co., *Öyvind Fahlström*, 3.
94. Marcoci, "Perceptions at Play," 9.
95. Stonard, "Gabriel Orozco"; Ebony, "Improbable Games," par. 2.
96. Orozco, "Games," par. 2.
97. Bennett, "Aesthetics of Intermediality," 432.
98. Joselit, "Gabriel Orozco."

99. Orozco, "Games," par. 8.

100. Parlett, *The Oxford History of Board Games*, 168. A reworded account from Pinckard's translation of the poem in *The Go Player's Almanac*.

101. Ball, "Artists Statement, *GO ECO,*" par. 3.

102. Ibid., par. 2.

103. The first Western scholarly account of chess was written in 1689 by Thomas Hyde (1636–1702), who published *Historia shailudii* (History of Chess). In 1694, Hyde published *De Ludis Orientalibus*. Sir William Jones (1746–1794), a poet and lingust, published the paper "On the Indian game of Chess" (1790), which identified India as the birthplace of chess. Later, Duncan Forbes (1798–1868), a professor of Oriental languages, published *The History of Chess* (1860), confirming his theory that India was the birthplace of chess five thousand years earlier. In 1913 H. J. R. Murray wrote *A History of Chess*, a classic.

104. Tronzo, "Moral Hieroglyphs," 18.

105. Ibid., 19.

106. Basulto, Camuñez, and Ortega, "Azar Game in the Book of the Dice of Alfonso X The Learned."

107. Tronzo, "Moral Hieroglyphs," 21.

108. Ibid., 23.

109. Yalom, *The Birth of the Chess Queen*.

110. Franklin, "The Morals of Chess."

111. Marcoci, "Perceptions at Play," 7.

112. Schwarz, "Game of Precision."

113. Murray, *A History of Chess*.

114. Breton, *Free Rein*, 75.

115. Pearce, "Games AS Art."

116. Yoshimoto, *Into Performance*, 129.

117. Ibid., 126.

118. Ibid., 128.

119. Munroe et al., *Y E S Yoko Ono*.

120. Allison, "Board Meetings."

121. Ibid.

122. Benjamin, "Critique of Violence."

123. This sense of nuance is also present to some extent in the game of Go. Though the game outcome is a single winner, the winning is far less spectacle-oriented, and functions within part of a whole, as a percentage of the board. In chess, winning is constituted by taking each piece, and by the usefulness of the pieces. Due to their almost heroic abilities, pieces seem to be taken in individual "murders."

124. Murray, *Hamlet on the Holodeck*, 126.

4 Language Games

1. Crystal, *Language Play*.
2. As mentioned, each of these categories could be theorized in book-length volumes. Several forms will not be explored much at all, including the categories of riddles. But I do wish to note that the riddle may have been used historically as a critical form of play, though there are many examples of simple whimsy. For instance, a riddle appears in an ancient Babylonian text: "Who becomes pregnant without conceiving, who becomes fat without eating?" (a rain cloud). See Augarde, *The Oxford Guide to Word Games*, 1. Anagrams, riddles, palindromes, acrostics, chronograms, spoonerisms, and pangrams each emerged in the earliest of languages, and flourished among Greek and Latin scholars. J. W. Shoemaker in his treatise *Practical Elocution* even elevated tongue twisters as "recreations in articulation."
3. Tse Bartholomew. *Hidden Meanings in Chinese Art*.
4. Picture-based puns are well documented. A decorative painting showing goldfish in a pond depicts the characters "gold fish fill the pond." But in the spoken language, this can also sound exactly like "may gold and jade fill your home," a proper good-luck wish. See Rudolph, "Notes on the Riddle in China," 68.
5. West, *Transcendental Wordplay*.
6. Shattuck, *The Banquet Years*, 199.
7. Ibid., 11.
8. Beaumont, *Alfred Jarry*.
9. Jarry, "Preface," *Ubu Roi*, 2.
10. Jarry, *The Ubu Plays*.
11. Ibid.
12. Thackary, *Vanity Fair*.
13. The Sator-Rotas square is discussed in reference to the square forming the acrostic "A PATERNOSTER O." Milburn, *Early Christian Art and Architecture*.
14. Some ancient language games like Sator-Rotas continue to puzzle classics scholars. The specific rebus containing the Latin SATOR AREPO TENET OPERA ROTAS (translating to the mysterious "Arepo holds the wheels with effort" (i.e., work) are written in a square. Not much is conclusively known about the square but it was left over much of the Roman Empire. For in-depth research, see Sheldon, "The Sator Rebus."
15. May, "Language-Games and Nonsense."
16. *Alice's Adventures in Wonderland* (1865), *Through the Looking Glass* (1872), and the subset of *Looking Glass*, *Jabberwocky*; the author was a graduate of Christ College and Oxford professor, an ordained deacon, amateur photographer, and mathematician. He was also a mystic interested in the occult. In 1857, he published "The Hunting of the Snark," a social satire, with the Snark standing in for the ever-elusive goal of societal "popularity" (White, "Biography," 553). Ludwig Wittgenstein, a noted

linguistic philosopher, argues that a language is a "language-game," and that the entirety of language is an assembly of many other, smaller language games; see Wittgenstein, *Philosophical Investigations*. In essence, Wittgenstein is interested in games because, like language, they are governed by rule-based activities.

17. Blake, *Play, Games, and Sport*, 56.

18. Fisher, *The Magic of Lewis Carroll*, 274.

19. This section is from Poe's "Silence: A Fable," available through public domain books, http://www.classic-literature.co.uk/american-authors/19th-century/edgar-allan-poe/silence-a-fable/. Poe's use of language games is more fully explored in Zimerman, *Edgar Allan Poe;* "Silence" is discussed as a palindrome on pages 264 and 265.

20. Erman, *Life in Ancient Egypt*, 396.

21. Noegel, *Nocturnal Ciphers*.

22. R. Mutt refers both to a mongrel dog, and to the Mott Street firm that made sanitation equipment where the work was allegedly created. Rosalind Krauss has argued that it was a pun for the German *armut*, meaning "poverty," which would change the meaning of the work entirely, but Duchamp refuted this claim in an interview, saying "Rosalind Krauss? The redhead? It isn't that at all." Harrison and Wood, *Art in Theory 1900–2000*, 1024.

23. Kuspit, "A Critical History of 20th-Century Art," par. 9.

24. Duchamp, *The Box in a Valise*, 125.

25. Adams Sitney, "Image and Title in Avant-Garde Cinema," 103.

26. Duchamp, *Anemic Cinema*.

27. Kuenzli, *Dada and Surrealist Film*, 52.

28. White, "Biography," 555.

29. Schwarz, *The Complete Works of Marcel Duchamp*.

30. This poem is available on Ubuweb, http://www.ubu.com/historical/mallarme/dice.html.

31. Shattuck, *The Banquet Years*, 309.

32. Apollinaire in Ibid., 309.

33. Ibid.

34. Ibid.

35. Stunned and enraged by the slaughter of modern warfare, Vaché committed suicide in 1919.

36. Tzara, "Seven Dada Manifestoes," 92.

37. Apollinaire, cited in Shattuck, *The Banquet Years*, 308–309, originally published in his own *Soirées* under a pseudonym.

38. Hausmann, cited in Benson, "Mysticism, Materialism, and the Machine in Berlin Dada," 50; originally printed in Raoul Hausmann, "Seelen-Automobil," *Der Dada* no. 3 (1920).

39. Ibid., 52.

40. Höch, cited in Ibid.

41. Lappin, "Dada Queen in the Bad Boys' Club"; Gammel, *Elsa*, and Sawelson-Gorse, *Women in Dada*.

42. Anderson founded *The Little Review* in 1914 in Chicago; it was the first publication to print Dadaist writing and artwork. The editors and staff moved the press to New York in 1917.

43. Hughes, "Camping Under Glass," 113.

44. Kuenzli, "Baroness Elsa von Freytag-Loringhoven," 458.

45. Rodker, "'Dada' and Else von Freytag von Loringhoven"; Hjartarson and Spettigue, *Baroness Elsa*.

46. Gammel, *Elsa*; Hjartarson and Spettigue, *Baroness Elsa*; Lappin, "Dada Queen in the Bad Boys' Club."

47. See Reilly, "Elsa von Freytag-Loringhoven," 30. Freytag-Loringhoven created portraits of Duchamp and others through photography and sculpture; her work and her personality permeated the work of other Dada artists. See Naumann, Venn, and Antliff, *Making Mischief*; Churchill, *The Little Magazine Others*.

48. Lappin, "Dada Queen in the Bad Boys' Club," 308. von Freytag-Loringhoven's two writing series, "Subjoyrides" and "Ready-Made Poems," were created as collages of advertising slogans she gathered from the New York City subway.

49. Ibid., par. 12

50. Brotchie and Gooding, *A Book of Surrealist Games*, 17.

51. Ibid., 10.

52. Gascoyne, *The Magnetic Fields*, 41.

53. Thodore Flournoy studied psychic Catherine Elise Muller, also known as Helene Smith, for five years and reports on this work in: Flournoy, *From India to the Planet Mars*.

54. Chénieux-Gendron, *Surrealism*, 111.

55. Breton, "Manifesto of Surrealism 1924."

56. Gascoyne, "Introduction," 48.

57. David, "Cadavre exquis."

58. Durozoi, *History of the Surrealist Movement*.

59. Martyniuk, "Troubling the 'Master's Voice,'" 61.

60. Irigaray, *This Sex Which Is Not One*, 1.

61. Martyniuk, "Troubling the 'Master's Voice.'"

62. Barnes, *The Book of Repulsive Women*.

63. Conley notes that the mental illnesses of both Carrington and Zürn were likely more "genuinely surreal" experiences than any of the psychological events and experiments carried out by male artists of the time, and that these women had a great impact on both future feminist writing (namely, Kristeva, Irigaray, and Cixous) as well as later avant-garde artists (Conley, *Automatic Woman*). See Zürn, *The*

Man of Jasmine & Other Texts, for the Man of Jasmine story. Regarding gender and Surrealist artists, Breton and Eluard's *L'Immaculee Conception* features woman as a powerful Virgin figure. Most images and texts about women from Surrealist men tend to fragment and sexualize the body, and specifically in the Bretonian Surrealist romance, *Nadja* (1928), present women as unknowable and often mad. The figure of woman, to many Surrealist artists, was a primary means to access the unconscious, but as such a means, the female becomes objectified. The women artists working in the movement included photographer Lee Miller and photographer-writer Claude Cahun, sculptors Meret Oppenheim and Maria Martins, painters Remedios Varo, Dorothea Tanning, Leonora Carrington, Leonora Fini, Kay Sage, and Frida Kahlo, and writers Djuna Barnes and Nancy Cunard, though this is in no way an exhaustive list.

64. Sutton-Smith, *The Ambiguity of Play*, 133.
65. Ibid., 134–135.
66. Fluxus was influenced primarily by Dada in that it shunned authority and produced works of nonsense and incongruity. Surrealism and its investigation of the unconscious and playful processes are also invoked. Other art movements also came into play, but are less instrumental to this participatory, playful history, including Bauhaus, the twentieth-century design school that redefined everyday objects and means of production, and the Situationists, who were interested in massive social change through large-scale, primarily social actions. In the movements discussed here, play and subversion are threads feeding each successive movement.
67. Deleuze, "What Is Becoming?"
68. Dempsey, *Art in the Modern Era*.
69. Ellipses mine. From the letter "George Maciunas to Tomas Schmit, January 1964," in Hendricks, *FLUXUS CODEX*, 37.
70. Jones, *Killing Monsters*.
71. Spencer is known as the inventor of the terminology *social structure* and *social function* in the contemporary sense—that is, acknowledging the framework of institutions in the West. See Spencer, *First Principles*, 694.
72. Munroe et al., *Y E S Yoko Ono*.
73. Ono, *Instruction Paintings*.
74. Ono, *Grapefruit*.
75. Higgins, *Fluxus Experience*, 118.
76. Ibid., 121.
77. Ibid.
78. Foster, *Compulsive Beauty*.
79. Guerrilla Girls, "Get Naked."
80. Utterback, "Unusual Positions," 226.
81. Ibid., 221.

82. See the feminist critiques of science and the theory of standpoint epistemology offered by Haraway, Harding, Harstock, and Hill Collins: Haraway, "Situated Knowledges"; Harding, *Whose Science? Whose Knowledge?*; Harstock, *The Feminist Standpoint Revisited*; and Hill Collins, *Black Feminist Thought*.
83. Braidotti, "Cyberfeminism with a Difference," par. 22.
84. Guattari, *Chaosmosis*, 21.

5 Performative Games and Objects

1. Huizinga, *Homo Ludens*, 28.
2. In fact, Roger Caillois critiqued Huizinga's approach as being far too general, and argued instead for the strengths of further classification so that granularity and specificity could be achieved in studying types of games. See: Caillois, *Man, Play and Games*.
3. Phalen, *The Unmarked*.
4. In 1990s performances, Stone would go through a process of separating out her sexual organs from her experience of orgasm. See also Stone, *The War of Desire and Technology*.
5. Csikszentmihalyi, *Flow*.
6. Cole and Knowles, *Researching Teaching*, 66.
7. Duchamp, *Salt Seller*.
8. Glimcher, *Logical Conclusions*, 7.
9. Marcel Duchamp, quoted in Judovitz, "Rendezvous with Marcel Duchamp," 202.
10. Decordova, *Picture Personalities*.
11. Wayne, *Crawford's Men*, 11.
12. Curtin, "Fanfiction.net Statistics," par. 1. In terms of contemporary digital fan culture, fan fiction on the web and its companion slash fiction are constantly growing phenomenon, fostered by the ease of distribution on the Internet. In 2003, fan sites such as fanfiction.net have surpassed one million original entries.
13. Matisse, "Notes d'un Peintre."
14. Kandinsky, *Concerning the Spiritual in Art*.
15. Paul, *Digital Art*.
16. Arp, *On My Way*. Artists including Arp, Hugo Ball and Emmy Hennings, Sophie Taeuber, and Hans Richter joined with Tristan Tzara.
17. Duchamp's readymades, which appeared first in France, and in New York City after 1915 include: a bicycle wheel (1913); a bottle rack (1914); a shovel (1915); a chimney cowl (1915); a comb (1916); a typewriter cover (1916); a hat rack (1917, New York); a coat rack (1917); and a urinal (1917).
18. Jean Arp, a classically trained German-French sculptor and painter, began exhibiting abstract paper and wood sculptures during World War I. *Collage Arranged According to the Laws of Chance* (1916–1917) explored chance operations in paintings, a

precursor to other art movements involving gaming. Dada, noted Arp, was a movement to "discover an unreasoned order" (*ordre déraisonnable*) (1948). Arp, like other Dada artists, was working against presumptions about artistic styles and voice, and even questioned the possibility of expression. The fascination with chance is important to subversion and, as will be argued in later chapters, becomes important to the feminist version of playculture.

19. Elderfield, *The Modern Drawing*, 108.
20. Ollman, "The Lives of Hannah Höch"; Lavin, *Cut with the Kitchen Knife*; Kimmelman, "Dada Dearest."
21. Nochlin, *Women, Art and Power*, 29.
22. Ollman, "The Lives of Hannah Höch"; Lavin, *Cut with the Kitchen Knife*; Kimmelman, "Dada Dearest."
23. Nochlin, *Women, Art and Power*, 28.
24. Parlor games went out of fashion as radio, film, and other mass-media forms emerged to occupy leisure time.
25. Ernst, from his journals (1925, 1991) and as featured in the video recording by Schamoni and Lamb, *Max Ernst*.
26. Rosemont, *Surrealist Women*.
27. Adamowicz, *Surrealist Collage*.
28. The Surrealists' deep engagement in Freudian thinking played a significant role in the development of their games, and war played no small part in their experience. Breton finally met Freud after the war in Vienna in 1921.
29. Breton, "Second Manifesto of Surrealism," 117.
30. Breton, Essays in *Médium*, 137.
31. Dali, "The Conquest of the Irrational," 49.
32. Dali's thoughts on the Paranoid-Critical method are collected in *Oui: The Paranoid-Critical Revolution—Writings 1927–1933* (Boston: Exact Change, 1998). Dali's desire for a thorough confusion is alluded to in "The Moral Position of Surrealism," 110. Originally published in 1971 in French.
33. Kay Sage, married to Yves Tanguy, or Jacqueline Lamba, married to Breton. Their marriages assisted them in acquiring some public recognition of their work, but also kept them from eclipsing the success of their partners.
34. Harris, *Surrealist Art and Thought*, 164–165.
35. Krauss, "The Photographic Conditions of Surrealism," 35.
36. Gamman and Marshment, *The Female Gaze*, 16.
37. Conley, citing John Roberts, in "Claude Cahun's Iconic Heads," 13.
38. Dean, "Claude Cahun's Double."
39. Knafo, "Claude Cahun"; Rice, *Inverted Odysseys*.
40. Tanaka and Kanayama, *Electrifying Art*.
41. Munroe, *Japanese Art after 1945*.

42. Munroe, *Japanese Art after 1945.*

43. Stevens, "Everything Is Illuminated," par. 3.

44. Ibid., par. 6.

45. Munroe, *Japanese Art after 1945.*

46. Tanaka and Kanayama, *Electrifying Art.*

47. Ibid.

48. Hendrix, "U.S. Teenage Girls Prefer Japanese Heroes."

49. Murakami, *Welcome to TakashiMurakami.com.*

50. Ibid.

51. Kon, *Paprika.*

52. Caillois, *Man, Play and Games,* 5.

53. Lewitt, "Paragraphs on Conceptual Art," 824.

54. Ibid., 422.

55. Guattari, *Chaosmosis,* 21.

56. Documentation of this work shows that Grooms's performance manifested essential links to the shocking performance work of Alfred Jarry's *Ubu Roi* creations, discussed in the last chapter. Pasty Man should be read as a reference to the Ubu character, a "gross, vulgar, stinking character fills the stage with his filth and relentlessly thrusts himself and his shiteness at us till the better end. No celestial or metaphysical forces direct Ubu, nor does he have a spiritual nature. He is not in the least capable of introspection" (Schumacher, *Alfred Jarry and Guillaume Apollinaire,* 57). Grooms also incorporated pop culture icons—the comic strip characters Dick Tracy and Little Orphan Annie made their way into his work.

57. Rosenthal, Rainbird, and Schmuckli. *Joseph Beuys.*

58. Macuinas, *Manifesto on Art.*

59. George Maciunas had Nam June Paik play his *Piano Piece #13 (Carpenter's Piece)* in 1962, and then directed him to hammer nails into every key of the piano until the instrument was destroyed.

60. Cook, "What? Institutional? Us?," par. 1.

61. Absolute Arts, "Fluxus Games Exhibition," par. 5.

62. MASS MoCA exhibition, "Fluxus Games," June 16–Dec. 30, 2001.

63. Alison Knowles noted this tendency of Duchamp at "I am 120: Marcel Duchamp's Birthday Party," Miguel Abreu Gallery, New York, July 27, 2007; it is this spirit, then, that makes gallery display of Fluxus work problematic. Take, for example, the more recent exhibition of Robert Filliou's *7 Childlike Uses of Warlike Material* (1970) in the Centre Pompidou. These objects appear more like a jumble of detritus than art, except for the sanctioning glow of the white gallery wall.

64. Cage, "An Autobiographical Statement," par. 25.

65. Knowles, cited in Robinson, *Sculpture of Interdeterminacy,* 3.

66. See Jones, *Killing Monsters.*

67. Spencer is known as the inventor of the terms *social structure* and *social function* in the contemporary sense, that is, acknowledging the framework of Western institutions. See: Spencer, *First Principles*, 694.

68. Knowles, *Bread and Water*.

69. Lefebvre, "The Everyday and Everydayness."

70. Knowles cited in Robinson, *Sculpture of Interdeterminacy*, 7.

71. Salen and Zimmerman, *Rules of Play*.

72. Elliot, "Interview (with Yoko Ono)," par. 9.

73. Nochlin, *Women, Art and Power*; see her essay, "Why Are There No Great Women Artists?"

74. Elam, *Taking It to the Streets*.

75. Mellencamp, *Indiscretions*; Elam, *Taking It to the Streets*.

76. Hyde, "André Cadere at Art," 192.

77. Birnbaum, "André Cadere," 271.

78. Hyde, "André Cadere at Art."

79. Birnbaum, "André Cadere," 271.

80. Ibid.

81. *America's Army* cost over $3 million and was created by professional game makers for the U.S. military.

82. Schleiner, *O.U.T.* (text). http://www.opensorcery.net/OUT/htm/project.htm, 2004, par. 3.

83. Barthes, "The Death of the Author," 145 (italics in original).

84. Schleiner, "Cracking the Maze Curator's Note," par. 4.

85. The 2004 Whitney Biennial included *Super Mario Brothers: Clouds* by Cory Archangel; the New York Guggenheim included Archangel's *I Shot Andy Warhol* game in a 2004 exhibition; the Barbican Gallery in London showed the "Game On" exhibition in 2002; and the "Bang the Machine" computer gaming art exhibition was shown in early 2004 at the Yerba Buena Arts Center in San Francisco. It is interesting to note that several major computer gaming art exhibitions have taken place in London, for London's ICA was the site of the first computer arts exhibition in the world: "Cybernetic Serendipity," curated by Jasia Reichardt in 1968.

86. Ostojic, "Looking for a Husband with a EU passport," par. 1.

87. See Gajjala, "Third-World Critiques of Cyberfeminism"; Sundén, "What Happened to Difference in Cyberspace?"

88. Critical Art Ensemble. *Digital Resistance*.

89. Martin et al., "Now the SI."

90. The Yes Men, *The Yes Men*, par. 1.

91. Ibid.

92. Ibid.

93. The Yes Men, *Vivoleum*, par. 3–4.

94. Salen and Zimmerman, *Rules of Play*, 528.
95. Fluegelman, *The New Games Book*, 9.
96. Ibid., 137.
97. Murray, *Hamlet on the Holodeck*, 126.
98. Readings, *Introducing Lyotard*, 69.
99. Guattari *Chaosmosis*, 34.
100. Harris, *Surrealist Art and Thought*, 127.
101. Maciunas, *Manifesto on Art/Fluxus Art-Amusement*.
102. Caillois, *Man, Play and Games*, 5.
103. Ibid., 5–6.
104. Recent game scholars' definitions of games are located in chapter 1, where definitions such as "a system in which players engage in an artificial conflict, defined by rules, that results in a quantifiable outcome" are described by contemporary scholars Salen and Zimmerman, *Rules of Play*, 80.
105. Nochlin, *Women, Art and Power*, 147–158.
106. Shade Regan, "Whose Global Knowledge?" 61.
107. Ibid.
108. Bourriaud, *Relational Aesthetics*, 58.

6 Artists' Locative Games

1. This chapter was first presented at the Digital Arts and Culture Conference, Perth, Australia, 2007. Portions may have subsequently been published in the Leonardo Electronic Almanac, through proceedings.
2. For more on the Situationists, see Debord, "Introduction to a Critique of Urban Geography."
3. Tuters and Varnelis, "Beyond Locative Media."
4. Broeckmann, "Exhibiting Locative Media."
5. de Certeau, *The Practice of Everyday Life*, xix.
6. Ibid.
7. Artists and workers employ tactical maneuvers of "la perruque" (a worker does his or her own work while "on the job") and "bricolage" (a piecing together of materials and ideas to create new cultural forms from the ground up) in their everyday challenges to authority (de Certeau, *The Practice of Everyday Life*). These ideas are closely aligned with practice techniques described later in the thesis, in which particular opportunities for subversions, interventions, or disruptions are necessarily designed into games. De Certeau's theory described action in physical spaces but can easily be applied to movement and action in games, as games, too, create their own spaces (Fuller and Jenkins, "Nintendo and New World Travel Writing").
8. de Certeau, *The Practice of Everyday Life*, 37.
9. Symons, *Aura*, par. 3.

10. Breitsameter, "Sound as Multi-User-Choreography."
11. Symons, *Aura*.
12. Breitsameter, "Sound as Multi-User-Choreography," par. 5.
13. Huizinga, *Homo Ludens*, 4.
14. One counter argument to this claim might be that the international prevalence of simple, nonverbal games such as rock, paper, scissors (RPS) transcends space and culture. When all else fails, many people can, at the very least, play RPS together. But the rules, the counting, and even the reason to play in the first place are still culturally specific. The author has been baffled by local variations of RPS, including one with over fifty extra gestures thrown in, a true RPS mod with levels, new weapons/invisible scoring, over the top performances, and intense scoring systems.
15. Serlin, "Disabling the *Flâneur*."
16. Wollen, "Situationists and Architecture," par. 9.
17. Debord, "Report on the Constructions and the International Situationist Tendency's Conditions of Organization and Action," 705.
18. Debord designed and created a board game in 1978 called *The Game of War*, unusual for its grand strategies that seem to fly in the face of psychogeographic approaches.
19. Ibid., 704.
20. Paulos et al., "Metapolis and Urban Life," par. 1.
21. Benford et al., "Coping with Uncertainty in a Location-Based Game"; McGonigal, "'This Is Not a Game'"; McGonigal, "SuperGaming."
22. "The Beast" game is documented by Lee and Stewart and Jane McGonigal. For more information on la fuga, see Negone, *La Fuga*; 42 entertainment, *I Love Bees*; Newt Games, *Mogi*; and Lantz and Slavin, *ConQuest, Numb3rs*, and *Crossroads*.
23. Gitman and Gomez de Llarena, *Noderunner*.
24. Lantz et al., *Pacmanhattan*.
25. Chang and Goodman, "Asphalt Games."
26. The *B.U.G.* project was initiated to explore more participatory methods for urban planning. See: Design Institute, *Big Urban Game*.
27. Heyward, *Traces*; Snap-Shot-City's *Snap Shot City*; Blast Theory's *Can You See Me Now, Uncle Roy All Around You*, and *I Like Frank*.
28. Paulos et al., "Metapolis and Urban Life."
29. Rheingold, *Smart Mobs*.
30. Wollen, "Situationists and Architecture," par. 9.
31. Blast Theory, *Can You See Me Now?*, par. 4.
32. Richards, "Ars Electronica: Interface Futures," par. 9.
33. Lefebvre, *The Production of Space*.
34. Judd, "Visitors and the Spatial Ecology of the City," 34.
35. Paulos et al., "Metapolis and Urban Life," par. 14.

36. As the author of this book, I've avoided discussion of my own work for the most part. It is the case, however, that much of my work parallels the various concerns in this book, which developed in parallel to my own creative practice.

37. Kwon, *One Place After Another*.

38. One of the key characteristics of modernist and postmodernist art is the premise of interrogation, or of calling into question the role of art, the role of the artist, and how artwork fits into economic and political issues. Many artists have challenged institutions, of course, but many also challenge the very media in which they work. From painters as diverse as "image makers" Monet, Picasso, and Cezanne, to "sculptor" Duchamp, to "poet" Gertrude Stein, a formalist deconstruction of the medium is historically an inherent principle behind much work in any medium in the last century. It is this key attribute that joins the artist and the activist, the person who plays with the very notion of the medium in which they work, and the person challenging or disrupting social and institutional norms. It is a very different task, however, for artist/activists, or those outside various media industries, to infiltrate and critique the medium for artistic concerns, and subsequently, use that medium for larger social critique. The most potent artistic/activist projects bring an awareness of the medium to the project, and an awareness of context. In fact, historically speaking, the less transparent the artist's role, the better, so there can be no mistaking critique with mainstream media production; think of Paper Tiger TV and early video art, which used rough hand-me-down cameras and less-than-ideal conditions to disrupt the mainstream consumption of video. For many years artists strove to achieve more professional results, with the bottom line being that they couldn't without the technology, team, time, or funding. In contemporary media art circles, however, this oppositional low-tech mode of working is not necessarily central to current practices. Many video artists shoot beautiful images in high definition, and produce high-quality media for consumption. Also, even "home-brew" game makers can mod existing games, using the textures and models by others or creating these themselves, and many such mods could in fact model the real game spaces quite closely.

39. Doherty, *From Studio to Situation*.

40. Come Out and Play, "Come Out and Play," 1.

41. McGonigal and Bogost, *Cruel 2 B Kind*, par. 5.

42. Ibid., par. 3.

43. Anne Herbert, a *Whole Earth Review* contributor, coined the expression, "Practice random kindness and senseless acts of beauty" in 1982. These acts are meant to surprise or be performed for others for no apparent reason but generosity. See Herbert, Pavel, and Oda, *Random Kindness & Senseless Acts of Beauty*.

44. Holmes, "Income Disparity Between Poorest and Richest Rises."

45. The game *Massively Multiplayer Soba* (2008) by the Tiltfactor laboratory addressed this question of inclusivity by not only holding the events in diverse communities

outside of central Manhattan (the game was planned for Jackson Heights, the nation's most diverse neighborhood) but was designed to include meaningful interactions with passers by as well as an invitiation to dinner to the strangers who help the players along the way. See Tiltfactor.org for more information.

46. A second example of appropriating space as a game board is in the live series of "Graveyard Games" in 2005 across the United States. The games occurred in Historic Elmwood Cemetery in Kansas City; the Italian Cemetery in San Francisco; the Historic Congressional Cemetery in Washington, DC; and cemeteries in New York, Atlanta, and Los Angeles. At the Hollywood Forever cemetery, sixty people convened for the grand end to a game of "Last Call Poker." In the middle of the poker tournament, instructions arrived via the Internet that players were to set out on a hunt through the cemetery for a series of specific graves. Players could receive bonus points by completing "favors" to the graveyard, such as cleaning, and documenting these favors in an email to Patricia Pizer, the lead designer on "Last Call Poker." The game's final instructions were for participants to gather around the grave of a little boy and pay homage by offering "Last Call Poker" chips worth $500 or more (Terdiman, "'Last Call Poker' Celebrates Cemeteries"). In arguing for the benefit of the game, organizer McGonigal noted, "It's only in the last 100 years that we've treated cemeteries as very separate spaces and not a part of everyday lives. . . . Prior to the twentieth century, they were the original parks and recreation areas" (Ibid., par. 6.) While organizers had permission to run the games in the cemeteries, "some relatives of people buried in the Italian Cemetery where the event was held objected to the notion of a game being played in what they consider to be a sacred space" (Ibid., par. 4).

47. Chang and Goodman, "Asphalt Games"; Tuters and Varnelis, "Beyond Locative Media"; ISEA, "Call for Participation."

48. Barnard, "The Legacy of the Situationist International," 107.

49. Activist theatre director Augusto Boal's public games methods were derived from his work while creating *The Theatre of the Opressed*, developed during the 1950s and 1960s in Brazil. Boal incorporated games that could serve to "act out" problematic social situations that directly affected participants' rights.

50. Tuters and Varnelis, "Beyond Locative Media," 362.

51. Sutton-Smith, *The Ambiguity of Play*.

52. See Blumenberg, *The Legitimacy Of The Modern Age*; Bruckner, *The Temptation Of Innocence*; Carse, *Finite and Infinite Games*; Csikszentmihalyi, *Beyond Boredom and Anxiety*; Sutton-Smith, *The Ambiguity of Play*.

53. Sutton-Smith, *The Ambiguity of Play*, 174.

54. Ibid.

55. Sutton-Smith's notion that play can cure children of the hypocrisies of adult life was mentioned in chapter 1. Sutton-Smith argues that children's play, spanning from

early childhood to teenage years, offers narratives that negotiate the risks of the real world. Sutton-Smith, *Interview with Brian Sutton-Smith*. To Sutton-Smith, play objects tend to be a simulation of the objects of the real world, having more or less abstracted relationships to known things; see Sutton-Smith, *Toys as Culture*.

56. Judd, "Visitors and the Spatial Ecology of the City."
57. Chang and Goodman, "Asphalt Games."
58. Flanagan, "The 'Nature' of Networks."
59. ISEA, "Call for Participation."
60. Montola and Waern, "Ethical and Practical Look at Unaware Participation."
61. Ibid., 190.
62. Lefebvre, *The Production of Space*, 41.
63. Butt, "Local Knowledge," 324.
64. Particularly citing the work of Lev Manovich and his detailing of the distinctive properties of new media, including discrete and recombinatory representation, numerical representation/algorithmic manipulation, automation, and variability, i.e., objects existing in different versions. See Manovich, *The Language of New Media*.
65. Debord, "Theory of the Dérive."
66. Glowlab, *Conflux*.
67. Wollen, "Situationists and Architecture," 9, also citing Debord.
68. Ibid.
69. Duc et al., *You Are Not Here*.
70. Boal, *The Rainbow of Desire*, 12.
71. Bey, *The Temporary Autonomous Zone*.
72. Ibid., 98.
73. Ibid.
74. Mitchell, "The End of Public Space?"
75. Nowacek, Salen, and Zurkow, *Karaoke Ice*.
76. Miranda Zúñiga, from the artist's website, http://www.ambriente.com/cart/about .html.
77. Similar games work by Raphael Fajardo also engages with questions of migration.
78. Bhabha, *Nation and Narration*, 294.
79. Bhabha, *The Location of Culture*, 9.
80. de Certeau, *The Practice of Everyday Life*, 28.
81. Butler, *Gender Trouble*, 9.

7 Critical Computer Games

1. Annual retail sales of video games in the United States in 2004, for example, exceeded $6.2 billion, not including hardware, peripherals, and related products. In 2007, video game and PC game sales exceeded $18.8 billion. See the NPD group report, "2007 U.S. Video Game and PC Game Sales Exceed $18.8 Billion."

2. Helen Nissenbaum and I have written about this in our 2006 CHI paper. For myriad debates on these areas, see at least: Anderson, "An Update on the Effects of Playing Violent Video Games"; Anderson and Dill, "Video Games and Aggressive Thoughts, Feelings, and Behavior in the Laboratory and Life"; Johnston, "Doom Made Me Do It"; Media Education Foundation, *Game Over*; Melillo, "Video-Game Group Creates Ads to Deflect Criticism."

3. CAWAMSET, *Land of Plenty*.

4. U.S. Department of Commerce, *How Americans Are Expanding Their Use of the Internet*.

5. See Wardle, Martin, and Clark, "The Increasing Scarcity of Women in Information Technology Is a Social Justice Issue." A similar challenge exists in the United Kingdom within technological fields such as the computer gaming industry: Natalie Hanman notes that women are on the sidelines in game play and employment, constituting only 17 percent of the games industry workforce in 2005.

6. See Koster, *A Theory of Fun for Game Design*, and Slagle, "Women Make Small Inroads in Video Game Industry."

7. Rosler, "Out of the Vox," 218.

8. International Game Developers Association, *Game Developer Demographics Report*.

9. Lenhart et al., *Teens, Video Games, and Civics*.

10. Ibid.

11. Gibbs, "Girls Got Game."

12. See Corneliussen and Walker Rettberg, *Digital Culture, Play, and Identity*.

13. More than two and one half million copies of *EverQuest* and its expansion packs have been sold since 1999; for more information, see Miller, "Players, Dollars, Keep Online Worlds Turning." For information on *World of Warcraft*, see Kirkpatrick, "World of Warcraft Hits 10 Million Subscribers."

14. Kiplinger's Personal Finance Magazine. "Women Play More Games Online."

15. Oser, "Moms are Unsung Players in Gaming World."

16. Roberta Williams has been a prolific designer, with game design credits such as *Phantasmagoria* (1995), *The Dark Crystal* (1982), and the *King's Quest* series (1980s).

17. Even though in this text I've documented Alison Knowles's electronic writing, is it part of the "canon" of digital media development? In current texts, her contributions are not often highlighted. I would argue that this should change.

18. Note, for example, the inherent racism in the game *Manhunt* (2003) from Rockstar Games, in which players can choose which ethnic group to chase and kill.

19. See Bookchin, "The Best of Natalie Bookchin." Portions of this chapter have previously been published in "Next Level" by the author.

20. Chesher, "Layers of Code," par. 5.

21. Ibid., par. 84.

22. Mary K. Jones, producer for Edmark software, notes in an interview that while it is too simple to blame video games for cultural violence, games do offer a unique encounter with violent imagery when compared to other media; "I think the trouble with computer-game violence is that you actually cause it to happen . . . you make choices in computer games." In Gillespie 2000, 17.
23. Mountford is cited in Utterback, "Unusual Positions," 218.
24. Franck, "A Feminist Approach to Architecture," 295.
25. For a video of Fort Paladin in operation, see Stern's website, http://www.eddostern .com/fort_paladin.html.
26. Vanouse, *The Relative Velocity Inscription Device*, par. 3
27. Ibid.
28. Fuller, *Thomas Kuhn*; and Kuhn, *The Structure of Scientific Revolutions*.
29. Caps in original; Flatfile Galleries, *Media Alert May 2007*.
30. Digg, "One Room, One Paintball Gun."
31. Petrilla, *United American Committee*, par. 2.
32. Bilal, "Virtual Jihadi," par. 3.
33. Ibid., par. 4. For more information on Bilal, see his forthcoming book from City Lights Press.
34. Frasca, "Videogames of the Oppressed."
35. Crawford, "What Is a Game?,"par. 21.
36. Frasca, "September 12th, a Toy World," par. 2–3.
37. Frasca, in Isbister, *Better Game Characters by Design*, 19.
38. Ibid.
39. Player post from GameGirlAdvance.com, ibid.
40. The Values at Play exercise is called "Grow a Game," and was created to help game designers take human values into account. See http://www.valuesatplay.org.
41. Antonisse et al. as cited in the press release for the Better Game contest for the Values at Play project; see http://valuesatplay.org/?p=247#more-247.
42. Bogost, "Persuasive Games."
43. See the feminist critiques of science and the theory of standpoint epistemology offered by Haraway, Harding, Harstock, and Hill Collins. See: Haraway, "Situated Knowledges; Harding, *Whose Science? Whose Knowledge?*; Harstock, *The Feminist Standpoint Revisited*; and Hill Collins, *Black Feminist Thought*.
44. Braidotti, "Cyberfeminism with a Difference."
45. Woods, "Loading the Dice," par. 1.
46. Here the term *serious games* is used in a way that is aligned with games researchers and practitioners such as the Serious Games Summit 2004 participants including Jim Dunnigan, John Wilson, Ian Bogost, Gonzalo Frasca, Aaron Thibault, and others.
47. Crawford, from "What Is a Game?," par. 35.
48. Lee, "I Lose, Therefore I Think," par. 2.

49. Keating et al., "Darfur Is Dying," par. 1–3.
50. This is text from one of the many losing scenarios in the game, playable at the website, http://www.darfurisdying.com/.
51. At http://www.peterpacket.org.
52. Lee, "I Lose, Therefore I Think," sec. 1.
53. The very existence of social impact games functions as a critique of the prevailing tendencies of the gaming industry itself.
54. Ibid., sec. 7.
55. Frasca, "Videogames of the Oppressed," par. 20.

8 Designing for Critical Play

1. Csikszentmihalyi and Bennett, "An Exploratory Model of Play."
2. McLuhan, *Understanding Media*, 242.
3. Bhabha, *The Location of Culture*, 1994.
4. Schleiner, "Operation Velvet Strike," par. 11.
5. Here, I should note I have taken on socially engaged design projects since the 1990s, particular in designing for girls and underrepresented groups. I also create artwork that has elements of play. At the moment I'm also working with Dr. Helen Nissenbaum on Values at Play, a research project to broaden these themes and see how game designers might design for human values. See http://www.valuesatplay.org.
6. The theme of critical play emerged be my dissertation work 2001–2005, and comes from my considerable work in activist design and a creative practice aligned with the avant-garde. My collaborator, Helen Nissenbaum, and I have more recently developed a method for taking human values into account, called the Values at Play method. The Critical Play Method is definitely informed by this work; appreciation and credit must go to Helen for introducing the term *values* and all it implies to the process. I hope I can adequately summarize by saying that Helen is interested in how values are embedded in various technologies, and I am more interested in the array of values brought forward in a game; how the system, the conditions of play, and the participants each bring values that are constantly "at play" with one another. This idea is both the name of our project, and a continual source of inspiration.
7. I have discussed contemporary computer games before in terms of the problematic representation of female characters, epistemological concerns, spatial concerns, etc. See: Flanagan, "The 'Nature' of Networks"; "My Profile, Myself in Playculture"; "The Bride Stripped Bare"; "Hyperbodies, Hyperknowledge."
8. Zimmerman, "Play as Research."
9. Schön, *The Reflective Practitioner*, 155.
10. For example, P. E. Agre, Introduction.
11. Laurel, *Utopian Entrepreneur*, 103.
12. The iterative process is best documented in Fullerton's *Game Design Workshop*.

Notes to Pages 258–262 |

13. Bødker and Grønbæk, "Cooperative Prototyping"; Shneiderman, "Universal Usability"; Freeman-Bensen and Borning, "YP and Urban Simulation."
14. Deleuze, 1989, 20.
15. Ibid., pp. 20–21.
16. Rancière, *The Politics of Aesthetics*, 19.
17. Guattari, *Chaosmosis*, 21.
18. Scott, *Seeing Like a State*, 1990, xi.
19. Sutton-Smith, *The Ambiguity of Play*, 114.
20. Laurel, *Utopian Entrepreneur*, 103.
21. Here I extend McLuhan's ideas to include the creative response that games represent. See McLuhan, *Understanding Media*, 235.

Bibliography

Film, Video, Artworks, Games

42 Entertainment. *I Love Bees.* 2004. http://ilovebees.com/.

Blast Theory. *Can You See Me Now?* 2001. http://www.blasttheory.co.uk/bt/work_cysmn .html.

Blast Theory. *Uncle Roy All Around You.* 2003. http://www.blasttheory.co.uk/bt/work_cysmn .html.

Blast Theory. *I Like Frank.* 2003. http://www.blasttheory.co.uk/bt/work_cysmn.html.

Center for Tactical Magic. *Tactical Ice Cream Unit.* 2005.

Duc, Thomas, Laila El-Haddad, Kati London, Dan Phiffer, Andrew Schneider, Ran Tao, and Mushon Zer-Aviv. *You Are Not Here.* 2006. http://www.youarenothere.org/.

Duchamp, Marcel. *Anemic Cinema (A Palindrome)* (seven-minute film). 1926.

Ernst, Max. *Max Ernst: Journey into the Subconscious.* 1925. Dir. Peter Schamoni and Dr. C. Lamb. Narrated by Max Ernst. Video recording. Harriman, NY, and Peasmarsh, East Sussex, UK: The Roland Collection of Films & Videos on Art, 1991.

Flanagan, Mary. *[mapscotch]* (performance/game). 2007.

Kon, Satoshi. *Paprika* (film). Sony Pictures, 2006.

Lantz Frank, Amos Bloomberg, Kate Boelhauf, Dennis Crowle, Christopher Hall, Will Lee, Morekwe Molefe, Mike Olson, Megan Phalines, Mattia Romeo, Oli Stephensen, Pakorn Thienthong, Peter Vigeant. *Pacmanhattan.* 2004. http://www.pacman hattan.com/.

Lantz, Frank, and Kevin Slavin. *ConQuest.* 2004. http://www.playareacode.com/.

Lantz, Frank, and Kevin Slavin. *Crossroads.* 2006. http://www.playareacode.com/.

Lantz, Frank, and Kevin Slavin. *Numb3rs.* 2007. http://www.playareacode.com/.

Looui, Suyin. *Transition Algorithm* (performance/instruction set). 2006. See box 6.1, this volume.

McGonigal, Jane, and Ian Bogost. *Cruel 2 B Kind.* 2006. http://www.comeoutandplay.org/ 2006/08/06/cruel-2–b-kind/.

Media Education Foundation. *Game Over: Gender, Race & Violence in Video Games* (DVD). 2001.

Miranda Zúñiga, Ricardo. *Vagamundo: A Migrant's Tale*. http://www.ambriente.com/cart/about.html.

Négone. *La Fuga*. 2005. http://www.negone.com/web/5_claves.

Newt Games. *Mogi*. 2003. http://www.mogimogi.com/.

Schleiner. Anne-Marie. *Operation Urban Terrain (OUT): A Live Action Wireless Gaming Urban Intervention*. August 2004. New York City.

Schamoni, Peter, and Dr. C. Lamb. *Max Ernst: Journey into the Subconscious*. Video recording. Narrated by Max Ernst. Harriman, NY, and Peasmarsh, East Sussex, UK: The Roland Collection of Films & Videos on Art, 1991.

Smith, Samara. *Chain Reaction* (performance/instruction set). 2006. See box 6.2, this volume.

Snap-Shot-City (group). *Snap-Shot-City*. 2006. http://www.snap-shot-city.com/.

Souzis, Ariana. *Cellphone TAZ*. 2006.

Stanley's March Across the Dark Continent for the Relief of Emin Pasha (board game). French school engraving, 1890.

Stern, Eddo. *Best . . . Flame War . . . Ever*. 2007.

Stern, Eddo. *Cockfight Arena*. 2001.

Stern, Eddo. *Dark Game*. 2006.

Stern, Eddo. *Fort Paladin: America's Army*. 2003. http://www.eddostern.com/fort_paladin.html.

Stern, Eddo. *RUNNERS: Wolfenstein*. 2002.

Stern, Eddo. *Tekken Torture Tournament*. 2001.

Vanouse, Paul. *The Relative Velocity Inscription Device*. http://www.contrib.andrew.cmu.edu/~pv28/rvid.html.

The Yes Men. *Hijinks*. 2007. http://www.theyesmen.org/en/hijinks.

The Yes Men. *The Yes Men*. 2007. http://www.theyesmen.org/.

The Yes Men. *Vivoleum*. 2007. http://www.theyesmen.org/en/hijinks/vivoleum.

Tiltfactor. *Massively Multiplayer Soba*. Tiltfactor Laboratory, 2008. http://www.tiltfactor.org.

Williams, Roberta, and Ken Williams. *Mystery House*. On-LineySystems/Sierra On-Line, 1980 (1982).

Written Works

Absolute Arts. "Fluxus Games Exhibition Mixes Hijinks and High Art." *Absolute Arts* (June 16, 2001). http://www.absolutearts.com/artsnews/2001/06/16/28719.html.

Adamowicz, Elza. *Surrealist Collage in Text and Image*. Cambridge, UK: Cambridge University Press, 1998.

Adams Sitney, P. "Image and Title in Avant-Garde Cinema." *October* 11, Essays in Honor of Jay Leyda (Winter 1979): 97–112.

Agre, P. E. "Introduction." In *Technology and Privacy: The New Landscape*, ed. P. E. Agre and M. Rotenberg, 1–28. Cambridge, MA: MIT Press, 1997.

Agudoawu, Kofi C. *Rules for Playing Oware*. Ashtown, Kumasi, Ghana: KofiTall, 1991.

Allison, Rebecca. "Board Meetings: Artists Put a Different Slant on Chess." *The Guardian* (Manchester, UK), June 9, 2003, 9.

Anderson, Craig A. "An Update on the Effects of Playing Violent Video Games." *Journal of Adolescence* 27 (2004): 113–122.

Anderson, Craig A., and Karen E. Dill. "Video Games and Aggressive Thoughts, Feelings, and Behavior in the Laboratory and Life." *Journal of Personality and Social Psychology* (April 2000): 772–790.

Anspach, Ralph. *Anti Monopoly*. 1999. http://www.antimonopoly.com/the_full_story.html.

Antonisse, Jamie. Values at Play press release for *Hush* for the Better Game contest. January 2008. http://valuesatplay.org/?p=247#more-247.

Aragon, Louis, Antonin Artaud, Jacques Baron, Joë Bousquet, J.-A. Boiffard, André Breton, Jean Carrive, René Crevel, Robert Desnos, Paul Élaurd, Max Ernst, et al. "The Surrealist Manifesto: The Declaration of January 27, 1925." In *The History of Surrealism*, ed. Maurice Nadeau, 240–241. Cambridge, MA: Belknap Press, 1989.

Armstrong, Frances. "The Dollhouse as a Ludic Space, 1690–1920." *Children's Literature* 24 (1996): 23–55.

Arnheim, Rudolf. "Brunelleschi's Peepshow." *Zeitschrift für Kunstgeschichte* 41, no. 1 (1978): 57–60.

Arnold Herstand & Co. *Öyvind Fahlström*. Exhibition catalog. New Haven, CT: Eastern Press, 1984.

Arp, Jean. *On My Way, Poetry and Essays 1912–1947*. New York: Wittenborn, Schultz, 1948.

Augarde, Anthony J. *The Oxford Guide to Word Games*. 2nd ed. Oxford: Oxford University Press, 2003.

Austin, R. G. "Roman Board Games I." *Greece & Rome* 4, no. 10 (October 1934): 24–34.

Austin, R. G. "Roman Board Games II." *Greece & Rome* 4, no. 11 (February 1935): 76–82.

Ball, Hugo. *Flight Out of Time: A Dada Diary*. Ed. John Elderfield, trans. Ann Raimes. Berkeley: University of California Press, [1926] 1996.

Ball, Lillian. "Artists Statement, *GO ECO*." *Queens Museum of Art*. 2007. http://www.queensmuseum.org/exhibitions/goeco.htm.

Barnard, Adam. "The Legacy of the Situationist International: The Production of Situations of Creative Resistance." *Capital & Class* 84 (2004): 103–124.

Barnes, Djuna. *The Book of Repulsive Women*. Yonkers, NY: Lincoln Press, [1915] 1948.

Barthes, Roland. "The Death of the Author." In *Image, Music, Text*, trans. Stephen Heath, 142–148. New York: Noonday Press, [1967] 1977.

Basulto, Jesùs, José Antonio Camuñez, and Francisco Javier Ortega. "Azar Game in the Book of the Dice of Alfonso X The Learned. Its Relation with the Hazard Games of Montmort, Cotton, Hoyle, De Moivre and Jacob Bernoulli," trans. S. Basulto Pardo. *Mathematics and Social Sciences* 44, no. 174 (June 28, 2006): 5–24. http://msh.revues.org/document3295.html.

Batchelor, David, Briony Fer, and Paul Wood. *Realism, Rationalism, Surrealism: Art Between the Wars*. New Haven, CT: Yale University Press, 1983.

Beaumont, Keith. *Alfred Jarry: A Critical and Biographical Study*. New York: St. Martin's Press, 1984.

Bell, John. "Puppets and Performing Objects in the Twentieth Century." *Performance Art Journal (PAJ): A Journal of Performance and Art* 19, no. 2 (1997): 29–46.

Bell, Robbie, and Michael Cornelius. *Board Games round the World: A Resource Book for Mathematical Investigations*. Cambridge, UK: Cambridge University Press, 1988.

Benford, Steve R., M. Anastasi, C. Flintham, N. Greenhalgh, M. Tandavanitj, and J. Row-Farr Adams. "Coping with Uncertainty in a Location-Based Game." In *IEEE Pervasive Computing Journal* 2, no. 3 (September 2003): 34–41.

Benjamin, Walter. "Critique of Violence." In *Reflections*, ed. Peter Demetz, 277–300. New York: Schocken, [1921] 1986.

Bennett, Jill. "Aesthetics of Intermediality." *Art History* 30, no. 3 (June 2007): 432–450.

Benson, Timothy O. "Mysticism, Materialism, and the Machine in Berlin Dada." *Art Journal* 46, no. 1 (Spring 1987): 46–55.

Bergen, Doris. *Play as a Medium for Learning and Development*. Portsmouth, NH: Heinemann, 1988.

Best, Elsdon. "Notes on a Peculiar Game Resembling Draughts Played by the Maori Folk of New Zealand." *Man* 17 (January 1917): 14–15.

Bettelheim, Bruno. "Play and Education." *The School Review* 81, no. 1 (1972): 1–13.

Bey, Hakim. *The Temporary Autonomous Zone, Ontological Anarchy, Poetic Terrorism*. New York: Autonomedia, [1985] 1991.

Bezolla, Tobia. *André Breton: Dossier Dada*. Ostfildern-Ruit, Germany: Hatje Cantz, 2005.

Bhabha, Homi K. *The Location of Culture*. London: Routledge, 1994.

Bhabha, Homi K. *Nation and Narration*. London: Routledge, 1990.

Bilal, Wafaa. "Virtual Jihadi." 2008. http://www.wafaabilal.com/.

Birnbaum, Daniel. "André Cadere." *Artforum* 46, no. 5 (January 2008): 271.

Bittanti, Matteo, and Mary Flanagan. *Similitudini. Simboli. Simulacri* (SIMilarities, Symbols, Simulacra). Milan: Edizioni Unicopli, 2003.

Blake, Kathleen. *Play, Games, and Sport: The Literary Works of Lewis Carroll*. Ithaca, NY: Cornell University Press, 1974.

Blanchard, Kendall A., and Alyce Cheska. *The Anthropology of Sport: An Introduction*. South Hadley, MA: Bergin and Garvey, 1984.

Blumenberg, Hans. *The Legitimacy of the Modern Age*. Cambridge, MA: MIT Press, 1985.

Boal, Augusto. *The Rainbow of Desire*. Trans. Adrian Jackson. London: Routledge, 1995.

Boal, Augusto. *Theater of the Oppressed*. Trans. Charles A. and Maria Odilia Leal McBride. New York: Theatre Communications Group, 1985.

Boal, Mark. "Three Days in the Most Surreal Game on Earth: Me & My Sims." *Village Voice* 29 (March 2000). http://www.villagevoice.com/issues/0013/boal.php.

Bødker, Susanne, and Kaj Grønbæk. "Cooperative Prototyping: Users and Designers in Mutual Activity." *International Journal of Man-Machine Studies* 34 (1991): 453–478.

Bogost, Ian. "Persuasive Games: Videogame Vignette." *Gamasutra* (February 12, 2008). http://www.gamasutra.com/view/feature/3537/persuasive_games_videogame_.php.

Bolton, Henry Carrington. "The Game of Goose." *The Journal of American Folklore* 8, no. 29 (April–June 1895): 145–150.

Bookchin, Natalie. "The Best of Natalie Bookchin." 2000. http://www.calarts.edu/~bookchin/.

Borer, Alain. *The Essential Joseph Beuys*. Cambridge, MA: MIT Press, 1997.

Bourriaud, Nicholas. *Relational Aesthetics*. Dijon: Les Presses du Reel, [1998] 2002.

Bowdidge, John S. "Toys and Sporting Goods." In *Manufacturing: A Historical and Bibliographical Guide* 1 (Handbook of American Business History), ed. D. Whitten. New York: Greenwood Press, 1990.

Braidotti, Rosi. "Cyberfeminism with a Difference." 1996. http://www.let.uu.nl/womens_studies/rosi/cyberfem.htm. Also published in *Zones of Disturbance*, ed. Silvia Eiblmayer, 112–120. Graz, Austria: Steirischer Herbst, 1997.

Bredekamp, Sue, ed. *Developmentally Appropriate Practice in Early Childhood Programs Serving Children from Birth Through Age 8*. Washington, DC: National Association for the Education of Young Children, 1998.

Breitsameter, Sabine. "Sound as Multi-User-Choreography: Steve Symons in Conversation with Sabine Breitsameter." *AudioHyperspace*. March 2005. http://www.swr.de/swr2/audiohyperspace/engl_version/interview/symons.html.

Breton, André. Essays in *Médium*, no. 2 (February 1954). Excerpted in *The Book of Surrealist Games*, ed. Alastair Brotchie and Mel Gooding, 137–138, 154. Boston: Shambhala Redstone Editions, 1995.

Breton, André. *Free Rein (La Clé des champs)*. Trans. Michel Parmentier and Jacqueline d'Ambroise. Lincoln: University of Nebraska Press, [1953] 1996.

Breton, André. "Manifesto of Surrealism 1924." In *Manifestoes of Surrealism*, trans. Richard Seaver and Helen R. Lane, 1–48. Ann Arbor: University of Michigan Press, 1971.

Breton, André. "Second Manifesto of Surrealism." In *Manifestoes of Surrealism*, trans. Richard Seaver and Helen R. Lane, 117–194. Ann Arbor: University of Michigan Press, [1930] 1969.

Breton, André. *What Is Surrealism?* 1932. http://www.Surrealist.com/new/what_is_surrealism.asp.

Breton, André, Soupault, Paul, and Phillipe Eluard. *The Magnetic Fields and the Immaculate Conception*. Trans. David Gascoyne. New York: Consortium Books, 1998.

Broeckmann, Andreas. "Exhibiting Locative Media." *CRUMB Discussion Postings*, ed. Beryl Graham. Post 7 (April 14, 2004). http://www.metamute.org/en/Exhibiting-Locative-Media-CRUMB-discussion-postings.

Brotchie, Alastair, and Mel Gooding. *A Book of Surrealist Games*. Boston: Shambhala Press, 1995.

Bruckner, Pascal. *The Temptation of Innocence: Living in the Age of Entitlement*. New York: Algora Publishing, 2000.

Brumbaugh, Robert S. "The Knossos Game Board." *American Journal of Archaeology* 79, no. 2 (April 1975): 135–137.

Bruner, Jerome. "Play, Thought, and Language." *Peabody Journal of Education* 60, no. 3 (1983): 60–69.

Brusati, Celeste. *Artifice and Illusion: The Art and Writing of Samuel van Hoogstraten*. Chicago: University of Chicago Press, 1995.

Busch, Akiko. *Geography of Home*. New York: Princeton Architectural Press, 1999.

Business Wire (BW). "*The Sims* Becomes the Best Selling PC Game of All Time." *Business Wire* (March 21, 2002). http://www.findarticles.com/p/articles/mi_m0EIN/is_2002 _March_21/ai_84043760.

Butler, Judith P. *Bodies that Matter: On the Discursive Limits of "Sex."* New York: Routledge, 1993.

Butler, Judith P. *Gender Trouble: Feminism and the Subversion of Identity*. New York: Routledge, 1990.

Butt, Danny. "Local Knowledge: Place and New Media Practice." *Leonardo* 39, no. 4 (2006): 323–326.

Cage, John. "An Autobiographical Statement." *Southwest Review* (1991). The John Cage Trust, New York. http://www.newalbion.com/artists/cagej/autobiog.html.

Cahun, Claude. *Disavowals: or Cancelled Confessions*. Trans Susan de Muth. Cambridge, MA: The MIT Press, 2008.

Caillois, Roger. *Man, Play and Games*. Trans. Meyer Barash. New York: The Free Press, 1961.

Candeloro, Dominic. "The Single Tax Movement and Progressivism, 1880–1920." *American Journal of Economics and Sociology* 38, no. 2 (April 1979): 113–127.

Carroll, Lewis. *Logical Nonsense: The Works of Lewis Carroll; Now, for the First Time, Complete*, ed. Philip C. Blackburn and Lionel White. New York: G. P. Putnam's Sons, 1934.

Carse, James P. *Finite and Infinite Games: A Vision of Life as Play and Possibility*. New York: Random House, 1986.

Castells, Manuel. *The Rise of the Network Society*. Oxford, UK, and Malden, MA: Blackwell Publishers, 1996.

Chadwick, Whitney, ed. *Mirror Images: Women, Surrealism and Self-Representation*. Cambridge, MA: MIT Press, 1998.

Chang, Michele, and Elizabeth Goodman. "Asphalt Games: Enacting Place Through Locative Media." *Leonardo Electronic Almanac* 14, no. 3 (2006). http://leoalmanac.org/ journal/Vol_14/lea_v14_n03–04/changoodman.asp.

Chénieux-Gendron, Jacqueline. *Surrealism*. Trans. Vivian Folkenflik. New York: Columbia University Press, 1990.

Chesher, Chris. "Layers of Code, Layers of Subjectivity." *Culture Machine* 5 (2003). http://culturemachine.tees.ac.uk/Cmach/ Backissues/j005/ Articles/CChesher.htm.

Christensen, Clayton M. *The Innovator's Dilemma: When New Technologies Cause Great Firms to Fail*. Boston: Harvard Business School Press, 1997.

Christensen, Clayton M., Erik A. Roth, and Scott D. Anthony. *Seeing What's Next: Using the Theories of Innovation to Predict Industry Change*. Cambridge, MA: Harvard Business School Press, 2004.

Churchill, Suzanne W. *The Little Magazine Others and the Renovation of American Poetry*. Aldershot, UK, and Burlington, VT: Ashgate, 2006.

Cole, Ardra L., and Gary Knowles. *Researching Teaching: Exploring Teacher Development through Reflexive Enquiry*. Boston: Allyn and Bacon, 2000.

Come Out and Play (CO&P). Come Out and Play (event). 2006. http://www.comeoutandplay.org/.

Commission on the Advancement of Women and Minorities in Science, Engineering, and Technology Development (CAWMSET). *Land of Plenty: Diversity as America's Competitive Edge in Science, Engineering and Technology*. 2000. http://www.nsf.gov/od/cawmset/report.htm.

Conley, Katharine. *Automatic Woman: The Representation of Woman in Surrealism*. Omaha: University of Nebraska Press, 1996.

Conley, Katharine. "Claude Cahun's Iconic Heads: From 'The Sadistic Judith' to Human Frontier." *Papers of Surrealism*, no. 2 (Summer 2004). http://www.surrealismcentre.ac.uk/papersofsurrealism/ journal2/acrobat_files/conley_article.pdf.

Consalvo, Mia. *Cheating: Gaining Advantage in Videogames*. Cambridge, MA: MIT Press, 2007.

Cook, Greg. "What? Institutional? Us? Fluxus Gets the Harvard Treatment." *The Phoenix* (March 20, 2007). http://thephoenix.com/article_ektid35744.aspx.

Corneliussen and Walker Rettberg, *Digital Culture, Play, and Identity*.

Costell, Matthew J. *The Greatest Games of All Time*. New York: Wiley Science Editions, 1991.

Costikyan, Greg. "I Have No Words & I Must Design." *Interactive Fantasy* 2 (1994). http://www.costik.com/nowords.html.

Crawford, Chris. *The Art of Computer Game Design*, 1984. *The Art of Computer Game Design, Online Version*, maintained by Sue Peabody. City: Washington State University Press, 1997. http://www.vancouver.wsu.edu/fac/peabody/game-book/Coverpage.html.

Critical Art Ensemble. *Digital Resistance: Explorations in Tactical Media*. New York: Autonomedia, 2003. http://www.critical-art.net/books/digital/.

Cross, Gary. *Kids' Stuff: Toys and the Changing World of American Childhood*. Cambridge, MA: Harvard University Press, 1997.

Crystal, David. *Language Play*. Chicago: University of Chicago Press, 2001.

Csikszentmihalyi, Mihaly. *Beyond Boredom and Anxiety: The Experience of Play in Work and Games*. San Francisco: Jossey-Bass, 1975.

Csikszentmihalyi, Mihalyi. *Flow: The Psychology of Optimal Experience*. New York: Perennial Press, 1991.

Csikszentmihalyi, Mihalyi. "Some Paradoxes in the Definition of Play." In *Play as Context*, ed. Alyce Taylor Cheska, 14–25. West Point, NY: Leisure Press, 1979.

Csikszentmihalyi, Mihaly, and Stith Bennett. "An Exploratory Model of Play." *American Anthropologist, New Series* 73, no. 1 (February 1971): 45–58.

Curtin, Mary Ellen. "Fanfiction.net Statistics." January 2003. http://www.alternateuni verses.com/ffnstats.html.

David, Jean-Marie. "Cadavre exquis." *Dictionnaire des Littératures Policières* 1, no. A-I, ed. Claude Mesplède (November 2007): 337–338.

Dali, Salvador. "The Conquest of the Irrational." In *Salvador Dali: A Panorama of His Art*, ed. A. Reynolds Morse. Cleveland: Salvador Dali Museum, [1936] 1974.

Dean, Carolyn. "Claude Cahun's Double." *Yale French Studies* 90 (1996): 71–92.

Debord, Guy. "Introduction to a Critique of Urban Geography." *Les Lèvres Nues* 6, trans. Ken Knabb (September 1955). http://library.nothingness.org/articles/SI/en/display/2.

Debord, Guy. "Perspectives for Conscious Alterations in Everyday Life." In *Situationist International Anthology*, ed. and trans. Ken Knabb, 68–75. Berkeley, CA: Bureau of Public Secrets, [1961] 1981.

Debord, Guy. "Report on the Constructions and the International Situationist Tendency's Conditions of Organization and Action." 1957. http://www.cddc.vt.edu/sionline/si/report.html. Also in *Theories and Documents of Contemporary Art: A Sourcebook of Artist's Writings*, ed. Peter Selz and Kristine Stiles, 704–706. Berkeley: University of California Press, 1996.

Debord, Guy. "Theory of the Dérive, Internationale Situationniste #2." In *Situationist International Anthology*, ed. and trans. Ken Knabb. Berkeley, CA: Bureau of Public Secrets, [1958] 1981.

de Certeau, Michel. *The Practice of Everyday Life*. Trans. Steven Rendall. Berkeley: University of California Press, 1984.

Decordova, Richard. *Picture Personalities: The Emergence of the Star System in America*. Urbana: University of Illinois Press, 1990.

Deleuze, Gilles. *The Logic of Sense*. Trans. Mark Lester and Charles Stivale, ed. Constantin V. Boundas. New York: Columbia University Press, 1990.

Deleuze, Gilles. "What Is Becoming?" In *The Deleuze Reader*, trans. Constantin V. Boundas, 39–41. New York: Columbia University Press, 1993.

Dempsey, Amy. *Art in the Modern Era: A Guide to Styles, Schools & Movements*. New York: Harry N. Abrams, 2002.

Design Institute, University of Minnesota. *Big Urban Game*. 2003. http://design.umn.edu/bug/index.jsp.

Dickerman, Leah, ed. "Zurich." In *Dada*. Washington, DC: National Gallery of Art, 2005.

Digg Online Aggregator "One Room, One Paintball Gun Controlled Via the Web, and One Iraqi-American." Anonymous comments on Digg.com (May 19, 2007). http://digg.com/politics/One_room_one_paintball_gun_controlled_via_the_Web_and_one_Iraqi_American.

Doherty, Claire. *From Studio to Situation: Contemporary Art and the Question of Context*. London: Black Dog, 2004.

Douglas, Ann. *The Feminization of American Culture*. New York: Noonday Press, 1998.

Duchamp, Marcel. *The Box in a Valise*. Trans. David Britt. New York: Rizzoli, 1989.

Duchamp, Marcel. *Marcel Duchamp, Notes*. Ed. Paul Matisse. Boston: G. K. Hall & Co, 1983.

Duchamp, Marcel. *Salt Seller: The Writings of Marcel Duchamp*. Ed. Michel Sanouillet and Elmer Peterson. New York: Oxford University Press, 1973.

Duchamp, Marcel. *The Writings of Marcel Duchamp*. Cambridge, MA: Da Capo Press, 1989.

Durai, H. G. "Pallanguli: A South Indian Game." *Man* 28 (November 1928): 185–186.

Durozoi, Gérard. *History of the Surrealist Movement*. Chicago: University of Chicago Press, 2002.

Ebony, David. "Improbable Games." *Art in America* (November 1, 1996). http://www.highbeam.com/doc/1G1-18823753.html.

Echols, Alice. *Daring to Be Bad: Radical Feminism in America, 1967–1975*. Minneapolis: University of Minnesota Press, 1989.

Elam, Harry Justin. *Taking It to the Streets: The Social Protest Theater of Luis Valdez and Amiri Baraka*. Ann Arbor: University of Michigan Press, 2001.

Elderfield, John. *The Modern Drawing: 100 Works on Paper from The Museum of Modern Art*. New York: The Museum of Modern Art, 1983.

Elliot, Anthony. "Interview (with Yoko Ono)." *Time Out Magazine* (London) (1968). http://pers-www.wlv.ac.uk/~fa1871/yoko.html.

Erman, Adolf. *Life in Ancient Egypt*. Trans. H. M. Tirard. Mineola, NY: Dover, [1894] 1971.

Eskin, Blake. "Pass Go, Collect a Ticket to Paradise," *New York Times* (late edition, November 14, 2004): section 2, page 38.

Fahlström, Öyvind. "On Monopoly Games." New York: The Solomon R. Guggenheim Foundation, [1971] 1982.

Fairbairn, John T. "Go in Ancient China." London. 1995. http://www.pandanet.co.jp/English/essay/goancientchina.html.

Fairbairn, John T. *Invitation to Go*. Oxford, Glasgow, and New York: Oxford University Press, 1977.

Feminist Pedagogy Working Group (FPWG). "Decentering Authority!" In *Feminist Geography in Practice: Research & Methods*, ed. Pamela Moss. London: Blackwell, 2002.

Fer, Briony. *Realism, Rationalism, Surrealism: Art Between the Wars*. New Haven, CT: Yale University Press, 1993.

Fernández, María. "Is Cyberfeminism Colorblind?" *ArtWomen.org* (July 2002). http://www .artwomen.org/cyberfems/fernandez/fernandez1.htm.

Fisher, John, ed. *The Magic of Lewis Carroll*. New York: Simon & Schuster, 1973.

Flanagan, Mary. "The Bride Stripped Bare." In *Data Made Flesh*, ed. Phillip Thurtle and Robert Mitchell, 359–388. New York: Routledge, 2003.

Flanagan, Mary. "Hyperbodies, Hyperknowledge: Women in Games, Women in Cyberpunk, and Strategies of Resistance." In *reload: rethinking women + cyberculture*, ed. Mary Flanagan and Austin Booth, 425–454. Cambridge, MA: MIT Press, 2002.

Flanagan, Mary. "The 'Nature' of Networks: Space and Place in the Silicon Forest." In *Nature et Progrès: Interactions, Exclusions, Mutations*, ed. Pierre Lagayette. Paris: Presses de l'Université, Paris-Sorbonne, 2006.

Flanagan, Mary. "Next Level: Women's Digital Activism through Gaming." In *Digital Media Revisited*, ed. Andrew Morrison, Gunnar Liestøl, and Terje Rasmussen, 359–388. Cambridge, MA: MIT Press, 2003.

Flanagan, Mary. "My Profile, Myself in Playculture." In *Exploring Digital Artefacts*, ed. Johan Bornebusch and Patrik Hernwall, 20–29. Stockholm: M3 Publication, 2006.

Flanagan, Mary. "SIMple & Personal: Domestic Space and The Sims." In *Proceedings of the Fifth International Digital Arts and Culture Conference*, May 19–23, 2003. Melbourne, Australia: RMIT, 2003. http://hypertext.rmit.edu.au/dac/papers/Flanagan.pdf.

Flatfile Galleries. *Media Alert* (May 2007). http://www.crudeoils.us/wafaa/html/closingme dia.html.

Flournoy, Theodore. *From India to the Planet Mars*. Trans. Sonu Shamdasani, intro. Mireille Cifali. Princeton, NJ: Princeton University Press, 1994.

Fluegelman, Andrew, and Shoshana Tembeck, eds. *The New Games Book*. San Francisco: Headlands Press, 1976.

Formanek-Brunell, Miriam. *Made to Play House: Dolls and the Commercialization of American Girlhood, 1830–1930*. New Haven, CT: Yale University Press, 1993.

Formanek-Brunell, Miriam. "Fatherland." In *The Material Culture of Gender/The Gender of Material Culture*, ed. Katherine A. Martinez and Kenneth L. Ames, 111–136. Hanover, NH: University Press of New England, 1997.

Foster, Hal. "Armor Fou." *October* 56 (1991): 64–97.

Foster, Hal. *Compulsive Beauty*. Cambridge, MA: MIT Press, 1993.

Foucault, Michel. *The Archeology of Knowledge*. Trans. A. Sheridan. New York: Pantheon, [1969] 1972.

Foucault, Michel. "Intellectuals and Power: A Conversation between Michel Foucault and Gilles Deleuze." Originally in *L'Arc* 49 (1972): 3–10. http://info.interactivist.net/ article.pl?sid= 03/01/13/0056200.

Foucault, Michel. *Discipline and Punish: The Birth of the Prison*. Trans. Alan Sheridan. New York: Vintage Books, 1977.

Foucault, Michel. *The History of Sexuality: An Introduction, Volume 1*. Trans. Robert Hurley. New York: Pantheon, 1978.

Foucault, Michel. *Language, Counter-Memory, Practice: Selected Essays and Interviews*. Oxford: Basil Blackwell, 1977.

Foucault, Michel. *Politics, Madness and Civilization: A History of Insanity in the Age of Reason*. Trans. Richard Howard. New York: Vintage, 1988.

Foucault, Michel. *Politics, Philosophy and Culture: Interviews and Other Writings, 1977–1984*, ed. Lawrence D. Kritzman. New York: Routledge, 1988.

Foucault, Michel. *Power/Knowledge: Selected Interviews and Other Writing, 1972–1977*, ed. Colin Gordon. London: Harvester Wheatsheaf, 1980.

Fox Keller, Evelyn. *Reflections on Gender and Science*. New Haven, CT: Yale University Press, 1985.

Franck, Karen A. "A Feminist Approach to Architecture: Acknowledging Women's Ways of Knowing." In *Gender, Space, Architecture*, ed. Jane Rendell, Barbara Penner, and Ian Borden, 295–305. London: Routledge, 2000.

Franklin, Benjamin. "The Morals of Chess" (1750). In *The Writings of Benjamin Franklin* 7, ed. Albert H. Smyth, 357–362. New York: Macmillan, 1905–1907.

Frasca, Gonzalo. "Madrid Game." *Newsgaming.com* (May 13, 2007). http://www.news gaming.com/games/madrid/.

Frasca, Gonzalo. "September 12." *Newsgaming.com* (2003). http://www.newsgaming.com/ games/index12.htm.

Frasca, Gonzalo. "September 12th, a Toy World: Political Videogame about the War on Terror." *Newsgaming.com-Press* (September 29, 2003). http://www.newsgaming.com/ press092903.htm.

Frasca, Gonzalo. In *Better Game Characters by Design: A Psychological Approach*, ed. Katherine Isbister, 17–20. Burlington, MA: Morgan Kaufmann, 2006.

Frasca, Gonzalo. "Videogames of the Oppressed." In *First Person: New Media as Story, Performance, and Game*, ed. Noah Wardrip Fruin and Pat Harrigan, 85–94. Cambridge, MA: MIT Press, 2004.

Freeman-Bensen, Bjorn N., and Alan Borning. "YP and Urban Simulation: Applying an Agile Programming Methodology in a Politically Tempestuous Domain." In *Proceedings of the Conference on Agile Development*, 2. City: Publisher, 2003.

Freud, Sigmund. *Psychopathology of Everyday Life. The Basic Writings of Sigmund Freud*. Trans. A. A. Brill. New York: Random House, 1938.

Freud, Sigmund. "The Uncanny." In *The Standard Edition of the Compleat Psychological Works of Sigmund Freud* 17, ed. and trans. James Strachey, 218–256. London: Hogarth, 1955.

Bibliography

Fuller, Mary, and Henry Jenkins. "Nintendo and New World Travel Writing: A Dialogue." In *CyberSociety: Computer-Mediated-Communication and Community*, ed. Steven G. Jones, 57–72. Thousand Oaks, CA: Sage Publications, 1995.

Fuller, Steve. *Thomas Kuhn: A Philosophical History for Our Times*. Chicago: University of Chicago Press, 2000.

Fullerton, Tracy. *Game Design Workshop*. San Francisco, CA: Morgan Kaufmann, 2008.

Gajjala, Radhika. "Third-World Critiques of Cyberfeminism," *Development in Practice* 9, no. 5 (1999): 616–619.

Gamman, Lorraine, and Margaret Marshment, ed. *The Female Gaze: Women as Viewers of Popular Culture*. Seattle, WA: Real Comet Press, 1989.

Gammel, Irene. *Elsa: Gender, Dada, and Everyday Modernity: A Cultural Biography*. Cambridge, MA: MIT Press, 2003.

Gascoyne, David. "Introduction." *The Magnetic Fields*, trans. David Gascoyne. In *The Automatic Message*, ed. André Breton, Paul Eluard, and Philippe Soupault. London: Atlas, [1985] 1997.

Geertz, Clifford. *The Interpretation of Cultures*. New York: Basic Books, 1973.

Gibbs, Colin. "Girls Got Game." *RCR Wireless News* 24, no. 6 (February 7, 2005): 1.

Gitman, Yuri, and Carlos Gomez de Llarena. *Noderunner*. 2002. http://noderunner.omni step.com/play.php.

Glimcher, Marc. *Logical Conclusions: 40 Years of Rule Based Art*. New York: PACEWIL-DENSTEIN, 2005.

Glowlab. Conflux (event). 2006. http://confluxfestival.org.

González, Jennifer A. *Subject to Display: Reframing Race in Contemporary Installation Art*. Cambridge, MA: MIT Press, 2008.

Goodfellow, Caroline G. *A Collector's Guide to Games and Puzzles*. Secaucus, NJ: Chartwell Books, 1991.

Goodman, Lizbeth. *Contemporary Feminist Theatres: To Each Her Own*. London and New York: Routledge, 1993.

Gramsci, Antonio. *Modern Prince and Other Writings*. New York: International Publishers, 1959.

Gramsci, Antonio. *Prison Notebooks, Volume 1*. Ed. Joseph A. Buttigieg, trans. A. Callari. New York: Columbia University Press, 1992.

Gramsci, Antonio. *Selections from the Prison Notebooks*. New York: International Publishers, 1971.

Graner Ray, S. *Gender Inclusive Game Design: Expanding the Market*. Hingham, MA: Charles River Media, 2004.

Guattari, Félix. *Chaosmosis: An Ethico-Aesthetic Paradigm*. Trans. Paul Bains and Julian Pefanis. Bloomington: Indiana University Press, 1995.

Guerrilla Girls. "Get Naked." 1989. http://www.guerrillagirls.com/posters/getnaked.shtml.

Hamilton, Claire. *The Celtic Book of Seasonal Meditations*. Newburyport, MA: Red Wheel/ Weiser Press, 2003.

Hanman, Natalie. "Jobs for the Girls." *The Guardian* (Manchester, UK) (June 23, 2005): http://www.guardian.co.uk/technology/2005/jun/23/games.shopping2.

Haraway, Donna. *Simians, Cyborgs, and Women: The Reinvention of Nature*. New York: Routledge, 1991.

Haraway, Donna. "Situated Knowledges: The Science Question in Feminism and the Privilege of Partial Perspective." *Feminist Studies* 14 (Fall 1988): 575–599.

Harding, Sandra G. *Whose Science? Whose Knowledge? Thinking from Women's Lives*. Ithaca, NY: Cornell University Press, 1991.

Hardt, Michael, and Antonio Negri. *Empire*. Cambridge, MA: Harvard University Press, 2001.

Harris, Steven. *Surrealist Art and Thought in the 1930s: Art, Politics, and the Psyche*. New York and Cambridge, UK: Cambridge University Press, 2004.

Harrison, Charles, and Paul Wood, ed. *Art in Theory 1900–2000: An Anthology of Changing Ideas*. Malden, MA: Wiley-Blackwell, 2002.

Harstock. *The Feminist Standpoint Revisited and Other Essays*. Boulder, CO: Westview Press, 1988.

Haslam, Malcolm. *The Real World of the Surrealists*. New York: Rizzoli, 1978.

Hebdige, Dick. *Subculture: The Meaning of Style*. London: Methuen, 1979.

Hendricks, Jon. *FLUXUS CODEX*. New York: Harry N. Abrams, 1988.

Hendrix, Grady. "U.S. Teenage Girls Prefer Japanese Heroes." *Women's eNews* (August 24, 2005): 20. http://www.alternet.org/wiretap/24174/.

Herbert, Anne, Margaret M. Pavel, and Mayumi Oda. *Random Kindness & Senseless Acts of Beauty*. Volcano, CA: Volcano Press, 1993.

Heyward, Megan. *Traces*. 2005. http://tracesheyward.blogspot.com/.

Higgins, Dick. "Statement on Intermedia." In *Theories and Documents of Contemporary Art: A Sourcebook of Artists' Writings*, ed. Kristine Stiles and Peter Selz, 728–729. Berkeley: University of California Press, [1966] 1996.

Higgins, Hannah. *Fluxus Experience*. Berkeley: University of California Press, 2002.

Hill Collins, Patricia. *Black Feminist Thought: Knowledge, Consciousness, and the Politics of Empowerment*. New York: Routledge, 1990.

Hillier, Mary. *Automata and Mechanical Toys: An Illustrated History*. London: Bloomsbury Books, 1998.

Hindman, Sandra. "Pieter Bruegel's Children's Games, Folly, and Chance." *The Art Bulletin* 63, no. 3 (September 1981): 447–475.

Hjartarson, Paul I., and Tracy Kulba, eds. *The Politics of Cultural Mediation: Baroness Elsa von Freytag-Loringhoven and Félix Paul Greve*. Edmonton, Alberta: The University of Alberta Press, 2003.

Hjartarson, Paul I., and Douglas O. Spettigue, eds. *Baroness Elsa: The Autobiography of Baroness Elsa von Freytag-Loringhoven*. Ottawa: Oberon, 1992.

Hofer, Margaret K. *The Games We Played: The Golden Age of Board and Table Games*. New York: Princeton Architectural Press, 2003.

Holmes, Steven. "Income Disparity Between Poorest and Richest Rises." *The New York Times* (June 20, 1996): section A, page 1.

Holzer, Jenny. *Please Change Beliefs*. 1999. http://adaweb.walkerart.org/project/holzer/cgi/pcb.cgi.

Hughes, Robert. "Camping Under Glass: The Ghost of Florine Stettheimer, Remote and Glittering, Evokes a Period Between the Wars in a New Show at the Whitney." *Time* (September 18, 1995). http://www.time.com/time/magazine/article/0,9171,983445,00.html.

Huizinga, Johan. *Homo Ludens: A Study of the Play Element in Culture*. Boston: Beacon Press, [1938] 1955.

Hutchison, Sharla. "Convulsive Beauty: Images of Hysteria and Transgressive Sexuality: Claude Cahun and Djuna Barnes." *symploke* 11, no. 1–2 (2003): 212–226.

Hyde, James. "André Cadere at Art: Concept." *Art in America* 93, no. 10 (November 2005): 192.

International Game Developers Association (IGDA). *Game Developer Demographics Report*. 2005. http://www.igda.org/diversity/report.php.

Irigaray, Luce. *This Sex Which Is Not One*. Trans. Catherine Porter. Ithaca, NY: Cornell University Press, 1985.

Isbister, Katherine. *Better Game Characters by Design a Psychological Approach*. Burlington, MA: Morgan Kaufmann, 2006.

ISEA (Inter-Society for Electronic Arts). "Call for Participation." 2006. http://www.urban-atmospheres.net/ISEA2006.

Ito, Setsuko. "The Muse in Competition: Uta-awase Through the Ages." *Monumenta Nipponica* 37, no. 2 (Summer 1982): 201–222.

Jameson, Frederick. *Postmodernism, or, the Cultural Logic of Late Capitalism*. Durham: Duke University Press, 1992.

Jarry, Alfred. "Preface." In *Ubu Roi*, trans. Beverly Keith and Gershon Legman. New York: Dover, [1953] 2003.

Jarry, Alfred. *The Ubu Plays*, ed. Simon Watson Taylor. London: Methuen, 1968.

Jenkins, Henry. "Complete Freedom of Movement: Video Games as Gendered Play Spaces." In *From Barbie to Mortal Kombat: Gender and Computer Games*, ed. Justine Cassell and Henry Jenkins, 262–297. Cambridge, MA: MIT Press, 1998.

Jenkins, Tiffany. "Reviews: Spotlight the Last Colonial Museum?" *The Independent* (August 20, 2004). http://findarticles.com/p/articles/mi_qn4158/is_20040820/ai_n12806467.

Jensen, Jennifer. "Teaching Success through Play: American Board and Table Games, 1840–1900." *Antiques* 160 (December 2001): 812–819.

Johnston, Chris. "Doom Made Me Do It." *Electronic Gaming Monthly* (July 1999): 26.

Jones, Gerard. *Killing Monsters: Why Children Need Fantasy, Super Heroes, and Make-Believe Violence.* New York: Basic Books, 2003.

Joselit, David. "Gabriel Orozco." *Artforum International* (September 1, 2000).

Judd, Dennis R. "Visitors and the Spatial Ecology of the City." In *Cities and Visitors: Regulating Tourists, Markets, and City Space*, ed. Lily M. Hoffman, Susan S. Fainstein, Dennis R. Judd, 23–38. Malden, MA: Blackwell, 2002.

Judovitz, Dalia. "Rendezvous with Marcel Duchamp: Given." In *Marcel Duchamp: Artist of the Century*, ed. Francis Naumann and Rudolf Kuenzli, 184–202. Cambridge, MA: MIT Press, 1989.

Juul, Jesper. "Games Telling Stories? A Brief Note on Games and Narratives." *Game Studies* 1, no. 1. (2001). http://www.gamestudies.org/0101/juul-gts/.

Kahn, Eve. "Murder is Merely Child's Play: Book Captures Homicide Scenes on Dollhouse Scale." *San Francisco Chronicle* (October 20, 2004): 8EB.

Kakuchi, Surundrini. "Tokyo Treasure Hunt: Exhibition of Sugoroku Board Game: Edo-Tokyo Museum." *Eastern Economic Review* 161, no. 13 (March 26, 1998): 56.

Kandinsky, Wasily. *Concerning the Spiritual in Art.* Trans. Michael T. H. Sadler. Project Gutenberg text. 1912. http://www.gutenberg.org/etext/5321.

Kaprow, Allan. "Untitled Guidelines for Happenings." In *Theories and Documents of Contemporary Art. A Sourcebook of Artists' Writings*, ed. Kristine Stiles and Peter Selz, 709–714. Berkeley: University of California Press, 1966.

Keating, Noah, Susana Ruiz, Kellee Santiago, Mike Stein, and Ashley York. "About the Game." 2006. *Darfur Is Dying 2007* (May 14, 2007). http://www.darfurisdying.com/aboutgame.html.

Keating, Noah, Susana Ruiz, Kellee Santiago, Mike Stein, and Ashley York. "Darfur Is Dying." *Darfur Is Dying 2007* (May 14, 2007). http://www.darfurisdying.com/.

Kelley, Mike. "Myth Science." *Öyvind Fahlström: The Complete Graphics, Multiples, and Sound Works.* Vienna: BAWAG Foundation, [1995] 2001. http://www.fahlstrom.com/texts_mike.asp?id=7&subid=10.

Kimmelman, Michael. "Dada Dearest: Artist Alone with Her Calling: Exhibit of Photomontages by Hannah Höch." *The New York Times* 146 (February 28, 1997): C1.

Kiplinger's Personal Finance Magazine. "Women Play More Games Online." *Kiplinger's Personal Finance Magazine* 58 (September 2004): 9.

Kirkpatrick, Marshall. "World of Warcraft Hits 10 Million Subscribers" January 22, 2008. http://www.readwriteweb.com/archives/world_of_warcraft_hits_10_mill.php

Knafo, Danielle. "Claude Cahun, The Third Sex." *Studies in Gender and Sexuality* 2, no. 1 (January 15, 2001): 29–62.

Knowles, Alison. *Events by Alison Knowles* (1962–1964). http://www.nutscape.com/Fluxus/homepage/aknowles.html.

Knowles, Alison. *Journal of the Identical Lunch*. San Francisco: Nova Broadcast Press, 1971.

Knowles, Alison. *Bread and Water*. New York: Left Hand Books, 1994.

Koster, Raph. *A Theory of Fun for Game Design*. Phoenix, AZ: Paraglyph, 2006.

Krauss, Rosalind. "The Photographic Conditions of Surrealism" (1981). In *The Originality of the Avant-Garde and Other Modernist Myths*, 87–118. Cambridge, MA: MIT Press, 1985.

Kuenzli, Rudolf E. *Dada and Surrealist Film*. Cambridge, MA: MIT Press, 1996.

Kuenzli, Rudolf E. "Baroness Elsa von Freytag-Loringhoven and New York Dada." In *Women in Dada: Essays on Sex, Gender, and Identity*, ed. Naomi Sawelson-Gorse, 442–477. Cambridge, MA: MIT Press, 2001.

Kuhn, Thomas S. *The Structure of Scientific Revolutions* (1961). Chicago: University of Chicago Press, 1996.

Kuspit, Donald. "A Critical History of 20th-Century Art." *Artnet* (2006). Chapter two, part three, available online at http://www.artnet.com/magazineus/features/kuspit/kuspit3-17-06.asp, 2006.

Kuznets, Lois R. "Taking Over the Dollhouse: Domestic Desire and Nostalgia in Toy Narratives." In *Girls, Boys, Books, Toys: Gender in Children's Literature and Culture*, ed. Beverly Lyon Clark and Margaret R. Higonnet, 142–153. Baltimore: Johns Hopkins University Press, 1999.

Kwon, Miwon. *One Place After Another: Site-Specific Art and Locational Identity*. Cambridge, MA: MIT Press, 2002.

Lappin, Linda. "Dada Queen in the Bad Boys' Club: Baroness Elsa Von Freytag-Loringhoven." *Southwest Review 89* (Spring–Summer 2004): 307–320.

Laurel, Brenda. *Utopian Entrepreneur*. Cambridge, MA: MIT Press, 2001.

Lavin, Maud. *Cut with the Kitchen Knife: The Weimar Photomontages of Hannah Höch*. New Haven, CT: Yale University Press, 1993.

Lee, Elan, and Sean Stewart. *The Beast*. 2001. http://www.cloudmakers.org/.

Lee, Shuen-Shing. "I Lose, Therefore I Think: A Search for Contemplation Amid Wars of Push-Button Glare." *Game Studies: International Journal of Computer Game Research* 3, no. 2 (2003). http://www.gamestudies.org/0302/lee/.

Lefebvre, Henri. "The Everyday and Everydayness," trans. Christine Levich, Alice Kaplan, and Kristin Ross. *Yale French Studies* 73 (1987): 7–11.

Lefebvre, Henri. *The Production of Space*. Trans. Donald Nicholson-Smith. Malden, MA: Blackwell Publishing, 1991.

Lenhart, Amanda, Joseph Kahn, Ellen Middaugh, Alexandra Rankin MacGill, Chris Evans, and Jessica Vitak. *Teens, Video Games, and Civics. Family, Friends & Community*. September 16, 2008. Pew Internet and American Life Project. October 5, 2008. http://www.pewinternet.org/ppf/r/263/report_display.asp.

Levy, Richard C., and Robert O. Weingartner. *The Toy and Game Inventor's Handbook*. Indianapolis: Alpha Books, 2003.

Lewitt, Sol. "Paragraphs on Conceptual Art." In *Theories and Documents of Contemporary Art*, ed. Kristine Stiles and Peter Selz, 822–826. Berkeley: University of California Press, [1967] 1996.

Lichtenstein, Therese. *Behind Closed Doors: The Art of Hans Bellmer*. Berkeley: University of California Press, 2001.

Lo, Andrew. "The Game of Leaves: An Inquiry into the Origin of Chinese Playing Cards." *Bulletin of the School of Oriental and African Studies, University of London* 63, no. 3 (2000): 389–406.

Lucy, William H., and David L. Phillips. *Tomorrow's Cities, Tomorrow's Suburbs*. New York: APA Planners Press, 2006.

Maciunas, George. "George Maciunas to Tomas Schmit, January 1964." In *FLUXUS CODEX*, ed. Jon Hendricks, 193. New York: Harry N. Abrams, 1988.

Maciunas, George. *Manifesto on Art/Fluxus Art-Amusement*. 1964. http://www.artnotart.com/Fluxus/gmaciunas-artartamusement.html.

Marcoci, Roxana. "Perceptions at Play: Giacometti through Contemporary Eyes." *Art Journal* 64 (December 22, 2005): 7.

Martin, J. V., Jan Strijbosch, Raoul Vaneigem, and René Viénet (August 1964). "Now the SI." In *Situationist International Anthology*, ed. and trans. Ken Knabb, 134–147. Berkeley, CA: Bureau of Public Secrets, 2007.

Martyniuk, Irene. "Troubling the 'Master's Voice': Djuna Barnes's Pictorial Strategies." *Mosaic* 31, no. 3 (1998): 61–82.

Matisse, Henri. "Notes d'un Peintre." *La Grand Revue* 52, no. 24 (December 1908): 731–745.

May, Leila Silvana. "Language-Games and Nonsense: Wittgenstein's Reflection in Carroll's Looking-Glass." *Philosophy and Literature* 31, no. 1 (April 2007): 79–94.

McGonigal, Jane. "SuperGaming: Ubiquitous Play and Performance for Massively Scaled Community." *Modern Drama* 48, no. 3 (2005): 471–491.

McGonigal, Jane. "'This Is Not a Game': Immersive Aesthetics & Collective Play." DAC 2003 Conference, Melbourne Australia.

McLuhan, Marshall. *Understanding Media: The Extensions of Man* (1964). Cambridge, MA: MIT Press, 1994.

Melillo, Wendy. "Video-Game Group Creates Ads to Deflect Criticism." *Adweek Eastern Edition* (November 15, 1999): 5.

Mellencamp, Patricia. *Indiscretions: Avant-garde Film, Video & Feminism*. Bloomington: Indiana University Press, 1990.

Milam, Jennifer D. *Fragonard's Playful Paintings: Visual Games in Rococo Art*. Manchester, UK: Manchester University Press, 2007.

Milam, Jennifer D. "Playful Constructions and Fragonard's Swinging Scenes." *Eighteenth-Century Studies* 33, no. 4 (2000): 543–559.

Milburn, Robert. *Early Christian Art and Architecture*. Berkeley and Los Angeles: University of California Press, 1988.

Miller, Stanley A. II. "Players, Dollars, Keep Online Worlds Turning." *Milwaukee Journal Sentinel* via *Knight Ridder/Tribune News Service* (April 27, 2004): K5063.

Miranda Zúñiga, Ricardo. "About Vagamundo." *Vagamundo Site*. October 2003. http://www.ambriente.com/cart/about.html.

Mitchell, Don. "The End of Public Space? People's Park, Definitions of the Public and Democracy." *Annals of the Association of American Geographers* 85, no. 1 (March 1995): 124.

Montola, Markus, and Annika Waern. "Ethical and Practical Look at Unaware Participation." In *Gaming Realities: A Challenge for Digital Culture: Proceedings from the Medi@ Terra* 2007, 185–193. Athens, Greece: Publisher, 2007.

Moore, Alan. "Dada Invades New York at the Whitney Museum." *Artnet* (December 9, 1996). http://www.artnet.com/magazine/features/moore/moore12-09-96.html.

Moore College of Art Gallery. *Öyvind Fahlström* Exhibition catalog. Philadelphia: Moore College of Art Gallery, 1973.

Morris, Meaghan. "Banality in Cultural Studies." *Discourse* 10, no. 2 (Spring/Summer 1988): 3–29.

Mulvey, Laura. "Visual Pleasure and Narrative Cinema." *Screen* 16, no. 3 (1975): 6–18.

Munroe, Alexandra. *Japanese Art after 1945*. New York: Harry Abrams, 1994.

Munroe, Aleandra, Yoko Ono, Yoko, Jon Hendricks, Bruce Altshuler, David A. Ross, Jann S. Wenner, Kevin C. Concannon, Reiko Tomii, Murray Sayle, and Edward M. Gomez. *Y E S Yoko Ono*. New York: Japan Society, Harry N. Abrams, 2000.

Murakami, Takashi. "Welcome to TakashiMurakami.com." 2007. http://www.takashimurakami.com.

Murray, H. J. R. *A History of Chess*. Northampton, MA: Benjamin Press, [1913] 1986.

Murray, H. J. R. *A History of Board Games Other than Chess*. Oxford: Oxford University Press, 1952.

Murray, Janet. *Hamlet on the Holodeck: The Future of Narrative in Cyberspace*. Cambridge, MA: MIT Press, 1997.

Nadeau, Maurice. *The History of Surrealism*. Cambridge, MA: Belknap Press, 1989.

Nakamura, Lisa. *Cybertypes: Race, Ethnicity, and Identity on the Internet*. New York: Routledge, 2002.

Nakamura, Lisa. *Digitizing Race: Visual Cultures of the Internet*. Minneapolis: University of Minnesota Press, 2008.

Naumann, Francis M., Beth Venn, and Allan Antliff. *Making Mischief: Dada Invades New York*. New York: Whitney Museum Press, 1996.

Nochlin, Linda. *Women, Art and Power and Other Essays*. New York: Westview Press, 1988.

Noegel, Scott B. *Nocturnal Ciphers: The Allusive Language of Dreams in the Ancient Near East.* American Oriental Series 89. New Haven, CT: American Oriental Society, 2007.

Nowacek, Nancy, Katie Salen, and Marina Zurkow. *Karaoke Ice.* 2006. http://karaokeice.com/home/.

NPD Group. "2007 U.S. Video Game And PC Game Sales Exceed $18.8 Billion Marking Third Consecutive Year of Record-Breaking Sales." January 31, 2008. http://www.npd.com/press/releases/press_080131b.html.

O'Brien, Richard. *The Story of American Toys: From the Puritans to the Present.* New York: Abbeville Press, 1992.

Ollman, Bertell. *Class Struggle Is the Name of the Game: True Confessions of a Marxist Businessman.* New York: William Morrow, 1983.

Ollman, Bertell. *Class Struggle Rules.* http://www.nyu.edu/projects/ollman/game_rules.php.

Ollman, Leah. "The Lives of Hannah Höch: Walker Art Center, Minneapolis MN." *Art in America* 86, no. 4 (April 1998): 100–106.

Ono, Yoko. *Grapefruit.* New York: Simon and Schuster, [1964] 2000.

Ono, Yoko. *Instruction Paintings.* New York: Weatherhill, 1995.

Oser, Kris. "Moms Are Unsung Players in Gaming World; 43% of Gamers Are Women; 28% Over Age 40 Play Online Games Late Night." *Advertising Age* 75, no. 22 (May 31, 2004): 56.

Ostojic, Tanja. "Looking for a Husband with a EU Passport, 2000–2005." *My Own Private Reality: Exhibition Catalog.* Co-curated by Sabine Himmelsbach and Sarah Cook. Edith Russ Site for Media Art, Oldenburg, Germany, May 12–July 1, 2007. http://myownprivatereality.wordpress.com/tanja-ostojic/.

Orbanes, Philip E. *Game Makers: The Story of Parker Brothers, from Tiddledy Winks to Trivial Pursuit.* Cambridge, MA: Harvard Business School Press, 2003.

Orozco, Gabriel. "Games: Ping Pong, Billiards, and Chess (Interview)." *Art* 21. http://www.pbs.org/art21/artists/orozco/clip1.html.

Oxford English Dictionary. 2nd ed, vol. 8. New York: Oxford University Press, 1989.

Oxford English Dictionary. 2nd ed., vol. 17. New York: Oxford University Press, 1989.

Parlett, David. *The Oxford History of Board Games.* Oxford: Oxford University Press, 1999.

Paul, Christiane. *Digital Art.* London: Thames & Hudson, 2003.

Paulos, Eric, Ken Anderson, Michele Chang, and Anthony Burke. "Metapolis and Urban Life." *The Seventh International Conference on Ubiquitous Computing (UbiComp05),* Tokyo, Japan, September 10–14, 2005. http://berkeley.intelresearch.net/paulos/pubs/papers/ Metapolis%20Workshop%20(UbiComp%202005).pdf.

Pearce, Celia. "Games AS Art: The Aesthetics of Play." *Visible Language* 40, no. 1, special issue: Fluxus after Fluxus (January 2006): 90–112.

Pellegrini, Anthony D. *The Future of Play Theory: A Multidisciplinary Enquiry into the Contributions of Brian Sutton-Smith.* Albany: SUNY Press, 1995.

Pellegrini, Anthony D. *School Recess and Playground Behavior: Educational and Developmental Roles*. Albany: SUNY Press, 1995.

Pellegrini, Anthony D., and Peter K. Smith. *The Nature of Play: Great Apes and Humans*. New York: Guilford Press, 2004.

Petrilla, Jesse. *United American Committee: Working for a Better, Safer Tomorrow*. September 19, 2006. http://www.unitedamericancommittee.org/quest_game.htm.

Phalen, Peggy. *The Unmarked: The Politics of Performance*. New York: Routledge, 1993.

Piaget, Jean. *Play, Dreams, and Imitation in Childhood*. New York: Norton, 1962.

Piccione, Peter A. *Senet, Gaming with the Gods: The Game of Senet and Ancient Egyptian Religious Beliefs*. Herndon, VA: Brill Academic Publishing, 2007.

Pitcher, George. *The Philosophy of Wittgenstein*. Englewood Cliffs, NJ: Prentice-Hall, 1965.

Plant, Sadie. *Zeroes + Ones: Digital Women + the New Technoculture*. New York: Doubleday, 1997.

Powell, Earl A., Glenn Lowry, and Bruno Racine. "Foreword." *eDada*, ed. Leah Dickerman, ixx. Washington, DC: National Gallery of Art, 2005.

Provenzo and Provenzo. *Favorite Board Games You Can Make and Play*. Mineola, NY: Dover, 1990.

Rancière, Jacques. *The Politics of Aesthetics*. Trans. Gabriel Rockhill. London: Continuum, 2004.

Readings, Bill. *Introducing Lyotard: Art and Politics*. London: Routledge, 1991.

Reilly, Eliza Jane. "Elsa von Freytag-Loringhoven." *Woman's Art Journal* 18, no. 1 (Spring–Summer 1997): 26–33.

Rheingold, Howard. *Smart Mobs: The Next Social Revolution*. New York: Perseus, 2002.

Rice, Shelley. *Inverted Odysseys: Claude Cahun, Maya Deren, Cindy Sherman*. Cambridge, MA: MIT Press, 1999.

Richard, Frances. "Oyvind Fahlstrom." *Artforum* 41, no. 9 (May 2003): 167–168.

Richards, Kate. "Ars Electronica: Interface Futures." *RealTime* 58 (December 2003–January 2004). http://www.realtimearts.net/rt58/richards.html.

Robinson, Julia. *Sculpture of Interdeterminacy: Alison Knowles' Beans and Variations*. Glen Ellyn, IL: Gahlberg Gallery, McAninch Arts Center, College of DuPage, 2004.

Rodker, John. "'Dada' and Else von Freytag-Loringhoven." *The Little Review* 7 (July–August 1920): 33–36. In *The Little Review Anthology*, ed. Margaret E. Anderson. New York: Horizon Press, 1953.

Rollefson, Gary O. "A Neolithic Game Board from 'Ain Ghazal, Jordan." *Bulletin of the American Schools of Oriental Research* 286 (May 1992): 1–3.

Roos, Bonnie. "Oskar Kokoschka's Sex Toy: The Women and the Doll Who Conceived the Artist." *Modernism/Modernity* 12, no. 2 (2005): 291–309.

Rose, Gillian. *Feminism and Geography: The Limits of Geographical Knowledge*. Minneapolis: University of Minnesota Press, 1993.

Rosemont, Penelope. *Surrealist Women: An International Anthology.* Austin: University of Texas Press, 1998.

Rosenthal, Mark, Sean Rainbird, and Claudia Schmuckli. *Joseph Beuys: Actions, Vitrines, Environments.* London: Tate Modern, 2004.

Rosler, Martha. "Out of the Vox: Martha Rosler on Art's Activist Potential." *Artforum International* 43, no. 1 (2004): 218–220.

Roth, Rodris. "Scrapbook Houses: A Late Nineteenth-Century Children's View of the American Home." In *The American Home: Material Culture, Domestic Space, and Family Life*, ed. Eleanor McD. Thompson. Hanover, NH: University Press of New England, 1998.

Rudolph, Richard C. "Notes on the Riddle in China." *California Folklore Quarterly* 1, no. 1 (January 1945): 65–82.

Russ, Larry. *The Complete Mancala Games Book: How to Play the World's Oldest Board Games.* New York: Marlowe & Co., 2000.

Sadler, Simon. *The Situationist City.* Cambridge, MA: MIT Press, 1999.

Salen, Katie, and Eric Zimmerman. *Rules of Play: Game Design Fundamentals.* Cambridge, MA: MIT Press, 2003.

Sawelson-Gorse, Naomi, ed. *Women in Dada: Essays on Sex, Gender, and Identity.* Cambridge, MA: MIT Press, 1998.

Schleiner, Anne-Marie. "Cracking the Maze Curator's Note." 1998. http://www.opensorcery.net/note.html.

Schleiner, Anne-Marie. "Does Lara Croft Wear Fake Polygons?" *Leonardo* 34, no. 3 (2001): 221–226.

Schleiner, Anne-Marie. "Operation Velvet Strike." 2002. http://www.opensorcery.net/velvet-strike/about.html.

Schön, Donald. *Reflective Practice.* New York: Basic Books, 1983.

Schumacher, Claude. *Alfred Jarry and Guillaume Apollinaire.* New York: Grove Press, 1985.

Schwarz, Arturo. "Game of Precision, An Aspect of the Beauty of Precision." In *The Complete Works of Marcel Duchamp.* New York: Abrams, 1969.

Schwarz, Arturo. *The Complete Works of Marcel Duchamp.* 3rd ed. New York: Delano Greenidge Editions, [1969] 1997.

Serlin, David "Disabling the *Flâneur.*" *Journal of Visual Culture* 5, no. 2 (2006): 193–208.

Shade Regan, Leslie. "Whose Global Knowledge? Women Navigating the Net." *Development* 46, no. 1 (2003): 61–65.

Shattuck, Roger. *The Banquet Years: The Origins of the Avant-Garde in France 1885 to World War I.* Garden City, NY: Doubleday, [1955] 1961.

Sheldon, Rose Mary. "The Sator Rebus: An Unsolved Cryptogram?" *Cryptologia* 27, no. 3 (2003): 233–287.

Shneiderman, Benjamin. "Universal Usability." *Communications of the ACM* 43, no. 5 (2000): 84–91.

Silverstone, Robert, ed. *Visions of Suburbia*. London and New York: Routledge, 1997.

Simms, Eva-Maria. "Uncanny Dolls: Images of Death in Rilke and Freud." *New Literary History* 27, no. 4 (1996): 663–677.

Slagle, Matt. "Women Make Small Inroads in Video Game Industry." *ABQ Journal* (September 13, 2004). http://www.abqjournal.com/venue/videogame_news/apgame _women09-13-04.htm.

Slavin, Robert E. *Educational Psychology: Theory into Practice*. Englewood Cliffs, NJ: Prentice-Hall, 1988.

Smith, Peter K. "Does Play Matter? Functional and Evolutionary Aspects of Animal and Human Play." *Behavioral and Brain Sciences* 5 (1982): 139–184.

Spain, Daphne. *Gendered Spaces*. Chapel Hill: University of North Carolina Press, 1992.

Spencer, Herbert. *First Principles*. 4th ed. New York: D. Appleton and Co., [1855] 1896.

Spencer, Herbert. *Principles of Psychology*. New York: Appleton, 1896. Cited in Sutton-Smith, Brian. *The Ambiguity of Play*. Cambridge, MA: Harvard University Press, [1855] 1997.

Spiegel, Lyn. *Make Room for TV: Television and the Family Ideal in Postwar America*. Chicago: University of Chicago Press, 1992.

Spivak, Gayatri Chakravorty. *In Other Worlds: Essays in Cultural Politics*. New York: Methuen, 1987.

Sterling, Bruce. *The Hacker Crackdown: The Hacker Crackdown. Law and Disorder on the Electronic Frontier*. 1994. http://www.cs.indiana.edu/classes/a106/readings/sterling.html.

Sterling, Bruce, ed. *Mirrorshades: A Cyberpunk Anthology*. New York: Ace, 1987.

Stern, Eddo. *Fort Paladin: America's Army*. 2003. http://www.eddostern.com/fort_paladin .html.

Stevens, Mark. "Everything Is Illuminated." *New York Metro Magazine* (September 27, 2004). http://nymag.com/nymetro/arts/art/reviews/9937/.

Stevens Heininger, Mary Lynn. *A Century of Childhood, 1820–1920*. Rochester, NY: Margaret Woodbury Strong Museum, 1984.

Stonard, John Paul. "Gabriel Orozco." *Grove Art Online*. New York: Oxford University Press. http://www.tate.org.uk/servlet/ArtistWorks?cgroupid=999999961&artistid =2685&page=1&sole=y&collab=y&attr=y&sort=default&tabview=bio.

Stone, Allucquère Rosanne. *The War of Desire and Technology at the Close of Mechanical Age*. Cambridge, MA: MIT Press, 1995.

Subrizi, Carla. "Art Actions from Everyday Life." *NY Arts Magazine* 76 (May 2003). http:// nyartsmagazine.com/76/art.htm.

Sue, Eugène. *The Wandering Jew* (in three volumes). New York: The Century Company, 1903.

Sundén, Jenny. "What Happened to Difference in Cyberspace? The (Re)turn of the She-Cyborg." *Feminist Media Studies* 1, no. 2 (July 1, 2001): 215–232.

Sutton, Laurel A. "Cocktails and Thumbtacks in the Old West: What Would Emily Post Say?" In *Wired Women: Gender and Realities in Cyberspace*, ed. Lynn Cherney and Elizabeth Reba Weise, 169–181. Seattle: Seal Press, 1996.

Sutton-Smith, Brian. *Toys as Culture*. New York: Gardner Press, 1986.

Sutton-Smith, Brian. *The Ambiguity of Play*. Cambridge, MA.: Harvard University Press, 1997.

Sutton-Smith, Brian. Interview by Eric Zimmerman. The Digital Games Research Association Level Up Conference, Utrecht, Netherlands, November 4–6, 2003.

Symons, Steve. *Aura*. 2004. http://www.muio.org/projects/aura.html.

Tanaka, Atsuko, and Akira Kanayama. "Electrifying Art" (lecture). The Japan Society, New York City, September 14, 2004.

Taylor, Sue. *Hans Bellmer: The Anatomy Of Anxiety*. Cambridge, MA: MIT Press, 2000.

Terdiman, Daniel. "'Last Call Poker' Celebrates Cemeteries." *ZDNet News.com* (November 20, 2005). http://news.zdnet.com/2100–1040_22–5963346.html.

Thackary, William Makepiece. *Vanity Fair: A Novel without a Hero*, ed. Peter L. Shillingsburg. New York: Garland, 1989.

Townsend, Chris. *The Art of Rachel Whiteread*. London: Thames and Hudson, 2004.

Tronzo, William L. "Moral Hieroglyphs: Chess and Dice at San Savino in Piacenza." *Gesta* 16, no. 2 (1977): 18.

Tse Bartholomew, Terese. *Hidden Meanings in Chinese Art*. San Francisco: Asian Art Museum, 2006.

Turim, Gayle. "American His-toy-ry." *Americana* 17, no. 6 (1990): 64–66.

Turner, Victor W. "Body, Brain, and Culture." *Zygon: Journal of Religion and Science* 18, no. 3 (1983): 221–245.

Turner, Victor W. "Liminal to Liminoid, in Play, Flow, and Ritual: An Essay in Comparative Symbology." In *Play, Games and Sports in Cultural Contexts*, ed. J. C. Harris and R. J. Park, 20–60. Champaign, IL: Human Kinetics, 1983.

Tuters, Marc, and Kazys Varnelis. "Beyond Locative Media: Giving Shape to the Internet of Things." *Leonardo* 30, no. 4 (2006): 357–363.

Tzara, Tristan. "Seven Dada Manifestoes." In *The Dada Painters and Poets: An Anthology*, ed. Robert Motherwell and Jack D. Flam, 74–98. Boston: G. K. Hall & Co, [1951] 1981.

Urizenus (user name). "Maxis Is Deleting In-Game References to *Alphaville Herald*." *The Second Life Herald, formerly the Alphaville Herald* (December 8, 2003). http://www.alphavilleherald.com/archives/000049.html.

U.S. Department of Commerce. *How Americans Are Expanding Their Use of the Internet*. Washington, DC: National Telecommunication and Information Administration, 2002. http://www.ntia.doc.gov/reports/anol/index.html.

Utterback, Camille. "Unusual Positions—Embodied Interaction with Symbolic Spaces." In *First Person: New Media as Story, Performance, and Game*, ed. Noah Wardrip-Fruin and Pat Harrigan, 218–226. Cambridge, MA: MIT Press, 2004.

Vanouse, Paul. "THE RELATIVE VELOCITY INSCRIPTION DEVICE by Paul Vanouse, 2002."http://www.contrib.andrew.cmu.edu/~pv28/rvid.html.

Veblen, Thorstein. *The Theory of the Leisure Class: An Economic Study of Institutions*. 1899. http://www.gutenberg.org/dirs/etext97/totlc11.txt.

Vygotsky, Lev S. "Play and Its Role in the Mental Development of the Child." In *Play: Its Role in Development and Evolution*, ed. Jerome S. Bruner, Allison Jolly, and Kathy Sylva, 537–544. New York: Basic Books, 1976.

Wallace Adams, David, and Victor Edmonds. "Making Your Move: The Educational Significance of the American Board Game, 1832 to 1904." *History of Education Quarterly* 17, no. 4 (Winter 1977): 359–383.

Wardle, Caroline, C. Dianne Martin, and Valerie A. Clark. "The Increasing Scarcity of Women in Information Technology Is a Social Justice Issue." In *Challenges for the Citizen of the Information Society: Proceedings of 7th International Conference, ETHICOMP 2004*, 983–903. Syros, Greece: Publisher, 2004.

Wark, McKenzie. "Suck on this, Planet of Noise!" In *Critical Issues in Electronic Media*, ed. Simon Penny, 7–26. Albany: State University of New York Press, 1995.

Wayne, Jane Ellen. *Crawford's Men*. New York: Prentice Hall, 1988.

Webb, Peter, and Robert Short. *Hans Bellmer*. London: Quartet Books, 1985.

Weber, Evelyn. *Ideas Influencing Early Childhood Education*. New York: Teachers College Press, 1984.

West, Michael. *Transcendental Wordplay: America's Romantic Punsters and the Search for the Language of Nature*. Athens: Ohio University Press, 2000.

White, Lionel. "Biography." In *Logical Nonsense: The Works of Lewis Carroll: Now, For the First Time, Complete*, ed. Philip C. Blackburn and Lionel White. New York: G. P. Putnam's Sons, 1934.

Williams, Juan. "Monopoly." NPR Report (November 25, 2002). http://www.npr.org/programs/morning/features/patc/monopoly/.

Williams, Patricia J. "L'Étranger." *Nation* 284, no. 9 (March 5, 2007): 11–14.

Williams, Raymond. *Culture and Society 1780–1960*. New York: Columbia University Press, 1958.

Williams, Raymond. *Television: Technology and Cultural Form*. New York: Schoken Books, 1975.

Williams, Raymond. *The Country and the City*. New York: Oxford University Press, 1975.

Williamson, Judith. "The Problems of Being Popular." *New Socialist* (September 1986): 14–15.

Willis, Paul. "Symbolic Creativity." In *The Everyday Life Reader*, ed. Ben Highmore, 282–294. New York: Routledge, [1990] 2002.

Winnicott, Donald Wood. *Playing and Reality*. New York: Basic Books, 1971.

Wittgenstein, Ludwig. *Philosophical Investigations*. Trans. G. E. M. Anscombe. New York: Macmillan, [1953] 1964.

Wollen, Peter. "Situationists and Architecture." *New Left Review* 8 (March–April 2001). http://newleftreview.org/A2315.

Wood, Gaby. *Edison's Eve: A Magical History of the Quest for Mechanical Life*. New York: Knopf, 2002.

Woods, Stewart. "Loading the Dice: The Challenge of Serious Videogames." *Game Studies* 4, no. 1 (2004). http://gamestudies.org/0401/woods/.

Yalom, Marilyn. *The Birth of the Chess Queen*. New York: Harper Collins, 2004.

The Yes Men. *Hijinks*. 2007. http://www.theyesmen.org/en/hijinks.

The Yes Men. *Vivoleum*. 2007. http://www.theyesmen.org/en/hijinks/vivoleum.

The Yes Men. *The Yes Men*. 2007. http://www.theyesmen.org/.

Yoshimoto, Midori. *Into Performance: Japanese Women Artists in New York*. New Brunswick, NJ: Rutgers University Press, 2005.

Zeisel, Hans. "The Surveys that Broke Monopoly." *University of Chicago Law Review* 50, no. 2 (Spring 1983): 896–909.

Zimerman, Brett. *Edgar Allan Poe: Rhetoric and Style*. Kingston, ON: McGill-Queen's University Press, 2005.

Zimmerman, Eric. "Play as Research: The Iterative Design Process." 2004. http://www.gmlb.com/articles/iterativedesign.html.

Žižek, Slavoj. "Looking Awry." *October* 50 (1989): 30–55.

Žižek, Slavoj. *Everything You Always Wanted to Know about Lacan (But Were Afraid to Ask Hitchcock)*. London: Verso, 1992.

Zürn, Unica. *The Man of Jasmine & Other Texts*. London: Serpent's Tale, 1994.

Index

Printed in the United States
by Baker & Taylor Publisher Services